WORDSWORTH CLASSICS
OF WORLD LITERATURE

*General Editor: Tom Griffith MA, MPhil*

# LIVES OF THE TWELVE CAESARS

# Suetonius
# *Lives of the Twelve Caesars*

Translated by H. M. Bird

With an Introduction by Tamsyn Barton

**WORDSWORTH CLASSICS**
**OF WORLD LITERATURE**

For customers interested in other titles from Wordsworth Editions

Visit our web-site at
www.wordsworth-editions.com

For our latest list and a full mail order service contact:

Bibliophile Books
5 Thomas Road, London E14 7BN

Tel: (0044) 020 7515 9222
Fax: (0044) 020 7538 4115
e-mail: orders@bibliophilebooks.com

The publishers would like to thank the Bodleian Library,
University of Oxford, for permission to re-set the edition
held in the library, shelfmark 23646.d.13.

This edition published 1997 by Wordsworth Editions Limited
8b East Street, Ware, Hertfordshire SG12 9HJ

ISBN 1 85326 475 X

© Wordsworth Editions Limited 1997

1 3 5 7 9 10 8 6 4 2

Wordsworth® is a registered trademark of
Wordsworth Editions Limited

Typeset by Antony Gray
Printed and bound in Great Britain by
Mackays of Chatham plc, Chatham, Kent

# CONTENTS

# INTRODUCTION

Suetonius is a name which may find few to recognise it in an age where an education in the classics is the exception rather than the rule. But many more will remember the classic BBC television serial, *I, Claudius,* which was based on Robert Graves's novelistic adaptation of Suetonius, starring the spectacularly stuttering Derek Jacobi in the title role. Who can forget Caligula dancing in his stage debut the night before his assassination, or the bumbling Claudius – the man 'whom Nature had not finished but had merely begun' according to his mother – pulled out from behind the curtain where he had been hiding after the murder of Caligula, and acclaimed emperor by the Praetorian Guard? Few would have guessed that this series in which 'Britain's finest character actors lie, murder and test each other's carnal knowledge'[1] was drawn in much of its detail from the biographies of the emperors written in the early second century AD.

The author of the *Lives of the Caesars,* Gaius Suetonius Tranquillus, was born around AD 67–72, and probably came from the town of Hippo Regius (now Annaba in Algeria), where an inscription recording his career has been found. He was of elite (equestrian) family, and the culture and society he enjoyed were those of the elite across the Empire, brought up in Greek literature, art and learning as well as in the Roman political, military and economic structures. Suetonius studied Roman law, a typical preparation for a political career, and was offered a military post, which could have set him on the path, by his patron Pliny (the Younger), a distinguished man of letters. Pliny may well have taken Suetonius on his staff when governor of the province of Bithynia-Pontus (northern Turkey) *c.* AD 100–112,

---

1 Advertisement for re-run of the series by Westminster Cable, 1996.

A Byzantine biography, describing him as a scholar, provides information on his writings (largely lost), and gives a notion of the range of his interests. His pieces on Greek games and Greek insults survive in summary and, along with works such as those on human physical defects, on types of clothes and on seas and rivers, can plausibly be reconstructed as scholarly dictionaries. His studies obviously catered to antiquarian tastes; he wrote about ancient Greek and Roman festivals and customs. To post-Byzantine posterity he is known as the greatest Roman biographer – we know that he wrote three major works of biography including *Lives of the Caesars*, *Famous Men* (a work of which the parts on scholars and orators survive), as well as the (sadly lost) *Lives of Whores*.

From the published *Letters* of his patron Pliny some more intriguing glimpses emerge – Suetonius begging for postponement of a case he was due to plead because he had been warned off by a bad dream, Suetonius getting financial assistance from Pliny to buy a small estate, being prodded to publish his first work, and changing his mind about the military post Pliny had obtained for him, deciding to give it to a relative instead.

It was most likely his own distinction as a writer which gave Suetonius his highest political appointments at the imperial court. It is from the inscription at Hippo that we know that he was Secretary of Studies, Director of the Imperial Libraries, and finally Secretary of the Imperial Correspondence. We learn from a later biography of Hadrian that the emperor dismissed his Secretary, along with his patron Septicius Clarus, Prefect of the Praetorian Guard (to whom Suetonius dedicates his *Lives of the Caesars*), on the grounds that they had been over-familiar with the Empress Sabina. This sounds a suitably lurid fall from grace for the chronicler of court scandal, but whether much of political significance lies behind the tale is uncertain, since the source tends to over-dramatise. At any rate, it is generally accepted that Suetonius was dismissed in 122, for behaviour which took place while Hadrian was on tour in Britain. Only an allusion in his work allows us to infer that Suetonius lived beyond 130 – how long thereafter is uncertain.

In the absence of other literary historical sources which are at all close to contemporary – apart from the great Tacitus – Suetonius' work is a key source of information about the early Roman Empire. Perhaps this is why Suetonius was long condemned as a poor historian. Because his is not a narrative history, there are tantalising glancing references to matters about which we would like to know much more. For instance, in his Life of Claudius he mentions the Jews being stirred up to revolt by one Chrestus – a rare secular reference to Jesus – and he is the sole source for most of our knowledge about the reign of Caligula, whose name he made a byword for perversion and cruelty. In avoiding explanation of his references, he imagined that readers would know the full story from other sources. Some historians, frustrated at the lack of key information, found it hard to forgive Suetonius' focus on trivial detail. Yet now that history's range has broadened, he is seen to have provided fascinating insights into the society and culture of his day. By comparison with the highly-coloured Tacitus, he seems to many an 'objective' source.

He also suffered slights to his literary reputation by comparison with Tacitus, whose prose style was imitated again and again across the centuries. More recently, Suetonius' originality in choosing to write biographies of the emperors is stressed more than his reliance on earlier Greek models of biography. Even then, however, his style has been dismissed as that of the impassive scholar, compiling his biographies somewhat indiscriminately from his variety of sources. The influence of the scholarly method is certainly detectable, with sections such as 'omens at birth', under which instances are cited. 'Not by chronology but by rubric', as he describes his method in the Life of Augustus, might be his motto. And his deliberately unadorned style, with the use of direct citations from documents and of Greek words, seems ostentatiously scholarly.

However, it is important to remember that Suetonius studied rhetoric, indeed studied oratory in his training as a barrister, and to note that his marshalling of the huge range of material about the emperors is often clearly done to make a case. The very ordering 'by rubric' was a recognised rhetorical device. In fact many of Suetonius' rubrics, such as ancestors, relations with family, physical appearance, eating, drinking, sexual habits and so on, were the topics outlined in rhetorical handbooks explaining how to damn opponents. A special category within rhetoric was 'praise and blame' – eulogies and character assassinations. Speeches of censure were made in court to undermine opponents, or in public in the case of quarrels between scholars, while eulogies were called for on a variety of occasions.

Speeches of eulogy were made to reigning emperors (Pliny's eulogy of Hadrian was preserved as a model), and by extension, emperors from an earlier dynasty, such as Tiberius, Nero and Domitian, could be the subjects of carefully-worked condemnation.

Suetonius gives no crudely one-sided accounts of his subjects, but that is not to say that he either strives for, or indeed accidentally achieves, objectivity. However, the scholarly style, with telling attention to detail, is very effective where he wishes to argue a case. On occasions, such as with his interpretation of Augustus' motives in selecting Tiberius as his successor, or his discussion of Nero's authorship of the poetry attributed to him, we know that he is arguing against Tacitus; in other instances we cannot be sure of the identity of the opponent, but we should be aware that there is a case he is pleading.

What is instructive is a comparison with Plutarch, the Greek biographer, who also wrote about Julius Caesar. Plutarch sets out an ethical programme for his works, claiming to provide instruction from his studies in virtue and vice. Suetonius, however scholarly, cannot be labelled didactic in his discussions of the virtues and vices of his subjects. Indeed, some find him rather too interested in the vice. One scholar viewed him as 'soiling the purple of the emperors'; while the translator of this volume, H. M. Bird, describes him as 'a gossipy old domestic'. Yet if he does go into extensive detail on such matters as Tiberius' sexual antics on the isle of Capri, he follows in a long and distinguished tradition of oratory, with exponents such as Cicero and Julius Caesar before him.

To see him as dry scholar is to miss the wit. Many of the most effective pieces of rhetoric against emperors are ironic jokes. The tale of Nero's marriage to the eunuch Sporus is told to lead up to the punch-line: people said 'the world would have been a happier place had Nero's father Domitius married such a wife'. Sometimes they are retailed as jokes, as with those about Caesar's homosexual relationship with the King of Bithynia. When Caesar spoke of his obligations to Nicomedes, Cicero cried: 'Enough! We know what you two gave each other!' Claudius' stupidity offers much comic potential. He draws attention to the fact that he is engaging in a marriage of dubious legality with his niece Agrippina by constant references to her in speeches, such as 'my daughter and foster-child, born and bred in my lap, so to speak'.

Suetonius' wit can be subtle. In the case of Nero's early reign, usually regarded as the Five Golden Years, there are a number of references to examples of good behaviour which are ironic in the context of what the readers would know and what is mentioned later. For instance, Nero ensures on succession that his adoptive father Claudius is deified, which looks forward to the chapter where Nero reveals his complicity in poisoning Claudius with a dish of mushrooms, appreciatively quoting the Greek proverb: 'Mushrooms are the food of the gods'. Nero's early building projects are discussed, and his biographer picks out his construction of platforms to fight fires! Which reader would not know the story that Nero set fire to Rome and sang the epic *Sack of Troy* from a tower overlooking the fire?

Suetonius has earned some appreciation for his set-pieces of dramatic narrative, such as the death-scenes, a contemporary literary genre. The vivid account of the last hours of the panic-stricken Nero suddenly takes on the point of view of the deposed emperor, struck by every detail. Domitian's increasing fear as the day when astrologers predicted his assassination approached, and frightening omens abounded, builds up to his final relieved exit to the bath in the belief that the fatal sixth hour had passed, only to meet his death exactly as he had been told.

A proper respect for Suetonius' rhetorical skills might seem to run the risk of undermining his worth as a historical source. But it would be too crude to dismiss his biographies as closer to art than life. His retailing of rumour about the murders and intrigue at court is precious as evidence of what did circulate, whether true or not, and incidentally provides a wealth of contextual information.

There is much irresistible detail, which gives us the material we expect from biography, throwing unusual light on his subjects, relaxing the stiff poses of the statues they wanted to represent them in public. The great Augustus, founder of the institution of the principate, is seen having his hair cut by two or three barbers at once to save time, playing dice with Moorish boys whose lisping Latin appealed to him, and wearing thick-soled shoes to make himself look taller. Julius Caesar, we learn, liked wearing the laurel wreath and combing forward his hair to cover his baldness, suffered from nightmares, and was too embarrassed to enter the amounts he paid for desirable slaves in his accounts.

There is an underlying pattern giving structure to each Life, with variations to prevent wearying repetition. We learn about emperors' literary productions, typical turns of phrase, the games and spectacles they put on for the people, their building projects. Under rubrics such as their writing, there are fascinating particulars – the reader learns how to break the code Caesar used for private letters, or where to find the three letters Claudius added to the Roman alphabet. The section on physical appearance is of interest, not just for the alternative to idealised portraiture, but for the framework used. It has been suggested that Suetonius was drawing on the discipline of physiognomics, which set out the rules for judging character from appearance, in his descriptions of the emperors' looks. If so, he was giving coded signs of character, and the apparently realistic details such as Augustus' slightly curly hair, were in fact, as we learn from technical treatises on the subject, references to his lion-like (i.e. kingly) character. Similarly, Caligula's hairy legs were signs of his goat-like (i.e. lustful) character, and his sunken eyes betrayed his panther-like effeminacy.

The descriptions of physical appearance in particular had a strong influence on literary imitators of Suetonius. The biographer set the pattern for later biographies of the emperors. A century after him, Marius Maximus continued from where Suetonius had left off, and was followed by a number of authors known as the Writers of the Augustan History, though they tended to favour more chronological accounts. There are some echoes in the hostile *Secret History* by Procopius of the reign of Justinian, but in the Byzantine period the dominant form of biography was hagiography, with lives of the saints the norm. Suetonius languished in obscurity. Only in the early ninth century was a copy of Suetonius, perhaps the only surviving copy in Western Europe, discovered in a German monastery and used as a model for a panegyrical *Life of Charlemagne*, the self-styled Holy Roman Emperor, by the Frankish scholar Einhard. William of Malmesbury was also influenced by Suetonius in his biography of William Rufus. But if his fame in literary circles in the Middle Ages did not seem to increase much in the Renaissance, he reached a wider audience in vernacular translation, such as that into English, published in 1606, by Philemon Holland.

It was Plutarch who was used by Shakespeare and his contemporaries. Only in the twentieth century, perhaps, in the new dramatic medium of television, has Suetonius come to life again.

TAMSYN BARTON

# FURTHER READING

Entries are listed roughly in order of usefulness to the general reader keen to know more. There is a dearth of books on Suetonius in English, so seminal articles are included.

A. Wallace-Hadrill, *Suetonius: the scholar and his Caesars*, 2nd edition, Bristol 1995.

R. Lounsbury, *The Arts of Suetonius*, New York 1987

G. B. Townend, 'Suetonius and his influence', in T. A. Dorey (ed.), *Latin Biography*, London 1959; and in T. J. Luce (ed.), *Ancient Writers: Greece and Rome*, New York 1982

B. Baldwin, *Suetonius*, Amsterdam 1983

M. Grant, *The Ancient Historians*, London and New York 1970

M. Grant, *The Twelve Caesars*, London and New York 1975

F. R. D. Goodyear in W. V. Clausen and E. J. Kenney (eds), *Cambridge History of Classical Literature II: Latin Literature*, Cambridge 1982

T. S. Barton, 'The inventio of Nero: Suetonius', in J. Elsner and J. Masters (eds) *Reflections of Nero*, Duckworth 1994

# DATES

The Romans dated events *Ab Urbe Condita* (or A.U.C.), which means 'from the founding of the city'. Tradition has it that Rome was founded in 753 BC, so A.U.C. 670, at the beginning of the life of Julius, represents the year 83 BC.

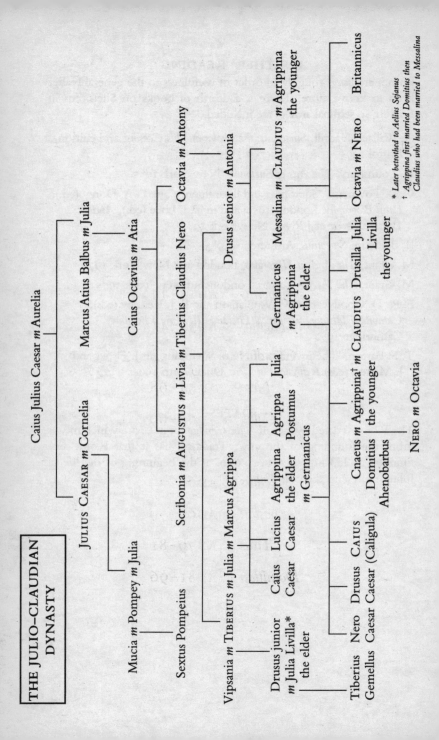

THE JULIO–CLAUDIAN DYNASTY

Caius Julius Caesar m Aurelia

Mucia m Pompey m Julia

JULIUS CAESAR m Cornelia

Sextus Pompeius

Marcus Atius Balbus m Julia

Caius Octavius m Atia

Scribonia m AUGUSTUS m Livia m Tiberius Claudius Nero

Octavia m Antony

Drusus senior m Antonia

Vipsania m TIBERIUS m Julia m Marcus Agrippa

Drusus junior m Julia Livilla* the elder

Caius Caesar

Lucius Caesar

Agrippina the elder m Germanicus

Julia

Agrippa Postumus

Germanicus m Agrippina the elder

Messalina m CLAUDIUS m Agrippina the younger

Tiberius Gemellus

Nero Caesar

Drusus Caesar

CAIUS Caesar (Caligula)

Cnaeus Domitius Ahenobarbus m Agrippina† the younger

CLAUDIUS

Drusilla Julia Livilla the younger

Octavia m NERO

Britannicus

NERO m Octavia

\* Later betrothed to Aelius Sejanus
† Agrippina first married Domitius then Claudius who had been married to Messalina

# THE TWELVE CAESARS

| | |
|---|---|
| *Julius Caesar* | 49–44BC |
| *Augustus* | 31BC–AD14 |
| *Tiberius* | AD14–37 |
| *Caius (Caligula)* | AD37–41 |
| *Claudius* | AD41–54 |
| *Nero* | AD54–68 |
| *Galba* | AD68–69 |
| *Otho* | AD69 |
| *Vitellius* | AD69 |
| *Vespasian* | AD69–79 |
| *Titus* | AD79–81 |
| *Domitian* | AD81–96 |

# LIVES OF THE TWELVE CAESARS

# *Foreword*

Caius Suetonius Tranquillus was born towards the close of the reign of Vespasian, when the events that he was to chronicle were still reflected on the political horizon. He was the son of a Roman knight who commanded a legion on the side of Otho, and this circumstance provided him with much of that vivid anecdotage that makes of his great work a series of intimate memoirs rather than a history.

It is regrettable that there was none to do for Suetonius – and hence for posterity – what he performed so ably for the Caesars. One would like to know something of the personality of the man beyond what is revealed by inference from his literary style. But there is very little to gratify the reader's curiosity. It would appear that he was on terms of cordial friendship with the younger Pliny, who wrote that 'the nearer he was brought into communion with him, the more he loved him.' This happy condition was not repeated, however, in the case of the Emperor Hadrian, whom Suetonius served for some time in the capacity of private secretary. For we next learn that he was dismissed from his secretarial duties on the charge of having conducted himself unbecomingly toward the Empress Sabina in Hadrian's absence – the exact nature of his offence being nowhere particularly set forth.

During his attendance upon the emperor, Suetonius had access to many important documents in the imperial archives, which, together with his numerous social contacts, furnished voluminous material for the writing of his projected history. Upon this engaging task he occupied himself when his exile from court placed him socially 'under a cloud'; and the eventual emergence of a document altogether unique in literary history turned the occasion to a happy use.

Of the result, Pio Baroja, in his brilliant miscellany, *Youth and Egolatry*, has this to say: 'It is the greatest collection of horrors in history. You leave it with the imagination perturbed, scrutinising your soul to discover whether you may not be yourself a hog or a wild beast.' The reaction to the work is necessarily personal because the manner is intensely so. The larger historical aspects of events are not considered, nor do we get a complete picture of the society of the times. The happenings of each reign, from that of Julius to that of Domitian, are touched upon only as they shed light on the personality of the emperor. It is not as a military annalist, nor as a civil servant, nor yet as an astute biographer, that Suetonius writes; but rather as a gossipy old domestic, with a born genius for story-telling, on whom every momentous happening in the outside world of affairs impresses itself mainly as it affects his master's temper when he has doffed his toga and donned his dressing-gown and slippers. The banquet hall and the bedchamber figure more largely in his narrative than do the Forum and the camps. And, as the real man lurks inevitably beneath the purple which conceals him, this method gives us a series of indelible portraits; not drawn, be it observed, with a psychological brush which blurs the individual outline by relating it to the human whole, but with the objective art of the skilled cartoonist who sharply differentiates individuals by stressing their most prominent characteristics.

It is difficult to say whether Suetonius' matter-of-fact relation of the gross and the horrific, or his solemn insistence upon the homely and the intimate, is the more diverting. We see, for example, the Divine Julius seizing the privilege of wearing the laurel wreath as the most grateful item in his triumph because it conceals his baldness. That excellent and courtly prince, Augustus, is caught in the act of ordering his shoes made with over-thick soles that he might appear taller than he was. There is grim humour in the mad antics of Nero and Caligula: the one posturing as a great artist, and the other as a military hero. And, though the sometimes world-splitting battles are treated with the brevity and indifference that they perhaps deserve, not a single side-splitting comment by any wit or sage of the period would seem to have been omitted. Thus succeeding generations of readers have reason to be grateful for the nice balance that is maintained in these matters when they reflect that while Suetonius' omissions are adequately supplied elsewhere (for he was contemporaneous with Tacitus and Dio Cassius), Suetonius' achievement is nowhere paralleled.

# Caius Julius Caesar

When Julius Caesar was sixteen years old, his father Caius died; and in the year following he received the honour of being elected High Priest of Jupiter. About this time he repudiated Cossutia to whom he had been affianced during his childhood, and who, although she belonged only to the equestrian order, was a very wealthy lady. He then married Cornelia, daughter of Cinna who filled the consulship four times; and she, soon after, gave birth to his daughter Julia.

Sulla, the dictator, was much displeased by Caesar's conduct, and tried to force him to put Cornelia aside; but Caesar resisted, upon which he suffered the penalty of being deprived of his sacred office, of his wife's dowry and all his heritages, and was moreover accused of being sympathetic to the adverse faction under Marius, leader of the people. He was compelled to flee Rome, and wandered about for some time in the Sabine territory, changing his hiding place almost every night, though he was sorely afflicted with the quartan ague. He finally obtained his release by bribing the officers who pursued him; and through the intercession of the Vestal Virgins, and of Mamercus Aemilius and Aurelius Cotta, his near kinsfolk, he at length won a pardon. It is certainly known, however, that Sulla, after he had denied a good while the pleas of his own best friends, persons of rank and influence, in Caesar's behalf, at last yielded to their entreaties in these words, which were touched either by divine prescience or shrewd conjecture:

'Take him then, my masters, since ye needs must have it so; but know this, that he whose life you so much desire will one day be the overthrow of the party of nobles, whose cause you have sustained with me; for in this one Caesar, you will find many a Marius.'

## 2

Caesar served in the wars for the first time in Asia, under the praetor, M. Thermus; and being sent by him into Bithynia to levy a fleet, he made his abode with King Nicomedes. His long sojourn there gave rise to the foul rumour that he entered into immoral relations with the king: which rumour he himself augmented by coming again into Bithynia within a few days of his departure, under the pretext of collecting money due to a freedman, his client. The rest of his service he carried with better fame; and at the winning of Mytilene in the isle of Lesbos, Thermus bestowed on him the honour of a civic garland.

## 3                                                        A.U.C 676

He served also under Servilius Isauricus, in Cilicia, but not for long; for upon hearing of Sulla's death, he returned in all haste to Rome, prepared for anything that might follow from a new dissension stirred up by Marcus Lepidus, who, being consul with Q. Catulus Lutatius, proceeded to repeal all of the acts of Sulla. But notwithstanding large offers and fair promises, he decided against joining Lepidus, partly from distrust of his nature, which was variable and indiscreet, and partly because the present opportunity seemed less favourable for the accomplishment of this project than he had at first believed.

## 4

Soon after this civil discord was quieted by the death of Lepidus, he brought a charge of extortion against Cornelius Dolabella, a man who had been consul and honoured with a triumph. But when the defendant was found innocent and acquitted, he determined to retire to the city of Rhodes, not only to appease the public indignation he had incurred but also to win leisure to learn the art of oratory under Apollonius Molon, the most renowned of rhetoricians in that day. It was winter time when he set sail and as he drew near to the isle of Pharmacusa, he had the misfortune to be captured by pirates, who kept him in custody, to his great resentment, for nearly forty days, during which time he was attended only by a physician and two chamberlains. The rest of his companions and servants belonging to his train, he had dispatched into the Asiatic cities to procure him money with all speed for his ransom. Upon the payment of fifty talents, his captors released him upon the shore. Losing no time, he put his fleet to sea again and did not cease pursuing these pirates until he had overtaken them; and no sooner were they in his power than he made good a threat he had many times given in jest, and put them all to death. Now while Mithridates was ravaging the countries adjoining, in order that he might not be thought lax while danger threatened the allies of Rome, he passed over into Asia, and gathering a power of auxiliary forces he expelled the king's governor, and re-established in their loyalty those cities which were wavering and at the point of revolt.

## 5

Being elected military tribune, the first dignity conferred upon him by the voice of the people after his return to Rome, he greatly assisted those who stood for the restitution of their tribunician authority, the force and strength whereof Sulla had abated. Moreover, by virtue of an act which Plotius, a tribune of the people, proposed at his suggestion, he effected the recall of Lucius Cinna, his wife's brother, and others with him who had taken part in the civil disturbances on the side of Lepidus, and who, after that consul's death, had fled to Sertorius, the commander in Spain; and it was decreed that they might now return safely into the city and enjoy their freedom. Respecting this matter, he himself made an oration before the people.

## 6

During his quaestorship, he pronounced funeral orations from the rostra, as the ancient custom was, in praise of Julia, his aunt on his father's side, and of his wife, Cornelia. And in the commendation bestowed on his aunt, he related the following concerning her own and his father's descent: 'Mine aunt Julia is lineally descended by her mother from kings, and by her father from the Immortal Gods; for, from Ancus Marcius are derived the Marcii, surnamed Reges, that is, Kings, which name my mother held; and from Venus the Julii are derived, of which house and name is our family. So then, in this stock there concur and meet the sanctity and majesty of kings, who among men are most powerful, and the religious supremacy of the gods, in whose power kings themselves are.' In the place of Cornelia, he wedded Pompeia, daughter of Quintus Pompeius, and granddaughter of Lucius Sulla. But he afterwards divorced her upon suspicion that she had been dishonoured by Publius Clodius, of whom persistent rumour went abroad that he, in woman's disguise, had access to her secretly during the celebration of the rites of the Bona Dea, in which only women took part; upon this, the Senate directed an inquiry into the pollution of those sacred ceremonies.

7

As quaestor, it fell to him by lot to execute his office in Farther Spain. One day, as he was riding the circuit of this province at the command of the praetor, Antistius Vetus, for the administration of justice, he came to Gades: where, beholding a statue of Alexander the Great in the Temple of Hercules, he sighed deeply, as if burdened with his own slothfulness in that he had performed no memorable act in his thirty-three years, what time Alexander had required to conquer the whole world. Presently, therefore, he sued earnestly for his discharge and license to depart, that he might take the first opportunity that should present itself in the city for entering upon greater enterprises. Being moreover much disquieted by a dream of the night before, in which he had imagined himself in carnal company with his own mother, he consulted the diviners, who incited him to hopes of most glorious achievements by interpreting his dream as an omen that he would possess the sovereignty of the whole world: considering that the mother he had imagined beneath him could augur nothing less than the subjection of the earth, which is counted the mother of all things.

8

Departing from the province, therefore, before his time was fully expired, he went into the Latin colonies, which were now devising means of effecting their freedom from the City of Rome; and he would have incited them to attempt some tumult and trouble in the State, but that the consuls, for the prevention of this very danger, kept back for a while the legions which were enrolled for service in Cilicia.

9 A.U.C. 688

And yet he soon thereafter projected greater designs within the City itself. For, not many days before he entered upon his aedileship, he fell under suspicion of having been engaged in a conspiracy with Marcus Crassus, a man of consular rank, with whom likewise were Publius Sulla and Lucius Autronius, who, after they had been chosen consuls, were condemned for bribery. The plan of the conspirators was to fall upon the senate in the beginning of their year, and massacre as many as seemed necessary; whereupon Crassus should usurp the dictatorship, and appoint Caesar his Master of the Horse; and so when they had settled the State at their pleasure, Sulla and Autronius should be restored again to their consulship. Of this conspiracy, Tanusius Geminus makes mention in his history, Marcus Bibulus in his edicts, and Curio, the father, in his orations. Cicero likewise seems to dwell upon it in a certain epistle to Axius, wherein he reports that Caesar established in his consulship that royal government which he had plotted to secure when he was aedile. Tanusius writes further that Crassus, either from repentance or fear, was not present upon the day appointed for the massacre, and therefore Caesar did not give the signal which he should have given; which agreement, Curio says, was that he should let his toga fall from his shoulders. The same Curio and M. Actorius Naso write that he conspired also with Cnaeus Piso, a noble young gentleman, who being under suspicion in connection with a conspiracy within the City, had the province of Spain bestowed upon him out of the regular order. It is said to have been agreed between them that Piso should lead a revolt in the provinces, and that Caesar at Rome should make an insurrection to alter the state, using as their instruments the Lambrani and the tribes beyond the Po. But the execution of this design was frustrated at both ends by reason of Piso's death.

10 A.U.C. 689

While he was aedile, he beautified not only the Comitium and the rest of the Forum, with the adjoining halls, but he graced the Capitol also by erecting temporary galleries for the public shows and plays: wherein he displayed for the view of all men the superabundant collection of images, statues, and pictures he had gathered from all parts for their amusement. As for the chasing and baiting of wild beasts, the stage plays and games, he exhibited them both in conjunction with his companion in office, Marcus Bibulus, and also independently. Whereby it appeared that he earned the sole honour and thanks, although the charges of these entertainments were borne in common; insomuch that M. Bibulus observed that his lot was like that of Pollux: 'For consider,' said he, 'the temple erected in the common market place of Rome unto both the twin-brethren, Castor and Pollux, bears the name of Castor alone: even so, the munificence which Caesar and I provide jointly goes under the name of Caesar only.'

Caesar exhibited also a fight of gladiators; but he brought into the place fewer couples of champions than he had purposed, for he had bought up such a great company of fighters that his adversaries of the other faction, in great alarm, caused a special act to be passed by the state which fixed the number of gladiators that a man might retain in Rome.

## II                    A.U.C. 690

Thus when he had gained the hearts and favour of the people, he made attempt through his power with some of the tribunes to have the province of Egypt conferred upon him by an act of the people: the occasion of his suit for this extraordinary government being that the Alexandrians had driven out of his realm their king, Ptolemy Auletes (father of Cleopatra), whom the senate had given the title of ally and friend of the Roman people. Although the people generally were indignant over the outrage, he did not carry the suit because of the opposition of the faction of the nobles. In order, therefore, to infringe and impair their authority by all means in his power, he restored the trophies in honour of Caius Marius, for his victories over Jugurtha, the Cimbrians, and the Teutons, which had been demolished by Sulla; also, in sitting upon a commission for the examination of murderers, he reckoned among them those who, in the time of the proscription, had received money out of the public treasury for bringing in the heads of Roman citizens, although they were excepted by virtue of the Cornelian laws.

## 12

Moreover, he suborned someone to indict for treason Caius Rabirius, by whose help especially some years before the senate had discovered and restrained the seditious tribune, Lucius Saturninus; and being by lot chosen a judge delegate to pass sentence on the prisoner, he was so willing to condemn him that when Rabirius appealed to the people, nothing stood so much in his favour as the extraordinary rigour of the judge.

## 13                                    A.U.C. 691

Having resigned all hope of gaining Egypt for his province, he became candidate for the office of Pontifex Maximus, and to further his prospects used the persuasive powers of lavish bribery. Considering how deeply he engaged himself in debt, he is said to have told his mother, when she kissed him as he left that morning to go into the assembly for the election, that he would never return home unless chosen pontiff. And so far did he outweigh his two most mighty competitors (who surpassed him both in age and in rank), that he carried in their own tribes alone more votes than both had in all tribes throughout.

## 14

After he was created praetor, although not yet entered into office, the conspiracy of Catiline was detected; and although the senate generally recommended no lighter punishment than death for the parties to the crime, he alone proposed that their goods should be confiscated and they themselves put into several free cities and buroughs under the people of Rome, there to be kept in ward. And furthermore he instilled so great a fright into those that had voted for heavier punishment, and so forcibly pointed out the censure which their course would call down upon them from the Roman people, that Decimus Silanus, consul-elect, was very ready to mollify his own pronouncement with a gentle exposition, as if it had been falsely construed in a harder sense than he had intended, and so avoided the shame of eating his own words. Caesar would certainly have prevailed in this matter, for many were already drawn to his side, (among the rest, Quintus Cicero, the consul's brother), had not a speech made by Marcus Cato emboldened the whole house, and confirmed all the senators in their former sentence after they had been at the point of yielding to him. Yet he ceased not to hinder their proceedings until a troop of Roman Knights, who stood in armed defence of the consul and senate, threatened to dispatch him out of the way if he continued in his obstinate contumacy; and they shook their drawn swords so near him that those who sat with him moved away and a few friends with great difficulty protected him by throwing their arms about him, and putting their togas between him and his assailants, thus saving him from violence. Alarmed at this display, he not only yielded to them but refrained from coming again to the senate house for the remainder of that year.

## 15    A.U.C. 692

The first day of his praetorship, he summoned Quintus Catulus before the body of the people to render an account of the improvements of the Capitol, proposing at the same time a decree for transferring the office of curator to another person, namely Pompey; for he did not desire that the honour of re-edifying and dedicating the Capitol, consumed by fire, should go to Catulus. But being unable to withstand the opposition of the aristocratic party, whom he perceived quitting in great numbers their attendance upon the new consuls, and fully determined to make resistance, he relinquished this project.

## 16

Afterwards he showed himself a stout abettor and maintainer of Caecilius Metellus, a tribune of the people, who proposed most turbulent and seditious laws in defiance of his colleagues; and so resolutely did he bear him out in his cause that both of them were by an injunction and decree of the senators removed from the administration. He presumed nevertheless to continue in his magistracy and to execute his jurisdiction, until he learned that some were ready to obstruct him by force of arms, whereupon he sent away his sergeants, cast off his purple robe and retired to his own house, there to keep himself quiet during these troubled times. And when, two days afterward, the people flocked to him of their own accord, promising in a very tumultuous manner their help and assistance in the recovery of his former place and dignity, he calmed them. This happening contrary to all expectation, the senate, who were hastily convened on the subject of the riot, gave him hearty thanks, and sent for him by some of the noblest members among them. After high commendation of his conduct, they reversed their former decree and restored him fully to his office.

## 17

He fell soon again into fresh trouble, however, being called into question as one of the Catiline conspirators, both before the Quaestor Novius Niger in his house by Lucius Vettius, the informer, and also in the senate, by Quintus Curius: to whom a reward had been voted, for having first detected the designs of the conspirators. Curius deposed that he had received his intelligence from Catiline; and Vettius even promised to produce Caesar's own handwriting, given to Catiline. But this indignity Caesar found in no way tolerable; and he appealed to Cicero, by whose testimony it was shown that he himself, of his own accord, had given some information to him of the conspiracy; and by prevailing in this he deprived Curius of the reward. As for Vettius, he had him heavily fined and his property seized; after which he was maltreated in the open assembly of the multitude even before the rostra, and then cast into prison. In the same manner he served Novius the quaestor, because he suffered him, a superior magistrate of state, to be accused and defamed in his house.

## 18                                              A.U.C. 693

At the expiration of his praetorship, he obtained by lot the farther province of Spain; and he quieted his creditors, who would have detained him, by providing sureties, of whom Crassus was named as one, for his debts. Contrary to both law and custom, however, he took his departure before the usual outfit and equipage were prepared; whether this was done from fear of some judicial proceeding intended against him while he was a private person, or because he might the more speedily succour the allies of the Romans, who craved help, is uncertain. He had no sooner settled the province in

peace, however, than he made haste to depart, without waiting for
the arrival of his successor; and he returned to Rome, to sue for a
triumph in recognition of his victories in Galicia and Lusitania, and
also to take on the consulship. But the day of election having already
been fixed by proclamation, he could not legally be admitted a
candidate unless he entered the City as a private citizen. He was
thereby placed in the dilemma that if he aspired to a triumph, he must
remain outside of the walls until it took place, while as a candidate for
the consulship he must be resident in the City. Upon his solicitation
that the law be laid aside in his behalf, Cato and his followers
withstood him, so that he was forced to forgo his triumph for fear of
being disappointed in the consulship.

## 19

Of the two competitors with him for the consulship, to wit, Lucius
Lucceius and Marcus Bibulus, he chose the former to be his
companion in office, upon condition that Lucceius, being a man of less
interest but greater affluence, should promise money to the electors in
their joint names. Which compact being known, the party of nobles,
fearing that once he became consul with a colleague at his beck to
approve and fortify his measures, he would both dare and do anything:
they persuaded Bibulus to promise the voters as much as the other, and
the most part of them contributed toward the expense. Cato himself
did not oppose the expedient, conceding that this largesse stood for the
good of the people. He was thereupon elected consul jointly with
Bibulus. Actuated still by the same motives, the party of nobles and
principal persons of the City gave order that the consuls for that year
should have only the provinces and commissions of least importance,
such as the administration of forests and roads. Caesar taking this
indignity most to heart, paid flattering court immediately to Cnaeus
Pompey, who had taken offence at the senators for not sooner
ratifying his acts and decrees following his triumph over Mithridates.
He reconciled also Pompey and Marcus Crassus, who had been
enemies since their joint consulship, a time of much jarring and
disagreement. He entered likewise into a compact with them both that
nothing should be done in the administration of the commonweal that
was displeasing to any of the three. It was this notorious alliance that
bred the civil war which ensued between Caesar and Pompey.

20

Having entered upon his consulship, he inaugurated the practice of having recorded and published all of the daily acts of the senate as well as the people, so that a history of every matter should be preserved. He also revived the ancient custom that on the alternate months when the fasces were not carried before him, a public officer should precede him and his lictors follow. Having promulgated an agrarian law for the division of some public lands, he was opposed by his fellow-consul whom he then drove out of the Forum by violence. The next day, when Bibulus complained in the senate of this outrage and due to the great confusion prevailing found not one having the hardihood to bring the matter forward or move a censure (which had often been done in cases of lighter disturbance), he was very much cast down; so much so indeed that he quit his magistracy and retired within his own house, where he did nothing but issue edicts to obstruct his colleague's proceedings. From that time forward, Caesar alone managed all the affairs of state, an arrangement very much to his liking; insomuch that divers citizens, whenever they signed any writings as witnesses, were moved to the merry conceit of putting down that such a thing was done, not when Caesar and Bibulus, but when Julius and Caesar, were consuls; and soon after these verses were commonly current abroad:

> Caesar of late did many things, but Bibulus not one:
> For naught by Consul Bibulus can I remember done.

The land of Stellas, held consecrated by our ancestors to the gods, together with the Campania territory left subject to tribute for the support of the expenses of the government, he divided without casting lots, among twenty thousand citizens who had each of them three or more children. The publicans entering a plea for relief, he eased them of a third part of their rents which they had agreed to pay; at the same time warning them openly, that in the letting of the new commodities and revenues of the City, they should not bid so prodigally. Many other pleas likewise he granted to those who approached him, without meeting opposition at any hand; for if any sought to thwart him they were quickly put down. Marcus Cato, who attempted to arrest his proceedings, he caused to be violently removed from the senate-house by an officer and committed to prison. As Lucius Lucullus also ventured to oppose his doings, he intimidated him so greatly by the threat of sundry acts and criminations that he was glad to come and fall upon his knees before him. And when Cicero, pleading upon an occasion in court, lamented the woeful state of these times, the very same day at the ninth hour he transferred Publius Clodius, his enemy, from a patrician to a plebeian family: a measure for which he had long supplicated in order that he might be a candidate for the tribuneship of the people. Last of all it is credibly reported that he by great rewards induced Vettius to profess that he had been solicited by certain persons to murder Pompey; this device having for its purpose the intimidation of those of the opposite party; and when Vettius was brought before the rostra to designate those who had set him to this work, (as it had been agreed between them), and had named one or two of them to no purpose, thus giving rise to suspicions of fraud, Caesar, despairing of the success of his rash project, poisoned Vettius, whom he had suborned, and so released him from telling any more tales.

## 21

About the same time he married Calpurnia, the daughter of Lucius Piso who was to succeed him in the consulate, and affianced his own daughter Julia to Cnaeus Pompey, rejecting Servilius Caepio to whom she had been contracted and by whose help especially a little while before he had impugned Bibulus. At the same time he promised in marriage to the repudiated suitor the daughter of Cnaeus Pompey. Following this new alliance, he began, in his deliberations in the senate, to ask Pompey's opinion first, an honour he had been wont to accord Crassus; and this was contrary to the usual custom that the consul should observe throughout the year, namely that of conferring with the senate which he adopted on the kalends of January.

## 22

Being supported now by the favour and assistance of his wife's father, Piso, and his son-in-law, Cn. Pompey, he made choice of Gaul, among all the provinces, as being especially fitted by reason of its wealth to provide him with occasions for triumphs; for, as it was truly said, the Romans triumphed oftener over the Gauls than over all the other nations combined. At first, by virtue of a decree proposed to the people by Vatinius, he received only the government of Cisalpine-Gaul, together with Illyricum; but soon afterwards he obtained from the senate Gallia-Comata also, for the nobles feared that if they denied him this, the people would bestow it upon him. So much did joy inflate him at this success that he could not restrain his pride, but boasted in the crowded senate-house that he had now realised his desires despite his adversaries and much against their will; and that he would thenceforward bend them to his pleasure. Whereupon one of the senators caustically observing that 'It was no easy matter for a woman so to do', (alluding in this manner to certain scandals that were rife concerning Caesar), he retorted merrily that 'Even in Assyria there had reigned for some time Queen Semiramis; and that the Amazons in times past held a great part of Asia in subjection', thus turning the taunt to another signification.

## 23                                                    A.U.C. 696

When he had served his term of consulship, Caius Memmius and Lucius Domitius, the praetors, brought into question the transactions of the year past, whereupon he referred the examination and censure thereof to the senate. Seeing, however, that they would not undertake the task after three days spent in vain altercation, he departed into his province. Immediately, then, for the purpose of bringing trouble upon him, his quaestor was indicted upon certain crimes. Soon after, a charge was also brought against Caesar by Lucius Antistius, a tribune of the people; but by making an appeal to the college of the tribunes, he arranged that he should not be liable to the accusation during his absence on the affairs of the state. For his better security, therefore, in times to come, he insinuated himself into the good favour of the magistrates at the annual elections; and he would aid with his interest no candidates for office except such as entered into compact with him to defend and uphold him in his absences, which were frequently of longer duration than the law prescribed. To bind this compact he did not hesitate to demand of certain ones an oath and even a written agreement.

But when Lucius Domitius, a candidate for the consulship, threatened openly, that once he should become consul, he would effect that which he could not while he was praetor, and divest him of his armies, he sent for Crassus and Pompey to Lucca, a city in his province; and persuaded them, in order to repulse Domitius, to sue again for the consulship and maintain him in his command for five years longer; and these aims he effected. Reassured by this accomplishment, he presumed to add at his own expense other legions to those which he had received from the state. And one legion among them, drawn from one of the countries beyond the Alps, he called by a Gallic word, Alauda, which referred to the feathers on their helmets resembling the crest of a lark; and this legion he trained and armed in the Roman fashion and afterwards enfranchised throughout and made free of Rome. From this time forward he avoided no occasion of war, no matter how unjust or dangerous; and attacked with equal zeal those nations that were allied with Rome and those that were enemies, thereby provoking them to take arms. Upon this, the senate issued a decree for sending ambassadors to inquire into conditions in Gaul; and some members, namely, Cato and Plutarch, were even of opinion that he should be delivered into the hands of the enemy. But by reason of the success that had attended all his undertakings, he was granted more days of supplication, and at more frequent intervals, than any commander had ever had before him.

25

During his nine years of provincial government he performed the following acts: he reduced to the form of a province all that part of Gaul which is enclosed within the Pyrenean forest, the Alps, Mount Gebenna, and the two rivers, the Rhine and the Rhone, a territory of about 3200 miles, excepting only the nations allied with the republic and such as had deserved his favour. Upon this new acquisition he imposed a yearly tribute of forty millions of sesterces. He of all Romans was the first to cross by means of a bridge into the Germanic country beyond the Rhone; and the inhabitants thereof he defeated in many encounters. He also marched against the Britons, a people unknown before that time, whom he conquered utterly and from whom he exacted tribute and hostages. Amid so many prosperous exploits he tasted thrice only of adverse fortune: once in Britain when his fleet was nearly destroyed in a violent tempest; a second time in Gaul, where one of his legions was routed; and a third time in the land of the Germans, when Titurius and Aurunculeius, his lieutenants, were caught in ambush and put to the sword.

## 26

During this period he lost his mother, Aurelia, whose death was followed by that of his daughter, Julia, and, not long afterwards, of his granddaughter. Meanwhile, the republic being much dismayed at the murder of Clodius by Milo, and the senate passing a vote that only one consul, namely Cnaeus Pompeius, should be elected for the ensuing year, he prevailed with the tribunes of the people who intended that he should be the colleague in office with Pompey, to propose to the people that they should grant him the right, when the term of his government drew toward an end, to become a candidate for his second consulship, without departing out of his province before the conclusion of the war. Having triumphed in this measure, carrying his aims still higher, and jubilant with the hopes of success, there was no opportunity of ingratiating himself into popular favour that he neglected to take full advantage of; and to this end he directed many acts of kindness and liberality, both in public and private. He began to build a new Forum with money which he raised from the spoils of war; and the plot of ground whereon it should stand cost him over a hundred millions of sesterces. He promised the people a public entertainment of gladiators, and a feast in memory of his daughter, such as no one before him had ever given. And to heighten the expectation of these celebrations, although he had agreed with victuallers of all kinds for his feast, he made yet further arrangements in private homes. He issued an order that the most famous gladiators, if at any time during the combat they should incur the displeasure of the public, should be immediately carried off by force, and reserved for some future occasion. Young gladiators he trained, not in any public school, nor under professed masters of that art, but in the houses of Roman gentlemen and even senators, who were skilled in the use of arms; and these he besought earnestly, as appears from his letters to them, to take these beginners in their charge, discipline them, and give them the word during their exercises. The pay of the legions he doubled in perpetuity; and he allowed them corn, when it was in plenty, without stint or measure, and sometimes he bestowed upon every soldier in his army a slave and a portion of land.

## 27

Moreover, to strengthen the bonds which united him with Pompey, he offered him in marriage his sister's granddaughter Octavia, who had been wedded to Caius Marcellus, and requested for himself his daughter, who was lately promised to Faustus Sulla. He likewise secured under obligations all those about him, even a great number of the senators, by lending them money, either without interest or at a very slight rate; and to all others who came to wait upon him, either by invitation or of their own accord, he dispensed liberal bounty; and he did not except even the freedmen and slaves, who were favourites with their masters and patrons. He befriended and succoured also, divers persons who were being prosecuted at law, such as were deeply in debt, or were young spendthrifts. He excluded from his benevolent care only those who were criminally guilty, or who were so deeply involved either in poverty or luxury, that they could not possibly be relieved by him. For these, he proclaimed openly, could not be benefited save by civil war.

## 28 A.U.C. 703

Neither did he spare any effort to win the loyalty of princes and provinces in every part of the world; to some offering in free gift thousands of captives, and to others sending aid secretly by means of troops without the authority of the senate or the people. Moreover he adorned with excellent buildings the most powerful cities, not only of Italy, Gaul, and Spain, but of Greece and Asia; until all people, being now astonished, were casting about in their minds for the purpose of these things, and Claudius Marcellus, the consul, proclaiming first by way of preamble to his edict, that he intended to voice a measure of the utmost importance to the people, proposed to the senate that some one be chosen to succeed Caesar in his province, before the time of his command was expired, seeing that the war was

now ended, and peace established; also, that the victorious army
ought by right to be disbanded. He further suggested that in the
assembly for the consuls' election, his name should not be admitted,
considering that Pompey, in his law relating to the choice of chief
magistrates, had forgot to except Caesar in the article in which he
proclaimed all such as were not present incapable of being candidates
for any office; but soon afterwards, when the law was engraven in
brass and so laid up in the treasury, he corrected his error. Marcellus,
not content to deprive Caesar of his provinces and the privilege
intended him by Pompey, made a motion also that those inhabitants
whom by the Vatinian law Caesar had settled at New Como, should
lose the freedom of the city of Rome, which they had, because this
prerogative of theirs had been granted them with ambitious views,
and was beyond the provisions of the law.

## 29

A.U.C. 704

Caesar, highly displeased by these proceedings and judging it, as he
was heard many times to observe, a harder matter for him, the chief
man in the state, to be deposed from the highest rank of citizens to
the second than from the second into the lowest of all, resisted with
all his might and power, partly by the opposition and negative voice
of the tribunes and partly through Servius Sulpitius, the other consul.
Also in the year following, when C. Marcellus, who succeeded his
cousin Marcus in the consulship, pursued the same course, he
contrived by means of a great bribe to secure the allegiance of
Aemilius Paulus, his companion in office, and Caius Curio, the most
violent of the tribunes. But seeing that events went against him more
obstinately than before, and that the new consuls–elect took an
opposing stand, he wrote a letter to the senate, humbly beseeching
them not to suffer the benefits granted him by the people to be taken
from him, or else that the other generals should likewise resign the
command of their armies; presuming confidently, it is thought, that
he could more readily assemble his veteran soldiers than Pompey
could levy new ones. At the same time, he made his adversaries an
offer to disband eight of his legions and give up Transalpine-Gaul,
upon condition that he might retain two legions, with the Cisalpine
province, or but one legion with Illyricum, until such time as he
should be created consul.

## 30

But perceiving that the senate declined to interpose their authority in the matter and that his enemies refused to enter into any compromise affecting the commonweal, he passed into Hither-Gaul; and, having gone the circuit for the administration of justice, he stopped at Ravenna, fully determined to be revenged by open war in case the senate should pass a decree against the tribunes of the people who had espoused his cause. This was his avowed pretext for the civil war, yet many ascribed to him other causes and motives. Cnaeus Pompey was wont to say that inasmuch as Caesar was unable, with his own private wealth, to complete the works he had begun, or to realise the vast expectations which he had aroused in the people, he therefore tried to create a distracting confusion. Others say that he feared he would be called to account for those things which he had done in his first consulship against the auspices, laws, and protests of the tribunes: especially his violent dealing with his fellow-consul Bibulus. Indeed, Marcus Cato had threatened, and that upon oath, that he would bring forward charges against him as soon as ever his army should be disbanded; and it was commonly spoken abroad that if he returned as a private citizen, he would, like Milo, have to plead his cause before the judges, with a guard of armed men surrounding him. This conjecture is made to seem the more probable by Asinius Pollio, who writes that Caesar, in the battle of Pharsalia, when he beheld his adversaries slain and put to flight, uttered these words: 'Lo, this was their intention: I, Caius Caesar, after so many worthy exploits achieved, must have been condemned had I not sought help of my army.' Some hold that, being so long inured to sovereign command, and weighing his own power with that of his enemies, he took that occasion to usurp the absolute dominion which he had craved from his youth; and this is the view, apparently, that was taken by Cicero, who writes in his third book of Offices, that Caesar used often to have in his mouth two verses of Euripides, which he thus translates:

> For if thou must do wrong by breach
> Of laws, of right and equity,
> 'Tis best thereby a crown to reach,
> In all things else keep piety

## 31

When word, therefore, was brought to him that the interposition of the tribunes in his behalf had been put aside and that they themselves had fled from the city, he immediately sent forward some cohorts, but privately, so that no suspicion might arise; and he dissimulated the matter further by attending a public game, viewing the model of a fencing-school which he proposed to build, and according to his usual custom, sitting down to table with his friends. But after sunset, he had mules put to his carriage from a neighbouring mill, and set forward on his journey with all possible privacy, and a few attendants; and when, by reason of the lights going out, he lost his way, he wandered about for a long time and at length met a guide, as day was breaking, by whose help through narrow footpaths he regained the road. When he had overtaken his cohorts at the river Rubicon, which was the boundary of his province, he stopped and rested for a little while; then, when he had reflected in his own mind upon the magnitude of the undertaking which he contemplated, he turned to those about him, and said: 'As yet, my friends, we may still go back; but once we pass over this little bridge, there will be no dealing but by force of arms and power of sword.'

## 32

As he thus stood doubtful and uncertain what to do, he chanced to see a strange sight. Suddenly there appeared to him, close at hand, a person of extraordinary stature and aspect, playing upon a pipe. Now when not only shepherds and herdsmen, but many soldiers, with some trumpeters among them, also ran from their posts to listen, Caesar caught a trumpet from one of them, ran to the river with it, and blowing a mighty blast to sound the battle, he crossed to the other side. Then he cried to them: 'Let us march on, and go whither the omens of the gods and the injurious dealings of our enemies call us. Come what will of it.'

## 33

Having thus conveyed his army over the river, he joined the tribunes of the people who, upon their expulsion from the city, had come to meet him; and in the midst of that assembly, with tears in his eyes, and rending his garment from his breast, he besought his troops to pledge him their fidelity. It is supposed also that he promised to every soldier a knight's estate; but that is founded upon a false report. For when in his exhortation to them, he showed ever and anon the ring finger of his left hand and promised that, for the reward of those who should uphold him in defence of his honour, he would willingly pluck the ring from off his own finger: those soldiers that stood at a distance, and could more easily see him than hear his words, formed their conception of what he said by the eye and not the ear; and so the report became current that he had promised to each of them the dignity of wearing the gold ring, together with 400,000 sesterces, the value of a knight's estate.

## 34

The order of events which followed this occasion proceeded thus: he seized and held Picenum, Umbria, and Etruria. Lucius Domitius, who had been nominated in a factious tumult to be his successor, and who held Corsinium with a garrison, he subdued and forced to yield: and when he had dismissed him, he marched along the coast of the Upper Sea, to Brundisium, whither the consuls and Pompey were fled with the intention of crossing the sea with all speed. After he had attempted by all manner of means to stop their passage, and all in vain, he turned his steps toward Rome. And when he had courteously appealed to the senate on the present state of public affairs, he then set out for Spain, where Pompey had powerful forces under the command of three lieutenants, Marcus Petreius, Lucius Afranius, and Marcus Varro; having openly professed among his friends, that 'he was going against an army without a captain, and would return thence against a captain without an army'; as if Petreius, Afranius, and Varro were without the smallest skill, and Pompey alone a worthy adversary. Although his journey was retarded both by the siege of Marseilles, which shut her gates against him, and by an exceeding scarcity of corn, yet within a short time he overcame and subdued all.

## 35

From thence having returned to Rome and passed over into Macedonia, after he had held Pompey besieged for nearly four months within a mighty line of trenches and strong ramparts, he at last defeated him in the battle of Pharsalia, and pursued him hotly as he fled to Alexandria. There he was told of his murder, and he perceived likewise that he himself was now engaged, under all the disadvantages of time and place, in a very dangerous war with King Ptolemy, who had lain in wait for him with designs upon his life. It was then winter-time, and he found himself within the walls of a very wealthy and subtle enemy, in distress by reason of the lack of many things, and wholly unprepared to fight. Nevertheless he achieved the victory, and granted the kingdom of Egypt to Cleopatra and her younger brother, being afraid to reduce it to the form of a province lest, under an ambitious governor, it might breed revolt. From Alexandria he went over into Syria, and so from thence into Pontus, upon urgent news that he had received concerning Pharnaces; this prince, notwithstanding that he was the son of the great Mithridates, had taken advantage of the opportunity which the times offered for making war upon his neighbours, and his presumption grew with his manifold victories and successes. Caesar, however, within five days after his arrival in that country and four hours after coming in sight of him, vanquished him utterly in only one battle. Afterwards, he many times descanted to his friends upon the excellent fortune of Pompey, who had won his military reputation chiefly by victory over so feeble an enemy. He afterwards defeated Scipio and Juba, who were rallying the remains of the party in Africa, as well as Pompey's sons in Spain.

## 36

In all the civil wars, he sustained no loss or overthrow except by defection of his lieutenants; of whom Caius Curio fell in Africa, Caius Antonius was taken captive in Illyricum, Publius Dolabella lost a fleet in the same Illyricum, and Cnaeus Domitius Calvinus his army in Pontus. Those battles fought under his own command were always fortunate, and never was the outcome even doubtful save in two instances: once before Dyrrachium, when, being obliged to give ground, and Pompey not following in pursuit, he said of him that he knew not how to use a victory; and once again in Spain at the last battle which he fought, when, being in great despair, he was tempted to kill himself.

## 37

Having finished all his wars, he rode in five triumphs: to wit, four times in one month, when he had vanquished Scipio, each triumph succeeding the former by an interval of a few days; and once again after the conquest of Pompey's sons. His first and most excellent triumph was for the victories gained in Gaul; the next for that of Alexandria, the third for the reduction of Pontus, the fourth for his African victory, and the last for that in Spain; and they all differed from each other in their arrangement and ornamentation. On the day of the Gallic triumph, as he rode along the street called Velabrum, he narrowly escaped being shaken out of his chariot by the breaking of the axle-tree. He mounted up into the Capitol by torch-light, having forty elephants on his right and left, bearing torches. In his Pontic triumph, among the pageantry and shows, he caused to be carried before him a tablet having the inscription: Veni, Vidi, Vici, I came, I saw, I conquered; signifying, not so much the acts accomplished as the expeditious manner in which they were done.

## 38

Throughout the legions of old soldiers, he gave in the name of pillage, to every footman, over and above the 2000 sesterces paid him in the beginning of the civil war, 20,000 more; and to the horsemen 24,000 apiece. He also assigned lands to them, but not in contiguity, so that the former owners might not be entirely thrust out. Among the people of Rome, besides ten modii of corn, and as many pounds of oil, he distributed 300 sesterces a man, which he had promised in times past, and a hundred more apiece for the delay in time. He remitted moreover one year's house rent to the treasury, for such houses in Rome as did not pay above two thousand sesterces a year; and through the rest of Italy, for all such as did not exceed in yearly rent 500 sesterces. Furthermore, he gave them a great feast and a portion of meat; and after his victory in Spain he gave two public dinners. For, deeming the former of them to have been niggardly and not beseeming his liberality, he bestowed upon them five days afterwards another dinner, which was most plenteous.

## 39

He exhibited shows of sundry sorts; namely, a combat of gladiators, and stage plays in several quarters of the City, acted in different languages, to gratify all strangers that flowed to Rome; likewise Circensian games, wrestlers, and the representation of a sea-fight. In the contest of gladiators held in the Forum, Furius Leptinus, a man of praetorian family, entered the lists as a combatant, as did also Quintus Calpenus, formerly a senator, and a pleader of causes. The Pyrrhic dance was performed by some youths who were sons to persons of the first distinction in Asia and Bithynia. In the plays, Decimus Laberius, who had been a Roman knight, acted in his own piece; and being presented on the spot with five hundred thousand sesterces and a gold ring, he went from the stage, through the orchestra, and resumed his place in the seats allotted for the equestrian order. In the Circensian games, for which the circus was enlarged on both sides and a moat sunk around it, several of the young nobility drove chariots, drawn, some by four, and others by two horses, and also rode races on single horses. The warlike Trojan game was acted by a two-fold troupe of boys, one differing from the other in age and rank. The hunting of wild beasts was presented for five days successively. And the last day of all, a battle was fought by five hundred foot, twenty elephants, and thirty horse on each side. And that they might have more room for this engagement, the goals were removed and in their space two camps were pitched, confronting one another. Wrestlers likewise performed for three days together in a place set out and built for that purpose in the Campus Martius. A lake having been dug in the little Codeta, a meadow beyond the Tiber, ships of the Tyrian and Egyptian fleets, containing two, three, and four banks of oars, with a number of men on board, gave a spirited representation of a sea-fight. To behold these sights, such a number of people gathered from all parts, that most of the strangers were obliged to lodge in tents erected in the streets, or along the roads near the

City. Several were caught helpless in the press and crushed to death, among whom were two senators.

## 40

Afterwards turning his attention to the reforming of the common-wealth, he corrected the calendar, with the aid of Sosigenes, an Egyptian philosopher; this had for some time been much confused, through the fault of the pontiffs, who had the liberty of interlacing months and days at their pleasure, so that neither the festival holidays of harvest fell out in summer, nor those of the vintage in autumn. And he arranged the year according to the course of the sun, ordaining that in future it should consist of 365 days, without any intercalary month; and that every fourth year an intercalary day should be inserted.

To the end that the year might thenceforth commence regularly with the kalends, or first of January, he inserted two months between November and December; so that the year in which this regulation was made consisted of fifteen months, including the month of intercalation which, according to the division of time then in use, happened that year.

## 41

He filled up the vacancies in the senate by conferring patrician rank upon several plebeians; and also increased the number of praetors, aediles, quaestors, and inferior magistrates. Such as were displaced by the censors or convicted of bribery at elections, he restored to their former power. The choice of magistrates he so divided with the people that, excepting only the candidates for the consulship, they nominated half of them, and he the other. His manner in these cases was to recommend such persons as he had pitched upon, by bills dispersed through the several tribes to this effect: 'Caesar the dictator to such a tribe (naming it), I commend to you, such a one and such a one (naming likewise the persons), that by virtue of your votes they may attain to the dignity for which they sue.' He also admitted to honourable offices the sons of those who had been proscribed. The trial of causes he restricted to two orders of judges, the equestrian and senatorial; and he utterly abolished as judges the tribunes of the treasury who had before made a third class. The revised census of the people, which was ordinarily taken by the censors with the public notaries in the Campus Martius and Villa Publica, he ordered to be taken street by street, and by the principal landlords of the several quarters of the city; and whereas 320,000 citizens had received corn at the public cost, he now reduced the number to 150,000. To the end that no riots should occur on account of the census, he ordained that every year, in the place of those that were deceased, the praetor should fill up the vacancies by casting lots among those who were not enrolled for the receipt of corn.

## 42

Eighty thousand citizens having been distributed in foreign colonies, principally Carthage and Corinth, he made the following law for replenishing the population of the city of Rome: That no citizen above twenty years of age, and under forty, unless he were a sworn soldier to the state, should remain away from Italy for more than three years at a time; that no senator's son should go abroad, unless in the retinue of some high officer; and that among shepherds and herdsmen, no less than a third of the number of their tenders of cattle, free-born, should be youths. All professors of physic in Rome and all teachers of the liberal arts, he enfranchised citizens, in order to attach them to the city and draw others to settle there. As to debts incurred, he disappointed the expectation which was generally entertained and frequently proposed, either by the tribunes of the people, or the debtors themselves, that these would be totally cancelled; and he decreed that all debtors should satisfy their creditors, according to the valuation of their estates, at the rate at which they were purchased before the commencement of the civil war, deducting from the principal what had been paid for interest either in money or in bonds; by which condition, about a fourth part of the money due was lost. All the societies and colleges, saving those that were of ancient foundation, he dissolved. The penalties of heinous crimes he augmented; and the rich being more easily induced to commit them, because they were only liable to banishment, without the forfeiture of their property, he stripped murderers, as Cicero writes, of their whole estates, and other offenders of one-half.

## 43

He administered justice and decided matters in law with great rigour and severity. Such as were convicted of bribery and extortion he removed from the senate. He dissolved the marriage of a man of praetorian rank who had wedded a lady two days after her divorce from a former husband, although there was no suspicion of any illicit relationship. He ordained customs and imposts on foreign goods. The use of litters for travelling, the wearing of purple robes and jewels, he prohibited, except to persons of a certain age and station, and on particular days. The sumptuary laws, which repressed extravagance of the table, he executed with great strictness; and for this purpose he set officers about the markets where victuals were sold, with instructions to seize and deliver to him any meats offered contrary to the rules. Sometimes he even dispatched his soldiers to fetch from the very dining-halls such victuals as had escaped the notice of the officers, even when they were already placed upon the board.

## 44

Every day he had more matters in hand, concerning his purpose to beautify the city of Rome and his plans to guard and extend the empire. First, he intended to construct a temple in the honour of Mars, the like of which was nowhere to be seen. To this end, he contemplated filling up the lake on which he had entertained the people with the mock sea-fight. He also purposed to erect a vast theatre adjacent to the Tarpeian mount; and projected a plan to reduce the civil law to a reasonable compass and out of that immense and undigested mass of statutes to extract the best and most vital parts into a few books; to make as large a collection as possible of works in the Greek and Latin languages, for the public use; committing to Marcus Varro the province of providing and arranging these volumes. He intended further to drain the Pomptine marshes, to cut a channel for the discharge of the waters of the lake Fucinus, to form a road from the Upper Sea through the ridge of the Appennine to the Tiber; to make a cut through the isthmus of Corinth, to reduce the Dacians, who had over-run Pontus and Thrace, within their proper limits, and then to make war upon the Parthians, through the Lesser

Armenia, but not to risk a general engagement with them until he had made some trial of their strength. But in the midst of all his enterprises and designs, death came to him; concerning which event it may not be impertinent to withhold further speech and give some account of his person, dress, and manners, together with details relating to his pursuits, both civil and military.

## 45

His stature is said to have been tall, his complexion light and clear, with eyes black, lively, and quick, set in a face somewhat full; his limbs were round and strong, and he was also very healthy, except towards his latter days when he was given to sudden swoons and disturbance in his sleep; and twice in the conduct of military affairs, he was seized with the falling sickness. In the care of his person, his scrupulousness almost approached the fantastical; for he not only kept the hair of his head closely cut and had his face smoothly shaved, but even had the hair on other parts of his body plucked out by the roots, a whim for which he was often twitted. Moreover, finding by experience that his baldness exposed him many times to the jibes of his enemies, he was much cast down because of it, and was wont to bring forward the thin growth of hair from his crown to his forehead; hence, of all the honours bestowed upon him by the senate and people, there was none which he accepted or used with greater alacrity than the privilege of wearing constantly a laurel crown. It is said also that in his apparel he was noted for a certain singularity; for he wore his senatorial purple-bordered robe trimmed with fringes about the wrists, and always had it girded about him, though rather loosely. This habit gave rise to the saying of Sulla, who admonished the nobles often to 'beware of the ill-girt boy'.

## 46

He dwelt at first in the Suburra, but after he was raised to the pontificate he occupied a palace belonging to the state in the Via Sacra. Many writers say that he was exceedingly addicted to elegance in his house and sumptuous fare at his table; and that he entirely demolished a villa near the grove of Aricia, which he had built from the foundation and finished at great cost, because it did not exactly realise his taste, although at that time he possessed but slender means and was deeply in debt. Finally, it is said that in his military expeditions he carried about him tessellated and marble slabs to grace the floor of his tent.

## 47

He made a voyage (as they say) into Britain in the hope of finding pearls; for the rumour was current that excellent pearls of all colours, but chiefly white, were found in the British seas; and he would compare the size of these and poise them in his hand to ascertain their weight. He was most eager, also, to purchase, at any cost, gems, carved works, statues, and pictures, executed by the eminent masters of antiquity. And for young, finely set-up slaves, he would pay a price so great that out of shame for his own extravagance he forbad its being recorded in the diary of his accounts.

## 48

It is reported of him that in all the provinces he governed, he feasted continually and maintained two tables, one for the officers of the army and the gentry of the country, and the other for Romans of the highest rank and provincials of the first distinction. He was so precise in his domestic arrangements, both great and small, that he once imprisoned a baker for serving to his guests bread of a lesser quality than to himself; and he put to death a freedman who was a particular favourite, for dishonouring the wife of a Roman knight, although no complaint had been made to him of the matter.

## 49

His reputation for continence and a clean life was unblemished save by the occasion of his intimacy with Nicomedes; but that was a foul stain that remained with him always and provoked many taunts and reproaches. I will not dwell at length on the notorious verses of Calvus Licinius, beginning:

> Whate'er Bithynia and her lord possess'd, –
> Her lord who Caesar in his lust caress'd –

I pass over the invectives and accusations of Dolabella, and Curio the father; in which Dolabella dubs him 'the queen's rival, and the inner side of the royal couch', and Curio, 'the brothel of Nicomedes, and the Bithynian stew'. I likewise pass over the edicts of Bibulus, wherein he proclaimed his colleague under the name of 'the queen of Bithynia', adding that 'he had formerly been in love with a king, but now coveted a kingdom'. At which time, as Marcus Brutus relates, there was one Octavius, a man of disordered brain and one given to overbroad jests, who, in a crowded assembly, after he had saluted Pompey by the title of king, addressed Caesar as queen. Caius Memmius likewise upbraided him with serving the king at table among the rest of his catamites, in the presence of a large company in which were some merchants from Rome, the names of whom he mentions.

But Cicero, not content with writing in certain of his letters that Caesar, having been conducted by the royal attendants from his own bedchamber to that of the king, was there laid upon a bed of gold with a covering of purple, where the flower of youth and innocence of him who was descended from Venus became defiled in Bithynia; but upon Caesar's pleading the cause of Nysa, the daughter of Nicomedes, before the senate, and there recounting the king's kindnesses to him, he replied: 'Pray tell us no more of that; for it is well known, both what he bestowed upon you and also what you gave to him.' Finally, in the Gallic triumph, his soldiers recited these verses among the others which they chanted merrily upon such occasions, and they have since that time become commonly current:

> The Gauls to Caesar yield, Caesar to Nicomede,
> Lo! Caesar triumphs for his glorious deed,
> But Caesar's conqueror gains no victor's meed.

## 50

It was generally believed that he was given to carnal pleasures and in this way spent much of his substance; also, that he dishonoured many ladies of noble houses, among whom were Postumia, the wife of Servius Sulpicius, Lollia, the wife of Aulus Gabinius, Tertulla, the wife of Marcus Crassus, and Mucia, the wife of Cnaeus Pompey.

Certain it is, that not only the Curios, both father and son, but many others also reproached Pompey, 'That to gratify his ambition, he married the daughter of a man upon whose account he had divorced his wife, after having had three children by her; and whom he used, with a deep sigh, to call Aegisthus.' For it was Aegisthus who, like Caesar, was a pontiff, and who dishonoured Clytemnestra while Agamemnon was engaged in the Trojan war; in like manner did Caesar to Mucia, the wife of Pompey. But above all the rest, he loved Servilia, the mother of Marcus Brutus, for whom he purchased, in his first consulship after the commencement of their intrigue, a pearl that cost him six millions of sesterces; and also to whom, during the civil war, in addition to many other gifts, he sold for a very trifling consideration, some valuable farms that were offered at public auction. And when many persons marvelled that they went so cheap, Cicero pointedly remarked: 'To acquaint you with the real value of the purchase (between ourselves), Tertia was deducted.' For Servilia was thought to have prostituted her own daughter to Caesar; and her name, signifying 'a third', gives added grace to the jest.

## 51

Nor did he avoid the wives of men in the provinces which he governed, as appears from this distich, which was as much repeated in the Gallic triumph as the other:

> Look to your wives, ye citizens, a lecher bald we bring,
> In Gaul adultery cost thee gold, here 'tis but borrowing.

For, as Caesar 'borrowed' of other men, so he also 'loaned', in that his own wife, Pompeia, as is thought, was maintained by P. Claudius.

## 52

He was enamoured also of certain queens, among whom was Eunoë, a Moor, the wife of Bogudes, to whom and her husband he made, as Naso reports, many handsome presents. But among these his liveliest fancy was for Cleopatra, with whom he often revelled all night until break of day; and he would have accompanied her through Egypt in dalliance as far as Ethiopia, in her luxurious galley, had not the army refused point blank to follow. He afterwards received her in Rome, whence he sent her back rich with honours and presents, and also gave her permission to name after him a son which she bore, and who, according to Greek historians of the times, was very like him both in shape and gait. Mark Antony avowed in the senate that Caesar had acknowledged the child to be his own; and that Caius Matias, Caius Oppius, and the rest of Caesar's friends knew it to be true. Of these, Caius Oppius, (as if the matter were so weighty as to require some apology) issued a book designed to show 'that the child which Cleopatra fathered upon Caesar was not his'. Helvius Cinna, tribune of the people, confessed to many persons that he had a law drawn out and in readiness, which Caesar had ordered him to prepare in his absence, to the effect that it might be lawful for him to take any wife he pleased, and as many as he desired, for the purpose of leaving issue. And that no man might have any doubt how infamous he was for sodomy and adulteries, Curio, the father, calls him in one of his orations, 'Every woman's husband and every man's wife.'

## 53

That he was a most sparing drinker of wine, his very enemies did not deny. Whereupon arose the remark of Marcus Cato, 'that Caesar was the only sober man among all those who tried to overthrow the state'. In the matter of diet, Caius Oppius reports him so indifferent, that when a person in whose house he was entertained, had served him with rancid instead of fresh, sweet oil for his vegetables, and the rest of the company would not touch it, he alone partook heartily that he might not be thought to blame his host either for negligence or rusticity.

## 54

From other men's goods, however, he did not abstain, neither when he had the command of armies abroad, nor when he held office at Rome; for (as some have recorded), he took money from the proconsul, Tubero, who was his predecessor in Spain, and from the Roman allies in that quarter, for the discharge of his debts; and certain towns of the Lusitanians, he sacked at the point of the sword, although they did not rebel at his commands but opened their gates to him upon his arrival. In Gaul he robbed and spoiled the very chapels and temples of the gods, which were full of rich gifts and oblations. As for cities, he demolished them more often for the sake of their spoil, than for any ill they had committed. In this way, he got such an abundance of gold, that he exchanged it through Italy and the provinces of the empire for three thousand sesterces the pound. In his first consulship, he stole out of the Capitol three thousand pounds' weight of gold, and left in its place the same quantity of gilt brass. He bartered likewise to foreign nations and princes, for gold, the titles of allies and kings, with the honours and privileges that accompanied them; and he exacted from Ptolemy alone nearly six thousand talents, in the name of himself and Pompey. He afterwards supported the expense of the civil wars, and of his triumphs and public spectacles, by the most flagrant rapine and sacrilege.

## 55

In eloquence and warlike achievements, he equalled if he did not surpass the greatest of men. After his accusation of Dolabella, he was indisputably reckoned one of the most distinguished advocates. Cicero, in recounting to Brutus the famous orators, avers, 'that he does not see that Caesar gave place to any of them', and further, 'that he had a manner of pleading that was at once elegant and gay, with much in it of magnificence and nobility'. And in a letter to Cornelius Nepos, he writes of him in the following terms: 'What should a man say more, – which of all the orators that have practised nothing else but oratory, will you prefer to Caesar? – who is there more quick or more profound in his thought, or more gallant and elegant in his sentences?' From his youth he seems to have followed the form of eloquence laid down by Strabo Caesar, out of whose oration in behalf of the Sardinians he transcribed some passages literally into his Divination. It is said that in his delivery he had a high and shrill voice, and his gestures were most animated, though not without grace. He has left behind him some orations, among which are included a few that are not genuine, such as that on behalf of Quintus Metellus. These Augustus deems, not without good reason, to have been written rather by notaries, who either took down his words incorrectly, or were unable to keep pace with him, than publications of his own. For in certain copies I find that the title is not *For Metellus*, but *What he wrote to Metellus*; whereas the speech is

delivered in the name of Caesar, vindicating Metellus and himself
from the aspersions cast upon them by their common defamers. The
oration addressed *To his soldiers in Spain,* Augustus considers likewise
as spurious. There are two under this title; one made, as is alleged, in
the first battle, and the other in the last; at which time, Asinius Pollio
says, he had not leisure to address the soldiers, on account of the
suddenness of the enemy's attack.

## 56

He left commentaries also of his own actions both in the war in Gaul
and in the civil war with Pompey. The authorship of the accounts of
the Alexandrine, African, and Spanish wars is uncertain, although
some think it was Oppius; others say Hirtius, who also compiled the
last book of the Gallic war, which, however, is imperfect.
Concerning the commentaries, Cicero, in his *Brutus,* writes: 'He
wrote exceeding well, I assure you, and in most pleasing fashion; his
commentaries are naked, straight and upright, yet graceful and lovely,
too, being divested of all ornaments and tricks of style. But while his
intention was to leave the materials wherewith others might write a
complete history, to some foolish ones he gave opportunity to curl
and frizzle the plain narrative with their crisping pins; but surely the
wiser sort he discouraged altogether from ever attempting the
subject.' Of the same commentaries, Hirtius gives this report: 'They
are, in the judgment of all men, so approved, that it seems he hath
prevented writers, rather than given them any help. And yet, we have
greater reason to admire him than others; for they only know how
well and purely they were penned, while we know also the facility
and expedition with which he wrote them.' Pollio Asinius thinks that
they were compiled with small care and diligence, and with as little
regard also of sound truth: saying that Caesar was very ready of belief
concerning what was performed by others under his orders; and that
he reported wrongly also those things which he himself achieved,
either from design or default of memory; he believed, also, that
Caesar intended to rewrite and correct these memoirs.

He left also two books of *Analogy,* with the same number under the
title of *Anti-Cato,* and a poem entitled *The Itinerary;* of these he
composed the first two in his passage over the Alps, as he was
returning to the army after making his circuit in Hither-Gaul, the

second about the time of the battle of Munda, and the last during the twenty-four days he employed in his journey from Rome to Farther Spain. There are extant epistles of his written to the senate in a manner never practised by anyone before him; for they are distinguished into pages in the form of a memorandum book: whereas the consuls and commanders before him used constantly in their letters to continue the line quite across the sheet, without any folding or distinction of pages. There are also missives of his written to Cicero and to familiar friends concerning home affairs; in which, if there were occasion for secrecy, he wrote in cipher; that is, he placed the letters in such order that they could not be made out. The proper manner of deciphering these was to exchange the fourth for the first letter, as d for a, and so for the other letters respectively. Furthermore there are certain works of his abroad said to have been written by him when a very young man: as, namely, *The Praises of Hercules*, *The Tragedy of Oedipus*, and also, *Collects of Sayings and Apophthegms*; all of which pamphlets Augustus forbad to be published, in one of his epistles, a short and plain one to Pompeius Macer, who was appointed by him in the disposing and ordering of his libraries.

## 57

He was very skilful in the use of arms, a cunning horseman, and able to endure fatigue beyond all belief. He would march ahead of his troops, sometimes mounted, but more often on foot, and with his head bare whether the sun shone or the clouds poured rain. He made very long journeys with incredible speed, covering as many as a hundred miles a day riding in some hired carriage if the baggage were light; and if he was hindered in his passage by floods in the rivers, he swam across or floated on skins inflated with wind; so that he often arrived in advance of the messengers who brought intelligence of his coming.

## 58

In his expeditions, it is doubtful whether he was better known for his caution or for his daring. He never led his army at any time over roads favourable for ambuscades, without having previously explored the condition by means of scouts; nor did he cross over to Britain, until he had carefully examined in person, the navigation, the harbours, and the most convenient point of landing in the island. Yet, circumspect as he was, when news was brought to him that his camp was besieged in Germany, he made his way to his soldiers, through the enemy's stations, in a Gaulish dress. He sailed the sea in winter, through the midst of the enemy's fleets, from Brundisium and Dyrrachium; and when his own forces which he had commanded to follow him, lingered in their movements, although he had sent messengers repeatedly to hurry them and to no avail, he at last went secretly and alone, aboard a small vessel, in the night time, with his head hooded; nor did he reveal himself, or suffer the pilot to give way to the tempest that came strong against them, until they were well-nigh overwhelmed with the waves.

## 59

No religious fear of unfavourable omens ever kept him from embarking on any enterprise, or stayed him in the prosecution of one that he had in hand. Once when he was about to offer a sacrifice, the beast made its escape; yet he did not defer his expedition against Scipio and Juba. And when it chanced that he fell prone on the ground, as he stepped out of the ship, he construed the accident in a lucky sense, by exclaiming: 'I take possession of thee, O Africa.' Moreover, to make a mockery of the prophecies which were extant that the name of the Scipios was, by the decrees of fate, fortunate and invincible in that province, he retained with him in his camp the most base and abject fellow of all the Cornelian family, and who, by reason of his disgraceful life, was surnamed Salvito.

## 60

He did not often fight pitched battles, but made sudden attacks when occasions arose: often at the end of a march, and sometimes during the most violent storms, when nobody could imagine he would stir. Nor did he ever hold off from fighting, except in his latter days; being then of the opinion that the oftener he had got victories, the less he should tempt fortune, and that nothing a victory could offer him would compensate for what he might lose by disaster. He never overcame the enemy without driving them from their camp, and giving them no time to rally their forces. When in doubtful or dangerous straits, it was his practice to send away the horses, and his own first, so that, with all means of flight taken away, they would be under the greater necessity to hold their ground.

## 61

The horse he rode was strangely marked, having feet like those of a man, with hooves cloven like toes. This horse he had bred himself, and the soothsayers having prophesied that his owner would win empire over the whole world, he was very careful about his rearing, and broke him in himself, as the beast would suffer no one else to mount him. A statue of this horse was afterwards erected by Caesar's order before the temple of Venus Genetrix.

## 62

Many a time he alone stood his ground when the battle was going against him, and he would block the way of those of his troops who fled, holding them back one by one, and even seizing their throats to turn them back towards the enemy. He dealt thus with his own troops even when they were panic-stricken and threatening in their multitude; and once when he had stopped in this manner a standard-bearer, the latter thrust at him with his spear-head; and another, upon a like occasion, left the silver eagle in Caesar's hand.

# 63

The following examples of his resolution are equally, if not more, remarkable. After the battle of Pharsalia, when he had sent his forces before him into Africa, and as he himself was crossing the seas through the straits of Hellespont in a ferryboat, he met with Lucius Cassius, one of the opposite party, with ten ships of war; and so far from endeavouring to escape, he went alongside the ship, and affronting Cassius, began to exhort him to yield; and so upon the submission of Cassius and his humble supplication, he received him aboard.

# 64

At Alexandria, in the attack of a bridge, being forced by a sudden sally of the enemy into a boat, and several others hurrying in with him, he leaped into the sea, and by swimming almost a quarter of a mile, reached the next ship: bearing up his left hand all the while, for fear of wetting some papers which he held in it, and drawing his general's cloak after him with his teeth, so that it might not become the spoils of the enemy.

# 65

His soldiers he regarded, not for their manners nor wealth, but only for their courage and strength; and he treated them with a blending of severity and indulgence; for his supervision was not always strict, but only when the enemy was near; and then he was most exacting in his discipline, insomuch that he would not even give them warning of a march or a battle until the moment of action, keeping them meanwhile always ready and prepared; and he would many times draw them out of camp without any cause, especially in rainy weather, and upon festival days. Sometimes, after admonishing his soldiers to keep their eyes upon him, he would suddenly depart by day or by night, and lengthen the marches so as to tire them out, as they followed him at a distance.

## 66

When at any time his soldiers were terrified by rumours of the strength of the enemy, his manner of restoring their courage was not to deny or diminish the facts, but, on the contrary, to exaggerate them to the highest degree of credibility. Once when his men were greatly perturbed at the expected coming of King Juba, he called them together, and addressed them thus: 'Be it known to you all that within a very few days the King will be here with a power of 10 legions of 30,000 men of arms, a hundred thousand light-armed foot, and three hundred elephants. Forbear, therefore, to inquire further in the matter, or indulge in conjectures, but give credit to me, that know this for a truth; or else I shall put such men as disobey me in the oldest ship I can find and cause them to be carried away with any wind, into what lands or countries it shall be their fortune to fall upon.'

## 67

The trespasses and delinquencies of his soldiers he did not inquire into particularly, nor punish after the regular manner of military discipline. But for deserters and mutineers he made the most diligent inquiry and proceeded against with rigour; at other offences he would wink. Sometimes, after a great battle had ended victoriously, he released them all of military duties and permitted them to revel in all manner of licentiousness; being wont to boast, that his soldiers fought none the less valiantly for being perfumed with sweet oils. He never addressed them in his orations as plain 'Soldiers' but by the more familiar and pleasing name of 'Fellow-soldiers'; and he maintained them in such brave array that their arms were ornamented with silver and gold, not merely for show, but in order that their beauty and value would cause the men to fight more resolutely for fear of losing or damaging them. Moreover he loved his soldiers so much, that when he heard of the overthrow of Titurius and his legions, he neither cut his hair nor shaved his beard until he had revenged their fate upon the enemy. By these means, he both won the devotion of his soldiers, and raised their valour to the highest pitch.

# 68

When he entered upon the civil war, the centurions of every legion offered, each of them, to maintain a horseman at his own expense, and the whole army agreed to serve freely, without either corn or wages; the wealthier ones among them undertaking the maintenance of the poorer. No one of them, during the whole course of the war, revolted from his command; and many of those who were taken captive, and having life offered to them upon condition that they would bear arms against him, refused to betray him. They endured hunger and other hardships which necessarily follow war, not only when they were besieged themselves, but also when they besieged others, with so much resolution, that Pompey, when blocked up in the neighbourhood of Dyrrachium, upon seeing a sort of bread made of a herb, which they lived upon, said: 'I have to deal with wild beasts,' and he commanded that it be taken away immediately, without any one seeing it, lest his own soldiers' spirits be daunted by perceiving the endurance and constancy of their enemies. Of their bravery in battle, this instance may testify: after an unsuccessful engagement at Dyrrachium, they voluntarily offered to be executed therefore; insomuch that their general was more concerned about comforting than punishing them. In other encounters, though their numbers were sometimes fewer than their enemies, they easily prevailed. In fact, one cohort of the sixth legion held out a fort against four legions belonging to Pompey, during several hours; being almost every one of them wounded by the vast number of arrows discharged against them, and of which there were found within the ramparts a hundred and thirty thousand. This is not a matter for marvelling, when one considers the conduct of some persons among them: such as that of Cassius Scaeva, a centurion, or Caius Acilius, a common soldier, to cite only two. Scaeva, when his eye was smitten out, his thigh and shoulder shot through, and his buckler pierced with the shot of 120 arrows, yet defended the guard of the fort committed to his charge, and yielded it not. Acilius, in a fight at sea at Marseilles, after his right hand was cut off as he caught the poop of his enemy's ship, followed the memorable example of Cynegirus among the Greeks, and leaped onto the ship, driving all before him with the boss of his shield.

## 69

They never once mutinied during all the ten years of the Gallic war, but were sometimes rebellious in the course of the civil war. Yet they were always reclaimed quickly, and returned again to their duty, not so much through the indulgence, but in submission to the authority, of their general; for he never would yield one jot to them in their seditious tumults, but always withstood their demands. He cashiered the whole ninth legion, and sent them away with shame, at Placentia, even though Pompey was still in arms in the field; and he would not restore them again to their places, even upon their humble prayers and supplications, until the leaders of the revolt had been punished.

## 70

When the soldiers of the tenth legion at Rome earnestly called for their discharge from warfare and rewards for their service, with mighty threats and no small danger to the whole city, although the war was then raging in Africa, he did not hesitate, contrary to the advice of his friends, to meet the legion and disband it. But addressing them by the title of 'Quirites' (Roman citizens), instead of 'Milites' (Soldiers), he by this single word gently and effectually changed their hearts and their determination, so that they cried out at once that they were his 'soldiers' still; and they followed him of their own accord into Africa, although he had refused their services. And yet he punished the most mutinous among them with the loss of a third of their share in the spoils, and the land appointed for them.

## 71

In affectionate care and protection of his dependants, he was not wanting even in his youth. He defended the cause of a noble youth, Masintha, against King Hiempsal, so vigorously, that in the altercation which took place upon that occasion, he flew upon Juba, the king's son, and caught him by the beard, which was a very great offence among the barbarians, who allowed their beards to grow very long; and when Masintha was pronounced tributary to Hiempsal, he forthwith rescued him out of the hands of those who would have carried him away, and also kept him close in his house for a long time; and soon after his praetorship there expired, and he went into Spain, he took the young gentleman away with him in his own litter, in the midst of his lictors bearing the fasces, and others who had come to attend and take leave of him.

## 72

His friends he treated at all times with so great courtesy and tender respect, that when Caius Oppius, who accompanied him in his journey through a wild forest, fell suddenly ill, he gave him the only place there was to shelter them at night, and lay upon the ground in the open air. Moreover, when he became sovereign lord of all, he advanced some of his faithful followers, though of humble origin, to the highest place of honour. And when he was reproached for this partiality, he professed openly, that if he had used the help of robbers, of cutters and swash-bucklers in maintaining his own dignity, he would not fail to requite them for their services.

## 73

He never entertained malice and hatred against any man so deeply that he would not willingly renounce it when occasion offered. Although Caius Memmius had made most bitter invectives against him, and he had answered with equal bitterness, yet he afterwards assisted him with his vote and interest when Memmius stood candidate for the consulship. When C. Calvus, after promulgating some scandalous epigrams upon him, endeavoured to bring about a reconciliation through the mediation of friends, he of his own accord wrote the first letter. And when Valerius Catullus, who had, as he himself observed, fixed such a stain upon his character in his verses upon Mamurra as never could be effaced, he asked his pardon, invited him to supper the same day, and continued to take up his lodging with his father occasionally, as he had been wont to do.

## 74

Moreover, in his temper he was by nature most mild. Those pirates by whom he was taken prisoner, although when he had captured them he dealt with them as he had sworn, namely that he would crucify them, he nevertheless commanded that their throats be cut first, so that they might be spared the more cruel death. He could never bear the thought of doing any harm to Cornelius Phagitas, who had pursued him in the night when he was sick and a fugitive, with the design of carrying him to Sulla, and from whose hands he had escaped with some difficulty by giving him a bribe. Philemon, his secretary, who had promised his enemies to take his life by giving him poison, he punished only by swift death, without any torment. Being called upon to bear witness against Publius Clodius, his wife Pompeia's gallant, who was accused of polluting certain sacred ceremonies, he denied that he knew anything whatsoever of the matter, or that he was able to bring in any evidence, although both his mother Aurelia, and his sister Julia, had related before the court a full and simple account of the circumstances. And being asked thereupon why he had put away his wife? – 'Because,' said he, 'those of my household should not only be clear of guilt, but even from the suspicion of it.'

## 75

The moderation and clemency which he showed, not only in his administration but in his conduct toward the vanquished party in the civil war, was most admirable. When Pompey announced that he would regard as enemies those who did not take arms in defence of the republic, he for his part proclaimed openly, that he would regard as his friends those who remained neutral. As to all those to whom he had, on Pompey's suggestion, given any command in the army, he left them entire liberty to go over to him, if they desired. When some proposals were made at Ilerda for a surrender, which gave rise to a free correspondence between the two camps, and Afranius and Petreius, upon a sudden change of front, had put to the sword all Caesar's men who were found in the camp, he scorned to imitate the perfidious treachery which they had dealt out to him. At the battle of Pharsalia, he cried out to the soldiers 'to spare their fellow-citizens', and afterwards granted to every one of his own soldiers permission to save an enemy. None of them, so far as appears, lost their lives but in battle, excepting only Afranius, Faustus, and young Lucius Caesar; and it is said that even they were put to death without his consent. Afranius and Faustus had borne arms against him, after obtaining their pardon; and Lucius Caesar, for his part, had not only in the most cruel manner destroyed by fire and sword his freedmen and slaves, but cut to pieces the wild beasts which he had prepared for the entertainment of the people. To conclude, in his latter days, he permitted all whom he had not before pardoned, to return into Italy, and to bear offices, both civil and military. He even erected again the statues of Sulla and Pompey, which the people had overthrown. And after this, when there was any plot hatched or word spoken against him by his adversaries, he chose rather to repress than to revenge it. And so, having detected certain conspiracies and nocturnal assemblies, he went no further than to proclaim that he knew of them, and as for those that gave out bitter speeches concerning him, he thought it sufficient to admonish them, in a public manner, not to persist therein. He bore with great moderation a virulent libel written against him by Aulus Caecinna, as well as the abusive lampoons of Pitholaus, which did great damage to his reputation; and he took the matter no more to heart than one citizen would have done at another's malice.

## 76

The rest of his deeds and words, however, so far outweigh all his excellent qualities, that it is thought he abused his power, and was justly cut off. For he not only appropriated excessive honours, such as the consulship every year, the dictatorship for life, and the censorship, but also the title of emperor, and the surname of Father of his Country, besides having his statue among the kings, and a lofty couch in the theatre; he even suffered some honours to be decreed to him, which were not becoming to the most exalted of mankind: namely, a golden throne in the senate-house and on his tribunal, a consecrated chariot, and banners in the Circensian procession, temples, altars, statues among the gods, a bed of state in the temples, a priest, and a college of priests dedicated to himself, like those of Pan; and that one of the months should be called by his name. There were, indeed, no honours which he did not either assume himself, or confer upon others, at his will and pleasure. In his third and fourth consulship, he used only the title of the office, being content with the absolute power of dictatorship decreed unto him with the consulship; and in both years, he substituted other consuls in his room, during the last three months; so that, in the meanwhile, he held no assemblies of the people for the election of magistrates, excepting only tribunes and aediles of the people; and appointed officers, under the name of prefects, instead of the praetors, to administer the affairs of the city during his absence. And upon the very last day of the year, to wit, next before the kalends of January, the office of consul having become vacant by a sudden death, he conferred it upon one that requested it of him, for a few hours, namely Caninius Rebitus. Of this consulship, Cicero made many jests, as: 'A vigilant consul we have had in Caninius, who in all his office never slept a wink.' And, 'A consul we have had so severe and Caesar-like, that during his governance, no man dined, nor supped, nor even so much as slept.' With equal disregard of the customs of his country, he appointed magistrates to continue in office for many years successively. To ten persons of praetorian rank, he granted the insignia of the consular dignity. He admitted into the senate some men who had been made free of the city, and even natives of Gaul, who were little better than barbarians. Furthermore, over the mint and the public revenue of the state, he placed in charge some servants of his own household; and gave over the command of three legions, which he left at Alexandria, to Rufio, an old catamite of his, the son of one of his freedmen.

## 77

He was guilty of the same presumptuousness in the language he publicly used, as Titus Ampius reports; according to whom he said, 'That the republic was nothing but a name, without substance or reality; that Sulla was altogether an ignorant fellow to abdicate the dictatorship; that men ought to consider what is becoming in talking with him, and look upon what he says as law.' To such a pitch of arrogance did he proceed, that when a soothsayer announced to him the unfavourable omen that the entrails of a victim offered for sacrifice were without a heart, he said: 'The entrails will be more favourable when I please; and it ought not to be regarded as a prodigy that a beast should be found wanting a heart.'

## 78

But the act of his which aroused the greatest censure and hostility was his failure to rise when he received the whole body of the conscript fathers before the temple of Venus Genetrix, where they waited upon him with a number of decrees, conferring on him the highest dignities. Some say that he attempted to rise, but that Cornelius Balbus restrained him; others believe that he not only made no move at all, but frowned upon Caius Trebatius, who suggested the propriety of standing up to receive the senate. This ungraciousness was thought the more intolerable in him, because, when one of the tribunes of the people, Pontius Aquila, would not rise up to him as he passed by the tribunes' seat during his triumph, he was very indignant, and cried out: 'Well then, you tribune, Aquila, wrest the commonwealth out of my hands'; and for some days afterwards, he never promised a favour to any person, without this proviso: 'If Pontius Aquila will give me leave.'

## 79

To this drastic gesture of contempt for the senate, he added another affront still more audacious. For when, after the sacred rites of the Latin festival, he was returning home amid the immoderate and unusual acclamations of the people, a man in the multitude placed on one of his statues a laurel crown encircled with a white fillet, the insignia of royalty, and Epidius Marullus, a tribune of the people, together with his colleague Caesetius Flavus, ordered the fillet to be removed from the crown, and the man to be taken to prison; Caesar, taking very much to heart either the notion that the idea of royalty had been suggested to so little purpose, or, as was said, that he was thus deprived of the merit of refusing it, reprimanded the tribunes very severely, and dismissed them from their office. From that day forward, he was never able to efface the scandal of affecting the name of king, although he replied to the people, when they saluted him by that title: 'I am Caesar, and no king.' And at the feast of the Lupercalia, when the consul Antony placed a crown upon his head in the rostra several times, he as often put it away and sent it to the Capitol for Jupiter Optimus Maximus. Moreover, a rumour was rife that he contemplated withdrawing to Alexandria or to Ilium, whither he would transfer the imperial power and drain Italy by new levies, leaving the government of the city to be administered by his friends. To this report it was added that in the next meeting of the senate, Lucius Cotta, one of the fifteen persons appointed to inspect and expound the Sibylline books, would move that, as there was in these books a prophecy that the Parthians would never be vanquished but by a king, therefore Caesar should be styled king.

## 80

This gave occasion to the conspirators to hasten the execution of their design lest they should be driven to give their assent to the proposal. Instead, therefore, of convening separately, in small groups dispersed here and there, they now combined their counsels; for the people themselves were discontented with the present state of things, both privately and publicly condemning the despotism under which they lived and calling earnestly for protectors and maintainers of their liberties. Upon the admission of aliens into the senate, a hand-bill was posted up in these words: 'A good deed! let no one show a new senator the way to the house.' These verses, also, were commonly chanted:

> The Gauls in triumph Caesar leads,
> In senate they anon
> No sooner laid their breeches off,
> But purpled robes put on.

When Quintus Maximus, who had been his deputy in the consulship for the last three months, entered the theatre, and the lictor, as the custom was, bid the people take notice who was coming, they all cried out: 'He is no consul.' After the removal of Caesetius and Marullus from their office, they were found to have a great many votes at the next election of consuls. Someone wrote under the statue of Lucius Brutus 'Would you were now alive!' and under the statue of Caesar himself these lines:

> Brutus for expelling the Kings, was created Consul the first.
> This man for expelling the Consuls is become King, the last.

There conspired against him more than sixty persons, under the leadership of Caius Cassius, and Marcus and Decimus Brutus. It was at first disputed among them, whether they should attack him in the Campus Martius when he was taking the votes of the tribes, and some of them should throw him off the bridge, while others should be ready to stab him upon his fall; or else in the Via Sacra, or at the entrance of the theatre. But after public notice had been given by proclamation for the senate to meet in the court of Pompey upon the ides of March, they approved both of the time and place, as being meet for their purpose.

## 81

Caesar had warning given him of his death by many strange signs. A few months before, when the colonists, settled at Capua by virtue of the Julian law (promulgated by himself), were demolishing some old sepulchres in building country houses, and were the more eager at the work because they came upon certain vessels of antique workmanship, a tablet of brass was found in a tomb in which Capys, the founder of Capua, was said to have been buried, with an inscription in the Greek language to this effect: 'Whenever the bones of Capys come to be discovered, a descendant of Iulus will be slain by the hands of his kinsmen, and his death revenged by fearful disasters throughout Italy.' Lest any person should regard this anecdote as a fabulous or silly invention, it was revealed by Cornelius Balbus, an intimate friend of Caesar's. On the day immediately preceding his death, he learned that the horses which, upon his crossing the Rubicon, he had consecrated and turned loose to graze without a keeper, turned away from their food and shed abundant tears. Also, as he offered sacrifice, the soothsayer Spurinna warned him, by certain ominous portents in the appearance of the offering, that he should take heed of danger which threatened him, and which would not be deferred beyond the ides of March. The day before the ides, birds of various kinds from a neighbouring grove, pursuing a wren which flew into Pompey's senate house with a sprig of laurel in its beak, tore it in pieces. That night, he dreamed at one time that he was soaring above the clouds, and at another that he had joined hands with Jupiter. His wife, Calpurnia, likewise had a dream in which she imagined that the pediment of the house was falling down and her husband stabbed on her bosom; and suddenly thereupon the chamber doors flew open. Pondering these omens, as well as his infirm health, he was in some doubt as to whether he should stay at home and put off those matters which he had purposed to debate before the senate, or no. At last, however, Decimus Brutus persuading him that he should not disappoint the senators who were now numerously gathered and awaiting his coming, he set forth about the fifth hour. On his way, some person thrust into his hand a paper warning him of the conspiracy upon his life, and he mixed it with some other documents which he carried in his left hand, intending to read it at leisure. Victim after victim was slain at the sacrifice, without any favourable appearances in the entrails; but he entered the Curia of Pompey, laughing at Spurinna as a false prophet, because the ides of March were come, without any harm having befallen him. To this the soothsayer made answer: 'They are come, indeed, but not past.'

## 82                                          A.U.C. 710

When he had taken his seat, the conspirators stood round him, under colour of paying their compliments; and immediately Tullius Cimber, who had been his great friend and loyal adherent and who had undertaken to commence the assault, stepped nearer than the rest, as though to make some application. Caesar, making a sign that he should defer his business until some other time, found himself seized by the toga at both shoulders; whereupon as he cried out, 'This is violence', one of the Cassii wounded him a little below the throat. Caesar, catching Cassius by the arm, thrust it through with his style; and attempting to rush forward was checked by another wound. When he perceived that he was beset on every side with drawn daggers, he covered his head with his gown, and at the same moment drew the skirt about his legs with his left hand that he might conceal thereby the lower part of his body and fall more decently. He was stabbed with three and twenty wounds, during which time he groaned but once, and that at the first thrust, but uttered no cry; although some writers have said that when Marcus Brutus fell upon him, he exclaimed: 'What! art thou, too, one of them? Thou, my son!' The whole assembly instantly dispersing, he lay for some time after he expired, until three of his slaves laid the body on a litter and carried it home, with one arm hanging down over the side. With all his wounds, there was, as Antistius the surgeon reported, none that was mortal, except the second, which he received in the breast. The conspirators meant to drag his body into the Tiber as soon as they had killed him; to confiscate his estate, and rescind all his enactments; but they were prevented by fear of Mark Antony and Lepidus, Caesar's Master of the Horse, and abandoned their intentions.

## 83

At the instance of Lucius Piso, his father-in-law, his will was opened and read in Mark Antony's house. He had made it on the ides of the preceding September, at his Lavican villa, and committed it to the care of the chief of the Vestal Virgins. Quintus Tubero writes that in all the wills he had signed from the time of his first consulship to the breaking out of the civil war, Cnaeus Pompey was appointed his heir, and that this had been publicly announced to the army. But in his last will, he named three heirs, the grandsons of his sisters; namely, Caius Octavius for three-fourths of his estate, and Lucius Pinarius and Quintus Pedius for the remaining fourth. Other heirs (in remainder) were named at the close of the will, in which he also adopted Caius Octavius, who was to assume his name, into his family; and named most of those who were concerned in his death among the guardians of his son, if he should have any; as well as Decimus Brutus among his heirs of the second order. He bequeathed to the Roman people his gardens near the Tiber, and three hundred sesterces to each man.

## 84

The occasion of his burial having been solemnly proclaimed, a pile of wood for his funeral fire was erected in the Campus Martius, near the tomb of his daughter Julia. Before the rostra was placed a gilded tabernacle, on the model of the temple of Venus Genetrix, within which was an ivory bed, covered with purple and cloth of gold, and at the head of which was a trophy, with the bloodstained robe in which he was slain. It being considered that the whole day would not suffice for carrying the funeral oblations in solemn procession before the corpse, orders were issued for every one, without regard to order, to carry them from the city into the Campus Martius by what way they pleased. In the plays performed at the funeral, there was sung a passage from Pacuvius's tragedy, entitled *The Trial for Arms,* in order to inspire pity and indignation for his murder:

> Men servasse, ut essent qui me perderent?

> Alas the while, that I these men should save:
> By bloody death, to bring me to my grave.

And some lines also from Attilius's tragedy of *Electra*, to the same effect. Instead of a funeral panegyric, the consul Antony ordered a herald to proclaim to the people the decree of the senate, in which they had bestowed upon him all honours, both divine and human; with the oath by which they had engaged themselves for the defence of his person; and to these he added only a few words of his own. The magistrates and others who had formerly filled the highest offices, carried the bier from the rostra into the Forum. While some proposed that the body should be burnt in the sanctuary of the temple of Jupiter Capitolinus, and others in Pompey's senate-house; on a sudden, two men, with swords by their sides and spears in their hands, set fire to the bier with lighted torches. The multitude immediately heaped upon it dry faggots, the tribunals and benches of the adjoining courts and whatever else came to hand. Then the musicians and players stripped off the dresses they wore on the present occasion, taken from the wardrobe of his triumph at spectacles, rent them, and threw them into the flames. The legionaries of his veteran bands also cast in their armour, which they had put on in honour of his funeral. Most of the ladies did the same with their ornaments, and with the bullae and mantles of their children. In this public mourning there joined a multitude of foreigners, expressing their sorrow according to the fashion of their respective countries; especially the Jews, on whom Caesar had conferred great benefits, and who for several nights together frequented the spot where the body was burnt.

## 85

The common people ran from the funeral, with torches in their hands, to the houses of Brutus and Cassius, from whence, being repelled with difficulty, they came upon Helvius Cinna, and mistaking him for Cornelius Cinna, who had, in a speech of the day before, reflected bitterly upon Caesar, they slew him, and carried his head about the city on the point of a spear. Afterwards they erected in the Forum a column of Numidian marble, formed of one stone nearly twenty feet high, and inscribed upon it these words: To the Father of His Country. At this column they continued for a long time to offer sacrifices, make vows, and decide controversies, in which they swore by Caesar.

## 86

Caesar left behind him in the minds of certain friends a suspicion that he neither desired nor cared to live any longer, on account of his failing health, and for that reason slighted all the omens of religion, and the warnings of his friends. Others are of opinion, that thinking himself secure in the late decree of the senate, and their oaths, he dismissed the Spanish guards who attended him with drawn swords. Others again suppose that he chose rather to face at once the dangers which threatened him on all sides than to be forever on the watch against them; protesting the while that the safety of his person concerned the commonwealth more than himself, for he had been for some time satiated with power and glory, whereas the commonwealth, if anything should befall him, would have no rest and, being involved in another civil war, would be in a worse state than before.

## 87

There is one thing, however, upon which all are commonly agreed; that his death was in many respects such as he would have chosen. For upon reading the account delivered by Xenophon, how Cyrus in his last illness gave instructions respecting his funeral, Caesar deprecated a lingering death and wished that his own might be sudden and swift. And the day before he fell, the conversation at supper in the house of Marcus Lepidus turning upon what was the most preferable end of a man's life, he spoke in favour of one that was sudden and unlooked-for.

## 88

He died in the fifty-sixth year of his age and was canonised among the gods, not only by a formal decree but in the belief of the common people. For during the first games which Augustus, his heir, consecrated to his memory, a comet blazed for seven days together, arising always about the eleventh hour of the day; and it was supposed to be the soul of Caesar, received into heaven; for which reason, also, he is represented on his statue with a star on his brow. The senate house in which he was slain was ordered to be shut up, and a decree made that the ides of March should be called parricidal and that the senate should never more assemble on that day.

## 89

Of his murderers, not one survived him above three years or died a natural death. All were condemned by the senate, and by some mishap or other were taken off; some perished in shipwreck, others in battle; and some slew themselves with the same dagger wherewith they had stabbed Caesar.

# Octavius Caesar Augustus

That the family of the Octavii was of the first distinction in Velitrae, there is much evidence to show; for not only was there a street in the most frequented part of the town which bore the name Octavius, but there was also to be seen an altar, consecrated to one Octavius, who being chosen general in a war with some neighbouring people, had brought to him, while he was sacrificing to Mars, the news of a sudden attack by the enemy; and he immediately snatched the entrails of the victim from off the fire and offered them half raw upon the altar; after which, he entered into battle and returned victorious. This incident resulted in a law, which decreed that in all future times the entrails should be presented to Mars in like manner and the rest of the sacrifice carried to the Octavii.

## 2

This family, as well as several in Rome, was admitted into the senate by Tarquinius Priscus and soon afterwards placed by Servius Tullius among the patricians; but in process of time it transferred itself to the plebeian order, and, after the lapse of a long interval, was restored by Julius Caesar to the rank of patricians. The first person of the family to be raised by the suffrages of the people to the magistracy was Caius Rufus, who obtained the quaestorship. He had two sons, Cnaeus and Caius, from whom are descended the two branches of the Octavian family, which have had very different fortunes. For Cnaeus and his descendants, in uninterrupted succession, attained to places of the highest honour; but Caius and his posterity, whether from their circumstances or their choice, remained in the equestrian order until the time of the father of Augustus. The great-grandfather of Augustus served as a military tribune in the second Punic war in Sicily, under the command of Aemilius Papus; his grandfather, contenting himself with bearing the public offices of his own municipality, grew old in the tranquil enjoyment of an ample patrimony. Such is the report made by various authors. Augustus himself, however, tells us nothing more than that he was descended of an equestrian family, both ancient and rich, of which his father was the first who obtained the rank of senator. Mark Antony upbraidingly tells him that his great-grandfather was a freedman of the territory of Thurium in Magna Graecia, and a ropemaker, and his grandfather a usurer. This is all the information I have anywhere met with, concerning the ancestors of Augustus by the father's side.

## 3

Caius Octavius, his father, was from his very youth a person of great wealth and reputation: so that I cannot but marvel at those who say that he was a money-dealer. He was employed in distributing bribes and canvassing for the candidates at elections in the Campus Martius. For, having been brought up in all the affluence of a great estate, he attained with ease to honourable posts and discharged the duties of these with much distinction. Presently, upon his praetorship, the province of Macedonia fell to his lot. And in his journey thither the fugitives, to wit, the relics of the armies of Spartacus and Catiline, who had possessed themselves of the territory of Thurium, were met and defeated by him; for he had received from the senate an extraordinary commission to that end. In his government of the province, he conducted himself with equal justice and fortitude. For, having discomfited in a great battle the Bessians and Thracians, he dealt with the allies of the republic in such a manner, that there are extant letters from M. Tullius Cicero, in which he advises and exhorts his brother Quintus, who then held the proconsulship of Asia with no great reputation, to imitate the example of his neighbour Octavius, in gaining the affections of the allies of Rome.

## 4

After quitting Macedonia, before he could profess himself a candidate for the consulship, he died suddenly, leaving behind him a daughter, the elder Octavia, by Ancharia; and another daughter, Octavia the younger, as well as Augustus by Atia, who was the daughter of Marcus Atius Balbus, and Julia, sister to Caius Julius Caesar. Balbus was, by the father's side, of a family who were natives of Aricia, and many of whom had been in the senate. By the mother's side he was closely related to Pompey the Great; and after he had borne the office of praetor, was one of the twenty commissioners appointed by the Julian law to divide the land in Campania among the people. But Mark Antony, treating with contempt Augustus' descent even by the mother's side, says that his great grandfather was of African descent and at one time kept a perfumer's shop, and at another, a bakehouse, in Aricia. And Cassius of Parma, in a letter, taxes Augustus with being the son of one who was not only a baker but a usurer. These are his words: 'Thou art a lump of thy mother's meal, which a money-changer of Nerulum taking from the newest bakehouse of Aricia, kneaded into some shape, with his hands all sullied by telling and exchanging money.'

## 5

Augustus was born when M. Tullius Cicero and Caius Antonius were consuls, upon the ninth day before the kalends of October (the 23rd September), a little before sunrise, in the palatine quarter of the city, at a place called Capita Bubula, where now stands a chapel dedicated to him, built a little after his death. For, as it is recorded in the proceedings of the senate, when Caius Laetorius, a young man of a patrician family, in pleading before the senators for a lighter sentence upon his being convicted of adultery, alleged, beside his youth and quality, that he was the possessor and as it were the guardian, of the ground which the Divine Augustus first touched upon his coming into the world; and entreated that he might find favour for the sake of that deity, who was in a peculiar manner his: an act of the senate was passed for the consecration of that part of his house in which Augustus was born.

## 6

His nursery is shown to this day, in a villa belonging to the family in the suburbs of Velitrae; being a very small place, and much like a pantry; and an opinion prevails in the neighbourhood, that he was also born there. Into this place no person presumes to enter, unless upon necessity and with great devotion; for it is a belief from olden times that such as enter it rashly are seized with great horror and fearfulness, which a short while since was confirmed by a remarkable incident. For when a new inhabitant of the house had, either by mere chance, or to try the truth of the report, taken up his lodging in that apartment, he was thrown out by some sudden violence, he knew not how, and was found in a state of stupefaction, with the coverlid of his bed, before the door of the chamber.

# 7

While he was yet an infant, he was surnamed Thurinus, in memory of the place of his ancestors; or because, soon after he was born, his father Octavius had vanquished the fugitive slaves, in the country near Thurium. That he was surnamed Thurinus, I can affirm upon sufficient evidence, for when a boy I had a small bronze statue of him with that name upon it in iron letters, nearly effaced by age, which I presented to the emperor Hadrian, by whom it is now revered amongst the other tutelary deities in his chamber. He is often called Thurinus tauntingly by Mark Antony in his letters; to which he makes only this reply: that he marvelled that his former name should be objected to and made a reproach. Afterwards, he assumed the surname of Caius Caesar, and then of Augustus: the former in compliance with the will of his great-uncle, and the latter upon a motion of Munatius Plancus in the senate. For when some gave it as their opinion that he should be styled Romulus, as being, in a sense, a second founder of the city, Plancus prevailed in his assertion that he should rather be called Augustus, a surname not only new but of greater dignity, because places devoted to religion, and those in which anything is consecrated by augury, are denominated August, either from the word *auctus*, signifying augmentation, or from *ab avium gestu, gustuve,* from the flight and feeding of birds; as appears from this line of Ennius:

> When glorious Rome by august augury was built.

# 8

He was four years old when his father died; and, in his twelfth year, he pronounced a funeral oration in praise of his grandmother Julia. Four years later, having put on his virile robe, he was honoured with several military rewards by Caesar in his African triumph, although by reason of his youth he had not served in the war. Soon afterwards, when his uncle had gone into Spain against the sons of Pompey, he followed him, although he was scarcely recovered from a dangerous illness; and after being shipwrecked at sea and proceeding with very few attendants through roads that were infested with the enemy, he at last came up with him. By this fortitude and bravery he won the love of his uncle, who strongly approved such indications of character. When Caesar, after he had subjugated Spain, meditated an expedition against the Dacians and Parthians, Augustus was sent before him to Apollonia, where he applied himself to his studies; until, receiving intelligence that Caesar was slain, and that he was appointed his heir, he hesitated for some time whether he should call to his aid the legions stationed in the neighbourhood; but he abandoned that course as too hasty. But when he returned to Rome, he entered upon his inheritance, notwithstanding that his mother was apprehensive that such a measure might be fraught with danger, and his step-father, Marcius Philippus, a man of consular rank, very earnestly advised him against it. From this time, having gathered and assembled his forces, he first held the government jointly with Mark Antony and Marcus Lepidus (this being the famed Triumvirate), then with Antony only, for the space of nearly twelve years, and at last in his own hands during a period of four and forty.

# 9

Having thus given a very short summary of his life, I shall consider the several parts of it, not in order of time, but arranging his acts into distinct classes, for the sake of perspicuity. He waged five civil wars, namely those of Modena, Philippi, Perugia, Sicily, and Actium: the first and last of which were against Antony, the second against Brutus and Cassius, the third against Lucius Antonius, the triumvir's brother, and the fourth against Sextus Pompeius, the son of Cnaeus

Pompeius. In all these wars he was animated by the desire to avenge the murder of his uncle, and maintain the state of affairs which he had established: an enterprise in which he felt that both his honour and interest were involved.

## IO

No sooner had he returned from Apollonia than he formed the plan of attacking Brutus and Cassius secretly and forcibly; but they having foreseen the danger and fled from it, he resolved to proceed against them by an appeal to the laws in their absence, and indict them for murder. Meanwhile, those whose province it was to prepare the sports in honour of Caesar's last victory in the civil war, not daring to do it, he himself set them forth. And that he might carry into effect his other designs with greater authority, he professed himself a candidate in the room of a tribune of the people who happened to die at that time, although he was of a patrician family, and had not yet been in the senate. But the consul Mark Antony, from whom he had expected the greatest help, opposed his suit, and even refused to do him so much as common justice, unless persuaded by a consideration; whereupon he went over to the party of the nobles, to whom he perceived Antony was odious principally because he had endeavoured to drive Decius Brutus, whom he besieged in the town of Modena, out of the province which had been given him by Caesar and confirmed to him by the senate. Upon the advice of persons about him, he engaged some ruffians to murder Antony; but the plot being discovered, and fearing a similar attempt upon himself, he gained over Caesar's veteran soldiers by distributing among them all the money he could collect, for the defence of his own person as well as that of the state. And being appointed to lead this army he had gathered, with the rank of praetor, and in conjunction with Hirtius and Pansa, who had accepted the consulship, to carry assistance to Decius Brutus, he put an end to the war by two battles in three months. In the former of which, Antony writes that he fled, and two days afterwards made his appearance without his general's cloak and his horse; in the last battle, however, it is certain that he performed the part not only of a general, but a soldier; for, in the heat of battle, when the standard-bearer of his legion was severely wounded, he took the eagle upon his shoulders and carried it a good while.

## II

During this war, Hirtius being slain in battle and Pansa dying soon after of his wound, it was rumoured widely that they both were killed through his means, in order that, when Antony fled, the republic having lost its consuls, he might have the victorious armies entirely at his own command. And verily the death of Pansa was so deeply suspected that Glyco, his surgeon, was placed in custody, upon the belief that he had put poison into his wound. Aquilius Niger adds moreover that Augustus himself, in the confusion of the battle, killed Hirtius with his own hands.

## 12

But upon intelligence that Antony, after his defeat, had been received by Marcus Lepidus, and that the rest of the generals and armies had all allied themselves with the senate, he, without any hesitation, deserted from the party of the nobles: giving as the pretext for his change of mind, the actions and sayings of several among them; for some said, 'he was a mere boy', and others threw out, 'that he ought to be promoted to honours, and cut off', to avoid making any suitable acknowledgment either to him or the veteran legions. And the more to testify his regret for having attached himself to the other faction, he fined the Nursini a large sum of money, which they were unable to pay, and then expelled them from the town, for having inscribed upon a monument, erected at the public charge to their countrymen who were slain in the battle of Modena, that 'they fell in the cause of liberty'.

## 13

Having entered into a confederacy with Antony and Lepidus, he concluded the war at Philippi in two battles, although he was at that time weak and suffering from sickness. In the first battle he was driven from his camp, and with some difficulty made his escape to the wing of the army commanded by Antony. And now, intoxicated with triumph, he sent the head of Brutus (who slew himself upon being defeated) to be cast at the foot of Caesar's statue, and treated the noblest of the prisoners not only with cruelty, but with abusive language; insomuch that he is said to have answered one of them who humbly entreated that at least he might not remain unburied, 'That will be in the power of the birds.' Two others, father and son, who implored of him their lives, he ordered to cast lots which of them should live or settle it between themselves by the sword; and he beheld both their deaths, for the father offering his life to save his son, and being accordingly slain, the son voluntarily killed himself on the spot. Whereupon the rest of the prisoners, and among them Marcus Favonius, Cato's rival, being led up in fetters, after they had saluted Antony, the general, with much respect, reviled Octavius in the foulest terms. After this victory, dividing between them the offices of the state, Mark Antony undertook to restore order in the east, while Augustus conducted the veteran soldiers back to Italy and settled them in colonies on the lands belonging to the municipalities. But he found favour neither with the soldiers nor the owners of the lands: one party complaining of the injustice done them, in being violently ejected from their possessions, and the other that they were not rewarded according to their merit; one of the fugitives being Virgil, who having narrowly escaped being killed by the centurion Ario, was ejected from his farm.

## 14

At this time he forced Lucius Antony, who, presuming upon his own authority as consul and his brother's power, was raising new disturbances, to fly to Perugia, and there compelled him, by famine, to yield at last, although not without exposing himself to great jeopardy, both before the war and during its continuance. For a common soldier having got into the seats of the equestrian order in the theatre at the public spectacles, Caesar ordered him to be removed by an officer; and a rumour being thence spread by his enemies that he had put the man to death by torture, the soldiers flocked together in great wrath and indignation so that he barely escaped with his life. The only thing that saved him was the sudden reappearance of the soldier, safe and sound, no violence having been offered him. And while he was sacrificing under the walls of Perugia he nearly fell into the hands of a body of gladiators who sallied out of the town.

## 15

After the taking of Perugia, he proceeded to the execution of a great many of the prisoners, making only one reply to all who implored pardon, or endeavoured to excuse themselves: 'You must die.' Some write, that 300 of the two orders, to wit, senators and knights, chosen out of those who were captured, were killed as sacrifices before an altar raised to Julius Caesar upon the ides of March, the anniversary of his death. There have been others who wrote that he entered upon the war with no other view than that his secret enemies and those whom fear more than affection kept quiet, might be detected, by declaring themselves, now they had an opportunity, with Lucius Antony at their head; and that having defeated them, and confiscated their estates, he might be enabled to fulfil his promise to the veteran soldiers.

## 16

He soon commenced the Sicilian war, but it was protracted by various delays during a long period; at one time for the purpose of repairing his fleets, which he lost twice by storm even in the summer; at another, while patching up a peace, to which he was forced by the clamours of the people, in consequence of a famine occasioned by Pompey's cutting off the supply of corn by sea. But at last, having built a new fleet, and obtained twenty-thousand manumitted slaves who were given him for the oar, he formed the Julian harbour at Baiae, by letting the sea into the Lucrine and Avernian lakes; and having exercised his forces there during the whole winter, he overcame Pompey betwixt Mylae and Naulochus; although just as the battle broke out, he suddenly fell into such a profound sleep that his friends were obliged to wake him to give the signal. And this, I think, gave occasion for Antony's reproach: 'You were not able to take a clear view of the fleet, when drawn up in battle array, but lay like a senseless block on your back, looking up at the sky; nor did you get up and let your men see you until Marcus Agrippa had forced the enemies' ships to sheer off.' Others impute to him both a saying and an action which were indefensible, for, upon the loss of his fleets by storm, he is reported to have cried: 'I will conquer in spite of Neptune'; and at the next Circensian games, he would not suffer the image of that god to be carried in procession as was the custom. Indeed he scarcely ever ran more or greater risks in any of his wars than in this. Having transported part of his army to Sicily, and being on his return for the rest, he was overtaken unawares by Demochares and Apollophanes, Pompey's admirals, from whom he escaped with great trouble, and with one ship only. Likewise, as he was travelling on foot through the Locrian territory to Rhegium, seeing two of Pompey's vessels passing by that coast, and believing them to be his own, he went down to the shore, and was very nearly taken prisoner. On this occasion, as he was making his escape through byways and blind lanes, a slave of Aemilius Paulus, a companion of his, owing him a grudge for the proscription of Paulus, the father of Aemilius, and embracing the good opportunity for revenge now offered, attempted to kill him. After the flight of Pompey, one of his colleagues, Marcus Lepidus, whom he had called out of Africa to his aid, swelling with pride because he was in command of twenty legions, challenged the sovereignty over the rest, namely, Mark Antony and Octavius Augustus, and that in a menacing manner, he divested him of his authority; but, upon his humble submission and supplication, granted him his life, but banished him forever to Circeii.

## 17

A.U.C. 724

The alliance between him and Antony, which had always been uncertain, spasmodic, and ill-knit by repeated reconciliations, he at last brought to an end. And the better to prove to the world how far Antony had degenerated from the standards befitting a Roman citizen, he caused to be opened and read in a public assembly the will of Antony, which had been left at Rome, and wherein he had named among his heirs, some children of Cleopatra. Yet upon his being termed an enemy by the state, he sent to him all his relations and friends, among whom were Caius Sosius and Titus Domitius, at that time consuls. He likewise spoke favourably in public of the people of Bologna, for joining in the association with the rest of Italy to support his cause, because they had, in former times, been under the protection of the family of the Antonii. And not long afterwards he vanquished him in a naval battle near Actium, which continued until such a late hour in the evening that he was forced to sleep all night, conqueror as he was, on ship-board.

When he retired from Actium into the isle of Samos for the winter season, he was much disquieted by the news of mutiny among the soldiers he had chosen from the main body of his army sent to Brundisium after the victory; and learning of their demands for rewards for their service and a discharge, he returned to Italy. In his journey thither he twice met with violent storms, the first time between the promontories of Peloponnesus and Aetolia, and the other about the Ceraunian mountains; in both which a part of his Liburnian squadron was sunk, the spars and rigging of his own ship carried away and the rudder broken in pieces. He remained only twenty-seven days at Brundisium, until the exactions of the soldiers were appeased, and then departed by way of Asia and Syria, to Egypt, where, laying siege to Alexandria, whither Antony had fled with Cleopatra, he made himself master of it very quickly. And as for Antony, who now (all too late) sued for conditions of peace, he forced him to kill himself, and viewed him dead. Cleopatra he would gladly have saved alive to beautify his triumph; and when she was said to have been poisoned by an asp, he sent for the Psylli to suck the venom from her body. When the poison proved fatal, he accorded her and Antony the honour of being buried in one sepulchre, and ordered the tomb, which they had themselves begun, to be completed. The elder of Antony's two sons by Fulvia, he caused to be taken by force from the statue of Julius Caesar, to which he had fled, after many fruitless entreaties for his life, and put him to death. The same fate he dealt out to Caesario, Cleopatra's son by Caesar, as he pretended, who had fled for his life but was retaken. The children which Antony had by Cleopatra he saved, and brought up and cherished in a manner suitable to their rank, just as if they had been his own relations.

## 18

At this time he had a desire to see the sarcophagus and body of Alexander the Great, which, for that purpose, were taken out of the cell in which they rested; and after looking upon it for some time, he paid honours to the memory of that prince by offering a golden crown and strewing flowers upon it; and being asked if he wished to see the tombs of the Ptolemies also, he answered that he was desirous of seeing a king, not dead men. When he had reduced Egypt to the form of a province, to the end that it might be more fertile and more capable of supplying Rome with corn, he set his soldiers to scouring the canals, into which the Nile, upon its rise, overflows, but which, during a long series of years, had become choked with mud. And to make the memory of his victory at Actium more glorious, he built the city of Nicopolis on that part of the coast and ordained certain games to be celebrated there every five years. He enlarged also an old temple of Apollo, and adorned with naval trophies the place wherein he had encamped, consecrating it to Neptune and Mars.

## 19

He afterwards suppressed several tumults and insurrections, as well as certain conspiracies against his life, which were detected by the confession of accomplices before they were ripe for execution; and others subsequently. Such were those of the younger Lepidus, of Varro Murena, and Fannius Caepio; then that of Marcus Egnatius, afterwards that of Plautius Rufus, and of Lucius Paulus, his grand-daughter's husband; and beside these, another of Lucius Audasius, an old feeble man, who was accused of forgery; as also of Asinius Epicadus, a Parthinian mongrel, and at last that of Telephus, a lady's prompter; for Augustus was not free from the plots and conspiracies even of some of the lowest of the people against him. Audasius and Epicadus had formed the design of carrying off to the armies his daughter Julia and his grandson Agrippa, from the islands in which they were confined. Telephus, conceiving the mad dream that the government was decreed to him by destiny and the will of God, proposed to fall upon both Octavius and the senate. And more than that, there was once found standing before his chamber door in the night, a camp servant, who had passed the porters unobserved and made his way thither armed with a hunting-knife; but whether he was really disordered in his head, or only counterfeited madness, is uncertain; for no confession could be wrung from him by torture.

## 20

He led in person only two foreign wars: the Dalmatian, while he was yet a youth; and, after Antony's final defeat, the Cantabrian. In the Dalmatian war he was wounded in one battle, in his right knee by a stone, and at another time he was greatly hurt in one leg and both arms by the fall of a military bridge. His other wars he carried on through his lieutenants; but occasionally he visited the army, in some of the wars of Pannonia and Germany, or remained not far off, proceeding from Rome as far as Ravenna, Milan, or Aquileia.

## 21

He conquered, however, partly in person and partly by his lieutenants, Cantabria, in the north of Spain, Aquitania and Pannonia, Dalmatia, with all Illyricum and Rhaetia, beside the two Alpine nations, the Vindelici and the Salassii. He repressed also the incursions of the Dacians by cutting off three of their generals with vast armies, and drove the Germans beyond the river Elbe; removing two other tribes who submitted, the Ubii and Sicambri, into Gaul, and settling them in the country bordering on the Rhine. Other nations, also, who broke into revolt, he reduced to submission. But he never made war upon any people without just and necessary cause; and so far was he from desire of enlarging the empire, or advancing his own military glory, that he compelled certain princes of the barbarians to take an oath in the Temple of Mars the Revenger, that they would faithfully continue in their allegiance and not violate the peace which they had implored. Of some he demanded a new kind of hostages, to wit, their women, having perceived that they thought little of their men, when they had given them; but he always afforded them the means of getting back these hostages whenever they desired. Even those who engaged most frequently and with the greatest treachery in their rebellion, he never punished more grievously than by selling their captives, on the terms of their not serving in any neighbouring country, nor being released from their slavery before the expiration of thirty years. By virtue of his fame for justice and moderation, he induced even the Indians and Scythians, nations before known to the Romans by hearsay only, to sue for his friendship and that of the

Roman people, by ambassadors. The Parthians readily allowed his claim to Armenia; restoring at his demand, the standards which they had taken from Marcus Crassus and Mark Antony, and offering him hostages beside. Afterwards when a contest arose between several pretenders to the crown of that kingdom, they refused to acknowledge any one who was not chosen by him.

## 22

The temple of Janus Quirinus, always kept open in time of war, and which had been shut twice only from the era of the building of the city to his own time, he closed twice in a much shorter period; for he had established universal peace both by sea and land. Twice he rode into the city with the honours of an ovation, namely after the war of Philippi and again after that of Sicily. He also had three curule triumphs for his several victories in Dalmatia, at Actium, and Alexandria, each of which continued for three days together.

## 23                              A.U.C. 738–762

Of shameful overthrows he received only two in all his wars, and those in Germany under his lieutenants Lollius and Varus. That of Lollius had in it more of dishonour than of loss; but that of Varus threatened the security of the empire itself, inasmuch as three legions, with the commander, his lieutenants, and all the auxiliaries, were cut off. Upon receiving news of this misfortune, he gave orders for a strict watch over the city to forestall any public disturbance, and prolonged the appointments of the prefects in the provinces, that the allies might be kept in order by experience of persons to whom they were used. He made a vow to celebrate the great games in honour of Jupiter Optimus Maximus, 'if he would be pleased to restore the state to more favourable condition'. This had formerly been resorted to in the Cimbrian and Marsian wars. In short, we are informed, that he was in such troubled state that for several days he let the hair of his head and beard grow, and sometimes knocked his head against the doorposts, crying out: 'O, Quintilius Varus! Give me back my legions!' And ever after, he observed the anniversary of this calamity as a day of sorrow and lamentation.

## 24

In military affairs he made many alterations, introducing some practices entirely new and reviving others which had become obsolete. Military discipline he maintained most severely. He would not so much as permit any of his lieutenants, without much ado and reluctance, to visit their wives, and then only in the winter season. A Roman knight having cut off the thumbs of his two young sons to render them unfit for military service, he exposed both him and his estate to public sale. But upon perceiving the farmers of the revenue very greedy for the purchase, he assigned him to a freedman of his own, that he might send him into the country and suffer him to retain his freedom. The tenth legion, for being stubborn and unwilling to obey, he dismissed with ignominy; and did the same by some other legions which petulantly demanded their discharge, withholding from them the rewards usually bestowed on those who had served their stated time in the wars. Whole cohorts which yielded their ground in time of action, he decimated, and fed with barley. Centurions as well as common sentinels who forsook their posts when on guard, he punished with death. For other kinds of delinquency he inflicted upon them various shameful tasks, such as obliging them to stand all day before the praetorium, sometimes in their tunics only and without their belts, sometimes to carry poles ten feet long, or sods of turf.

## 25

After the civil wars, he never, in any of his military addresses or proclamations, greeted his soldiers by the name of 'Fellow-soldiers', but as 'Soldiers' only. Nor would he suffer them to be otherwise called by his sons, or step-sons, when they were in command; for he judged the former appellation to convey the idea of a degree of condescension inconsistent with military discipline, the maintenance of order, and his own majesty, as well as that of his house. Unless at Rome, in case of incendiary fires or under the apprehension of public disturbances, during a scarcity of provisions, he never employed freedmen in his army except on two occasions; once for the security of the colonies bordering upon Illyricum, and once to guard the banks of the river of Rhine. Although he compelled persons of fortune, both male and female, to give up their slaves, and they received their manumission at once, yet he kept them together under their own standard, unmixed with soldiers who were better born, and armed after a different fashion. Military rewards, such as trappings, collars, and other decorations of gold and silver, he distributed more readily than camp or mural crowns, which were reckoned more honourable. These he bestowed sparingly, without partiality, and frequently even on common soldiers. He presented M. Agrippa, after the naval victory in the Sicilian war, with a sea-green banner. Those who shared in the honours of a triumph, although they had attended him in his expeditions, and taken part in his victories, he judged it improper to distinguish by the usual rewards, because they also had the power to bestow such rewards to whom they would. Moreover, he deemed nothing less beseeming an accomplished general than precipitancy and rashness; and therefore he had frequently on his tongue these proverbs: 'Hasten slowly.' 'The cautious captain's better than the bold.' And also 'That is done fast enough which is done well enough.' He was wont to say that 'a battle or a war ought never to be undertaken unless the hope of gain was greater than the fear of damage; for men who pursue small commodities with no small risk resemble those who fish with a golden hook, for the loss of which, if the line should break, no draught of fish whatsoever could make amends.'

## 26

He attained to magistracies and other honourable places of government before the age at which he was legally qualified for them; and to some, also, of a new kind (as the triumvirate), and to others for life (as the censorship). He seized the consulship in his twentieth year, quartering his legions in a hostile manner near the city and sending deputies to demand it for him in the name of the army. When the senate demurred, a centurion named Cornelius, who led the chief deputation, throwing back his cloak and showing the hilt of his sword, dared to say openly in the senate-house: 'This will make him consul if ye will not.' His second consulship he filled nine years afterwards; his third, after the interval of only one year, and held the same office every year successively until the eleventh. From this period, although the consulship was frequently offered him, he always declined it, until, after a long interval, not less than seventeen years, he voluntarily stood for the twelfth, and two years after that for a thirteenth; his purpose being that he might successively introduce into the Forum, on their entering public life, his two adopted sons, Caius and Lucius, the natural children of his daughter Julia and C. Agrippa, while he was invested with the highest office in the state. In his five consulships from the sixth to the eleventh, he continued in office throughout the year; but in the rest, during only nine, six, four, or three months, and in his second no more than a few hours. For having sat for a short time in the morning, upon the kalends of January (1st January), in his curule chair, before the temple of Jupiter Capitolinus, he abdicated the office, and substituted another in his room. Nor did he enter upon them all at Rome, but upon the fourth in Asia, the fifth in the Isle of Samos, and the eighth and ninth at Tarragona.

## 27

For the space of ten years, he acted as one of the triumvirate, formed for the ostensible purpose of settling the commonwealth. In this capacity, he withstood for some time his colleagues' design of a proscription; but when it was once on foot, he executed it more sharply than either of them. For whereas they were exorable and would often yield to the entreaties of friends in behalf of certain persons and were prevailed upon to show mercy, he alone strongly insisted that no one should be spared. He even proscribed Caius Toranius, his guardian, who had been formerly the colleague of his father Octavius in the aedileship. Junius Saturnius adds this further account of him: that when, the proscription being over, Marcus Lepidus made an apology in the senate for their past proceedings and inspired hope of clemency for the future because there had been execution enough done already; he on the contrary professed openly that the only limit he had fixed to the proscription was, that he should be free to act as he would. Afterwards, however, repenting of his harshness, he honoured with the dignity of knighthood T. Vinius Philopoemen, who was reputed to have hidden his patron at the time he was proscribed. In this same office, he incurred in many ways the resentment and ill-will of the people. For, as he was one day making an harangue, observing among the soldiers, Pinarius, a Roman knight, admit some private citizens, and engaged in taking notes, he ordered him to be stabbed before his eyes, as a busybody and a spy. He so terrified with his menaces Tedius Afer, the consul elect, for having referred in malicious terms to something he had done, that he threw himself from a great height and met instant death. And when Quintus Gallius, the praetor, came to compliment him with a double tablet under his cloak, suspecting that it was a sword he had concealed and yet not daring to make a search lest it should be found to be something else, he caused him to be dragged from his tribunal by centurions and soldiers, and tortured like a slave: and although he made no confession, ordered him to be put to death, after he had, with his own hands, plucked out his eyes. Augustus himself writes, however, that Gallius sought a secret conference with him for the purpose of taking his life; that he therefore committed him to prison, but afterwards released him, and banished him from the city, when he perished, either in a storm at sea or by falling into the hands of robbers.

He accepted the tribunician power for life, but more than once chose a colleague in that office for two *lustra* successively. He also had the supervision of morality and observance of the laws for life, but without the title of censor; yet he thrice took a census of the people, the first and third time with a colleague, but the second by himself.

## 28

Twice he meditated giving up his absolute authority: first, immediately after he had put down Antony, remembering that he had often charged him with being the obstacle to the restoration of the republic; and secondly, by reason of a long and lingering illness, when he sent for the magistrates and the senate to his own house and delivered them a particular account of the state of the empire. But considering at the same time that it would be both hazardous to himself to return to the condition of a private person, and might be dangerous to the public to have the government placed again under the control of the people, he resolved to keep it in his own hands, whether for his own good or that of the commonwealth, is hard to say. His good intentions he often affirmed in private discourse and also published an edict, in which they were declared in the following terms: 'Oh, that I might establish the commonwealth safe and sound on her own proper basis, and thus reap the fruit which I desire: that of being reported the author of that happy state; so that, on leaving the world, I may carry with me the hope that the foundations which I shall lay, may continue steadfast for all time.' And indeed he did his best in every way to bring these things to pass. For the city, not being built in a manner worthy of the grandeur of the empire and liable to inundations of the Tiber as well as to fires, was so greatly beautified under his reign that it was his just boast that he 'found it of brick, but left it of marble'. He also made it secure for the time to come against such disasters, so far as could be foreseen by human wit and reason.

## 29

Of the great number of public buildings erected by him, the most considerable were a Forum, containing the temple of Mars the Avenger, the temple of Apollo on the Palatine hill, and the temple of Jupiter Tonans in the Capitol. The reason of his building a new Forum was the vast increase in the population and the number of causes to be tried in the courts, for which, the two already existing not affording sufficient space, it was thought necessary to have a third. It was therefore opened for public use before the temple of Mars was completely finished; and a law was passed, that causes should be tried, and judges chosen by lot, in that place. The temple of Mars was built in fulfilment of a vow made during the war of Philippi, undertaken by him to avenge his father's murder. He ordained that the senate should always assemble there when they met to deliberate respecting wars and triumphs; that thence should be dispatched all those who were sent into the provinces in the command of armies; and that in it those who returned victorious from the wars should lodge the trophies of their triumphs. He erected the temple of Apollo in that part of his house on the Palatine hill which had been struck with lightning and which, on that account, the soothsayers declared the god to have chosen. He added porticos to it, with a library of Greek and Latin authors; and when advanced in years, used to sit there many times in council with the senate, and also to review the rolls of the judges.

He consecrated the temple to Jupiter Tonans, in acknowledgment of his deliverance from a great danger in his Cantabrian expedition;

when, as he was travelling in the night, his litter was struck by lightning which killed the slave who carried a torch before him. He likewise constructed some public buildings in the name of others; for instance, his grandsons, his wife, and sister. Thus he built the portico and basilica of Lucius and Caius, and the porticos of Livia and Octavia, and the theatre of Marcellus. He also often exhorted other persons of rank to embellish the city by new buildings, or by repairing and improving the old, according to their means. By this encouragement many splendid edifices were raised: such as the temple of Hercules and the Muses by Marcus Philippus; the temple of Diana by Lucius Cornificius; the Court of Freedom by Asinius Pollio; a temple of Saturn by Munatius Plancus; a theatre by Cornelius Balbus; an amphitheatre by Statilius Taurus; and several other goodly buildings by Marcus Agrippa.

## 30

He divided the city into regions and districts, ordaining that the annual magistrates should take by lot the charge of the former and that the latter should be superintended by wardens chosen out of the people of each neighbourhood. He appointed a nightly watch to be on guard against accidents from fire; and to prevent the frequent inundations he widened and cleansed the bed of the Tiber, which had in the course of years been almost dammed up with rubbish, and the channel narrowed by the ruins of houses. To provide more commodious approaches to the city, he took upon himself the charge of repairing the Flaminian way as far as Ariminum, and distributed the repairs of the other roads among several persons who had obtained the honour of a triumph, to be defrayed out of the money arising from the spoils of war. Temples decayed by time, or destroyed by fire, he either repaired or rebuilt; and enriched them, as well as many others, with splendid offerings. On one occasion he deposited in the cell of the temple of Jupiter Capitolinus, sixteen thousand pounds of gold, with jewels and pearls to the amount of fifty millions of sesterces.

He assumed the office of Pontifex Maximus as soon as Lepidus was dead, for he could not bring himself to deprive him of it during his lifetime. All prophetical books, both in Latin and in Greek, the authors of which were either unknown or of no great reputation, he caused to be called in from all places. They reached the number of 2000 and above: and of these he burnt all except the Sibylline oracles, which he subjected to a strict examination to determine their authenticity. He then deposited them in two gilt coffers, under the pedestal of the statue of the Palatine Apollo. Seeing that the calendar, which had been corrected by Julius Caesar, had again fallen into disorder, inasmuch as the priests, in the interval of thirty-six years, had erroneously intercalated eleven days instead of nine: he brought it again to its former state of regularity. Upon that occasion, also, he renamed the month Sextilis (the sixth month, reckoning from March, in which the year of Romulus commenced), and called it by his own name, August, rather than September, in which he was born; because in it there befell his first consulship and all his notable victories. He increased the number, dignity, and revenues of the religious orders, and especially those of the vestal virgins. And when, upon the death of one of them, a new one was to be taken, and many persons entered the plea that their daughters' names might be omitted in the lists for election, he replied with an oath: 'If either of my own grand-daughters were old enough, I would have her presented.'

Certain ancient ceremonies which had fallen into disuse or were abolished, he restored again; such as the augury of public health, the office of high priest of Jupiter, the religious solemnity of the Lupercalia, with the Secular, and Compitalian games. At the Lupercalian ceremonies, he commanded that no beardless boys should run. Likewise, at the Secular plays, he forbad young folk of both sexes to frequent any show exhibited at night, unless in the company of some elderly relation. He was the first who ordained that the household gods should be adorned twice a year with spring and summer flowers in the Compitalian festival.

Next to the immortal gods, he paid the highest honours to the memory of those generals who had raised the Roman state from its low origin to so high and glorious a pinnacle. And therefore he repaired or rebuilt the public edifices erected by them, preserving the former inscriptions, and placing statues of them all, with triumphal emblems, in both the porticos of his Forum, issuing an edict on the occasion, in which he professed as follows: 'My design in so doing is that the Roman people may require from me, and all succeeding princes, a conformity to those illustrious examples.' He likewise removed the statue of Pompey from the senate house in which Caius Caesar had been killed, and placed it under a marble arch fronting the palace attached to Pompey's theatre.

## 32

He corrected many ill practices, which, to the detriment of the commonwealth, had either survived the licentious habits of the late civil wars, or else originated in the long peace. Bands of robbers showed themselves openly, completely armed, under colour of self-defence; and in different parts of the country travellers, freedmen and slaves without distinction, were forcibly carried off and kept to work in the houses of correction. Several associations were formed under the specious name of a new college, which had for their purpose the projection of all kinds of villainy. The banditti he suppressed by posting soldiers in suitable places; the houses of correction were subjected to a strict superintendence; all associations, those only excepted which were of ancient standing and recognised by the laws, were dissolved. He burnt all the notes of those who had been a long time in arrears with the treasury, as being the principal source of vexatious suits and prosecutions. Places in the city claimed by the public, where the right was doubtful, he adjudged to the actual possessors. He struck out of the list of criminals the names of those over whom prosecutions had been long impending, where nothing further was intended by the informers than to gratify their own malice by seeing their enemies humiliated; laying it down as a rule, that if any one chose to renew a prosecution, he should incur the risk of the punishment which he sought to inflict. And that crimes might not escape punishment, nor business be neglected by delay, he ordered the courts to sit during the thirty days which were spent in celebrating honorary games. To the three classes of judges then existing, he added a fourth, consisting of persons of inferior order, who were called *Ducenarii* and decided all litigations about trifling sums. He chose judges from the age of thirty years and upwards; that is, five years younger than had been usual before. And a great many declining the office, he was with much difficulty prevailed upon to allow each class of judges a twelve-months' vacation in turn, and the courts to be shut during the months of November and December.

## 33

He was himself assiduous in his functions as a judge and would sometimes prolong his sittings even unto the night: causes are mentioned the hearing of which was so protracted that lights were required, and sometimes they lasted, we are told, as long as eleven or twelve days: if he were indisposed, his litter was placed before the tribunal, or he administered justice reclining on his couch at home. He displayed always not only the greatest attention, but extreme leniency. To save a culprit, evidently guilty of parricide, from the extreme penalty of being sewn up in a sack, (because none were punished in that manner but such as confessed the fact), he is said to have interrogated him thus: 'Surely you did not kill your father, did you?' And when, in a trial of a cause about a forged will all those who had signed it were liable to the penalty of the Cornelian law, he ordered that his colleagues on the tribunal should not only be furnished with the two tablets by which they decided 'guilty or not guilty', but with a third likewise, ignoring the offence of those who should appear to have given their signatures through any deception or mistake. All appeals in causes between inhabitants of Rome, he assigned every year to the praetor of the city; and where provincials were concerned, to men of consular rank, to one of whom the business of each province was referred.

## 34

He abrogated some laws, and originated others: such as the sumptuary law, the one relating to adultery and pederasty, the law against bribery in elections, and likewise that for the encouragement of marriage. This last-named law he amended and reformed somewhat more precisely and with greater severity than the rest, so that he could not carry it through against the tumultuous objections of the people, who demanded that the penalties be abolished or mitigated, that an interval of three years be allowed after a wife's death during which the husband might live unmarried, and that the premiums on marriage be increased. The equestrian order clamoured loudly, at a spectacle in the theatre, for the total repeal of the statute; whereupon he sent for the children of Germanicus, and showed them partly sitting upon his own lap, and partly on their father's: intimating as well by the gesture of his hand, as by his countenance, that they ought not be loath to imitate the example of that young man. But perceiving that the force of the law was dallied with, and avoided by the immaturity of young espoused wives, and by frequent change of wives, he limited the time for consummation after espousals and imposed restrictions on divorce.

# 35

The number of senators having grown to a shameful and confused company of more than a thousand, some of them most unworthy persons who, after Caesar's death, had been chosen by dint of interest and bribery, and who were termed by the common people Charonites, in that they owed their office to one who had gone to Charon: he effected in two scrutinies the reduction of this number to the ancient 300. The first of these scrutinies was left to the senators themselves, each one naming another; but the last was conducted by himself and Agrippa. On this occasion, he is said to have taken his seat as president, with a coat of mail under his tunic, a sword by his side, and with ten of the stoutest men of senatorial rank, who were his friends, standing round his chair. Cordus Cremutius writes that no senator was suffered to approach him except singly, and after having his clothing searched for hidden weapons. Some he obliged to have the grace of declining the office; these he allowed to retain the privileges of wearing the distinguishing dress, and occupying the seats at the solemn spectacles in front of the orchestra, reserved for the senators, together with the honour of keeping their places at the public feasts. To the end that those who were chosen and approved of might perform their functions under more solemn obligations and with less inconvenience, he ordered that every senator, before he took his seat in the house, should pay his devotions, with an offering of frankincense and wine, at the altar of that god in whose temple the senate then assembled, and that their stated meetings should be only twice in the month, namely on the kalends and ides; and that in the months of September and October, a certain number only, chosen by lot, such as the law required to give validity to a decree should be required to attend. For himself, he resolved to choose every six months a new council, with whom he might consult previously upon such affairs as he judged proper at any time to lay before the full senate. He also took the votes of the senators upon any subject of importance, not according to custom, nor in regular order, but as it pleased himself, so that every man might bend his mind so attentively thereto, as always to be ready to give his opinion rather than a mere assent to another.

## 36

He also made several other alterations in the management of public affairs, among which were these: that the acts of the senate should not be published, thus going contrary to the established practice of Julius Caesar; that the magistrates should not be sent into the provinces immediately after the expiration of their office; that the proconsuls should have a certain sum assigned them out of the treasury, for mules and tents, which used before to be contracted for by the government with private persons; that the management of the treasury should be transferred from the city-quaestors to the praetors, or those who had already served in the latter office; and that the decemviri should call together the court of One Hundred, which had been formerly summoned by those who had filled the office of quaestor.

## 37

With the purpose of drawing more men to take part in the administrations of the commonwealth, he devised new offices: to wit, the surveying of the public buildings, of the roads, the aqueducts, and the bed of the Tiber; the distributing of corn to the people; the prefecture of the city; a triumvirate for the election of the senators; and another for reviewing the several troops of the equestrian order, as often as it was necessary. He revived the office of censor, which had been long disused, and whose duty it had formerly been to take an account of the number of the people and the value of their estates. The number of praetors he increased. He required also that whenever the consulship was conferred upon him, he might have two colleagues instead of one; but this measure he could not carry, inasmuch as all the senators cried out with one voice that his majesty was enough abridged already, in that he would not bear that office alone but shared it with another.

## 38

Neither was he sparing in granting honourable rewards for military prowess; for he bestowed upon more than thirty generals the honour of the greater triumph; besides which he took care to have triumphal decorations voted by the senate for more than that number. That the sons of senators might become early acquainted with the administrations of affairs, he permitted them, at the age when they took their virile robe, to wear likewise the senatorial gown with its broad border, and to be present at the debates in the senate-house. When they entered the military service, he not only gave them the rank of military tribunes of the legion, but also the command of the auxiliary horse. And that all might have an opportunity of acquiring military experience, he commonly joined two sons of senators in command of each troop of horse. He often reviewed the troops of the equestrian order, reviving the ancient custom of a cavalcade, which had been long laid aside. But he did not suffer any one to be obliged by an accuser to dismount while he passed in review, as had formerly been done. And to such as were infirm from age, or were in any way defective physically, he gave leave to send their horses before them and to come on foot to answer to their names when the muster roll was called soon afterwards. He permitted those who had passed the age of 45 years, and did not desire to keep their horses any longer, to have the privilege of giving them up.

## 39

With the assistance of ten senators, he required of each of the Roman knights that he give an account of his life. Of those who fell under his disapproval, some were punished, others he marked with shame and ignominy; the most part of them he only admonished, but not in the same terms. The easiest and lightest kind of admonition was the tendering to them publicly a pair of writing tablets, wherein were written all their faults, and the contents of which, confined to themselves, they were to read on the spot. Some also he rebuked and visited with disgrace for taking loans upon small interest and letting it out again for usurious gain.

## 40

In the election of tribunes of the people, if there was not a sufficient number of senatorial candidates, he created them from the equestrian order, granting them the liberty, after the expiration of their office, to continue in whichsoever of the two orders they pleased. As most of the knights had been much reduced in their estates by the civil wars, and therefore dared not sit to see the public games in the theatre in the seats allotted to their order, for fear of the penalty provided by the law in that case, he enacted that none were liable to it, who had themselves, or whose parents had ever, possessed a knight's estate. He took the census of the Roman people street by street; and that the people might not be too often taken from their business to receive the distribution of corn, it was his intention to deliver tickets three times a year for four months respectively; but at their request he continued the former regulation, that they should receive their share monthly.

He revived the former law of elections, endeavouring, by various penalties, to suppress the practice of bribery. Upon the day of election, he distributed to the freedmen of the Fabian and Scaptian tribes, in which he himself was enrolled, a thousand sesterces each, that they might look for nothing from any of the candidates. Considering it a matter of great consequence to keep the Roman people pure and untainted with any mixture of foreign or servile blood, he not only bestowed the freedom of the city with a sparing hand, but laid some restrictions upon the practice of manumitting slaves. When Tiberius requested of him by letter the freedom of Rome in behalf of a Greek client of his, he wrote to him in answer, 'I shall not grant it, unless he comes to me personally and satisfies me that he has just grounds for the application.' And when Livia begged the freedom of the city for a tributary Gaul, he denied it, but offered to release him from payment of taxes, saying: 'I shall sooner suffer some loss in my exchequer, than that the citizenship of Rome be rendered too common.' Not content with interposing many obstacles to either the partial or complete emancipation of slaves, by quibbles requesting the number, condition and difference of those who were to be manumitted, he likewise enacted that none who had been put in chains or tortured should ever obtain the freedom of the city in any degree. He endeavoured also to restore the old habit and dress of the Romans; and upon seeing once, in an assembly of the people, a crowd in grey or sullied gowns instead of white, he was very indignant, and cried out: 'Behold –

> Rome's conquering sons, lords of the wide-spread globe,
> Stalk proudly in the toga's graceful robe.'

And he charged the aediles not to suffer any person from thence-forward, to remain in the Forum or circus unless he laid aside his short coat, and appeared in the toga.

## 41

His liberality to all degrees of citizens was displayed as often as occasion offered. Moreover, upon his bringing the treasure belonging to the kings of Egypt into the city in his Alexandrian triumph, he made money so plentiful that usury languished, but the price of land rose considerably. And afterwards, as often as large sums of money came into his possession by means of confiscations, he would lend it free of interest for a fixed period, to such as could give security for the double of what was borrowed. The estate necessary to qualify a senator, instead of eight hundred thousand sesterces, the former standard, he ordered, for the future, to be twelve hundred thousand; and to those who had not so much, he made good the deficiency. He often gave largesses to the people, but generally of different sums; sometimes four hundred, sometimes three hundred, or two hundred and fifty sesterces; upon which occasions he extended his bounty even to young boys, who before were not used to receive anything, until they arrived at eleven years of age. He measured out also to the people supplies of corn, in times of scarcity, many times at a very low price, and sometimes freely; and doubled the number of the money tickets.

## 42

And that you may know he was a prince more concerned about thrift and wholesomeness than about popularity, he chided the people thus when they complained of the dearth and price of wine: 'My son-in-law Agrippa has taken care that men should not thirst, by conveying plenty of water into the city.' Upon their demanding a gift which he had promised them, he answered: 'I am a man of my word', and he performed his promise. But when they sued for a gift that he had not promised, he issued a proclamation, taxing them with their effrontery, and assuring them that the favour would not be granted them, although he had intended it.

With no less gravity and resolution, when upon a promise he had made of a donative, he found many slaves had been emancipated and enrolled among the citizens, he declared that no one should receive anything who was not included in the promise, and to all the rest he gave less than he had promised, in order that the amount he had set apart might be sufficient. On one occasion, when there was great scarcity of corn, which it was difficult to remedy, he ordered expelled from the city the troops of slaves brought for sale, the gladiators belonging to the masters of defence, and all foreigners, excepting physicians and the teachers of the liberal sciences; even some of the domestic slaves were likewise ordered to be dismissed. When the market began to mend, and food grew plentiful again, he wrote: 'I was much inclined to abolish forever the practice of doling out corn, because the people presume upon it so much that they neglect to till their lands; but I did not persevere in my design, as I felt sure that the practice would some time or other be revived by some one ambitious of popular favour.' However, he so ordered the matter ever afterwards, that as much account was taken of husbandmen and traders as of the idle populace.

## 43

In number, variety, and magnificence, the public shows which he exhibited surpassed all former examples. He writes himself that he treated the people with games upon his own account four-and-twenty times, and three-and-twenty times for such magistrates as were either absent, or not able to afford the expense. The performances took place sometimes in the different streets of the city, and upon several stages, by players in all languages. The same he did not only in the Forum and amphitheatre, but in the circus likewise, and in the Saepta; and sometimes he exhibited only the hunting of wild beasts. He entertained the people with wrestlers in the Campus Martius, where wooden seats were erected for the purpose; and also with a naval fight, for which he excavated the ground near the Tiber, where there is now the grove of the Caesars. During these two entertainments, he stationed guards in the city, lest it might be endangered by robbers taking advantage of the small number of people left at home. In the circus he exhibited chariot and foot races, and combats with wild beasts, in which the performers were often youths of the highest rank. His favourite spectacle was the Trojan game, acted by a select number of boys, in parties different in age and station: considering, that it was a practice both excellent in itself, and honoured by ancient custom, that the spirit of the young nobles should be displayed in such exercises. Caius Nonius Asprenas, who was lamed by a fall in this diversion, he rewarded with a gold collar and permitted both himself and his posterity to bear the surname of Torquatus. But soon afterwards he gave up the representation of such pastimes because Asinius Pollio, the orator, made a grievous and invidious complaint in the senate house, of the fall that Aeserninus, his grandson, sustained, by which he had broken his leg.

In the performance of his stage plays and gladiatorial fights, he sometimes employed the gentlemen and knights of Rome; but only before the practice was prohibited by a decree of the senate. Afterwards, the only exhibition he made of that kind was that of a young man named Lucius, born of a good family, who was not quite two feet in height, and weighed only seventeen pounds, but possessed an exceeding great voice. During one of the fights of gladiators that he set forth, he brought in the Parthian hostages, the first ever sent to Rome from that nation, through the middle of the amphitheatre, and placed them in the second tier of seats above himself. His habit was likewise, on days when there were no public entertainments, if anything strange or new were brought to Rome and worthy to be seen, to expose it to public view, in any place whatever. Among these sights were a rhinoceros in the Saepta, a tiger upon a stage, and a serpent fifty cubits long, in the Comitium. It

happened that during the great Circensian games, which he performed because of a vow, that he fell sick, and was obliged to attend
the Thensae reclining on a litter. Another time, in the games
celebrated for the opening of the theatre of Marcellus, the joints of his
curule chair happening to give way, he fell upon his back. And in the
games exhibited by his grandsons, when the people were in such
great fear by reason of an alarm raised that the theatre was falling that
all his efforts to calm them failed, he moved from his place and sat
down in that part of the theatre which was most suspected.

# 44

He reformed and regulated the confusion and disorder with which
the spectators took their seats at the public games; a measure to which
he was moved by the wrong done to a senator at Puteoli, who,
entering a crowded theatre, found no one who would grant him
room. Hereupon when a decree of the senate was procured by him,
that in all public spectacles, the first tier of benches should be left
empty for the accommodation of senators: he forbad even the
ambassadors of free nations and allies of Rome to sit in the orchestra,
because he had found that some manumitted slaves were sometimes
sent in embassage. He separated the soldiery from the rest of the
people and assigned to married plebeians their particular rows of seats.
To the boys he assigned their own benches, and to their tutors the
seats which were nearest it; ordering that none clothed in black
should sit in the centre of the circle. As for women, he would not
allow them to be present at the combats of gladiators, except from the
upper part of the theatre, although in times past they had mingled
freely with the rest of the spectators. To the Vestal Virgins he granted
a place apart from the rest within the theatre, opposite the praetor's
bench. But from the wrestlers' conflicts, he excluded the female sex
entirely: so that in the games which he exhibited upon his accession
to the office of high priest, he deferred producing a pair of
combatants which the people called for, until the next morning; and
made proclamation that his will and pleasure was, 'That no woman
should come into the theatre before the fifth hour of the day.'

For the most part, he beheld the Circensian games himself from the upper rooms of the houses of his friends or freedmen, sometimes from the place appointed for the statues of the gods, and sitting in company with his wife and children. From these shows he would be absent many hours together and sometimes whole days: but not without first having excused himself to the people and recommended substitutes. But when present, he never attended to anything else, either to avoid the reflections which he used to say were commonly made upon his uncle, Caesar, for perusing letters and memorials, and making rescripts during the spectacles; or else from the real pleasure he felt in seeing such pastimes, and which he never dissimulated but often frankly professed. This he manifested frequently by presenting honorary crowns and handsome rewards to the best players, in the games exhibited by others; and he never was present at any performance of the Greeks, without rewarding the most proficient, according to their merit. But most of all, he loved to see the pugilistic fights, especially those of the Latins, not only between combatants who had been trained scientifically whom he used often to match with the Greek champions, but even between mobs of the lower orders who fell together pell mell in the narrow streets, and though they had no skill at all in the art, yet could lay on lustily and offend their concurrents one way or another. In fine, he felt a warm interest in all sorts of people who contributed in any way to the success of the public entertainments and showed them especial respect and patronage. The privileges of the wrestlers he not only maintained, but amplified. He prohibited combats of gladiators where no quarter was given. He deprived the magistrates of the power of chastising or beating with rods the stage-players, which by an ancient law was allowed them at all times and in all places; restricting their jurisdiction entirely to the time of the plays and misdemeanours in the theatres. However, he would tolerate no slackness of the wrestlers and gladiators in their several matches, but exacted with the utmost rigour their greatest exertions. He went so far in restraining the licentiousness of stage-players, that upon discovering that Stephanio, a performer of the highest class, had a married woman with her hair cropped and dressed in boy's clothes, to wait upon him at table, he ordered him to be whipped through all the three theatres, and then banished. Hylas, an actor of pantomimes, upon a complaint against him by the praetor, he commanded to be scourged in the court of his own house, which, however, was open to the public. And Pylades he not only banished from the city but from Italy as well, for pointing with his finger at a spectator by whom he was hissed, and turning the eyes of the audience upon him.

## 46

Having in this manner ordered the civil affairs of Rome, he augmented the population of Italy by planting in it no less than twenty-eight colonies, which he furnished with public works and maintained by revenues. In rights and privileges, he made it equal in some respects to the city itself, by devising a new kind of suffrage which the principal officers and magistrates of the colonies might take at home, and forward under seal to the city against the time of elections. To increase the number of persons of condition and of children among the lower ranks, he granted the petitions of all those who requested the honour of doing military service on horseback as knights, provided their demands were seconded by the recommendation of the town in which they lived; and when he visited the several districts of Italy, he distributed a thousand sesterces a head to such of the lower class as could prove that they had sons or daughters.

## 47

As for those provinces which were more powerful than others, which could not with ease or safety be entrusted to the government of annual magistrates, he undertook the rule of them himself, distributing the rest by lot among the proconsuls; but sometimes he made exchanges and frequently visited most of both kinds in person. Certain cities allied to Rome, but which by their great licentiousness were running headlong to destruction, he deprived of their liberties. Others, which were deeply in debt, he eased, and rebuilt those that had been destroyed by earthquakes. To those that could produce any instance of their having deserved well of the Roman people, he presented the freedom of Latium, or even that of the city. There is not, I believe, a province except Africa and Sardinia, which he did not visit. After pursuing Sextus Pompeius into these provinces, he was indeed preparing to cross over from Sicily to them, but was deterred by continual and violent storms; and afterwards there was no occasion or call for such a journey.

## 48

All those kingdoms which he had won by the right of conquest, with but few exceptions, he either restored to their former monarchs as in the case of Herod, or else bestowed upon aliens. Between kings in alliance with Rome he encouraged most intimate union, being always ready to promote or favour any proposal of marriage or friendship among them; and, indeed, treated them all with as much consideration as if they were members and parts of the empire. To those princes who were of tender age, or deranged in mind, he appointed guardians to have charge of them until they arrived at age or recovered their wits. The sons of many of them he brought up and educated with his own.

## 49

Of his military forces, he distributed the legions and auxiliary troops throughout the several provinces. He stationed a fleet at Misenum, and another at Ravenna, for the protection of the Upper and Lower Seas. A certain number of the forces were selected for a guard, partly of the city and in part of his own person; but he discharged the Spanish guard, which he retained about him till the fall of Antony; and also the Germans, whom he had among his guards, until the defeat of Varus. Yet he never permitted a greater force than three cohorts in the city, and had no praetorian camps. The rest he quartered in the neighbourhood of the nearest towns, in winter and summer camps. All the troops throughout the empire he reduced to one fixed form and proportion of wages and rewards, determining these according to their rank in the army, the time they had served, and their private means; so that after their discharge they might not be tempted by age or want to join the agitators for a revolution. For the purpose of providing a fund always ready to meet their pay and pensions, he appointed a military exchequer, and appropriated new taxes to that object. In order to obtain the earliest intelligence of what was passing in the provinces, he disposed along the road posts, consisting at first of young men stationed at moderate distances along the military roads, and afterwards of regular couriers with fast vehicles; which appeared to him the most commodious, because the persons who were the bearers of dispatches, written on the spot, might then be questioned about the business, as occasion arose.

## 50

In sealing letters-patent, rescripts, or epistles, he at first used the figure of a sphinx, afterwards the head of Alexander the Great, and at last, his own, engraved by the hand of Dioscurides, a cunning lapidary and graver in precious stones; which practice was retained by the succeeding emperors. In all his missives his manner was to record precisely not merely the day but the exact time at which they were dispatched.

## 51

Of his clemency and affability, there are abundant and striking examples. For, not to reckon up how many and what persons of the adverse faction he pardoned, received into favour, and suffered to rise to the highest eminence in the state: he thought it sufficient to punish Junius Novatus and Cassius Patavinus, both plebeians, one of them with a fine and the other with an easy banishment, notwithstanding that Junius Novatus had published, in the name of young Agrippa, a most biting letter against him, and Cassius Patavinus had professed openly, and in broad terms, at a public feast, that he wanted neither courage nor inclination to stab him. In the trial of Aemilius Aelinaus, of Cordova, when, among other charges exhibited against him, it was particularly insisted upon that he used to calumniate Caesar, he turned round to the accuser, and said with an air and tone of passion, 'I wish you could make that appear; I shall let Aelianus know that I also have a tongue, and shall speak sharper of him than he ever did of me.' Nor did he, either then or afterwards, make any further inquiry into the affair. Likewise, when Tiberius, in a letter, complained of the affront with great earnestness, he returned him an answer in the following terms: 'Do not, my good Tiberius, on such occasion, follow and feed the humour of your age; nor take it too much to heart that one should speak ill of me; for it is enough, for us, if we can prevent any one from really doing us harm.'

## 52

Although he was well aware that it had been customary to decree temples in honour of the proconsuls, yet he would not permit them to be raised in any of the provinces, unless in the joint names of himself and of Rome. In the city itself, he declined this honour most resolutely; and he even melted down all the silver statues which had been set up for him, and converted the whole into tripods which he consecrated to the Palatine Apollo. When the people importuned him to accept the dictatorship, he fell upon his knees, cast his gown from off his shoulder, bared his breast, and besought them not to urge him further.

## 53

He always abhorred the title of Lord, as an ill-omened and reproachful term. And when, in a play performed at the theatre, at which he was present, these words were pronounced, 'O good and gracious Lord', and the whole assembly, with great joy and applause, approved them as applied to him, he immediately checked their indecent flattery, by a gesture of the hand and a frowning countenance; and the next day he reproved them most sharply by an edict; neither would he ever afterwards suffer himself to be called Dominus, even by his own children or grandchildren, either in jest or in earnest, and forbad them the use of all such extravagant expressions to one another. He rarely entered any city or town or departed from it, except in the evening or the night, to avoid giving any person the trouble of doing him honour by way of dutiful attendance. During his consulships he commonly went about the streets on foot; but at other times rode in a closed carriage. He admitted to court even plebeians, in common with people of the higher ranks; receiving the petitions of those who approached him with so much affability, that he once rebuked a man merrily, because in presenting a supplication, he did it as timorously 'as if he were offering a piece of money to an elephant'. On senate days, he used to pay his respects to the conscript fathers only in the house, addressing them each by name as they sat, without any prompter; and on his departure, he bade each of them farewell, while they retained their seats. In the same manner, he maintained with many of them a constant interchange of kindnesses and civilities, giving them his company upon occasions of any particular festivity in their families, until he was far advanced in years, and unable to withstand the press and throng of people at a wedding. When Gallus Terrinius, a senator, though not one of his familiar acquaintance, had suddenly lost his sight, and thereupon purposed resolutely to starve himself to death, he visited him personally, and by his consolatory admonitions diverted him from his design.

## 54

As he delivered a speech in the senate, one of the members said to him: 'I did not understand you,' and another, 'I would contradict you, could I do so with safety.' And when, upon occasions of excessive heat and altercation in the senate debates, he was about to quit the house in great disgust, some of them would arrest him with these words: 'Senators ought to have liberty to speak their minds concerning the commonweal.' Antistius Labeo, in the election of a new senate, when each, as he was named, chose another, nominated Marcus Lepidus, who had formerly been Augustus' enemy, and was then in exile. And being asked by him, 'Is there no other person more worthy?' he returned this answer: 'Every man has his own opinion.' Nor was anyone ever chastised for his free speech, although it was carried to the edge of insolence.

## 55

Even when some vicious libels against him were cast abroad in the senate house, he was neither disturbed nor did he give himself much trouble to refute them. He neglected even to make inquiry concerning the authors; but only proposed that, from thenceforward, those who published libels or lampoons in a borrowed name against any person, should be called to account. Furthermore, to deal with certain spiteful taunts which were designed to make him odious, he issued an edict against them. And yet, he restrained the senate from passing an act to curtail the liberties which were taken with others in people's wills.

## 56

Whenever he was present at the election of magistrates he went round the tribes with the candidates of his nomination and begged the votes of the people in the customary way. He likewise gave his own vote in his tribe, as one of the people. He suffered himself willingly to be called as a witness upon trials, and not only to be interrogated, but cross-examined, with the utmost patience. In building his Forum, he restricted himself as to site in order to avoid encroaching upon the neighbouring houses and compelling their owners to give up their property. He never recommended his sons to the people without the additional clause, 'if they deserve it'. Upon an occasion when the audience rose at their entrance into the theatre, although they were yet under age, and gave them applause in a standing position, he took it very ill and made complaint of the matter.

He desired that his friends should be great and powerful in the state, but have no exclusive privileges, or be exempt from the laws which governed others. When Asprenas Nonius, an intimate friend of his, was accused by Cassius Severus of administering poison, and pleaded for himself at the bar, he asked counsel of the senate as to what they thought was his duty in the matter: 'For I am in doubt,' quoth he, 'lest, if I should appear as an advocate, I should seem to espouse a guilty cause; and if I do not, to forsake and prejudge a friend.' Whereupon, with the full consent of the senate, he took his seat among his advocates for several hours, but spoke never a word in commendation of his friend's qualities, as the custom was in the trial of such cases. He likewise pleaded the causes of his clients; as on behalf of Scutarius, an old shieldbearer who had served him in the wars, and in whose behalf he spoke, when he was sued in an action for slander. He never delivered from prosecution any that were thus in trouble, except in a single instance, and that was the case of Castritius, who had given information of the conspiracy of Murena; and that he did, only by earnestly entreating the accuser, in open court, to drop his action.

# 57

How much he was beloved for his worthy conduct in all these matters is easy to estimate. The decrees of the senate in his honour I pass over, as these may seem to have been wrested from them by policy or deference. The Roman knights voluntarily, and with one accord, always celebrated his birth for two days together; and all ranks of the people, yearly, upon a solemn vow they had made, threw a piece of money into the Curtian lake, as an offering for the preservation of his life and health. They likewise, on the kalends (first) of January, presented for his acceptance New Year's gifts in the Capitol, though he was not present; out of which donations he purchased some costly images of the Gods, which he erected in several streets of the city: as that of Apollo Sandaliarius, Jupiter Tragoedus, and others. For the rebuilding of his house on the Palatine hill, which was accidentally consumed by fire, the old soldiers, the judges, the tribes, and even the people, contributed, according to the ability of each. However, he would touch only some small portion out of the several sums collected, and forbore to take from any one person more than a single denarius. Upon his return from any of the provinces, they acclaimed him not only with joyful and welcoming words, but also with songs. It is also said that as often as he entered the city the infliction of punishment was suspended for the time.

# 58                                        A.U.C. 758

The title of Father of His Country was presented to him by the whole body of the people, upon a sudden impulse, and with unanimous accord. It was offered to him first at Antium, by a deputation from the people, and upon his setting aside the honour, they tendered it a second time at Rome, in a full theatre, when all were crowned with laurel. The senate soon afterwards followed their precedent, not in the way of acclamation or decree, but by commissioning M. Messala, in an unanimous vote, to compliment him with it in the following terms: 'That which may be to the good and happiness of thee and thy house, O Caesar Augustus, (for in this wise, we think, we pray likewise for perpetual felicity and prosperity to the commonwealth), the senate, in accord with the people of Rome, do jointly salute thee by the name of Pater Patriae.' To this, Augustus, with tears standing in his eyes, made answer in these words (for I give them exactly, as I did those of Messala): 'Now that I have, mine honourable Lords, attained to the height of all my wishes, what remaineth else for me to crave of the Immortal Gods, but that I may carry with me this universal affection of yours unto my life's end?'

## 59

To the physician Antonius Musa, a freedman, who had cured him of a dangerous illness, they erected a statue near that of Aesculapius, by a general subscription. Some heads of families ordered in their wills that their heirs should lead victims to the Capitol, with a tablet carried before them, and pay their vows, 'because Augustus still survived'. Certain cities of Italy appointed the day of his first visit to be the beginning of their year. And most of the provinces, besides erecting temples and altars, instituted games to be celebrated in his honour every five years.

## 60

The kings, his friends and allies, built cities in their several kingdoms, to which they gave the name of Caesarea; and all with one consent resolved to finish, at their common expense, the temple of Jupiter Olympius at Athens, which had been begun long before, and to dedicate it to his Genius. And many times, these princes left their realms, laying aside their crowns and royal ornaments, and in the habit and manner of devoted clients, attended and paid their respects to him daily; not at Rome only, but also when he was travelling through the provinces.

## 61     A.U.C. 711–745

Having related what his public carriage was in civil and military matters, together with his management and administration of the empire, both in war and in peace: I shall now describe his private and domestic life, his habits at home and among his friends and dependants, from his youth to the day of his death. He lost his mother in his first consulship, and his sister Octavia, when he was in the fifty-fourth year of his age. And as he had shown them while living the greatest kindness and affection, so when they were dead, he did them the greatest honours he possibly could.

## 62

He had espoused when very young the daughter of Publius Servilius Isauricus; but upon his reconciliation with Antony after their first discord, the armies on both sides demanding a family alliance between them, he took to wife Antony's stepdaughter, Claudia, the daughter of Fulvia by Publius Claudius, who was a very young damsel, and scarcely marriageable; and upon some disagreement with Fulvia, his wife's mother, he put her away, as yet untouched and a virgin. Soon afterwards, he wedded Scribonia, who had before been married twice, each time to a man of consular rank, one of whom was Scipio, the father of Cornelia, the other being unknown; and she was a mother by one of them. This wife also he divorced, not able to endure, as he himself writes, the perverseness of her temper; and forthwith he took from Tiberius Nero, Livia Drusilla, his lawful wife, who was then with child; and her he loved entirely to the very end.

## 63

By Scribonia he had a daughter named Julia, but by Livia he had no issue, although he ardently desired it. She did, indeed, conceive once, but miscarried, and the infant was born before its time. Julia he gave in marriage to Marcellus, the son of his sister Octavia, although he had just emerged from childhood. When Marcellus died, he bestowed her on Marcus Agrippa, having by entreaty persuaded his sister to yield her son-in-law to his wishes; for at that time Agrippa was married to one of the Marcellas, and had children by her. When Agrippa died also, he cast about for a suitable union a long time, even considering some of the equestrian order, and at last chose for her his wife's son, Tiberius, whom he forced to put away a former wife then with child, and by whom he had been a father already. Mark Antony writes, 'That he first affianced Julia to his son, and afterwards to Cotiso, king of the Getae, demanding at the same time the king's daughter in marriage for himself.'

## 64

By Agrippa and Julia he had three grandsons, namely Caius, Lucius, and Agrippa; and two granddaughters, Julia and Agrippina. Julia he bestowed in marriage upon Lucius Paulus, the censor's son, and Agrippina to Germanicus, his sister's grandson. Caius and Lucius he adopted at home by the ceremony of purchase from their father, advanced them, while yet very young, to offices in the state, and when they were consuls-elect, sent them to visit the provinces and armies. His daughter and grand-daughters he brought up in the knowledge of domestic arts, even of spinning; and forbad them to say or do anything otherwise than openly before the family, that it might be set down in their day-books. He so strictly prohibited them from all converse with strangers, that he once wrote to Lucius Vinicius, a handsome young man of a good family, charging him with having passed the boundaries of modesty, in making a visit to his daughter at Baiae. His grandsons he taught himself, for the most part, in reading, writing, swimming, and other rudiments of knowledge; and he laboured for nothing more than to perfect them in the imitation of his hand-writing. He never supped but he had them sitting at the foot of his couch; nor ever went upon a journey but with them in a chariot before him, or riding at his side.

## 65

But as joyous and confident as he was in regard to his numerous family and the discipline of his house, fortune failed him in the proof of all. The two Julias, his daughter and granddaughter, abandoned themselves to such excesses of lewdness and dishonesty that he banished them both. Caius and Lucius both, he lost in the space of eighteen months, the first dying in Lycia, and the second at Marseilles. His third grandson, Agrippa, with his stepson Tiberius, he adopted in the Forum, by a law passed for the purpose by the sections; but he soon afterwards discarded Agrippa for his base disposition and unruly temper, and confined him at Surrentum. He bore the death of his relations with more patience than he did their disgraceful conduct. For, although he was not extremely cast down by the loss of Caius and Lucius, in the case of his daughter and her shameful pranks, he stated the facts to the senate in a message read to them by the quaestor, he not having the heart to be present himself; and indeed, he absented himself for a long time, for very shame, and had thoughts of putting her to death. It is certain that when one Phoebe, a freedwoman and one cognisant of Julia's naughtiness, hanged herself about the same time, he said: 'I had rather be the father of Phoebe than of Julia.' In her banishment he would not allow her the use of wine, nor any delicate adornment of the body; neither would he permit any man, slave or free, to have access to her without his permission, and having received an exact account of his age, stature, colour, and even the marks or scars he had about him. After five years, he removed her from the island where she was confined, to the continent and treated her with less harshness, but could never be prevailed upon to call her home again. When the Roman people besought him earnestly on her behalf several times, all the reply he gave was: 'I wish you had all such daughters and wives as she.' He likewise forbad the child of which his granddaughter Julia was delivered after she was condemned, to be either owned as a relation or brought up.

His grandson Agrippa, who was equally intractable and whose folly increased, instead of modifying, every day, was transported from Surrentum to the island Planasia, and placed under a guard of soldiers. He provided also, by an act of the senate, that he should be confined there for life. And when any mention was made of him or the two Julias, he would quote, with a heavy sigh,

'Would I were wifeless, or had childless died!'

## 66

He did not easily or quickly form friendship with any person, but maintained them with great constancy; not only honouring the virtues and merits of his friends as they deserved, but bearing likewise with their faults and vices provided they did not overpower the good in them. Among all his friends there is hardly to be found one who fell into disgrace with him except Salvidienus Rufus, whom he raised to the consulship, and Cornelius Gallus, whom he made prefect of Egypt; both of them men of the lowest origin. One of these, who engaged secretly in plotting sedition in the state, he delivered over to the senate for condemnation; and the other, on account of his ungrateful and malicious temper, he forbad his house, and his living in any of the provinces. But when Gallus, being denounced by his accusers, and sentenced by the senate, was driven to shorten his own life, Augustus commended, indeed, the attachment to his person of those who manifested so much indignation; but for Gallus's sake he wept, and complained of his own hard fortune, in that he alone might not be angry with his friends, or resent their misconduct in such a manner as he would wish. All the rest of his favourites flourished in power and wealth to the end of their lives, in the highest ranks of their several orders, notwithstanding occasional malcontent. For, not to mention others, he sometimes found a want of patience in M. Agrippa, and a tendency in Maecenas to babble; the first having thrown up all his employments and retired to Mytilene, on suspicion of some slight coolness, and from jealousy that Marcellus received greater marks of favour; and the second having revealed to his wife Terentia the secret of the detection of Murena's conspiracy.

He likewise required of his friends, at their deaths as well as during their lives, some proofs of mutual attachment. For although he would never lie in wait to catch at inheritances and in fact would never accept any legacy left him by a stranger, yet he weighed in a sober way the last words of his friends; and could never dissemble his grief if, in their wills, they made but a slight, or no very honourable mention, of him; nor his joy, if they remembered him thankfully and with love. And whatever legacies or shares of their property were left to him by such as were parents, he used to hand them over to their children; or if they were in their minority, to restore all to them, with interest, upon the day of their assuming their virile gowns, or of their marriage.

## 67

As a patron to his freedmen and a master to his servants, his attitude in general was gracious and gentle; although upon occasion he was known to show severity. Many of his freedmen he honoured with posts of great dignity and importance, as Licinus, Enceladus, and others. And when his slave, Cosmus, spoke bitterly of him, he chastised him no further than by hanging a pair of fetters at his heels; as for Diomedes, his steward, who, while walking with him and seeing a wild boar suddenly bearing down upon them, for very fear put his master between himself and the beast, he imputed to him timidity, rather than a breach of duty; and although it occasioned no small peril, yet he turned it into a jest, because there was no malice in his steward's conduct. Nevertheless, he put to death Procillus, one of his most favoured freedmen, for maintaining disorderly relations with other mens' wives. He broke the legs of his secretary, Thallus, for taking a bribe of 500 denarii to discover the contents of one of his letters. The tutor and other servants in attendance upon his son, Caius, who, taking advantage of his sickness and death, bore themselves with insolence and rapacity in the province he governed, he caused to be thrown headlong into a river, with heavy weights tied about their necks.

## 68

In the prime of his youth he incurred suspicion upon sundry occasions of leading a vicious and wanton life. Sextus Pompey railed at him as an effeminate person. Mark Antony laid to his charge that he earned his adoption from his uncle by suffering the immoral use of his body. Lucius Antony, brother of Mark, likewise accuses him, first of having prostituted himself for Caesar, and afterwards of having yielded to Aulus Hirtius in Spain in the same manner, for a consideration of three hundred thousand sesterces; adding, also, that he was wont to singe his legs with burnt nutshells so that the hair might grow in softer. Nay, the whole concourse of the people, at some public exhibition in the theatre, construed to his reproach, with great applause, this sentence, recited in allusion to the Gallic priest of the mother of the gods, beating a drum:

*Videsne ut cinaedus orbem digito temperet!*

See with his orb the wanton's finger play!

## 69

That he was an adulterer upon many occasions even his friends did not deny; but they offer in excuse for it, that he did not act thus through lust but from policy, that he might more easily detect the plots and plans of his adversaries, by means of intimate converse with their wives. Mark Antony objected, not only to his over-hasty marriage with Livia, but to his having taken the wife of a man of consular rank, under his very eyes, away from the table to his own bedchamber, from which he brought her again to the entertainment, with her hair all ruffled and her ears glowing red; also that he put away Scribonia, because she resented too openly the great ascendancy which one of his mistresses had obtained over him; that his friends were employed as procurers for him, in which capacity they examined, in the nude, the persons of both matrons and ripe virgins, in the same manner as if Thoranius, the slave-dealer, had them under sale. And before they came to an open break, he writes to him in a familiar manner, thus: 'Why are you changed towards me? Because I lie with a queen – who is my wife? And is this the first time? Have I not done so for these nine years? Alas, good sir, you that would have me in company only with Octavia, my wife, tell me true: do you, for your part, know none other women but Drusilla? May health and happiness attend you, as when you shall read this letter you be not in dalliance with Tertulla, Terentilla, Rufilla, or Salvia Titiscenia, or all of them. What matters it to you where, or upon whom, you spend your manly vigour?'

## 70

There was much talk abroad of a certain supper which he gave, commonly called the Supper of the Twelve Gods, at which the guests were dressed in the garb of gods and goddesses, and he himself personated Apollo; this was imputed to him not only by Antony in his letters, who likewise names with reproach all the parties concerned, but in these verses, of unknown authorship, which were familiar to all men:

> When Mallia late beheld, in mingled train,
> Twelve mortals ape twelve deities in vain;
> Caesar assumed what was Apollo's due,
> And wine and lust inflamed the motley crew.
> At the foul sight the gods avert their eyes,
> And from his throne great Jove indignant flies.

The ill fame of this banquet was heightened by the great dearth and famine at that time in Rome. The very next day a great cry was set up by the people, 'that the gods had eaten up all the corn; and that Caesar was indeed Apollo, but Apollo the Tormentor': under which title that god was worshipped in some parts of the city. Furthermore, he was taxed with greed as to pretentious furniture and costly Corinthian vessels, and also with being addicted to dice play. For, in the time of the proscription, there was written upon his statue:

*Pater argentarius, ego Corinthianus:*

My father was a silversmith, my dealings are in brass;

because it was believed that he had put some persons upon the list of the proscribed only to obtain their Corinthian vessels. And afterwards, in the Sicilian war, this epigram of him went abroad:

Twice having lost a fleet in luckless fight,
To win at last, he games both day and night.

## 71

These criminal imputations or malicious slanders (I know not which), concerning the unnatural filthiness aforementioned, he checked and refuted very easily by the chastity of his life, at the very time the talk was current, as well as ever afterwards. His demeanour likewise cancelled the charge of his indulgence in extravagant and sumptuous furniture; for, upon the taking of Alexandria, he retained for himself out of all the king's household stuff and rich implements, nothing more than one porcelain cup, and soon afterwards melted down all the vessels of gold, even such as were intended for common use. His amorous wantonness never abated one whit, however, and it is reported that he gave himself overmuch to the deflowering of young maidens, which were procured for him from all places, even by his own wife. It is thought that he was discovered with one of these victims *in flagrante delicto* by the poet Ovid, who was subsequently banished because of the embarrassing knowledge upon which he had blundered. Augustus had for many years affected a decency of behaviour, and he would, therefore, naturally be not a little disconcerted at the unseasonable intrusion of the poet. That Ovid had not expected to find Augustus in the place was beyond question; and the character of Ovid might have suggested to Augustus that the poet had sought out the room for some dalliance on his own account. From his own acknowledgment, Ovid's purpose seems to have been not wholly free from blame, for one of his verses contains this couplet:

> I know I cannot wholly be defended,
> Yet plead 'twas chance, no ill was then intended.

As for the rumours that ran of his dice-playing, he paid no attention to them; and he played in public, but purely for pleasure, even when he was well advanced in years; and not only in the month of December, wherein the feast Saturnalia was kept, and much liberty tolerated of gaming, feasting and revelling, but upon all days, whether festivals or not. There can be no doubt as to this, for in a certain letter written with his own hand, he says: 'I supped, my dear Tiberius, with the same men: there came moreover to bear us company, Vinicius, and Silvius the father. We gamed at supper like old fellows, both yesterday and today. And as any one threw upon the tali aces or sixes, he put down for every talus a denarius; all which was gained by him who threw a Venus.' At another time he wrote: 'We lived full merrily, my Tiberius, during the feast of Minerva: for we played every day, and kept the gaming table warm. Your brother played his hand with many shouts and outcries over his ill luck; but in the end he lost not much, for little by little he recovered beyond his expectations. I, for my part, lost twenty thousand sesterces; but then I was overliberal in my play, as my manner is; for had I insisted upon the stakes which I declined, or kept what I gave away, I should have won about fifty thousand. But this I like better: for the fame of my bounty exalts me into celestial glory.' In a letter to his daughter, he writes: 'I have sent you two hundred and fifty denarii, which I gave to every one of my guests, in case they were inclined at supper to divert themselves with the Tali, or at the game of Even-or-Odd.'

## 72

In other matters, it appears that he was moderate in his habits, and without suspicion of any kind of vice. He lived at first near the Roman Forum, above the Ring-maker's Stairs, in a house which had once been occupied by Calvus the orator. He afterwards moved to the Palatine Hill, where he occupied a small house, belonging to Hortensius, which was in no way striking either for spaciousness or adornment; the piazzas being but small, the pillars of Alban stone, and the rooms without anything of marble or fine paving. He continued to use the same bedchamber, both winter and summer, during forty years, for though he was conscious that the city did not accord with his health in the winter, he nevertheless stayed there constantly during that season. If at any time he wished to do anything secretly, and without interruption, he used a special room at the top of his house, which he called his Syracuse or Cabinet of Arts; or he went to some villa belonging to his freedmen near the city. But when he was indisposed, he commonly took up his residence in the house of Maecenas. Of all the places of retirement from the City, he frequented most those upon the sea coast, and the islands of Campania, such as Baiae, and the islands of Ischia, Procida, Capri, and others; or the towns nearest the City, such as Lanuvium, Praeneste, and Tibur, where he frequently would sit for the administration of justice, in the porticos of the temple of Hercules. He disliked greatly large and sumptuous palaces; and some which had been raised at a vast expense by his granddaughter, Julia, he tore down; his own, which were small in size, he adorned not so much with statues and pictures, as with walks and groves, and things which were curious either for their antiquity or rarity; such as, at Capri, the huge limbs of sea monsters and wild beasts, which some affect to call the bones of giants; and also the arms of ancient heroes.

## 73

His simplicity in the matter of furniture and household stuff appears even at this day from some beds and tables still remaining, most of which are scarcely elegant enough to satisfy the taste of a private citizen. Neither did he sleep, some say, upon a bed raised high and swelling with down, but upon a low cot, meanly spread. He seldom wore any apparel but what was made of common cloth, within his own house, by his wife, sister, daughter, and granddaughters. His togas were neither full nor scanty; and his senator's border neither overbroad nor narrow. His shoes were raised somewhat underneath that he might seem taller than he was. His raiment and shoes he had at all times laid in readiness in his bed chamber for any sudden or unlooked-for occasions.

## 74

He feasted daily, and never otherwise than with guests, whom he chose very carefully, however, with due respect to rank and character. Valerius Messala tells us that he never entertained any of his freedmen at table, except Menas, who was granted the privilege of citizenship for betraying Pompey's fleet. He himself writes that he invited to his table a person in whose villa he lodged, and who had once been employed by him as a spy. He sometimes came very late to table, and left early; on these occasions his guests would begin supper before he sat down, and continue sitting after he was gone. His suppers consisted of three dishes, or at most only six; but if he entertained his guests in no very sumptuous manner, yet his kindness and courtesy were very fine. For he would rally those who were silent, or spoke softly to their neighbours, and draw them into the general discourse; and he even introduced buffoons and stage players, and sometimes low performers from the circus, and very often itinerant humorists, to delight the company.

## 75

Festivals and holidays he usually celebrated at great expense, but sometimes with merriment and sport only. In the Saturnalia, and at other times when it pleased him, he distributed to his company clothes, gold and silver; sometimes coins of all stamps, even old pieces current in the time of the ancient kings of Rome and of foreign countries; sometimes nothing but towels, sponges, rakes and tweezers, and other articles of that kind, to which were appended tickets having an obscure or double meaning, the humour of which was derived from the use to which these articles were applied. He used likewise to sell by lot among his guests articles of which the value was most unequal, as well as pictures exposed on the wrong side, and so, by the uncertainty of the lot, disappoint or gratify the hope of the purchasers. This sort of traffic passed through the whole company, every one being obliged to buy something, and to run the chance of loss or gain in common with the others.

# 76

His diet (for I may not pass over so much as this) was very plain and scanty. His appetite favoured coarse bread, small fishes, new cheese made of cow's milk and pressed with the hand rather than in the cheese-press, so that it remained soft: and green figs, especially of that kind which bear fruit twice a year. His habit was to eat when and where he liked, without waiting for supper. These passages, taken from his own letters, bear out this report: 'I ate a little bread and some small dates, in my carriage.' Again: 'In returning home from the palace in my litter, I ate an ounce of bread, and a few raisins.' And once more: 'No Jew, my Tiberius, ever observed a more strict fast upon the Sabbath, than I have this day; for while in the bath, and after the first hour of the night, I ate only two biscuits, before I began to be rubbed with oil.' (From which it will be seen that his observation was at fault in the case of Jews, who assuredly do not fast upon the Sabbath.) Due to this great indifference about his diet, he used sometimes to take his supper alone, either before his guests were seated at table or after they had departed, and would then eat nothing at all when the feast was served.

# 77

He was by nature a very slight drinker of wine. Cornelius Nepos says that he used to drink only three times at supper in the camp at Modena; and when he drank the most, it was never more than a pint, for, if he went beyond, his stomach revolted. He delighted most in Rhaetian wine, but seldom ever drank any in the day-time. Instead of drinking, he used to take a piece of bread dipped in cold water, or a slice of cucumber, some leaves of lettuce, or a green, sharp, juicy apple.

# 78

After his light noonday repast, he used to take his repose, dressed as he was and with his shoes on, his feet stretched out and holding his hand before his eyes. After supper he retired to his study, a small closet, where he sat late, until he had put down in his diary all or most of the remaining affairs of the day, which he had not before recorded. He would then go to bed, but never slept above seven hours at the most, and that not without interruption, for he would wake three or four times during that period; and if he could not again fall asleep, as sometimes happened, he summoned one to read or tell him stories, until he became drowsy, and then his sleep was usually protracted till after day-break. He would never lie awake in the dark without someone sitting by him. Very early rising was apt to disagree with him; and if he was obliged to rise betimes, for any civil or religious occasion, in order to guard his own good health he used to stay at the house of some friend near the spot where the event was to take place. And as he was being carried through the streets, if a fit of drowsiness overcame him, he would have his litter set down while he indulged in a few moments' slumber.

## 79

In person he was well favoured and charming, and these qualities marked him at all stages of his life. Yet he was negligent in his dress, and so careless about the grooming of his hair that he usually had it done in great haste, by several barbers at a time, such as might be available, it mattered not whom; and one clipped, while another shaved his beard, during which time he either read or wrote, and attended not at all to the ceremony. His visage, whether he spoke or held his peace, was so mild, so pleasant, and lightsome, that one of the nobles of Gaul confessed to his countrymen that he was so struck by it as to be checked from throwing him down a precipice, in his passage over the Alps, after he had gained admittance to his presence under colour of a conference, for that very purpose. He also had very clear and shining eyes, wherein (as he was willing to have men believe) there shone a kind of divine vigour; and he was much pleased, when he looked steadfastly at people, if they dropped their lids, as if from the brightness of the sun. But in his old age, he could not see very well with the left eye. His teeth were thin set, small and scaly, his hair somewhat curled, and of a light yellow colour. His eyebrows came together, his ears were small, and his nose aquiline. His complexion was betwixt brown and fair; and his stature is said to have been short; yet Julius Marathus, his freedman, says he was five feet and nine inches in height. But although he seemed short when compared with some taller person standing beside him, this low stature was not ordinarily observable because of the admirable proportion of his limbs.

## 80

His body, by report, came into the world with many spots upon the breast and belly, dispersed in the manner, order, and number of the stars in the constellation of the Bear; he had besides several callosities resembling scars, occasioned by an itching in his body, and the constant and forcible use of the strigil in being rubbed. He had a weakness in his left hip, thigh, and leg, insomuch that he often halted on that side; but he was greatly eased by the use of a certain remedy of sand and reeds. Also, the forefinger of his right hand was sometimes found so weak, that when it was benumbed and contracted with cold, he was driven to use a circular piece of horn to strengthen it for writing. He complained also of trouble with his bladder, but upon voiding some stones in his urine, he was relieved of that pain.

## 81

All his life he experienced at certain times dangerous fits of sickness, especially after the conquest of Cantabria; when, his liver being injured by a defluxion upon it, he was thrown into such great discomfort that he was obliged to undergo a desperate and doubtful method of cure: for warm applications having no effect, his physician Antonius Musa recommended the use of cold. He was also subject to maladies which recurred at certain times every year. About his birthday (September 21st) he was commonly a little indisposed, and likewise in the beginning of the spring, when he was attacked with an inflation of the midriff; and when the wind was southerly, he suffered from a cold in his head. By all these troubles, his constitution was so weakened that he could not easily bear either heat or cold.

## 82

In winter, he went clad against the cold in a thick toga, four tunics, a shirt, a flannel stomacher, and swathings upon his legs and thighs. During the summer, he lay with the doors of his bedchamber open, and frequently in a piazza, refreshed by a bubbling fountain, and a fan manipulated by a servant. He could not endure even the winter's sun, and at home he never walked in the open air without a broad-brimmed hat on his head. He usually travelled in a litter, and by night; and so slowly, that if he went from Rome to Praeneste or Tibur, he made two days' journey of it. If he could reach any place either by land or sea, he preferred to sail thither. He strove valiantly to preserve his health against his many infirmities, avoiding chiefly the free use of the bath; but he was often rubbed with oil, and sweated in a stove; after which he was washed with tepid water, warmed either by a fire, or by being exposed to the heat of the sun. When, on account of his nerves, he had recourse to sea water, or the waters of Albula, (which, standing upon a vein of brimstone, were naturally hot), he contented himself with sitting over a wooden tub, which he called by a Spanish name *Dureta,* and plunging his hands and feet in the water by turns.

## 83

Riding and other military exercises in the Campus Martius he gave up immediately after the civil wars, and took to playing at handball or football. But soon afterwards he used no other exercise than that of going abroad in his litter, or walking; towards the end of his walk, he would run leaping, wrapped up in a short cloak or cape. For his recreation, he would sometimes angle, or play with dice, pebbles or nuts, with little boys collected from various countries, all that were lovely and amiable of person, and could prattle charmingly; he particularly favoured Moors and Syrians for these graces. But dwarfs, and such as were misshapen in any way, or deformed, he abhorred, as being the very mockeries of nature's work, and of unlucky presage.

# 84

Eloquence and other liberal arts he exercised from his childhood with great diligence. During the war of Modena, notwithstanding the weighty affairs which occupied him, he is said to have read, written, and declaimed every day. He never addressed the senate, the people, or the army, but in a premeditated speech, though he did not lack the gift of speaking extempore when the occasion arose. And lest his memory should fail him, or that he might spend too much time in learning by rote, he was wont to recite his written speeches. In his discourse with individuals, and even with his wife Livia, he never spoke without first having put down in writing all he wished to say, if the subject were important, so that he might say neither more nor less than was needful. He enunciated in a sweet and peculiar tone, which he acquired by the help of a master of elocution. But when he had a cold, he sometimes delivered his orations to the people by the mouth of a herald.

# 85

He made many compositions in prose on various topics, some of which he read in a meeting of his friends, as to an auditory. Among these was his *Rescript to Brutus respecting Cato*. Most of the pages he read himself, although weakened by old age; but becoming fatigued, he gave the rest to Tiberius to finish. He likewise read over to his friends his *Exhortations to Philosophy*, and the *History of His Own Life*, which he continued in thirteen books, as far as the Cantabrian war, but no further. He dealt in poetry only superficially. There is extant one book by him written in hexameter verse, of which both the subject and title is *Sicily*. There is also a book of epigrams, no larger than the last, which he composed almost entirely while he was in the bath. These are all his poetical works; for, though he began a tragedy (called *Ajax*) with great zeal, when he could not fashion his style to suit his taste, he obliterated the whole piece. And when some of his friends asked him, 'How fared Ajax?', he answered pleasantly, 'My Ajax has fallen upon a sponge', alluding to the circumstance that Ajax, in Sophocles' tragedy, fell upon his sword.

## 86

The eloquence that he cultivated was of a chaste and elegant kind, for he avoided extravagant and rough expressions as well as all words of an archaic and obscure import, which he called offensive. He took especial care to express his mind with clearness and simplicity; the better to effect this, and so that he might not perplex or retard the reader or hearer, he did not hesitate to add prepositions to verbs, or to reiterate his conjunctions; the omission of which breeds some obscurity, though yielding a better grace. Those that affected newly-made words, as well as those who used obsolete ones, he disliked and rejected as equally faulty, though in different ways. On this subject he resorted sometimes to jest, particularly with his friend Maecenas, whose myrrh-scented style (for these were his very words) he heartily loathed, and ridiculed by way of imitation. Nor did he spare Tiberius for searching out old words which were obscure and fantastic. Mark Antony he rated insane for writing that which men may rather wonder at, than understand, and mocking at his lewd and inconstant taste in the choice of words, he writes to him thus: 'And are you yet in doubt, whether Cimber Annius or Veranius Flaccus be more proper for your imitation? Whether you will adopt words which Sallustius Crispus has borrowed from the *Origines* of Cato? Or do you think that the rolling tongue of Asiatic orators, full of vain words, and void of pithy sentences, is fit to be transfused into our language?' And in a letter where he praises the ready wit of his granddaughter, Agrippina, he says: 'But you must take pains that neither in writing nor in speaking, you become affected and odious.'

## 87

In ordinary daily conversation, he had certain significant expressions of which he made frequent use, as is shown from letters written in his own hand; in which, now and then, when he means to imply that some persons would never pay their debts, he said, 'They will pay at the Greek Kalends.' And when he exhorted men to bear patiently the present state of affairs, whatever it was, he said: 'Let us be content with our Cato.' To describe anything done expeditiously, he said: 'It was sooner done than asparagus is boiled.' He constantly puts *baceolus* for *stultus, pullejaceus* for *pullus, vacerrosus* for *cerritus, vapide se habere* for *male,* and *betizare* for *languere,* which is commonly called *lachanizare.* Likewise *simus* for *sumus, domos* for *domus* in the genitive singular. With respect to the last two peculiarities, lest any person should imagine that they were only errors, and not customary with him, he never varies. I have also observed, especially in his manuscripts, that he never divides a word, so as to carry the letters which cannot be inserted at the end of a line to the next, but puts them below the other, enclosed by a bracket.

## 88

He did not observe meticulously the precise rules of orthography set down by grammarians, but seems to have followed rather the opinion of those who think that men should write as they speak. For, if he oftentimes exchanges or leaves out entirely, not letters only but also syllables, that is a common error among men. Neither should I have noted it at all, but that it appears strange to me that any person should have told us that he substituted another officer for a certain consular lieutenant of a province, whom he put down as a rude and illiterate fellow, because he had observed that he wrote *ixi* for *ipsi.* When he had occasion to write in cipher, he put b for a, c for b, and so forth; and for x, aa.

## 89

Nor was he less in love with the study of Greek literature in which he excelled, having had Apollodorus of Pergamus for his professor in rhetoric; whom, being now very aged, he took with him from the City to Apollonia, while he was himself very young. Afterwards, he was well instructed in various branches of learning through his association with Areus the philosopher, and his sons Dionysius and Nicanor; yet he never could speak readily in the Greek tongue, nor dared he attempt to compose in it. For if the need arose for him to express himself in that language, he drew up what he had to say in Latin, and gave it to another to be translated. He was not unacquainted with the poetry of the Greeks, and he took delight in the ancient comedy which he frequently exhibited upon the stage, in his public solemnities. In reading the Greek and Latin authors, he sought after nothing so much as wholesome precepts and examples, which served for public or private use; and those he used to reproduce word for word, and give to his servants, or else send them to the commanders of the armies, the governors of the provinces, or the magistrates of the City, when any of them seemed to need admonition. Moreover, he read whole books to the senate, and often made them known to the people by his edicts; such as the orations of Quintus Metellus, *For the Encouragement of Marriage*, and those of Rutilius, *On the Style of Building*; his object being to show them that he was not the first to concern himself with these matters, but that their forefathers likewise had a regard for them. The men of wit who flourished in his time he cherished in every way he could. He listened with courtesy and patience while they read their compositions before him; not only poetry and history, but also orations and dialogues. However, he was offended if anything were written of himself, unless it were done in a grave manner, and by men of the highest quality; and he charged the praetors not to suffer his name to be made vulgar in the trivial contests among orators and poets in the theatres.

## 90

It is reported that he was much affected by signs and omens. Thunder and lightning he feared so much that he always carried about him a seal's skin, which was considered a preservative remedy. And whensoever he apprehended a great storm, he would retire to some secret place underground, which was vaulted above; for he had at one time been greatly frightened by a flash of lightning which crossed his path as he journeyed at night, which event has before been related.

## 91

He neither disregarded his own dreams nor those of others relating to himself. At the battle of Philippi, although he had resolved not to step out of his tent because of sickness, he went forth because of a warning which came to him in a dream had by one of his friends. And it was well that he did so, for in the enemy's attack, his couch was pierced and cut to pieces, in the belief that he was lying there sick. In the spring, he had many frivolous and frightful dreams; but at other times of the year he dreamed not so often but to more effect. Upon his frequently visiting a temple near the Capitol, which he had dedicated to Jupiter Tonans, he dreamed that Jupiter Capitolinus complained that his worshippers were taken from him, and that upon this he replied, he had only given him The Thunderer for his porter. (For the temple of Jupiter Tonans was close by.) Whereupon soon afterwards he hung little bells around the summit of the temple, because such commonly hung at the gates of great houses to raise the porters. Because of a dream, too, he always begged alms of those who passed, on a certain day of the year, holding out his hand to receive the mite which was offered him.

## 92

Certain signs and omens he observed as infallible, to wit, if in the morning his shoe was put on wrong, for example, the left on the right foot, he feared ill luck; or, when he was to take any long journey by land or sea, if there happened to fall a mizzling rain, he took it for a good sign betokening a speedy and prosperous return. He was especially affected by uncouth or unnatural sights. A palm-tree which happened to spring forth between some stones in the court of his house, he transplanted into a court where the images of the household gods were placed, and took great care that it should thrive there. In the island of Capri, when some drooping and decayed boughs of an old ilex became fresh and upright again at his arrival, he was so overjoyed that he made an exchange with the Republic of Naples, of the island of Oenaria (Ischia), for that of Capri. He likewise observed certain days very religiously; as never to go from home the day after the Nundinae, nor to begin any serious business upon the nones; avoiding nothing else in it, as he writes to Tiberius, than its unlucky name.

## 93

The religious ceremonies of foreign nations, he regarded with all reverence, if they were established by ancient custom: but others he held in no esteem. For, having been initiated at Athens, and coming afterwards to hear a cause at Rome relative to the privileges of the priests of the Attic Ceres, when some of the mysteries of their sacred rites were to be introduced in the pleadings, he dismissed those who sat upon the bench as judges with him, as well as the bystanders, and heard the argument upon those points himself. But, on the other hand, he not only declined, in his progress through Egypt, to go out of his way to pay a visit to Apis, but he likewise commended his grandson Caius for not paying his devotions at Jerusalem in his passage through Judaea.

## 94

Seeing that we have proceeded thus far in our reports of this prince, it would not be impertinent to dwell on what happenings preceded and followed his birth, which gave hope of his future greatness and the felicity that constantly attended him. At Velitrae, a part of the wall having in former times been struck with lightning, the pronouncement of the soothsayers was that a native of that town would some time or other be ruler of the world. Believing this, the Velitraeans both then, and several times afterwards, made war upon the Roman people, to their own ruin. At length it appeared that the strange accident portended the ascendancy of Augustus.

Julius Marathus reports that a few months before his birth there happened at Rome a prodigy, by which was signified that Nature was in travail with a king for the Roman people; at which the senate, being affrighted, made an act that no child born that year should be brought up; but that those among them whose wives were with child, because each of them hoped to draw the honour to himself, took care that the decree of the senate should not be registered in the treasury.

I read in the theological books of Asclepiades the Mendesian that Atia, the mother of Augustus, upon attending at midnight a religious solemnity in honour of Apollo, when the rest of the matrons retired home, fell asleep on her couch in the temple, upon which a serpent immediately crept up to her, and soon after withdrew. She, awaking upon this, purified herself as she would have done after the embraces of her husband; and instantly there appeared upon her body a mark in the form of a serpent which she never after could efface, and which obliged her, during the rest of her life, to avoid the public baths. Augustus, it was added, was born in the tenth month after, and for this reason he was reputed to be the son of Apollo. The same Atia, before her delivery, dreamed that her entrails were heaved up to the stars and there stretched forth over the whole of heaven and earth. His father Octavius, likewise, dreamed that a sunbeam issued from his wife's womb.

The very day on which he was born, while the senate was debating on the conspiracy of Catiline, and Octavius, by reason of his wife's being in childbirth, coming late into the house, it is well known that Publius Nigidius, upon hearing the occasion of his coming so late, and the hour of his wife's delivery, said with confidence that there was born a sovereign lord of the world. Afterwards, when Octavius led his army through the deserts of Thrace, and consulted the oracle in the grove of father Bacchus with barbarous rites, concerning his son, he received from the priests the same answer; because, when they poured wine upon the altar, there arose from thence so great and shining a flame, that it surmounted the roof of the temple and ascended to the heavens: a token that had never before occurred except to Alexander the Great when he sacrificed upon the same altars. And next night he dreamed that he saw his son in a majestic aspect, above ordinary human dignity, holding a thunderbolt and a sceptre and the other attributes of Jupiter Optimus Maximus, having on his head a radiant crown, and mounted upon a chariot decked with laurel, and drawn by six pairs of milk-white horses.

While he was yet a babe, as Caius Drusus relates, being laid in his cradle by his nurse, in a low place, the next morning he was nowhere to be seen; and after long seeking he was found at last upon a lofty tower, lying with his face toward the rising sun. As soon as he began to speak, he commanded the frogs that happened to make a troublesome noise upon an estate belonging to the family near the town, to be silent; and there goes a report that frogs never croaked there since that time. About four miles from Rome, as he was dining in a grove on the Campanian road, an eagle suddenly snatched a piece of bread out of his hand and, soaring to a very great height, came gently down again most unexpectedly, and restored it to him.

Quintus Catulus dreamed for two nights successively after his dedication of the Capitol; the first night he thought that Jupiter, out of several boys of the order of the nobility who were playing about his altar, chose one from the rest, into whose bosom he put the public seal of the commonwealth which he held in his hand; and in his vision the next night, he saw in the bosom of Jupiter Capitolinus, the same boy, whom he ordered to be removed, but it was forbidden by the god, who commanded that he must be brought up to be the guardian of the state. The next day, chancing to meet with young Augustus, with whom till that hour he had not the least acquaintance, and looking at him with admiration, he said he was remarkably like the boy of whom he dreamed. Some tell the former dream of Catulus differently, saying that Jupiter, when several noble lads asked him for a guardian, pointed to one among them, to whom they were to refer all their requests; and putting his fingers to the boy's mouth to kiss, he afterwards lightly touched them to his own mouth.

Marcus Cicero, having accompanied Caius Caesar to the Capitol, happened to be telling some of his friends a dream which he had the night before, in which a boy of an ingenuous face and form was let down from heaven by a golden chain, and stood at the door of the Capitol, where a whip was put into his hands by Jupiter. And espying unawares little Augustus, who had been sent by his uncle Caesar to the sacrifice, and was as yet wholly unknown to most of the company, he avowed plainly that this boy was the one whose image he had seen in his dream. When he was putting on his virile gown, his senatorian tunic, becoming loose in the seam on each side, fell at his feet. Some interpreted this as an omen that the order, of which that was the badge of distinction, would some time or other be subject to him.

Julius Caesar, in cutting down a wood to make room for his camp near Munda, happened to light upon a palm-tree, and ordered it to be preserved as an omen of victory. From the root of this tree there sprung immediately certain shoots which in a few days grew so high as not only to equal, but overtop it, and afford room for many nests of wild pigeons which built in it, though that species of bird particularly avoids a hard and rough leaf. It is likewise reported, that Caesar was largely influenced by this prodigy to suffer none other than his sister's grandson to succeed him in the empire.

Augustus, during his retirement at Apollonia, went with his friend Agrippa to visit Theogenes, the astrologer, in his gallery on the roof. Agrippa, who first consulted the fates, having great and almost incredible fortunes predicted for him, Augustus concealed the date of his own nativity for a long while, for fear that his fortunes should be found inferior to those of Agrippa. Being persuaded, however, after many exhortations, to reveal it, Theogenes started up from his seat and worshipped him. Augustus, soon afterwards, conceived such great confidence in his fortunes, that he published his horoscope and struck a silver coin, bearing upon it the sign of Capricorn, under which influence he was born.

## 95

After Caesar's death, upon his return from Apollonia, as he was entering the City, suddenly in a fair, clear sky, a coronet in the form of a rainbow encircled the sun; and immediately afterwards, the tomb of Julia, Caesar's daughter, was blasted by lightning. In his first consulship, while he was observing the auguries, twelve vultures presented themselves, as they had done to Romulus. And when he offered sacrifice, the livers of all the victims were folded inward in the lower part: and there was present no man of skill who conjectured otherwise but that great prosperity and fame were thereby prognosticated.

## 96

Furthermore, he foresaw the outcome of all of his wars. When the troops of the Triumviri were assembled about Bologna, an eagle, which sat upon his tent, and was assailed by two crows, beat them both, and struck them to the ground, in the sight of the whole army; who thence inferred that discord would arise between the three colleagues, which would be attended with the like event; and it accordingly ensued. At Philippi, he was assured of success by a Thessalian, upon the authority, as he pretended, of the Divine Caesar himself, who had appeared to him while he was travelling in a byroad. At Perugia, the sacrifice not presenting any favourable intimations but quite the contrary, he ordered fresh victims; the enemy, however, carrying off the sacred things in a sudden sally, it was agreed among the augurs that all the perils and calamities which had threatened the sacrifice would fall upon the heads of those who had got possession of the entrails; and so indeed it fell out. The day before the naval battle near Sicily, as he walked upon the shore, a fish leaped out of the sea and lay at his feet. At Actium as he was going down to his fleet to enter the battle he was met by an ass with his driver; the man's name being Eutychus, meaning 'fortunate' and the beast's Nicon, signifying 'victorious'. After the victory, he set up a brazen statue to each in a temple built upon the spot where he had encamped.

## 97

His death, of which I shall now write, and his subsequent deification, were forecast by divers manifest prodigies. As he was finishing the census amid a great crowd of people in the Campus Martius, an eagle soared about him many times, and crossing at length to a neighbouring temple, settled upon the name of Agrippa, and at the first letter. Perceiving this, he ordered his colleague Tiberius to put up the vows, which it is usual to make on such occasions, for the succeeding Lustrum. For he professed himself reluctant to tamper with what it was evident he should never achieve, though the tables were ready drawn for it. About the same time, the first letter of his name, in an inscription upon one of his statues, was struck out by a flash of lightning; which was interpreted as a presage that he would live only a hundred days longer, the letter C denoting that number; and that he would be placed among the gods, as Aesar, the residue of the name Caesar, signifies in the Tuscan language a god. Being, therefore, about to send Tiberius into Illyricum, and intending to accompany him as far as Beneventum, when several persons detained him with respect to causes they had depending, he cried out (and it was afterwards reckoned as an omen of his death), 'Not all the business in the world shall keep me at Rome one moment longer'; and setting out upon his journey, he went as far as Astura whence, contrary to his custom, he put to sea in the night time, as there was a favourable wind.

## 98

His mortal illness proceeded from diarrhoea; notwithstanding which, he went round the coast of Campania and the adjoining islands and spent four days in that of Capri: where he gave himself up wholly to ease and enjoyment. It happened as he sailed by the bay of Puteoli, that the passengers and mariners aboard a ship of Alexandria, just then arrived, clad all in white, with chaplets upon their heads, and offering incense, heaped upon him praises and joyful acclamations, crying out 'By you we live, by you we sail securely, by you enjoy our liberty and our fortunes.' At which he was much cheered at heart, and distributed to each of those who attended him forty gold pieces, requiring from them an assurance on oath not to employ the sum given them in any other way than in the purchase of Alexandrian wares. And during several days afterwards, he distributed Togae and Pallia, among other gifts, on condition that the Romans should use the Greek, and the Greeks the Roman, dress and language. He likewise constantly attended to see the boys perform their exercises, according to an ancient custom still continued at Capri. He gave them also an entertainment in his presence, and not only permitted but required from them the utmost freedom in jesting, and scrambling for fruit, victuals, and other things which he threw among them. In a word, he indulged himself in all the ways of amusement he could contrive.

He called an island near Capri, Apragopolis, 'The City of the Dolittles', because of the indolent life which several of his party led there. A favourite of his, one Masgabas, he used to call by a Greek word, signifying founder or planter of the island. And observing from his room a great company of people with torches assembled at the tomb of this Masgabas, who died the year before, he pronounced aloud, in Greek, this verse which he made extempore.

Blazing with lights I see the founder's tomb.

And turning then to Thrasyllus, a companion of Tiberius, who reclined on the other side of the table, he asked him, who knew nothing about the matter, what poet he thought had made the verse? And on his remaining dumb, he added another:

Honour'd with torches Masgabas you see;

and put the same question to him concerning that likewise. But when Thrasyllus replied that, whoever the author might be, they were excellent verses, he fell into hearty laughter and became exceedingly merry over it. Soon afterwards, passing over to Naples, although at that time greatly enfeebled in his bowels by the frequent attacks of his disease, he nevertheless saw to the very end the exhibition of the gymnastic games which were held in his honour every five years; and so proceeded with Tiberius to the place intended. But on his return, his disorder increasing more and more, he at length yielded to it, stopping at Nola; where, having sent for Tiberius to come back again, he had a long and secret talk with him;

nor, from that time on, did he give his mind to any affair of any importance.

## 99

Upon his dying day, he inquired ever and anon, whether there was any stir and tumult in the city on his account; and calling for a mirror, he commanded his hair to be combed and his shrunk cheeks to be composed. Then, having admitted his friends to his presence, he asked them whether they thought he had acted well his part on the stage of life, and he immediately subjoined,

> If all be right, with joy your voices raise,
> In loud applauses to the actor's praise.

After which, having dismissed them all, while he was questioning some persons who were just arrived from Rome, concerning Drusus's daughter who was in a weak state of health, suddenly amid the kisses of Livia, and in these words, he gave up the ghost: 'Live mindful, Livia, of our wedlock, and so farewell.' Thus he died a very easy death, such as he himself had always wished for. For as often as he heard that any one had died quickly and without pain, he prayed that he and his might have the like Euthanasia (an easy death), for that was the word he made use of. He showed one sign only of being deranged in his mind before he yielded up his vital breath in that he was all of a sudden much frightened and complained that he was being carried away by forty tall and lusty young men. And that was rather a pregnant prevision than a disorder of the brain; for exactly that number of soldiers belonging to the praetorian cohort carried him forth dead upon their shoulders.

## 100 A.U.C. 767

He died in the same bedroom wherein his father Octavius left this life before him, when the two Sextus's, Pompey and Apuleius, were consuls, upon the fourteenth of the kalends of September (the 19th August), at the ninth hour of the day, being 76 years old lacking thirty-five days. His corpse was borne by the magistrates of the municipal towns and colonies, from Nola to Bovillae, and in the night time, because of the season of the year. During the day the body lay in some basilica, or great temple, of each town. At Bovillae it was met by the Equestrian Order, who carried it to the city and deposited it in the vestibule of his own house. The senate proceeded with so much zeal in the arrangement of his funeral, and paying honour to his memory, that, among several other proposals, some were for having the funeral procession made through the triumphal gate, preceded by the image of Victory which is in the senate house, and the children of highest rank and of both sexes singing the funeral dirge. Others proposed, that on the day of the funeral, they should lay aside their gold rings, and wear rings of iron; and others, that his bones should be collected by the priests of the principal colleges. One likewise moved to transfer the name of August to September, because he was born in the latter but died in the former. Another suggested that the whole period of time, from his birth to his death, should be called the Augustan age, and be inserted in the calendar under that title. But at length it was thought best to be moderate in the honours paid to his memory. Two funeral orations were pronounced in his praise, one before the temple of Julius, by Tiberius; and the other before the rostra, under the old shops, by Drusus, Tiberius' son. The body was then carried upon the shoulders of senators into the Campus Martius, and there burnt. A man of praetorian rank affirmed upon oath that he saw his spirit ascend from the funeral pile to heaven. The most honourable persons of the equestrian order, barefooted and with their tunics loose, gathered up his relics, and deposited them in the mausoleum, which had been built in his sixth consulship between the Flaminian Way and the bank of the Tiber; at which time likewise he gave the groves and walks about it for the use of the people.

## IOI

He had made a will one year and four months before his death, upon the third of the nones of April (the 11th of April), in the consulship of Lucius Plancus, and Caius Silius. It consisted of two skins of parchment, written partly in his own hand, and partly by his freedmen Polybius and Hilarion. The Vestal Virgins, to whose charge it had been committed, now brought it forth, together with three codicils under seal: all of which were opened and read in the senate. He named as his direct heirs, Tiberius for two-thirds of his estate, and

Livia for the other third, both of whom he appointed to bear his name. The heirs in remainder were Drusus, Tiberius' son, for one-third, and Germanicus with his three sons for the residue. In the third place, failing them, were his relations, and several of his friends. He left in legacies to the Roman people forty millions of sesterces; to the tribes three millions five hundred thousand; to the praetorian troops a thousand to each man; to the city cohorts five hundred; and to the legions and soldiers three hundred each; which several sums he ordered to be paid immediately after his death, having taken due care that the money should be ready in his exchequer. For the rest he ordered different times of payment. In some of his requests he went as far as twenty thousand sesterces, for the payment of which he allowed a twelvemonth; alleging for this procrastination his slight estate; and protesting that not more than a hundred and fifty millions of sesterces would come to his heirs: notwithstanding that during the twenty preceding years, he had received, in legacies from his friends, the sum of fourteen hundred millions: almost the whole of which, with his two paternal estates, those of his father Octavius and his adopted father, Julius Caesar, and others which had been left him, he had spent in the service of the state. He left orders that the two Julias, his daughter and granddaughter, should not be buried in his tomb. With regard to the three codicils before-mentioned, in one of them he gave orders about his funeral; another contained a summary of his acts, which he intended should be inscribed on brazen plates and placed in front of his mausoleum; in the third he had drawn up a concise account of the state of the empire; the number of troops enrolled, what money there was in the treasury, the revenue, and arrears of taxes; to which were added the names of the freedmen and slaves from whom the several accounts might be taken.

# *Tiberius Nero Caesar*

## I

The patrician family of the Claudii (for there was likewise a plebeian family of that name, in no way inferior to the other either in power or dignity) came originally from Regilli, a town of the Sabines. They journeyed thence to Rome soon after the building of the city, with a great retinue of dependants, under Titus Tatius, who reigned jointly with Romulus in the kingdom; or, perhaps, what is reported upon better authority, under Atta Claudius, the head of the family, who was admitted by the senate into the patrician order six years after the expulsion of the Tarquins. They likewise received from the state lands beyond the Anio for their followers, and a burying place for themselves near the Capitol; and after this period, in process of time, the family had the honour of twenty-eight consulships, five dictatorships, seven censorships, seven triumphs, and two ovations. Their descendants were distinguished by sundry forenames and surnames, but rejected by general consent the forename of Lucius because, of the two races who bore it, one person had been convicted of robbery, and another of murder. Among other surnames they assumed the addition of Nero, which in the Sabine tongue signifies strong or valiant.

Many of the Claudii earned the gratitude of the commonwealth by their excellent services, and many also were guilty of serious faults. To mention only the most conspicuous examples: Appius Caecus dissuaded the senate from agreeing to an alliance with Pyrrhus, as prejudicial to the state; Claudius Candex was the first man that passed over the straits of Sicily with a fleet, and drove the Carthaginians out of the island. Claudius Nero surprised and defeated Hasdrubal upon his arrival in Italy from Spain, with a great and powerful army, before he could join his brother Hannibal. On the contrary side of the picture, Claudius Appius Regillanus, one of the Decemvirs, attempted by violence to gain possession of a free virgin, of whom he was enamoured; and thereby gave occasion to the people to break off with the nobles for a second time. Claudius Drusus erected a statue of himself wearing a diadem at Appi Forum, and attempted with the help of his dependants to bring all Italy into his power. Claudius Pulcher, when the sacred pullets used for taking augury off the coast of Sicily refused to eat, caused them, in contempt of the omen, to be plunged into the sea that they might drink at least; and then, attacking the enemy, was vanquished. Being thereupon commanded by the senate to nominate a dictator, making a jest of the public calamity, he named Glycias, his apparitor.

There stand likewise upon record the examples of the women of this family, no less diverse in character than the men. For both the Claudias belonged to the race: she who, when the ship laden with things sacred to the Idaean Mother of the Gods, Cybele, stuck fast in the shallows of the Tiber, got it off, by praying to the goddess with a loud voice: 'Follow me, if I am a true and pure virgin'; and she also who, contrary to the usual practice in the case of women, was brought to trial by the people for treason: because, when her litter was halted by a great multitude in the streets, she openly exclaimed: 'I wish my brother Pulcher was alive now to lose another fleet, that Rome might be less thronged.' Moreover, it is very well known, that all the Claudii, (except Publius Claudius, who, to effect the banishment of Cicero, procured himself to be adopted by a plebeian, and one younger than himself), were always of the patrician party, as well as great sticklers for the honour and power of that order; and so violent and obstinate in their opposition to the plebeians, that not one of them, even in the case of a trial for life by the people, would ever condescend to put on mourning, according to custom, or make any supplication to them for favour; and some of them, in their contests, even proceeded to lay hands on the tribunes of the people. A Vestal Virgin of the family likewise, when her brother was resolved to have the honour of a triumph contrary to the will of the people, mounted the chariot with him, and attended him into the Capitol, that it might not be lawful for any of the tribunes to interfere and forbid it.

From this race is Tiberius Caesar descended, both by his father, from Tiberius Nero, and by his mother from Appius Pulcher, who were both sons of Appius Caecus. He likewise belonged to the family of the Livii, by the adoption of his mother's grandfather into it: which family, though plebeian, flourished notwithstanding and was highly reputed, having had the honour of eight consulships, two censorships, three triumphs, one dictatorship, and the office of master of the horse; and was renowned also for brave and notable men, particularly Salinator and the Drusi. Salinator, in his censorship, branded all the tribes for their inconstancy in that although they had condemned him to a heavy fine after his first consulship, they afterwards made him consul a second time, as well as censor. Drusus, by the killing in single combat of one Drausus, the enemy's general, procured for himself and his posterity a new surname. It is reported also that when he was pro-praetor in the province of Gaul, he recovered the gold which was formerly given to the Senones at the siege of the Capitol, and had not, as is said, been forced from them by Camillus. His great-great-grandson who, for his notable services against the Gracchi, was styled the 'Patron of the Senate', left a son, who, while plotting a sedition of the same nature, was treacherously slain by the adverse faction.

But the father of Tiberius Caesar, being quaestor to Caius Caesar, and admiral of his fleet in the war of Alexandria, contributed greatly to its success; whereupon he was made one of the high priests in the room of Publius Scipio and was sent to settle some colonies in Gaul, among which were Narbonne and Arles. After Caesar was slain, however, when the rest of the senators, for fear of public disturbances, were inclined to bury the affair in oblivion, he proposed a resolution for rewarding those who had killed the tyrant. Having filled the office of praetor, and at the end of the year there occurring an upheaval among the triumvir, he kept the badges of his office beyond the legal time; and following Lucius Antonius the consul, brother of the triumvir, to Perugia, when the rest yielded, he himself continued firm to the party, and escaped first to Praeneste and then to Naples; whence, having in vain invited the slaves to liberty, he fled over to Sicily. But resenting his not being immediately admitted to the presence of Sextus Pompeius, and being also debarred the use of the fasces, he went over into Achaia to Mark Antony; with whom, upon a reconciliation soon after brought about amongst the several contending parties, he returned to Rome; and, at the request of Augustus, gave up to him his wife Livia Drusilla, although she was then big with child, and had before borne him a son. He died not long after; leaving behind him his two sons, Tiberius and Drusus Nero.

5

A.U.C. 712

Some have believed that Tiberius was born at Fundi, lightly grounding their conjecture upon the circumstance that his mother's grandmother was of Fundi and that the image of Good Fortune was, by a decree of the senate, erected in a public place in that town in token of his nativity. But, as most reliable writers attest, he was born at Rome, in the Palatine quarter, upon the sixteenth of the kalends of December (16th November), when Marcus Aemilius Lepidus was second time consul, with Lucius Munatius Plancus, after the battle of Philippi; for so it stands upon record and in the public registers. Yet some have it that he was born the preceding year, in the consulship of Hirtius and Pansa; and others say, in the year following, during the consulship of Servilius Isauricus and Antony.

6

His infancy and childhood were spent in the midst of danger and trouble; for he accompanied his parents everywhere in their flight. And twice at Naples he nearly disclosed their whereabouts by his wailing when they were secretly hastening to a ship as the enemy suddenly rushed into the town; once, when he was snatched from his nurse's breast, and again, from his mother's bosom, by some of the company, who on the sudden emergency wished to relieve the women of their burden. He was carried away with them likewise through Sicily and Achaia, and entrusted for some time to the care of the Lacedaemonians, who were under the protection of the Claudian family; upon his departure thence then travelling by night, he ran the hazard of his life by a fire which, suddenly bursting out of a wood on all sides, surrounded the whole party so closely, that part of Livia's dress and hair was singed. The gifts bestowed upon him in Sicily by Pompeia, sister to Sextus Pompey, namely, a cloak with a clasp, and bullae of gold, are still in existence, and are shown at Baiae to this day. After his return to the city, being adopted by Marcus Gallius, a senator, in his will, he entered upon his inheritance; but soon afterwards declined the use of his name, because Gallius had been of the party opposed to Augustus. When only nine years of age, he pronounced a funeral oration in praise of his father upon the rostra; and afterwards, when he had nearly attained the age of manhood, he attended the chariot of Augustus, in his triumph for the victory at Actium, riding on the left-hand horse, while Marcellus, Octavia's son, rode that on the right. He presided, also, at the games held in honour of that victory; and in the Trojan games intermixed with the Circensian, he commanded a troop of the biggest boys.

# 7
A.U.C. 744

After assuming his virile robe, at seventeen years of age, he spent his youth and the rest of his life until he succeeded to the government, in the following manner: he exhibited an entertainment of gladiators in memory of his father, and another for his grandfather Drusus, at different times and in different places: the first in the Forum, the second in the amphitheatre; some gladiators who had been honourably discharged being induced to engage again, by a reward of a hundred thousand sesterces. He likewise exhibited public sports, which he did not himself attend. All these he performed with great magnificence, at the expense of his mother and father-in-law. He married Agrippina, the daughter of Marcus Agrippa and granddaughter of Caecilius Atticus, a Roman knight, the same person to whom Cicero has addressed so many epistles. And when he had begotten of her a son named Drusus, he was forced to put her away, although he loved her still and knew her to be again with child, in order to wed Julia, the daughter of Augustus; this he did, not without much grief and heartbreak, for not only did he still desire Agrippina, but he also disliked the demeanour of Julia, who had exhibited her fancy and disposition for him while she was the wife of a former husband, and who, it was generally thought, was a woman of free and inconstant character. He suffered so keenly at the parting with

Agrippina, and upon meeting her by chance afterwards he followed her with eyes so full of affection and longing, that great care was taken that she should never again cross his path. With Julia he lived at first in great concord and love; but discord soon arose between them which quickly took on the darkest aspect; so that after the loss of their son, the pledge of their union, who was born at Aquileia and died in infancy, he took to a separate bed and never slept with her any more. He also lost his brother Drusus in Germany and brought his body to Rome, travelling all the way on foot before it.

## 8

When he first turned his attention to civil matters, he pleaded at the bar in defence of King Archelaus, the Trallians, and the Thessalians, before Augustus, who sat as judge at the trials. He addressed the senate on behalf of the Laodiceans, the Thyatireans, and Chians, who had suffered great loss by an earthquake and sought relief from Rome. He arraigned for treason Fannius Caepio, who had conspired against Augustus, and caused him to be condemned. In all these affairs, he executed a double function: namely, that of supplying the City with corn, which was then very scarce, and that of clearing the houses of correction throughout Italy, the masters of which had fallen under the odious suspicion of seizing and keeping confined not only travellers, but those whom the fear of taking the military oath and of being enrolled had driven to seek refuge in such places.

## 9                                                      A.U.C. 728

His first service in the wars was in the expedition of Cantabria, as a military tribune. Afterwards, he conducted an army into the East, where he restored the kingdom of Armenia to Tigranes; and seated on a tribunal, put a crown upon his head. He likewise recovered from the Parthians the standards which they had taken from Crassus. He next governed, for nearly a year, the province of Gallia Comata, which was then full of troubles, partly on account of the incursions of the barbarians, and partly through the internal discord of the nobles of the country. He afterwards commanded in the several wars against the Rhaetians, Vindelicians, Pannonians, and Germans. In the Rhaetian and Vindelician wars, he subdued the nations in the Alps; and in the

Pannonian wars the Bruci, and the Dalmatians. In the German war, he transplanted into Gaul forty thousand of the enemy who had submitted, and assigned them lands near the banks of the Rhine. For which acts, he entered the city with an ovation, but riding in a chariot, and is said by some to have been the first that ever was honoured with this distinction. He filled early the principal offices of state; and passed through the quaestorship, praetorship, and consulate almost successively. After some interval, he was chosen consul a second time, and held the tribunician authority during five years.

IO           A.U.C. 748

In this confluence of so many prosperous ventures, in the full strength of his years and in perfect health, he suddenly conceived the purpose of retiring as far from Rome as he could. Whether this desire was due to weariness of the life he was leading with his wife, whom he neither dared accuse nor divorce, a condition that he was unable to endure any longer; or to prevent that indifference towards him which his continual residence in the city might produce; or in the hope of better maintaining and increasing his authority in the state by absenting himself, if at any time his services were needed; is uncertain. Some are of opinion, that as Augustus' sons were now well grown, he voluntarily yielded up to them the possession he had long enjoyed of the second place in the government, as Agrippa had done before him; who, when M. Marcellus was advanced to public offices, retired to Mytilene, that he might not seem to stand in the way of his promotion, or in any respect lessen him by his presence. The same reason likewise Tiberius gave afterwards for his retirement; but his pretext at this time was, that he was satiated with honours, and desirous of resting from the fatigue of public affairs, in consideration of which he sued for license to depart. And neither gave he any care to his own mother who humbly besought him to stay, nor to his father-in-law, who complained that he was being forsaken by him and left unsupported in the senate. Moreover, when they were determined to hold him back, he refused to take any sustenance for four days together. At last, having obtained leave to be gone, he left his wife and son behind him at Rome, and forthwith proceeded to Ostia; having spoken not so much as one word with any of those who attended him, and kissing very few of them at the parting.

## II

As he sailed from Ostia along the coast of Campania, upon receiving news of Augustus' weakness he halted awhile; but this giving rise to a rumour that he stayed with a view to something extraordinary, he sailed with the wind almost full against him, and arrived at Rhodes, having been struck with the pleasantness and healthfulness of the island at the time of his landing there on his return from Armenia. Contenting himself here with a small house and a villa not much larger, he led entirely a private life, taking his walks sometimes about the Gymnasia, without any lictor or other attendant, and returning the civilities of the Greeks with almost as much complaisance as if he had been upon a level with them. One morning, in settling the course of his daily excursion, he chanced to say that he was desirous of visiting all the sick in the city. These words were misconstrued by those about him, and all the diseased persons were brought into a public portico, where they were ranged in order, according to their several maladies. At which unexpected sight, being much troubled and perplexed, he was for sometime uncertain what to do; but at last, he went around to all of them, even the meanest, and made apology for the mistake that had been made. One instance only is mentioned, in which he appeared to exercise his tribunician authority. Being a constant attendant upon the schools and lecture rooms of the professors of the liberal arts, on occasion of a dispute among the wrangling sophists, in which he interposed to reconcile them, some person took the liberty to abuse him as an intruder, and partial in the affair. Upon this, withdrawing privately to his house, he came forth suddenly, attended by his officers, and summoning his accuser before his tribunal by a public crier, ordered him to be taken to prison. Afterwards, he received tidings that his wife Julia had been condemned for her incontinence and adulteries, and that a bill of divorce had been sent to her in his name by the authority of Augustus. Though he was glad at this intelligence, yet he thought it devolved upon him, as a point of decency, to endeavour by many letters to reconcile the father to his daughter, and to allow her to retain the presents which he had made her, notwithstanding the little regard she deserved from him. When the period of his tribunician authority expired, confessing at last that he had no other object in his retirement than to avoid all suspicion of rivalship with Caius and Lucius, he made suit that, since he was now secure in that respect, as they were come to the age of manhood and could easily maintain themselves in possession of the second place in the state, he might be permitted to return and see again his friends and acquaintances whose presence he missed and longed for. But he was not granted his plea; and was admonished to lay aside all concern for his friends and kinsfolk, whom he had been so willing before to abandon.

## 12

Against his will, therefore, he remained at Rhodes; and to cover his ignominy, he obtained, with difficulty, through his mother's intercession, the title of Augustus' lieutenant. He thenceforth lived, however, not only as a private person, but as one suspected and under apprehension, retiring into the interior of the country, and avoiding the visits of those who sailed that way, which were very frequent; for no one passed to take command of an army, or the government of a province, without touching at Rhodes. There were, besides, other grounds for fear and trouble presented him. For crossing over to Samos, on a visit to his stepson Caius, who had been appointed governor of the East, he found him to be estranged from him by the slanders of Marcus Lollius, his companion and director. He also incurred the suspicion of sending by some centurions who had been promoted by himself, upon their return to the camp after a furlough, mysterious messages to several persons there, intended apparently to incite them to rebellion. This jealousy respecting his designs being intimated to him by Augustus, he begged repeatedly to have some person of any of the three Orders placed as a spy upon him to observe all his deeds and words.

## 13

He neglected also his usual exercises of riding and arms; and laying aside the Roman habit, adopted the pallium and crepida of the Greeks. In this condition he continued almost two years, becoming daily an object of increasing contempt and odium; insomuch that the people of Nismes pulled down all the images and statues of him in their town; and upon mention being made of him at table one of the company said to Caius: 'I will sail over to Rhodes immediately, if you will give the word, and bring you the head of that exiled person' — for so he was commonly called. And being faced now, not only by fear but by real peril, he renewed his supplications for leave to return; and, enforced by the earnest prayers of his mother, he at last obtained his request, with the help, also, of good fortune. Augustus had resolved to determine nothing in the matter but with the consent of his eldest son. The latter was at that time displeased with Marcus Lollius and therefore easily disposed to favour the cause of his father-in-law. By the permission of Caius, therefore, he was called home, but upon the condition that he should not meddle in any way with the affairs of state.

## 14    A.U.C. 755

Thus, after an absence of eight years, he returned to Rome, full of great hopes for his future fortunes, which he had conceived in his youth, in consequence of various prodigies and predictions. For Livia, when she carried him in her womb, being anxious to know whether her offspring would be a son, among other experiments which she made, took an egg from a hen that was sitting, and kept it warm with her own hands and those of her maids, by turns, until a fine cock chicken, with a large comb, was hatched. Scribonius, the astrologer, prophesied great things of him when he was yet a child; namely, 'that he should one day reign as king, but without the usual marks of royalty'. (For, as yet, the rule of the Caesars was unknown.) When he entered upon his first expedition and led an army into Syria through Macedonia, it chanced that the altars which had been formerly consecrated at Philippi by the victorious legions, blazed suddenly with spontaneous fires. And soon after, as he was marching to Illyricum, he stopped to consult the oracle of Geryon, near Padua; where, having drawn a lot by which he was desired to throw golden tali into the fountain of Aponus for an answer to his inquiries, he did so and the highest numbers came up; and those very tali are to be seen at the bottom of the fountain. A few days before his leaving Rhodes, an eagle, a bird never before seen in that island, perched on the top of his house. And the day before he had intelligence of the permission granted him to return, as he was changing his attire, his tunic appeared to be on fire. He then likewise had a singular proof of the skill of

Thrasyllus, the astrologer, whom, for his proficiency in philosophical researches, he had taken into his family. For, upon sight of the ship which brought the tidings, he affirmed that joyful news was coming, whereas everything before having turned out badly and contrary to his predictions, Tiberius had fully purposed that very moment, when they were talking together, to throw him headlong into the sea as a false prophet and one to whom he had rashly entrusted his secret affairs.

## 15

Upon his return to Rome, having introduced his son Drusus into the Forum, he immediately removed from Pompey's house in the Carinae to the gardens of Maecenas on the Esquiline; where he gave himself wholly to a life of ease, performing only the common duties of civility in private, without any preferment in public affairs. But Caius and Lucius being both carried off by death in the space of three years, he was adopted by Augustus, along with their brother Agrippa, but was first compelled to adopt Germanicus, his brother's son. After his adoption, he never more acted as master of a family, nor exercised, in the smallest degree, the rights which he had lost by it. For he neither conferred gifts nor manumitted a slave; nor so much as received any estate left him by will, nor any legacy, without reckoning it as a part of his *peculium* or property held under his father. From that day forward nothing was omitted that might contribute to the advancement of his grandeur, and much more when, upon Agrippa being discarded and banished, it was evident that the hope of succession rested upon him alone.

## 16 A.U.C. 757

The tribunician authority was again conferred upon him for five years, and a commission given him to settle the affairs of Germany. The ambassadors of the Parthians, after having had an audience of Augustus, were ordered to apply to him likewise in his province. But upon the news that Illyricum was in revolt he went over to take charge of that new war, which proved the most serious of all the foreign wars since the Carthaginian. This he conducted during three years, with fifteen legions and an equal number of auxiliary forces, under great hardships, not the least of which was an extreme scarcity of corn. And though he was several times recalled, he nevertheless persisted, fearing lest an enemy so powerful, and so near, should fall upon the army in their retreat. His perseverance was well rewarded; for he at length fully subdued all Illyricum lying between Italy and the kingdom of Noricum, Thrace, Macedonia, the river Danube, and the Adriatic gulf.

## 17

The glory accruing to him by these exploits was further amplified by the conjuncture in which they occurred. For almost about that very time Quintilius Varus was cut off with three legions in Germany; and it was generally believed that the victorious Germans would have joined the Pannonians, had not the war of Illyricum been previously concluded. A triumph, therefore, beside many other honours, was decreed him; some moved that he should be surnamed 'Pannonicus', others suggested 'Invincible', and others, 'Pius'; but Augustus interposed his negative voice, promising in his behalf that he should rest content with that to which he would succeed upon his death. He himself put off his triumph until a later day because the whole state was in great sorrow over the defeat of Varus and his army. Nevertheless he entered the city in a triumphal robe, crowned with laurel, and mounting a tribunal in the Saepta, sat with Augustus between the two consuls, while the senate gave their attendance standing; whence, after he had saluted the people, he was attended by them in procession to the several temples.

## 18

The year following he went again to Germany, where he gathered that the overthrow of Varus was occasioned by the rashness and negligence of the commander; whereupon he did nothing at all without seeking the advice of a council of war, although at other times he used to follow the dictates of his own judgment and considered himself alone as sufficiently qualified for the entire direction of affairs. He likewise used more precautions than usual. Having to pass the Rhine, he restricted the whole convoy within certain limits and would not suffer the waggons to cross until he had considered (standing upon the very bank of the river) the load of each one, to see that they carried nothing but what was allowed or necessary. Beyond the Rhine he held strictly to this order of life which revived the simple habits of the times of the republic: he took his meals sitting on the bare ground and often passed the night without a tent; and his regular orders for the day, as well as those upon sudden emergencies, he gave in writing with this injunction, that in case of any doubt as to their import he should be approached at any hour, even in the night, for further exposition.

## 19

He maintained military discipline with great strictness and revived certain ancient customs relative to chastising and degrading offenders. He even set a brand of ignominy upon the commander of a legion for sending a few soldiers with one of his freedmen across the river for the purpose of hunting. In battle, though it was his manner to trust as little as might be in the power of fortune or chance, yet he entered upon it with much more resolution when, in his night watches, the lamp failed and went out of itself: relying, as he said, upon this sign which had always proved infallible both for him and his ancestors. But in the very thick of his good fortune in this province, he escaped very narrowly being slain by a certain Bructerian who, mingling with those about his person and being detected by his timorous gesture, was apprehended and forced by torture to confess his intended crime.

## 20 A.U.C. 765

After two years he returned from Germany to Rome and celebrated the triumph which he had deferred, attended by his lieutenants for whom he had obtained the honour of triumphal ornaments. Before he turned to ascend the Capitol he alighted from his chariot and knelt before his father, Augustus, who presided over the solemnities. Bato, the Pannonian chief, he sent to Ravenna, loaded with rich presents, in gratitude for his having suffered him and his army to retire from a position in which he had so enclosed them that they were entirely at his mercy. He afterwards gave the people a dinner where they sat at a thousand tables, bestowing also upon each man thirty sesterces. He likewise dedicated the temple of Concord and that of Castor and Pollux, which had been erected out of the spoils of the war, in his own and his brother's name.

Not long after, a law having been carried by the consuls for his being appointed a colleague with Augustus in the administration of the provinces and in taking the census, he performed these duties, and having finished, he went into Illyricum. But being hastily recalled during his journey, he found Augustus dangerously ill, though still breathing and conscious; and he was with him in private sitting a whole day. I know that it is generally believed that upon Tiberius' quitting the room after their secret conference, the chamberlains overheard Augustus voice these words: 'Oh, unhappy people of Rome, to be ground by the jaws of such a slow devourer!' Nor am I ignorant of its being reported by some that Augustus so openly and plainly disliked the sourness of his temper that sometimes, in the midst of pleasant and merry discourse, he would break off at Tiberius' entrance; and that he was only persuaded by the importunity of his wife to adopt him, or induced to do so by the ambitious view of enhancing his own memory by contrast with such a successor. Yet I cannot be persuaded to think otherwise than that Augustus, a most circumspect, considerate and prudent prince, did nothing, especially in such a weighty matter, without taking excellent counsel; and that, having duly weighed the vices and virtues of Tiberius, he esteemed his virtues of greater force; and this the rather since he swore publicly, in an assembly of the people, that 'he adopted him for the public good'. Besides, in several of his letters, he commends him as a most expert and valiant general and the only safeguard of the Roman people; out of which, I have thought well to quote certain passages: 'Farewell, most sweet Tiberius, and God bless your conduct, while you are warring for me and the Muses.' Again: 'Farewell, my most dear, and (as I hope to prosper) most gallant man, and accomplished leader.' Also: 'The disposition of your summer quarters? In truth, my dear Tiberius, I do not think, that amidst so many difficulties, and with an army so little disposed for action, any one could have performed better service than you have done. All those likewise who were with you, acknowledge that this verse is applicable to you:

One man by vigilance restored the state.'

'Whenever,' he says, 'anything happens that requires more than ordinary consideration, or I am out of humour upon any occasion, I still, by Hercules! long for my dear Tiberius; and those lines of Homer frequently occur to my thoughts:

> Bold from his prudence, I could ev'n aspire
> To dare with him the burning rage of fire.

When I hear and read that you are weakened and grown lean with incessant labour, may the gods confound me if my body does not quake and tremble. I pray you therefore, spare yourself, lest, if it come to our ears that you are sick, both I and your mother die of sorrow and the Roman people should be in peril for the safety of the empire. It matters nothing whether I be well or no, if you be not well. I beseech the gods to preserve you for us, and bless you with health both now and ever, if they love the Roman people.'

## 22

He did not divulge the death of Augustus until he had taken off young Agrippa, who was slain by a tribune in command of his guard upon reading a written order for that purpose. Whether this order was left behind by Augustus, who had written it before his death to prevent any occasion of public tumult afterwards; or whether Livia issued it, in the name of Augustus, and with the knowledge of Tiberius or without it, remains uncertain. It is known that when the tribune brought him word that his command had been executed, he replied: 'I gave you no such command, and you must answer for the deed to the senate'; avoiding, as it seems, the odium of the act for the present. And within a little while the matter was buried in silence.

## 23

Having assembled the senate by virtue of his tribunician authority, and begun to make a speech of consolation on the death of Augustus, suddenly, as if unable to master his grief, he fell into a fit of sighing and groaning; and wishing that not his voice only, but his vital breath, might fail him, he gave his written speech to his son Drusus to read aloud. Augustus' will was then brought in and read by a freedman; none of the witnesses to it being admitted but such as were of the senatorian order, the rest standing without the doors and there acknowledging their handwriting. The will began thus: 'Since my sinister fortune has deprived me of my two sons, Caius and Lucius, I will that Tiberius Caesar be mine heir to two-thirds of my estate.' By the preface thus affixed to the document, the suspicion felt by some, that Tiberius was chosen as his successor more out of necessity than desire, was augmented.

## 24

Though he made no scruple to enter upon his imperial authority immediately, and to exercise its rights by giving orders that he should be attended by the guards, who were the mainstay and insignia of absolute rule: yet he affected, by a most impudent imposture, to refuse it for a long time; one while sharply rebuking his friends who encouraged him to accept it, by representing to them, as those who knew it not, what a monstrous and untamed beast an Empire was; and another while keeping in suspense the senate, when they besought him and threw themselves at his feet, by ambiguous answers and a crafty kind of dissimulation; insomuch that some were out of patience, and one cried out, during the tumult: 'Let him either take it at once, or decline'; and a second openly upbraided him in these words: 'Others are slack in performing what they promise, but you are slack in promising what you actually perform.' In the end, as if under compulsion, and complaining of the miserable and burdensome servitude imposed upon him, he accepted the government; but not without giving hopes of some day resigning it. His exact words were these: 'Until the time shall come, when ye may think it meet to give some rest to my old age.'

## 25

The cause of his long demur was fear of imminent danger on every side, insomuch that he would often say: 'I have got a wolf by the ears.' For a slave of Agrippa's, Clemens by name, had gathered a considerable force to revenge his master's death; Lucius Scribonius Libo, a senator of the first rank, was secretly plotting sedition; and the troops both in Illyricum and Germany were mutinous. Both armies insisted upon high demands, particularly that their pay should be made equal to that of the praetorian guards. The army in Germany absolutely refused to honour a prince who was not their own choice, and with all their might and main urged Germanicus, who was then their general, to take the government on himself, though he stoutly refused to do so. Fearing the outcome of this controversy more than anything else, Tiberius requested the senate to assign him some part only in the administration, such as they should deem proper, since no man could be sufficient for the whole, without one or more to assist him. He feigned likewise to be in frail health, that Germanicus might the more patiently wait in hopes of speedily succeeding him, or at least of being admitted as a colleague in the government. When he had suppressed the mutinies in the armies, he brought Clemens under his power by a wily stratagem. That he might not begin his reign by a rigorous proceeding, he did not call Libo to an account before the senate until his second year, being content, in the meantime, with taking vigilant measures to protect his own welfare. For upon Libo's attending a sacrifice among the high priests, he ordered that instead of the usual knife, a lead one should be given him; and when Libo requested at one time a private conference with him, he would not grant it except on condition that his son Drusus should be present; and as they walked together, he held Libo fast by the right hand under colour of leaning upon him, until their conversation was ended.

## 26

But once delivered from his fears, he carried himself in an orderly and unassuming manner, much as if he were a private person. Of the many and great honours which were decreed to him, he accepted but few and such as were very modest. His birthday, which fell in the time of the Plebeian Circensian games, he would hardly suffer to be honoured with the addition of only a single chariot drawn by two horses. He forbad temples, flamens, or priests to be appointed for him, as likewise the erection of any statues or effigies for him, without his permission; and this he granted only on condition that they should not be placed among the images of the gods, but only among the ornaments of houses. He also interposed to prevent the senate from swearing to observe and keep his acts inviolably; and prohibited their calling the month of September, Tiberius, or October, Livia. The forename likewise of Emperor, with the cognomen of Father of his Country, and a civic crown in the vestibule of his house, he would not countenance. Even the name of Augustus, hereditary though it was, he would not use in any of his letters, except those addressed to kings and potentates. Nor had he any more than three consulships; one for a few days, another for three months, and a third, during his absence from the city, until the ides (15th) of May.

## 27

He detested flattery so much that he would never suffer any senator to approach his litter as he passed through the streets, either to pay him a civility, or upon any business. When a man of consular rank, by way of humbly entreating his pardon for some offence, essayed to kneel before him, he started back in such precipitation that he stumbled and fell on his back. If any address seemed in the least redolent of obsequiousness, either in private discourse or in a set speech, he would not scruple to interrupt the speaker both to reprimand him, and to correct such terms. Being once called 'Lord', by some person, he gave warning that he desired never more to be affronted in that manner. When another alluded to his occupations as 'sacred', and a third represented that he waited upon the senate 'by his authority', he charged them to change their expressions, the one by substituting 'persuasion' for authority, and the other by putting 'laborious' in place of 'sacred'.

## 28

In all instances of foul rumours, slanderous reports, and reviling verses which were spread against him or his relations, he remained firm and patient in his ruling that: 'In a free state, both the tongue and the mind ought to be free.' And when the senate earnestly besought him to consider these crimes, as well as the offenders themselves, he answered them: 'We have not so much leisure on our hands that we ought to involve ourselves in so many affairs. If you open this window once, you will soon have time for nothing else. All private quarrels will be referred to you, under that pretence.' There is also on record another statement made by him in the senate, which is equally civil of tone: 'If he speaks otherwise of me, I shall take care to behave in such a manner as to be able to give a good account of my words and actions: and if he persists, I shall hate him in my turn.'

## 29

These things were so much the more remarkable in him, because, in the respect he paid to individuals or the whole body of the senate, he went beyond all bounds. When he dissented one day from Quintus Haterius in the senate house, 'Pardon me, sir,' he said, 'I beseech you, if I shall, as a senator, speak my mind very freely in opposition to you.' And then, directing his speech to the whole house, he said: 'My Lords, I say it now, as I have often said it at other times, that a good and useful prince, whom you have invested with so great and absolute power, ought to be a slave to the senate, to the whole body of the people, and often to individuals likewise: nor am I sorry that I have said it. For I have always found you good, kind, and gracious masters, and still find you so.'

## 30

He likewise introduced a certain show of liberty, by preserving to the senate and magistrates their former majesty and power; neither was there any matter, either great or small, public or private, but he laid it before the senate; as namely, the taxes and monopolies, the erecting or repairing of edifices, levying and disbanding of soldiers, the disposal of the legions and auxiliary forces in the provinces, the appointment of generals for the management of extraordinary wars, and the answers to letters from foreign princes. He compelled the commander of a troop of horse, who was accused of robbery attended with outrage, to plead his cause before the senate. He never entered the senate-house but alone; and being once brought thither in a litter, because of illness, he dismissed his attendants at the door.

## 31

When some decrees were enacted against his expressed judgment, he did not even make any complaint. And notwithstanding that he thought no magistrates after their nomination should be permitted to absent themselves from the city, in order that they might receive their honours in person, a praetor-elect obtained liberty to depart under the honorary title of a legate-at-large. Again, when he proposed to the senate that the Trebians might have leave granted them to divert some money which had been left them by will for the purpose of building a new theatre, to that of making a road, he could not prevail to have the will of the testator set aside. And when, upon a division of the house, he went over to the minority, nobody followed him. All other matters of a public nature were likewise handled and debated by the magistrates, and in the usual forms; the authority of the consuls waxing so great, that some ambassadors from Africa applied to them, for dispatch, complaining that they were put off by Caesar to whom they had been sent. And small marvel: seeing that he himself would rise up as the consuls approached, and give them the way.

## 32

He rebuked some generals of armies, who were also of consular rank, for not writing to the senate an account of their exploits, and for consulting him about the distribution of military rewards: as if they themselves had not a right to bestow them as they deemed fit. He commended a praetor who, on entering office, revived an old custom of making honourable mention of his ancestors, in a speech to the people. He accompanied the corpses of certain persons of noble rank to the funeral pile, with the common multitude. He displayed like moderation with relation to persons and things of inferior importance. When he sent for the magistrates of Rhodes for having dispatched to him a letter on public business which was not subscribed, he gave them not so much as one harsh word, but only commanding them to subscribe it, he sent them away. Diogenes, the grammarian, who used to hold public disquisitions at Rhodes every sabbath day, once refused him admittance upon his coming out of course especially to hear him, and sent him a message by a servant, fixing his attendance on the next seventh day. When Diogenes afterwards came to Rome and stood before his gate at Rome to pay his respects to him, he sent him word to come again at the end of seven years. To some governors, who advised him to burden the provinces with taxes, he wrote: 'It is the part of a good shepherd to shear his sheep, not to flay them.'

## 33

By little and little he showed his princely majesty and exercised it for a long time with some variety of conduct, yet for the most part in a mild and gracious manner and in recognition of the public weal. At first he only interposed his absolute voice to check unjust measures. Therefore, he rescinded some decrees of the senate; and when the magistrates sat for the administration of justice, he would offer himself as an assistant in their councils, either taking his place indiscriminately among them, or seating himself in a corner of the tribunal. If a rumour went forth that any person under prosecution was likely to be acquitted by his favour, he would suddenly appear, and from the floor of the court, or the praetor's bench, remind the judges of the laws, of their oaths, and the nature of the charge brought before them. Also, if anything were amiss or faulty in the public morals, through neglect or evil custom, he undertook to reform it.

## 34

He abridged the expense of the plays and public spectacles by lowering the allowances to actors and reducing the number of gladiators. He complained grievously to the senate that the price of Corinthian vessels was become enormous, and that three mullets had been sold for thirty thousand sesterces: upon which he proposed that a new sumptuary law should be enacted that the butchers and other dealers in viands should be subject to an assize, fixed by the senate yearly; and the aediles commissioned to restrain eating houses and taverns, so far as not even to permit the sale of any kind of pastry. And to encourage frugality in the public by his own example, he would often, at his solemn feasts, have at his tables victuals which had been served up the day before, and were partly eaten, saying, that the side of a wild boar had in it the same savoury bits as the whole. He forbad expressly by an edict the practice of people's kissing each other when they met; likewise the exchange of New Year's gifts after the kalends (the first) of January was passed. He was himself in the habit of returning these offerings fourfold and with his own hand; but being annoyed by the continual interruption to which he was exposed during the whole month, by those who had not the opportunity of attending him on the festival, he never gave any after that day.

## 35

Married women guilty of adultery, though not prosecuted publicly, he authorised the nearest relations to punish by agreement among themselves, according to ancient custom. He released a Roman knight from his oath never to put away his wife, and allowed him to divorce her, upon her being taken in adultery with her son-in-law. Women infamous for loose conduct, divesting themselves of the rights and dignity of matrons, had now begun a practice of professing themselves prostitutes, that they might elude the penalties of the law; and the most profligate young men of the senatorian and equestrian orders, to secure themselves against a decree of the senate, which prohibited their performing on the stage, or in the amphitheatre, voluntarily drew upon themselves the note of infamy by committing lewd acts. Both these and the light women aforesaid, he banished, that none for the future might evade by such artifices the intention and efficacy of the law. He stripped a senator of the broad stripes on his robe upon intelligence of his having removed to his gardens before the kalends (the first) of July, in order that he might afterwards hire a house cheaper in the city. He likewise deprived of his quaestorship one who, having chosen a wife by lottery on one day, dismissed her on the next.

## 36

All foreign religions, including the Egyptian and Jewish rites, he prohibited: compelling those who practised that kind of superstition to burn their vestments and all their sacred utensils. He distributed the Jewish youths, under colour of a military oath, to sundry provinces noted, above other things, for an unwholesome and pestilential climate; the rest of that nation or such as were addicted to its practices, he banished out of Rome, under pain of perpetual bondage if they obeyed not. He expelled also the astrologers: but upon their earnest entreaty and promise to give over the practice of that art, he suffered them to remain.

## 37

He took especial care to keep the peace, and to preserve the state from outrages and robberies, as also from mutinies and seditions. He therefore increased the number of military stations throughout Italy; and formed a camp at Rome for the praetorian cohorts which, till then, had been quartered in the city. All insurrections of the people he punished most sharply; and took likewise much pains to prevent them. Some persons having been killed in a quarrel which broke out in the theatre, he banished the leaders of the parties, as well as the players about whom the fray had arisen; nor could all the entreaties of the people afterwards induce him to recall them. When the people of Pollentia would not suffer the corpse of a certain centurion of the first rank to be carried out of the Forum until they had forcibly extorted from his heirs a sum of money for a public exhibition of gladiators, he detached one cohort from the city, and another from the kingdom of Cottius: who, concealing the cause of their march, entered the town by different gates, with their arms suddenly displayed, and trumpets blaring; and, having seized the greatest part of the people and the magistrates, cast them into prison for life. He abolished everywhere the privileges of all places of refuge. The people of Cyzicus having committed an outrage upon some Romans, he deprived them of the liberty they had obtained for their good services in the Mithridatic war. The rebellions of foreign enemies he suppressed by his lieutenants, without ever going against them in person; nor would he even employ his lieutenants but with much reluctance, and when it was absolutely imperative. Kings who rebelliously took arms, or were suspected of seditious designs, he kept down more by threats and remonstrances than by force. Some whom he induced to come to him with fair words and promises, he never would permit to return home: as, namely, Maraboduus the German, Thrasypolis the Thracian, and Archelaus the Cappadocian, whose kingdom he even reduced to the form of a province

## 38

For two years together after he came into the empire, he never set foot once outside the gates of Rome. And in the years ensuing, went no farther from the city than to some of the neighbouring towns: his longest journey being to Antium, and that but infrequently and for a few days only – though he often gave out that he would visit the provinces and armies, and made preparations for it almost every year by taking up carriages and ordering provisions for his retinue in the municipia and colonies. He even, at the last, suffered vows to be put up for his good journey and safe return; insomuch that he was called, in jest, by the name of Callipides, who is noted in a Greek proverb to be always running, yet never gaining ground by one cubit.

## 39                                    A.U.C. 779

But after he was bereft of both his sons, of which Germanicus, the adopted, died in Syria, and Drusus, the natural, at Rome, he withdrew into Campania; at which time men were persuaded, and spoke of it commonly, that he would never return but would die soon after. Both predictions very nearly were fulfilled. For, in truth, he never more came to Rome; and a few days after leaving it, when he was at a villa of his called the Cave, near Terracina, during supper a great many huge stones fell from above and killed several of the guests and attendants; but he himself miraculously escaped.

## 40

After he had gone round Campania, and dedicated the Capitol at Capua and a temple to Augustus at Nola, where he had died, (which he pretended to have been the motive of his journey), he retired to Capri; being greatly delighted with the island, because there was but one way of access to it and that by a narrow beach; otherwise it was enclosed by craggy rocks and steep cliffs of a stupendous height, and by the deep sea. But soon after, when the people called him and urgently besought him to return, because of a disaster at Fidenae, where upwards of twenty thousand persons had been killed by the fall of the amphitheatre during a public spectacle of gladiators, he crossed over again to the continent and gave all people free audience with him; although, at his departure from the city, he had caused it to be proclaimed that no one should address him, and had declined admittance to any persons who approached him on the journey.

## 41

Returning to the island, he so far abandoned all care of the government that he never filled up the decuriae of the knights, never changed any military tribunes or prefects, or governors of provinces, and kept Spain and Syria for several years without any consular lieutenants. He likewise suffered Armenia to be seized by the Parthians, Moesia by the Dacians and Sarmatians, and Gaul to be ravaged by the Germans: to the great shame, no less than the danger, of the empire.

## 42

But having now the liberty of this secret place, and being removed from the eyes of the people of Rome, he at once poured forth and indulged all those vices which he had but half dissimulated for a long time; and of these I shall give a particular relation from the very beginning. While a young soldier in the camp, he was so notorious for his excessive greediness for wine that, for Tiberius, they called him Biberius; for Claudius, Caldius; and for Nero, Mero. And after he succeeded to the empire, and was invested with the office of reforming the morality of the people, he spent a whole night and two days together in feasting and drinking with Pomponius Flaccus and Lucius Piso; to one of whom he immediately gave the government of the province Syria and to the other the prefecture of the city: professing in his letters patent that they were 'most pleasant companions and friends for all occasions'. To Sestius Gallus, a lewd and spendthrift old fellow, who had in times past been disgraced by Augustus and reprimanded by himself but a few days before in the senate-house, he sent word that he would sup with him: upon this condition, that he altered nothing in his usual manner of entertainment and that they should be attended at table by naked girls. He preferred a very obscure candidate for the quaestorship, before the most noble competitors, only because he drank off, in pledging him at table, an amphora of wine at a draught. He presented Asellius Sabinus with two hundred thousand sesterces for writing a dialogue, by way of dispute, betwixt the truffle and the fig-pecker, the oyster and the thrush. To conclude, he instituted a new office, for the originating of unfamiliar carnal pleasures, over which he appointed Titus Caesonius Priscus, a Roman knight and one who had been censor.

## 43

In his retreat at Capri he also contrived a room with many couches and adapted to the purpose of secret wantonness, where he entertained companies of girls and catamites, and assembled from all quarters devisers of monstrous and unnatural lewdness whom he called Spintriae and who, the better to revive his fainting courage and feeble lust, were wont to link themselves together in three ranks and practise before his eyes their sensual arts. He had many bedchambers hung with pictures and statues representing figures in the most lascivious attitudes, and furnished with the books of Elephantis, that none might want a pattern for the execution of any filthy project that was prescribed him. He arranged in the woods and groves, here and there, recesses for the gratification of lust; where, within caves and hollow rocks, young persons of both sexes indulged their passions in the disguise of little Pans and nymphs; insomuch that he was publicly termed, by an abuse of the name of the island, Caprineus. For the name of Capri has a double meaning and signifies also a goat.

## 44

He incurred yet greater infamy for filthiness such as may not well be described and much less believed: to wit, that he taught fine boys, the tenderest and daintiest that might be had (whom he called his little fishes) to converse and play between his thighs as he was swimming, and prettily with tongue and teeth seem to nibble at his secret parts; and likewise that he took babies of good growth and strength, though not yet weaned, and set them to his private member as to the nipple of a breast, to suck. When a picture, painted by Parrhasius, in which the artist had represented Atalanta in the act of offering Meleager a peculiar assuagement for his lust, was bequeathed to him upon the condition, that if the matter shown was offensive to him, he might receive in lieu of it a million of sesterces, he not only chose the picture but hung it up in his bedchamber. It is also reported, that during a sacrifice, he took such an ardent fancy to the beautiful face and form of a youth who held a censer, that, before the religious rites were well over, he took him aside and abused his body; as also a brother of his who had been playing the flute; and soon afterwards broke the legs of both of them for upbraiding one another with their shame.

## 45

Moreover, his foul behaviour with women, even those of the highest birth and reputation, appeared very plainly by the death of one Mallonia who, being brought to his bed by force, but resolutely refusing to comply with his demands, he gave her up to the common informers to be falsely accused. Even when she was upon her trial, he called out to her and asked whether she repented not yet of her obstinacy, persisting so long that she, quitting the court, went home and stabbed herself, after having openly upbraided the beastly old lecher for his gross obscenity. Whereupon, in a farce called *Atellanicum Exodium,* there was an allusion to him which was received with great accord, and was rife in every man's mouth, that the 'old goat' was savouring the does.

## 46

He was very niggardly of his purse and never allowed his attendants, in his travels and expeditions, any remuneration but their diet. Once indeed he treated them liberally, at the instigation of his step-father, when, dividing them into three classes, according to their rank, he gave the first six, the second four, and the third two, hundred thousand sesterces; which last class he called not friends, but Greeks.

## 47

All the while he was Emperor, he never built any stately edifice; for the only things he did undertake, namely, building the temple of Augustus and restoring Pompey's Theatre, he left at last after many years unfinished. Nor did he ever entertain the people with public spectacles; and he was rarely present at those which were given by others, lest anything of that kind should be requested of him; especially after he was obliged to give freedom to the comedian Actius. Having relieved the poverty of a few senators, to avoid further demands he declared that he should for the future assist none but those who gave the senate full satisfaction as to the cause of their necessity. Upon this, most of the needy senators, from modesty and shame, declined troubling him; among these was Hortalus, grandson to the celebrated orator Quintus Hortensius who, marrying by the persuasion of Augustus, had brought up four children upon a very small estate.

## 48

He showed public munificence upon only two occasions. One was an offer to lend gratis, for three years, a hundred millions of sesterces to those who wanted to borrow; and the other, when, some large houses being burnt down upon Mount Coelius, he indemnified the owners. To the former of these he was compelled by the clamours of the people, in a great scarcity of money, when he had ratified a decree of the senate obliging all money-lenders to advance two-thirds of their capital on land, and the debtors to pay off at once the same proportion of their debts, and it was found insufficient to remedy the grievance. The other he did to alleviate in some degree the pressure of the times; for it was then that the calamity occurred at Fidenae, which caused the death of twenty thousand persons. Nevertheless, he esteemed so greatly his benefaction to the sufferers by fire, that he ordered the Caelian Hill to be called, in future, the Augustan. To the soldiery, after doubling the legacy left them by Augustus, he never gave anything, except a thousand denarii a man to the praetorian guards, for not joining the party of Sejanus; and some presents to the legions in Syria, because they alone had not paid reverence to the effigies of Sejanus among their standards. He seldom gave discharges to the veteran soldiers, calculating on their deaths from advanced age, and on what would be saved by thus getting rid of them, in the way of rewards or pensions. Nor did he ever relieve the provinces by any act of generosity, excepting Asia, where some cities had been destroyed by an earthquake.

# 49

In the course of a very short time, he turned his mind to sheer rapine. It is certain that Cnaeus Lentulus, the augur, a man of great wealth, was driven by him, in very fear and anguish of mind, to make him his heir; and that Lepida, a lady of a very noble family, was condemned by him to gratify Quirinus, a man of consular rank, extremely rich, and childless, who had divorced her twenty years before and now charged her with an old design to poison him. Several persons, likewise, of the first distinction in Gaul, Spain, Syria, and Greece, had their estates confiscated upon such slight and impudent pretences that against some of them no other charge was preferred, than that they held large sums of ready money as part of their property. Old immunities, the rights of mining and of levying tolls, were taken from several cities and private persons. And Vonones, king of the Parthians, who had been driven out of his dominions by his own subjects, and fled to Antioch with a vast treasure, claiming the protection of the Roman people, his allies, was treacherously robbed of all his money and afterwards slain.

# 50

The hatred that he bore his own kinsfolk was first manifested toward his brother Drusus, whom he betrayed by disclosing a letter to himself, in which Drusus proposed that Augustus should be forced to restore the public liberty; and toward the rest of his family, in process of time, he showed the same disposition. So far was he from according his wife Julia any courtesy or kindness, when she was banished, and, by her father's order, confined to one town, that he forbad her to stir out of the house or enjoy any intercourse with society. He proceeded so far as to deprive her of the dowry given her by Augustus, and of her yearly allowance, by taking advantage of a point of law, because no express provision was made for them in the will. Being harassed by his mother, Livia, who claimed an equal share in the government with him, he frequently avoided seeing her, or having long and secret conferences with her, that it should not be thought he was swayed by her counsel, which, notwithstanding, he sometimes sought and followed. He was much offended at the senate, when they proposed to add to his other titles that of the Son of Livia, as well as Augustus. He, therefore, would not suffer her to be called 'the Mother of her Country', nor to receive any extraordinary mark of honour. He many times admonished her, also, not to mix in weighty affairs and such as were not suited to women; especially when, upon the Temple of Vesta catching fire, she came thither in person, and encouraged the people and soldiers to do their best, as she had been used to do in the time of her husband.

## 51

By these degrees, he proceeded to an open rupture with her, but chiefly it is said, upon this occasion: she having frequently urged him to place among the judges a person who had been made free of the city, he flatly refused unless she would allow it to be inscribed on the roll: 'That the appointment had been extorted from him by his mother.' Highly displeased at this, Livia brought forth from her chapel some letters from Augustus to her, complaining of the perverse, bitter, and intolerable humour of Tiberius; and these she openly read. He was so much enraged, both that these letters had been preserved so long, and that she should cast them at him so spitefully, that some think this incident was the principal reason for his departure from the City. And during the three years which he spent apart from her, he saw her but once, and that for a few hours only. Afterwards, when she fell sick, he showed no inclination to visit her; and when she died he suffered her body to stay so long above ground (while friends deferred the funeral, hoping he would come), that it was in a state of decay and putrefaction before the interment; and he then forbad divine honours being paid to her, affecting to follow out her own wishes. He likewise annulled her will, and in a short time ruined all her friends and acquaintances, even those to whom, on her death-bed, she had recommended the care of her funeral; one of them, a man of equestrian rank, he even condemned to the treadmill.

## 52

He loved neither his own son, Drusus, nor his adopted one, Germanicus. Taking offence at the vices of Drusus, who was of an effeminate nature and given to a loose, idle mind, he was not greatly affected at his death; but, almost immediately after the funeral, resumed his ordinary duties and prohibited the customary vacation of the courts from being continued any longer. Moreover, when the ambassadors from the people of Ilium came somewhat late to offer their sympathy, he said to them by way of banter, 'and I heartily condole with you on the loss of your renowned countryman, the brave and noble Hector'. So much did he depreciate Germanicus, that he not only passed over his achievements as utterly insignificant, but spoke of his most glorious victories as being ruinous to the state. He also complained of him to the senate because he went to Alexandria without his knowledge upon occasion of a great and sudden famine at Rome. It was believed, too, that he was the cause of Germanicus' death, in that he took care to have him dispatched by Cnaeus Piso, his lieutenant in Syria, who was afterwards tried for the murder, and who would, as was supposed, have produced his orders, had they not been contained in a private and confidential dispatch. Tiberius was many times blamed in the matter, and often in the night this cry was heard: 'Give us back our Germanicus!', which words were likewise posted up in various places to confront him. The suspicion was afterwards upheld by his barbarous treatment of his wife and children.

## 53

His daughter-in-law Agrippina, after the death of her husband, once complained of him more boldly than usual; whereupon he took her by the hand and addressed her in a Greek verse to this effect: 'My dear child, do you think you are wronged, because you are not empress?' and never spoke to her again. Also, upon her refusing once at supper to taste some fruit which he presented to her, he never invited her to his table any more, pretending that she in effect charged him with a design to poison her; whereas the episode had been purposely prearranged, both that he should proffer the fruit, and that she should be forewarned that it would assuredly cause her death. At last, having her accused of a design to flee for refuge to the statue of Augustus, or to the army, he banished her to the island of Pandataria, whither the elder Livia was banished by Augustus; and as she railed at him for this, he caused a centurion to lash her across the face and to strike out one of her eyes. When she was fully determined to starve herself to death, he caused her mouth to be forcibly opened, and food crammed down her throat. But she, persisting in her resolution, died soon afterward. He then overwhelmed her memory with the basest aspersions and forced the senate to put her birthday among the number of unlucky days on the calendar. Furthermore, he took credit, as for a high favour done her, in that he had not caused her to be strangled and her body cast upon the Gemonian Steps; and in reward for such singular clemency, he suffered a decree of the senate to pass that thanks should be given to him and a present of gold consecrated to Jupiter Capitolinus.

## 54

By Germanicus he had three grandsons, Nero, Drusus, and Caius; and by his son Drusus one, named Tiberius. Of these, after the loss of his sons, he commended Nero and Drusus, the two eldest sons of Germanicus, to the senate; and celebrated their solemn presentation at the Forum by scattering money among the people. But when he found that on entering upon the new year, they were included in the public vows for his own welfare, he gave the senate to understand, 'that such honours ought not to be conferred but upon those who had been proved and were of more advanced years'. Thereby having laid bare his inner feelings towards them, he exposed them to the slanders and imputations of all men: when also, by subtle devices to provoke them to rail at and taunt him, that he might be provided with a pretext for destroying them, he charged them with it in a letter to the senate: at the same time accusing them, in the bitterest terms, of the most heinous offences. Upon their being judged enemies of the state, he starved them to death: Nero, in the island of Ponza, and Drusus in the vaults of the Palatium. Some think that Nero was driven to accomplish his own death by the executioner's showing him some halters and hooks, as if he had been sent to him by order of the senate. Drusus, it is said, was so ravenous with hunger, that he attempted to eat the chaff with which his mattress was stuffed. The relics of both were so scattered, that it was with difficulty they were collected.

## 55

Besides his old friends and intimate acquaintances, he demanded the assistance of twenty of the most prominent citizens of Rome as counsellors in the conduct of public affairs. Out of all this number, scarcely two or three came out alive; all the rest he persecuted and destroyed upon one pretence or another: among whom was Aelius Sejanus, whose fall was attended with the ruin of many others. He had advanced this minister to the highest place of authority, not so much from any real regard for him, as that by his base and sinister practices he might circumvent the children of Germanicus and so establish as heir apparent to the empire his own grandson by Drusus.

## 56

Nor did he accord any milder treatment to the Greek professors and artists who daily lived and conversed with him, even those in whom he took the greatest pleasure. Of one of them, named Zeno, when he used some unfamiliar phrase, he inquired: 'What harsh dialect is that?' Upon his answering 'The Doric', he banished him to Cinara, suspecting that he twitted him with his former residence at Rhodes, whose natives speak Doric. His manner being to propound questions at supper, suggested by what he had been reading in the day, and having learned that Seleucus, the grammarian, always inquired of his attendants what authors he was then studying and so came prepared for his enquiries, he first forbad him his house and then drove him to take his own life.

## 57

His cruel and unpliable nature was apparent when he was still a child; which Theodorus of Gadara, his master in rhetoric, first observed and expressed most fitly, when by way of chiding him he called him sometimes 'Clay soaked in blood'. But his disposition betrayed itself still more clearly on his attaining the imperial power, and even in the beginning of his administration, when he was endeavouring to win the favour of the people with a pretence of moderation. A certain wag, when a funeral passed through the streets, called out to the dead man: 'Tell Augustus that the legacies he bequeathed to the people are not yet paid.' Tiberius, ordering the man to be brought before him, caused him to be given the amount due him and then led to execution, that he might deliver the message to his father himself. Not long afterwards, when one Pompey, a Roman knight, persisted in his opposition to something he proposed in the senate, he threatened to send him to prison, and added: 'Of a Pompey, I shall make a Pompeian of you'; alluding, by this biting taunt, both to the man's name and the ill fortune of his party.

## 58

About the same time, when the praetor consulted him, whether it was his pleasure that the tribunals should take cognisance of accusations of treason, he replied: 'The laws ought to be put in execution'; and in truth he enforced them with extreme rigour. Some person had taken off the head of Augustus from one of his statues and replaced it by another. The matter was debated in the senate, and because some doubt arose as to the perpetrator of the deed, inquisition was made by torture. The one accused being found guilty and condemned, this kind of proceeding was carried so far that it became capital for a man to beat his slave, or change his clothes, near the statue of Augustus; to carry his head stamped upon the coin, or cut in the stone of a ring, into a house of necessity, or a brothel; or to reflect upon anything that had been either said or done by him. To conclude, a person was condemned to death for suffering some honours to be decreed to him in the colony where he lived, upon the same day on which they had formerly been decreed to Augustus.

## 59

He performed many barbarous deeds, under colour of discipline and reformation of manners, but in reality to gratify his own cruel nature; and this occasioned some verses which both deplored the present calamities and warned of the miseries to come:

> Obdurate wretch! too fierce, too fell to move
> The least kind yearnings of a mother's love!
> No knight thou art, as having no estate;
> Long suffered'st thou in Rhodes an exile's fate,
> No more the happy Golden Age we see;
> The Iron's come, and sure to last with thee.
> Instead of wine he thirsted for before,
> He wallows now in floods of human gore.
> Reflect, ye Romans, on the dreadful times.
> Made such by Marius, and by Sulla's crimes.
> Reflect how Antony's ambitious rage
> Twice scar'd with horror a distracted age.
> And say, Alas! Rome's blood in streams will flow,
> When banish'd miscreants rule this world below.

At first he would have these verses construed as resentful thrusts made by those who chafed under his absolute rule at Rome rather than as sincere expressions of honest feeling; and he would always say: 'Let them hate me, so long as they do but obey me.' At length, however, his actions proved that he was sensible they were too well founded.

## 60

Within a few days after his arrival at Capri, a fisherman coming up to him unexpectedly, when he was desirous of being alone and presenting him with a large mullet, he ordered the man's face to be scrubbed all over with the fish; being affrighted, no doubt, that the man had been able to creep upon him from the back of the island, over such rugged and steep rocks. And when the poor fellow, in the midst of his punishment, nevertheless rejoiced that he had not offered him a great lobster which he had also caught, he commanded that his face should be grated with the lobster likewise. He put to death one of the praetorian guards for having filched a peacock out of his orchard. In one of his journeys, his litter being obstructed by some bushes, he ordered the officer whose duty it was to ride on and examine the road, and who was a centurion of the first cohorts, to be laid on his face upon the ground and scourged almost to death.

## 61

Soon afterwards he broke out into all kinds of cruelty, never wanting occasions of one kind or another to serve as a pretext. He persecuted first the friends and acquaintances of his mother, then those of his grandsons and his daughter-in-law, and lastly those of Sejanus: after whose death he grew most incredibly cruel. From this it appeared that he had not been so much instigated by Sejanus, as supplied with occasions to serve his savage temper when he wanted them; however, in a short memoir which he composed of his own life, he conceived this impudent fiction, 'that he had executed Sejanus because he had found that he was bent upon the destruction of the children of his son Germanicus' – the one of whom, in truth, he himself murdered, when he began to suspect Sejanus, and the other after Sejanus was executed. To detail all his bloody projects and deeds would be well-nigh endless; it shall suffice therefore to set down a few examples, in their different kinds and degrees. Not a day passed without the punishment of some person or other, not excepting holidays, or those appropriated to the worship of the gods. Some were tried on New Year's Day. Of many who were condemned, their wives and children shared the same fate; and for those who were sentenced to death, the kinsfolk were forbidden to wear mourning. Considerable rewards were voted for the prosecutors, and sometimes for the witnesses also. The information of any person, without exception, was credited; and all offences were capital, even the speaking of a few simple words, without ill intent. A poet was charged with abusing Agamemnon, in a tragedy; and a historian, A. Cremutius Cordus, for calling Brutus and Cassius 'the last of the Romans'. The two authors were immediately called to account and their writings suppressed, notwithstanding that they had been well received some years before, and read in the presence of Augustus. Some who were thrown into prison were not only denied the solace of study, but debarred from all company and conversation. Many persons, when summoned to trial, stabbed themselves at home to avoid the distress and ignominy of a public condemnation, which they were certain would ensue. Others took poison in the senate house. The wounds were bound up, and all who had not expired, were carried, half-dead and panting for life, to prison. Those who were put to death were thrown down the Gemonian Steps and then dragged into the Tiber. In one day, twenty were treated in this manner; and among them women and boys. In the case of young girls, these were first deflowered by the executioner and afterwards strangled, because it was not lawful to execute virgins. Did any appear willing to die, they were forced to live. For he thought death was so light a punishment, that upon hearing that Carnulius, one of the accused, who was under prosecution, had killed himself, he exclaimed: 'Carnulius has escaped me!' In calling over his prisoners, when one of them besought him for speedy death, he retorted: 'Nay, you are not yet restored to favour, that I should show you such kindness.' A man of consular rank writes in his annals that once at a great feast, where he was himself present, when Tiberius was suddenly asked aloud by a dwarf standing among the buffoons, why Paconius, who was charged with treason, lived so long: he immediately reprimanded him for his impertinent tongue, but a few days later wrote to the senate to proceed with all speed towards the execution of Paconius.

## 62

Galled and fretted by news which he received of his son Drusus's death, he plunged into still greater excesses of cruelty; for, having imagined that he had died from the results of his intemperate life, when he learned that he had been poisoned by the design of his wife, Livilla, and Sejanus, he spared no one from torture and death. So immersed was he for whole days together with the examination of this matter, that when word came to him that the person in whose house he had lodged at Rhodes, and whom he had by friendly letters invited to Rome, was arrived, he ordered him immediately to be put to the torture, as a party concerned in the enquiry. Afterwards, when his error was discovered, he caused him to be put to death, that he might not make known the things done to him. The scene of his bloody carnage is still shown at Capri, where he ordered those who were condemned to die, after long and exquisite torments, to be flung headlong before his face into the sea; where, ready to deal with them, were a party of soldiers belonging to the fleet, who battered them with poles and oars, that no breath might remain in their bodies. He had devised moreover, among other kinds of torture, one which involved getting men very drunk with wine, upon which he caused their private members to be tied up with harpstrings, so that they became painfully swollen, both with the tightness of the ligature and the stoppage of their urine. Had it not been that death prevented him, and Thrasyllus, the astrologer, also prevailed upon him, designedly as some say, to forgo some of his monstrous designs in the hope of longer life, he would have destroyed many more, and perhaps not spared even the rest of his grandchildren; for he was jealous of Caius and hated Tiberius as having been conceived in adultery. It would seem most probable that he meditated these things, as people believed; for he used often to say: 'Happy Priam, who survived all his children!'

## 63

But how, amid these enormities, he lived not only in much fear and apprehension but also in odium and detestation, there is much evidence to show. He forbad the soothsayers to be consulted in private, and without some witnesses being present. He attempted to suppress the oracles in the neighbourhood of the city; but being affrighted by the divine authority of the Praenestine Lots, he abandoned the design. For though they were sealed up in a box and carried to Rome, yet they were not to be found in it, until it was returned to the temple of Fortune at Praeneste. More than one person of consular rank, appointed governors of provinces, he never ventured to dismiss to their respective destinations, but kept until several years after, when he nominated their successors, while they still remained present with him. In the meantime they bore the title of their office; and he frequently gave them orders, which they took care to have executed by their deputies and assistants.

## 64

His daughter-in-law Agrippina, and his grandsons, Drusus and Nero, after they were once condemned, he never removed to any place but in fetters and in a covered litter, closely attended by soldiers to hinder all who met them on the road from stopping to stare at them.

## 65

After Sejanus had plotted against him, though he saw that his birthday was solemnly kept by the public and divine honours paid to golden images of him in every quarter, yet he overthrew him at last, rather by craft and subtlety than by his princely authority. In the first place, to remove him from about his person, with some show of honour, he made him his colleague in his fifth consulship; which, although then absent from the city, he took upon him for that purpose, long after his preceding consulship. Then, having flattered him with the hope of an alliance by marriage with one of his own kindred, and the prospect of the tribunician authority, he suddenly, while Sejanus little expected it, charged him with treason in an abject and pitiful address to the senate; in which, among other things, he begged them 'to send one of the consuls to conduct himself, a poor solitary old man, with a guard of soldiers, into their presence'. Nevertheless, being still distrustful and apprehensive of an uprising, he ordered his grandson, Drusus, whom he still kept in confinement at Rome, to be set at liberty, and if occasion required, to head the troops. He also had ships rigged and prepared to transport him to any of the legions to which he might deem it prudent to make his escape. Meanwhile, he stood watching from the highest cliff accessible, for the signals which he had ordered to be flashed if anything occurred, lest the messengers tarried too long. Even when he had quite suppressed the conspiracy of Sejanus, he did not feel secure, and was so much harried by lingering fears that for the space of nine months he never once stirred out of the Villa Jovis.

## 66

Besides this great distress of mind, various and bitter taunts from all quarters reached him daily. Those who were condemned to die reviled him openly, both by the most opprobrious language to his face, and by handbills scattered in the senators' seats in the theatre. These he received in fitful and contradictory moods: sometimes, out of shame, he wished to have all smothered and concealed; at other times, he would disregard what was said and make it known himself. Furthermore, in the midst of all this scandal and outrage, he received a letter from Artabanus, king of the Parthians, charging him with parricides, murders, cowardice, and lewdness, and urging him to satisfy with a voluntary death the hatred of his own people, conceived so justly against him.

## 67

At last, being even weary of himself, he confessed his extreme misery in a letter to the senate, which began thus: 'What to write to you, Conscript Fathers, or how to write, or what not to write at this time? may all the gods and goddesses plague and confound me utterly, if I can tell, feeling myself perish, day by day, as I do.' Some believe that he had a foreknowledge of those things, from his skill in the science of prognostication, and that he foresaw long before also the great calamity and infamy that would one day befall him; and that for this reason, at the beginning of his reign, he had absolutely refused the title of the Father of his Country, and the proposal of the senate to maintain his acts, lest he should afterwards, to his greater shame, be found unworthy of such special honours. This indeed may be justly gathered from the speeches which he made upon both those occasions: as when he says, 'I shall ever be the same, and shall never change my conduct, so long as I retain my senses; but to avoid giving a bad precedent to posterity, the senate ought to beware of binding themselves to the acts of any person whatever, who might by some accident be induced to alter them.' And again: 'If ye should at any time entertain a jealousy of my conduct, and my entire affection for you, which heaven prevent by putting a period to my days, rather than that I should live to see such an alteration in your opinion of me, the title of "Father" will add no honour to me, but be a reproach to you, for your rashness in conferring it upon me, or inconstancy in altering your opinion of me.'

## 68

In person he was heavy-set and powerful, of a stature above the average, broad in the shoulders and chest, and the rest of his body of congruent proportions. His left hand was stronger and more nimble than his right; and his joints were so strong, that he could bore a fresh, sound apple through with his finger, and wound the head of a boy, or even a young man, with a fillip. His complexion was fair, and he wore his hair so long behind that it covered his neck; which was observed to be a fashion affected by his family. His face was ingenuous and well-favoured, but was often covered with pimples. His eyes, which were large, had a marvellous faculty of seeing in the night time, and in the dark, for a short time only, and immediately after awaking from sleep; but they soon grew dim again. He walked with his neck held stiff and upright, and with a countenance somewhat severe. For the most part he was silent; when he spoke with those about him, it was very slowly, and usually accompanied with a slight gesticulation of his fingers. All of which attributes being ungracious and full of arrogance, Augustus observed in him and endeavoured to excuse to the senate and the people, assuring them that they were defects and imperfections of nature, and not the vices of the mind. He enjoyed excellent health through his whole reign; though from the thirtieth year of his age, he preserved it by his own efforts, without any counsel from physicians.

## 69

He had little respect for the gods and matters of religion, being greatly addicted to astrology and fully persuaded that all things were governed by fate. Yet he was extremely afraid of lightning, and when the sky was in any way troubled, always wore a laurel crown on his head, because it is believed that the leaf of that tree is never touched by lightning.

## 70

The liberal arts, both Latin and Greek, he loved exceedingly. In his Latin prose he followed Corvinus Messalla, an aged and venerable man, to whom he had paid much respect in his own early years. But with much affectation and abstruseness he marred his style, so that he was thought to speak better extempore, than in a premeditated discourse. He composed also a lyric ode, under the title of *A Lamentation upon the Death of Lucius Caesar;* and also some Greek poems, in imitation of Euphorion, Rhianus, and Parthenius; in which poets he took much delight, and placed their works and statues in the public libraries among the principal authors of antiquity. On this account, most of the learned men of the time vied with each other in publishing observations upon them, which they addressed to him. His principal study, however, was the history of the fabulous ages; and he inquired into the smallest details relating to such matters, in a spirit of thoroughness that had its ludicrous side. For he used to try the grammarians, a class of men which, as I have already observed, he affected especially, with such questions as these: 'Who was Hecuba's mother? What name did Achilles assume among the virgins? What was it that the sirens used to sing?' And the first day that he entered the senate house after the death of Augustus, as if he intended to pay respect at once to his father's memory and to the gods, he made an offering of frankincense and wine, but without any music, in imitation of Minos upon the death of his son.

## 71

Though he was conversant with the Greek tongue, and spoke it with facility, he did not use it everywhere; most of all, he avoided it in the senate house, insomuch that having occasion to employ the word *monopolium* (monopoly), he first craved leave to adopt a foreign expression. And when, in a decree of the senate, the word 'emblem' was read in Greek, he proposed to have it changed, and that a Latin word should be substituted in its place; or, if no proper one could be found, to express the thing by circumlocution. A certain Greek soldier, who was examined as a witness upon a trial, he forbad to make reply unless it were in Latin.

## 72

During the whole time of his seclusion at Capri, twice only he made an effort to visit Rome. Once he came in a galley as far as the gardens near the Naumachia, but placed guards along the banks of the Tiber to keep off all who should offer to come to meet him. The second time he travelled on the Appian Way, as far as the seventh milestone from the city, but he immediately returned, without entering it, having only taken a view of the walls at a distance. For what reason he did not disembark in his first excursion is uncertain; but in the last, he was deterred from entering the city by a prodigy. Among other pastimes, he amused himself with a serpent, which, upon going one day to feed it with his own hand, according to custom, he found devoured by ants; from this, he took warning to beware of the violence of the multitude. On this account, returning with all speed to Campania, he fell ill at Astura; but recovering to some degree, went on to Circeii. And to give no suspicion of being in a weakened state, he was not only present at the sports in the camp, but when a wild boar was let loose in the arena, he attacked it with a javelin. Being immediately seized with a pain in his side, and catching cold upon his overheating himself in the exercise, he relapsed into a worse condition than he was before. He held out, however, for some time; and sailing as far as Misenum, omitted nothing in his usual mode of life, not even in his entertainments and other gratifications, partly from an intemperate appetite and partly to conceal his condition. When Charicles, a physician, having obtained leave of absence, took his hand upon rising from the table, intending to kiss it, Tiberius, supposing that he did it to feel his pulse, desired him to stay and resume his place, and continued the supper longer than usual. Nor did he omit his usual custom of taking his stand in the centre of the banquet room, with a lictor standing by him, while he took leave of each of the party by name.

Meanwhile, when he had read in the acts of the senate, 'that some persons under prosecution had been discharged without being brought to a hearing', for he had only written cursorily that they had been denounced by an informer, he complained in a great rage that he was treated with contempt, and resolved at all hazards to return to Capri, not daring to attempt anything until he found himself in a safe place. But being restrained as well by storms as by the increasing violence of his malady, he died shortly afterwards, at a villa formerly belonging to Lucullus, in the seventy-eighth year of his age, upon the seventeenth of the kalends of April (16th March), in the consulship of Cnaeus Acerronius Proculus and Caius Pontius Niger. Some think that a poison of slow operation was administered to him, little by little, by Caius Caligula. Others say that during the interval of the intermittent fever with which he happened to be seized, upon asking for food, it was denied him. Others report that he was stifled by a pillow thrown upon him, when, on his recovering from a swoon, he called for his ring which had been taken from him in the fit. Seneca writes, that realising he was dying, he took his signet ring from his finger, and held it a while as if he would give it to somebody; but afterwards put it again upon his finger and lay for some time, with his left hand clenched, and without stirring; when suddenly summoning his attendants, and no one answering the call, he rose; but his strength failing him, he fell down at a short distance from his bed.

## 74

Upon his last birthday, he had brought from Syracuse a full sized statue of the Timenian Apollo, a work of exquisite art, intending to place it in the library of the new temple of the Palatine Apollo; but he dreamed that the god appeared to him in the night, and assured him 'that his statue could not possibly be dedicated by him'. A few days before he died, the watch tower at Capri was thrown down by an earthquake. And at Misenum, some embers and live coals, which were brought in to warm his apartment, were mysteriously quenched, and after being quite cold for a long time, suddenly burst out into a flame again towards evening, and continued burning brightly for several hours.

## 75

The people were so overjoyed at his death, that when they first received the tidings, they ran up and down the city, some crying out 'Away with Tiberius to the Tiber'; others exclaiming, 'May the earth, the common mother of mankind, and the infernal gods, allow him no abode in death but among the wicked.' Others threatened his body with the hook and the Gemonian Steps, their anger at his former crimes being kindled anew by a fresh outrage. It had been provided that the execution of condemned criminals should always be deferred until the tenth day after the sentence. Now this fell on the very day when the news of Tiberius' death arrived, and in consequence thereof the unhappy men implored a reprieve, in mercy's name; but as Caius had not yet arrived and there was no one else to whom application could be made on their behalf, their guards, apprehensive of violating the law, strangled them and threw them down the Gemonian Steps. Thereupon the people's wrath against him increased, because his cruelty survived him. As soon as his corpse was begun to be moved from Misenum, many cried out for its being carried to Atella, and being half burnt there in the amphitheatre. It was, nevertheless, brought to Rome, and burnt with the usual ceremony.

## 76

About two years before, he had made his will in two states, one written by his own hand, the other by one of his freedmen; and both were witnessed by some persons of very mean rank. By virtue of this will, he appointed as co-heirs to his estate his two grandsons, Caius by Germanicus, and Tiberius by Drusus; and upon the death of one of them, the other was to inherit the whole. He gave likewise many legacies; among which were bequests to the Vestal Virgins, to all the soldiers, and each one of the people of Rome, and to the magistrates of the several quarters of the city.

# Caius Caesar Caligula

## I

Germanicus, father of Caius Caesar, and son of Drusus and the younger Antonia, was, after his adoption by his uncle Tiberius, preferred to the quaestorship five years before he was of legal age, and immediately upon the expiration of that office, to the consulship. Being sent to the army in Germany who, upon hearing of Augustus' death, obstinately refused to acknowledge Tiberius as emperor, and offered to place him at the head of the state, he declined and succeeded in restoring order; but whether his devotion to filial duty, or the firmness of his resolution, was greater, it is difficult to say. Soon afterwards he defeated the enemy, and obtained the honours of a triumph. Being then made consul for the second time, before he could enter upon his office, he was obliged to set out suddenly for the east, where, after he had conquered the king of Armenia, and reduced Cappadocia into the form of a province, he died at Antioch, of a lingering distemper, in the thirty-fourth year of his age, not without suspicion of being poisoned. For besides the livid spots which appeared all over his body, and a foaming at the mouth, his heart, after he was burnt, was found unconsumed and entire among the bones: its nature being such, as it is supposed, that when infected with poison, it cannot be destroyed by fire.

## 2

But, as the opinion of the world went, his death was contrived by Tiberius and effected through the means of Cnaeus Piso, who was about the same time prefect of Syria, and, not dissimulating the fact that he must either offend the father or the son, heaped upon Germanicus, even during his sickness, the most merciless abuse, both of word and deed. For this, when he returned to Rome, he closely

escaped being torn to pieces by the people, and was condemned to
death by the senate.

## 3

It is generally agreed that there were combined in Germanicus all the
good gifts of body and mind, and in greater measure than had ever
before fallen to any man: to wit, a well-favoured person, unusual
courage, great proficiency in eloquence and other branches of
learning; besides a singular humanity, and a disposition so gracious as
to win the confidence and love of all about him. His only defect was
a slenderness of leg that did not conform to the symmetry and beauty
of his physique; but he corrected this at length by regular riding after
meals. Many a time he engaged and slew an enemy in single combat.
He pleaded causes of great importance, even after he had the honour
of a triumph. Among other fruits of his studies, he left behind him
some Greek comedies. Both at home and abroad, his manner was
most civil and modest; insomuch that on entering any free and
confederate town, he was never attended by his lictors. Whenever he
heard, in his travels, of the tombs of illustrious men, he made
offerings over them to the infernal deities. He gave a common grave,
under a mound of earth, to the scattered relics of the legionaries slain
under Varus, and was the first to put his hand to the work of
collecting and bringing them to the place of burial. He was so
exceedingly mild and gentle to his enemies, wherever he lighted
upon them, or of whatever quality they were that, although Piso
rescinded his decrees, and for a long time severely harassed his
dependants, he never showed the smallest resentment, until he found
himself attacked by magical charms and imprecations; and even then,
he proceeded no farther against him than to renounce all friendship
with him, according to ancient customs, and to charge his servants to
avenge his death, if anything untoward should befall him.

## 4

He reaped the fruit of his virtues in abundance, being so loved and
esteemed by his friends, that Augustus (to say nothing of his other
relations), being a long time in doubt, whether he should not
appoint him his successor, at last ordered Tiberius to adopt him. He

was so highly favoured by the people, many authors tell us, that the crowds of those who went to meet him upon his coming to any place, or to attend him at his departure, were so prodigious, that his own life was sometimes endangered in the press; and that upon his return from Germany, after he had suppressed the mutiny in the army there, all the cohorts of the praetorian guards marched out to meet him, notwithstanding the order that only two should go; and that all the people of Rome, both men and women, of every age, sex, and rank, flocked as far as the twentieth milestone to attend his entrance.

## 5

Far greater and more assured testimony of men's love for him was displayed after his death. The day on which he died the temples were pelted with stones, and the altars of the gods cast down: for how could they be worthy of respect, when a man like Germanicus was permitted to die? The household gods, in some cases, were thrown into the streets, and newborn infants exposed: for to what end should children be reared, when Germanicus, than whom none had ever been finer, was taken by untimely death? And, what is more, the report goes that even barbarous nations, both those engaged in intestine wars, and those in hostilities against Rome, all agreed to a cessation of arms, as if they had been mourning for some very near and common friend; that some petty kings shaved their beards and their wives' heads, in token of their extreme sorrow; and that the very king of kings gave up his exercise of hunting and feasting with his nobles, which, among the Parthians, is equivalent to a cessation of all business in a time of public mourning with us.

## 6

At Rome, upon the first rumour of his sickness, the city was thrown into great consternation and grief, waiting impatiently for further intelligence; when suddenly, in the evening, a report, without any certain author, was spread, that he was well again, the people flocked with torches and victims to the Capitol, and were in such haste to pay the vows they had made for his recovery, that they almost broke open the doors; insomuch that Tiberius was awakened out of his sleep with the shouts and cries of the people rejoicing, and singing about the streets,

> *Salva Roma, salva Patria, salvus est Germanicus.*

Safe is Rome, safe is our country, safe is Germanicus.

When certain intelligence was received of his death, the public sorrow could neither be assuaged by consolation, nor restrained by edicts, but continued even during the holidays in the month of December. The glory and endearment of his memory was much augmented also by the outrages of the times ensuing; all men being of opinion, and not without reason, that the fierceness of Tiberius, which broke forth soon afterwards, was kept down by the fear and awe he had of him.

## 7

He wedded Agrippina, daughter of Marcus Agrippa and Julia; and by her he had nine children, two of whom died in their infancy, and another a few years after, when he was grown into a pretty, jolly boy, full of mirth and lively talk; an effigy of whom, in the character of a Cupid, Livia set up in the temple of Venus in the Capitol. Augustus also placed another statue of him in his bed-chamber, and used to kiss it as often as he entered the room. The rest survived their father: three daughters, Agrippina, Drusilla, and Livilla, who were born in three successive years; and as many sons, Nero, Drusus, and Caius Caesar. Nero and Drusus, at the accusation of Tiberius, were declared public enemies.

## 8                                              A.U.C. 765

Caius Caesar was born on the day before the kalends of September, during the consulship of his father and Caius Fonteius Capito. The place of his nativity, by the disagreement of writers, is left uncertain. Cnaeus Lentulus Gaetulicus writes that he was born at Tibur; Pliny the younger, in the country of the Treviri, at a village called Ambiatinus, above Confluentes; and alleges, as proof of it, that altars are there shown, with this inscription: 'For Agrippina's childbirth'. Some verses which were published in his reign, however, intimate that he was born in the winter quarters of the legions,

Born in the camp, and train'd in every toil
Which taught his sire the haughtiest foes to foil;
Destin'd he seem'd by fate to raise his name,
And rule the empire with Augustan fame.

I find among the public records that he was born at Antium. Pliny charges Gaetulicus as guilty of an arrant forgery, merely to soothe the vanity of a conceited young prince, by giving him the lustre of being born in a city sacred to Hercules; and says that he advanced this false assertion with the more assurance because, the year before the birth of Caius, Germanicus had a son of the same name born at Tibur; concerning whose amiable childhood and untimely death we have spoken before. Dates clearly confute Pliny, for the writers of Augustus' history all agree that Germanicus, at the expiration of his consulship, was sent into Gaul, after the birth of Caius. Nor will the inscription upon the altar confirm Pliny's opinion; because Agrippina was delivered of two daughters in that country, and any childbirth, without regard to sex, is called *puerperium,* as the ancients were used to call girls *puerae,* and boys *puelli.* There is also extant a letter written by Augustus, a few months before his death, to his granddaughter Agrippina, about the same Caius (for there was then no other child of hers living under that name) in these words: 'I gave orders yesterday for Talarius and Asellius to set out on their journey towards you, if the gods permit, with your child Caius, upon the fifteenth of the kalends of June (18th May). I also send with him a physician of mine, and I wrote to Germanicus that he may retain him if he pleases. Farewell, my dear Agrippina, and take what care you can to come safe and well to your Germanicus.' It appears sufficiently evident, I suppose, that Caius could not be born at a place to which he was carried from the City when almost two years old. The same considerations must likewise invalidate the evidence of the verses, and the rather because they are anonymous. The only authority that remains, upon which we can depend in the matter, is that of the acts and the public register; especially as he always preferred Antium to every other place of retirement, and loved it as one commonly loves one's native soil. It is said, too, that he once contemplated, upon growing weary of the city, the plan of transferring thither the seat of empire.

# 9

He got his surname Caligula, derived from *Caliga*, a kind of boot, by reason of a merry word passed around the camp, because he was brought up there in the dress of a common soldier. How much his education among them recommended him to their favour and trust was made known upon the death of Augustus, when the mere sight of him appeased their fury, though it had risen to a great height. For they did not cease their mutinous tumult until they perceived that he was about to be sent out of the way of danger, and appointed to a neighbouring city; then and not before, they began to repent, and, stopping the chariot in which he was to be conveyed, they earnestly prayed that he might stay and so avert the displeasure they had incurred.

# 10

He accompanied his father also in his expedition to Syria. After his return, he lived first with his mother, and, when she was banished, with his great-grandmother, Livia Augusta, in praise of whom, after her decease, though then only a boy, he pronounced a funeral oration in the rostra. He was then transferred to the family of his grandmother, Antonia, and afterwards, in the twentieth year of his age, being called by Tiberius to Capri, he in one and the same day assumed his virile gown, and shaved his beard, but without receiving any of the honours which had been paid to his brothers on a similar occasion. While he remained in that island, many insidious plans were devised to draw him into quarrels, and incite him to complaints against Tiberius; but by his circumspection he avoided falling into the snare. He passed over the calamities that attended his mother, brethren and near-friends, as if nothing had befallen any of them. As to his own sufferings, he endured them with incredible dissimulation, and was so obsequious and thoughtful towards his grandfather Tiberius, and all about him, that it was said of him, and not without good cause: 'A better servant and a worse master there never was.'

## II

Yet he did not entirely conceal his cruel and villainous disposition even then. He delighted in witnessing the infliction of punishments, and in frequenting taverns and brothels, disguised in a periwig and a long coat. He was passionately fond of the theatrical arts of singing and dancing, to which he gave much study. All these tendencies Tiberius readily suffered, in the hope that his fierce and savage nature might be thereby mollified and made tractable; and so well did he understand his grandson's real nature (for he was a shrewd old man, full of sagacity), that he often said: 'That Caius was destined to be the destruction of him and them all; and that he was cherishing a hydra for the people of Rome, and a Phaeton for all the world.'

## 12

Not long afterwards, he married Junia Claudilla, the daughter of Marcus Silanus, a man of the highest rank. Being then chosen augur in the room of his brother Drusus, before he could be inaugurated he was advanced to the pontificate, with no small commendation of his dutiful conduct and great capacity. The situation of the court likewise was at this time favourable to his fortunes, as it was now left destitute of support, Sejanus being suspected, and soon afterwards overthrown; and he was by degrees flattered with the hope of succeeding Tiberius in the empire. In order more effectually to secure this object, upon Junia's dying in childbed, he engaged in a criminal intercourse with Ennia Naevia, the wife of Macro, at that time prefect of the praetorian cohorts: promising to marry her if he became emperor, to which he bound himself, not only by an oath, but by a written obligation under his hand. Having by her means insinuated himself into Macro's favour, some are of opinion that he attempted to poison Tiberius, and ordered his ring to be taken from him before the breath was out of his body; and that, because he seemed to hold it fast, he caused a pillow to be thrown upon him, squeezing him by the throat at the same time with his own hand. One of his freedmen crying out at this cruel and horrible act, he gave order immediately to crucify him. And this episode seems to ring true, as some authors relate that afterwards, though he did not acknowledge his having a hand in the death of

Tiberius, yet he frankly confessed that he had once entertained such a design; and as a proof of his affection for his relations, he would often boast that, 'To revenge the death of his mother and brothers, he had entered the chamber of Tiberius, when he was asleep, with a poniard, but being seized with a fit of compassion, flung it away, and withdrew; and that Tiberius, though he had an inkling of his intention, dared not make any inquiries, nor attempt revenge.'

## 13                                                    A.U.C. 790

Having thus secured the imperial power, he realised the wish of the Roman people, or (I may venture to say) of all mankind; for he had long been the object of expectation and desire to the greater part of the provincials and soldiers, who had known him when a child; and to the whole people of Rome, from their affection for the memory of his father, Germanicus, and compassion for the family almost extinct. Upon his moving from Misenum, therefore, although he was in mourning, and reverently attending the corpse of Tiberius, he had to walk amid altars, victims, and lighted torches, with prodigious crowds of people everywhere hailing him in transports of joy, and calling him, beside other auspicious names, their 'star', their 'chick', their 'pretty puppet', and 'bantling'.

## 14

No sooner had he entered the city of Rome than by the joint acclamations of the senate and people, who rushed into the senate-house, Tiberius' will was set aside, with its provision that his other grandson, Tiberius, son of Drusus, then a minor, should be coheir with him, and the whole government and administration of affairs was placed in his hands; so much to the joy and gratitude of the people, that, in less than three months after, above a hundred and sixty thousand victims are said to have been sacrificed. Upon his going a few days afterwards to the nearest islands on the coast of Campania, vows were made for his safe return; every man emulously testifying their care and concern for his well-being. And when he fell sick, the people kept watch by night about the Palatium; some vowed, in public handbills, to risk their lives in the combats of the amphitheatre, and others to lay them down, for his recovery. To this

surpassing love of his own countrymen was added the notable favour
of foreign nations. Even Artabanus, king of the Parthians, who had
always manifested hatred and contempt of Tiberius, voluntarily
sought his friendship and came to hold a conference with his consular
lieutenant; passing the Euphrates, he paid the highest honours to the
eagles, the Roman standards, and the images of the Caesars.

## 15

Caligula himself enkindled still more the affections of his people, by
practising all the arts of popularity. After he had delivered, with
copious tears, a funeral oration in praise of Tiberius and buried him
with the highest honours, he immediately hastened over to Pandataria
and the Pontian Islands to transport thence the ashes of his mother
and brother, and that in most foul and tempestuous weather, so that
his tender regard for their memory might be the more marked.
Approaching their remains, he very reverently, with his own hands,
bestowed them in several pitchers. With no less solemnity, he
conveyed them to Ostia, with an ensign flying in the stern of the
galley, and thence up the Tiber to Rome where they were borne on
two biers by persons of the first distinction in the equestrian order,
into the mausoleum at noon-day when people were assembled there
in great numbers. In memory of them, he appointed yearly offerings
to be solemnly and publicly celebrated; as well as Circensian games in
honour of his mother, and a chariot with her image to be included in
the procession. In remembrance of his father, he called the month of
September, Germanicus. By a single act of the senate, he heaped
upon his grandmother, Antonia, all the honours which had ever been
conferred on the empress Livia. His uncle, Claudius, who till then
continued in the equestrian order, he took for his colleague in the
consulship. He adopted his brother Tiberius on the day he put on his
virile gown, and styled him 'Prince of the Youths'. As for his sisters,
he ordered these words to be added to the oaths of allegiance to
himself: 'Nor will I prize myself or my own children more dear than
I do Caius and his sisters': and commanded all resolutions proposed
by the consuls in the senate to be prefaced thus: 'May what we are
going to do prove fortunate and happy to Caius Caesar and his
sisters.' In the same vein of popularity, he restored all those who had
been condemned, confined, and exiled, and granted an act of

indemnity against all impeachments and past offences. To relieve the informers and witnesses against his mother and brother from all apprehension, he brought the records of their trials into the Forum and there burnt them, calling loudly on the gods to witness that he had not read or meddled with them. A pamphlet which was presented to him concerning his own life and safety, he would not receive, affirming 'that he had done nothing to make himself odious to any person, and that he had no ears for informers'.

## 16

The Spintriae, those panderers to unnatural lusts, he expelled from Rome, being with difficulty dissuaded from throwing them into the sea, as he had intended. The writings of Titus Labienus, Cordus Cremutius, and Cassius Severus, which had been suppressed by an act of the senate, he suffered to be sought out again, and read by all who would; observing 'that it would be for his own advantage to have the deeds of former times delivered to posterity'. He published accounts of the proceedings of the government – a practice which had been introduced by Julius, but discontinued by Augustus. He granted the magistrates a full and free jurisdiction, without any appeal to himself. He made a very strict and precise review of the Roman knights, but conducted it with moderation: publicly depriving of his horse every knight who lay under the stigma of anything base or dishonourable; but passing over, in reading the list of the order, the names of those knights who were culpable in smaller matters. To ease the labours of the judges, he added a fifth class to the former four. He attempted likewise to restore to the people their ancient right of voting in the choice of magistrates. He paid very honourably, and without any dispute, the legacies left by Tiberius in his will, though it had been set aside; as likewise those left by the will of Livia Augusta, which Tiberius had annulled. He remitted the hundredth penny due to the government in all auctions throughout Italy. He made up to many their losses sustained by fire; and when he restored their kingdoms to any princes, he likewise allowed them all the arrears of the taxes and revenues which had accrued in the interval; as in the case of Antiochus of Comagene, where the confiscation would have amounted to a hundred millions of sesterces. To prove to the world that he was ready to encourage good examples of every kind, he gave to a freedwoman eighty thousand sesterces for not discovering a crime committed by her patron, though she had been put to grievous torment for that purpose. For all these acts of beneficence, among other honours, a golden shield was decreed to him, which the colleges of priests were to carry annually upon a fixed day into the Capitol, with the senate attending, and the youth of the nobility of both sexes celebrating the praise of his virtues in songs. It was likewise ordained, that the day on which he succeeded to the empire should be called Palilia, implying thereby, as it were, a second foundation of the City.

## 17

A.U.C. 790

He bore the consulship four times: the first, from the kalends of July for two months: the second, from the kalends of January for thirty days: the third until the ides of January; and the fourth until the seventh of the same ides; of these, he held the two last successively. The third he assumed by his sole authority at Lyons; not, as some are of opinion, from pride or negligence; but because, at that distance, it was impossible for him to know that his colleague had died a little before the beginning of the new year. He twice distributed to the people a bounty of three hundred sesterces a man, and as often gave a splendid feast to the senate and the equestrian order, with their wives and children. In the latter, he presented to the men forensic garments, and to the women and children violet scarfs. To make a perpetual addition to the public joy, he lengthened the feast Saturnalia by one day, which he called Juvenalis (the juvenile feast).

## 18

He presented some combats of gladiators, which were held sometimes in the Amphitheatre of Taurus and sometimes in the Saepta, with which he intermingled troops of the best pugilists from Campania and Africa. He did not always preside in person upon those occasions, but sometimes assigned magistrates or friends to attend in his place. He frequently entertained the people with stage plays of various kinds, and in several parts of the city, sometimes by night, when he caused the whole city to be illuminated. He likewise scattered various small gifts to be scrambled for among the people, and presented to every man a basket of bread with other victuals. Upon this occasion, noticing a Roman knight, who was seated opposite to him, enjoying himself heartily by eating his fill, he sent him his own share; to a senator, who was occupying himself in like manner, he sent an appointment of praetor-extraordinary. He also exhibited a great number of Circensian games from morning until night; intermixed with the hunting of wild beasts from Africa, or the Trojan game. Some of these games were celebrated under novel conditions; the Circus being overspread with vermilion and chrysolite; and none drove in the chariot races who were not of the senatorian order. For some of these he suddenly gave the signal when, upon his viewing from the Gelotiana the preparations in the Circus, he was asked to do so by a few persons in the neighbouring galleries.

## 19

Furthermore, he devised a new kind of spectacle, such as had never been heard of before. He made a bridge about three miles and a half in length, from Baiae to the mole of Puteoli, collecting trading vessels from all quarters, mooring them in two rows by their anchors, and spreading earth upon them to form a viaduct, after the fashion of the Appian Way. This bridge he crossed and recrossed for two days together; the first day mounted on a horse richly caparisoned, wearing on his head a crown of oak leaves, armed with a battle-axe, a Spanish buckler and a sword, and in a cloak made of cloth of gold; the day following, in the habit of a charioteer, standing in a chariot drawn by two highbred horses, having with him a young boy, Darius by name, one of the Parthian hostages, with a cohort of the praetorian guards attending him, and a party of his friends in cars of Gaulish make. Most people, I know, are of opinion that this bridge was designed by Caius in imitation of Xerxes who, to the wonderment of the world, laid a bridge over the Hellespont, which is somewhat narrower than the distance betwixt Baiae and Puteoli; others, however, thought that he did it to strike terror in Germany and Britain, which he was upon the point of invading, by the fame of some prodigious work. But for myself, when I was a boy, I heard my grandfather say, that the reason assigned by some courtiers who were on terms of the greatest intimacy with him was this: when Tiberius was in some anxiety about the nomination of a successor and rather inclined to pitch upon his grandson, Thrasyllus the astrologer had assured him, 'that Caius would no more be emperor, than he would ride on horseback across the gulf of Baiae'.

## 20

He likewise presented public diversions in Sicily, Grecian games at Syracuse, and Attic plays at Lyons in Gaul: besides a contest for pre-eminence in the Grecian and Roman eloquence in which we are told that such as were baffled bestowed rewards upon the best performers and were obliged to compose speeches in their praise; but that those who performed the worst were forced to blot out what they had written with a sponge or their tongue, unless they chose rather to be beaten with a rock or plunged over head and ears into the nearest river.

## 21

The buildings left uncompleted by Tiberius, namely the Temple of Augustus and the Theatre of Pompey, he took in hand and finished. He began, too, the aqueduct from the neighbourhood of Tibur, and an amphitheatre near the Saepta; of which works, one was completed by his successor Claudius, and the other remained as he left it. The walls of Syracuse which had fallen to decay by length of time, he repaired, as he did also the temples of the gods. He formed plans for rebuilding the palace of Polycrates at Samos, finishing the temple of the Didymaean Apollo at Miletus, and building a town on a ridge of the Alps; but, above all, for cutting through the isthmus in Achaia; and even sent a centurion of the first rank to measure out the work.

## 22

Thus far we have spoken of him as a prince. What remains to be related bespeaks him rather a monster than a man. He assumed a variety of titles, such as 'Dutiful', 'The Pious', 'The Child of the Camp, the Father of the Armies', and 'The Greatest and Best Caesar'. Upon hearing some kings, who came to the city to pay him court, conversing together at supper about their illustrious descent, he cried out: 'Let there be but one prince, one king'; and there is small doubt that he would have taken the diadem and converted the form of government from imperial to regal; but being told that he far exceeded the grandeur of kings and princes, he began to arrogate to himself a divine majesty. He ordered all the images of the gods, which were famous either for their beauty or the veneration paid them, among which was that of Jupiter Olympius, to be brought from Greece, that he might take the heads off and put on his own. Having continued part of the Palatium as far as the Forum, and the temple of Castor and Pollux being converted into a kind of vestibule to his house, he often stationed himself between the twin brothers, and so presented himself to be worshipped by all votaries; some of whom saluted him by the name of Jupiter Latialis. He also instituted a temple and priests, with choicest victims, devoted to his peculiar worship. In his temple stood a statue of gold, executed in full proportion, and the exact image of himself, which was daily dressed in garments corresponding with those he habitually wore. The richest persons in the city offered themselves as candidates for the honour of being his priests and purchased it successively at an immense price. The victims were flamingoes, peacocks, bustards, guinea fowls, turkeys and pheasant hens, each sacrificed on their respective days. On nights when the moon was full, he was in the constant habit of inviting her to his embraces and his bed. In the day time he talked in private to Jupiter Capitolinus; one while whispering to him, and another turning his ear to him: sometimes he spoke aloud, and in chiding fashion. For he was overheard to threaten the god thus: 'Raise thou me up, or I'll transport thee to the land of Greece', until being at last persuaded by the entreaties of the god, as he said, to take up his abode with him, he built a bridge over the temple of the Deified Augustus, by which he joined the Palatium to the Capitol. Afterwards, that he might be still nearer, he laid the foundations of a new palace in the very court of the Capitol.

## 23

He would not abide being reputed the grandson of Agrippa, by reason of his obscure birth; and he was angry if anyone, either in prose or verse, ranked him (Agrippa) among the Caesars. He said that his mother was the fruit of an incestuous relation between Augustus and his own daughter Julia. And not content with this infamous imputation upon the memory of Augustus, he forbad his victories at Actium and on the coast of Sicily to be celebrated as usual; affirming that they had been most unlucky and injurious to the Roman people. Livia Augusta, his great-grandmother, he called 'Ulysses in a woman's dress', and had the indecency to reflect upon her in a letter to the senate, as of ignoble birth and descended, by the mother's side, from a grandfather who was only one of the municipal magistrates of Fondi; whereas it is certain, from the public records, that Aufidius Lurco held high offices at Rome. His grandmother Antonia desiring a private conference with him, he refused to grant it, unless Macro, the prefect of the praetorian guards, was present. Indignities of this kind, and ill-usage, were the cause of her death; but some think he also gave her poison. Nor did he pay the smallest respect to her memory after her death, but beheld from his dining chamber the burning of her funeral fire. He surprised his brother Tiberius, who looked for no violence, by sending a military tribune who rushed upon him suddenly and slew him. He forced Silanus, his father-in-law, to end his own life by cutting his throat with a razor. The pretext he urged for these murders was that Silanus had not followed him upon his putting to sea in stormy weather, but stayed behind with the view of seizing the city, if he should perish. Tiberius, he said, smelt of an antidote, as if he had thus protected himself from being poisoned by him. Whereas, in truth, Silanus merely avoided the terrors of sea-sickness and the disagreeableness of a voyage; and Tiberius had taken the odorous medicine as a remedy for an habitual cough, which was steadily growing worse. As for his successor, Claudius, he reserved him for nothing else but to make him a laughing-stock.

## 24

With all his sisters, he lived incestuously; and at table, when much company was present, he placed each of them in turns below him while his wife sat above. It is believed that he deflowered one of them, Drusilla, when he was still a boy, and was one time found in bed with her by his grandmother Antonia, with whom they were brought up together. When she was afterwards bestowed in marriage upon Lucius Cassius Longinus, a man of consular rank, he took her from him, and kept her openly as if she were his lawful wife. In a fit of sickness, he by his will appointed her heiress both of his estate and the empire. After her death, he ordered a public mourning for her, during which it was a capital crime for any person to laugh, use the bath, or sup with his parents, wife, or children. Being inconsolable under his affliction, he fled suddenly in the night time from the City; going through Campania to Syracuse, and then hastily returning without shaving his beard or trimming his hair. Nor did he ever afterwards, in matters of the greatest importance, not even in the assemblies of the people or before the soldiers, swear otherwise, than 'By the divinity of Drusilla'. His other sisters he did not regard with so much tenderness or respect, but frequently prostituted them to his catamites. He therefore the more readily condemned them in the case of Aemilius Lepidus, as guilty of adultery, and privy to that conspiracy against him. And he not only divulged their handwriting relative to the affair, which he procured by base and lewd means, but likewise consecrated to Mars the Avenger three swords which had been prepared to stab him, with an inscription over them setting forth the occasion of their consecration.

## 25

As for his marriages, one may hardly discern whether it was in the contracting, dissolving, or maintaining of them that he acted with greater infamy. Being at the wedding of Caius Piso with Livia Orestilla, he commanded the bride to be carried to his own house, but within a few days divorced her, and two years after banished her: because, it was thought, upon her divorce she hastened again to her former husband. Some say that being invited to the wedding-supper, he sent a messenger to Piso, who sat opposite to him, in these words: 'See that you sit not too close to my wife', and that he immediately carried her off. Next day be published a proclamation, 'That he had got a wife as Romulus and Augustus had done'; alluding, in the case of Romulus, to the rape of the Sabines; and in that of Augustus to his having taken Livia from her husband.

Lollia Paulina, who was married to a man of consular rank in command of an army, he suddenly called from the province where she was with her husband, upon mention being made that her grandmother was formerly very beautiful, and married her; but he soon afterwards parted with her, interdicting her from having ever afterwards any bodily relations with any man. He loved with a more ardent affection and constancy Caesonia, (though she was neither beautiful nor young, and was besides the mother of three daughters by another man), because of her lascivious nature and insatiable lust. Her he would frequently exhibit to the soldiers, dressed in a military cloak, with shield and helmet, and riding by his side. To his friends he would even show her quite naked. When she bore him a daughter, he honoured her with the title of wife; in one and the same day making it known both that he was her husband, and the father of her child. He named the babe Julia Drusilla, and carrying it round the temples of all the goddesses, laid it on the lap of Minerva, to whom he recommended the care of bringing up and instructing her. He had no surer sign for believing that she was his own child than her fierce and treacherous temper, which was so marked even in her infancy, that she would attack with her nails the face and eyes of the children at play with her.

## 26

It would be vain and tedious to narrate in detail the manner in which he treated his relations and friends; as Ptolemy, King Juba's son, his cousin (for he was the grandson of Mark Antony by his daughter Selene, born of Cleopatra), and especially Macro himself, and Ennia likewise, by whose help he had obtained the empire; all of whom, for their alliance and notable services, he rewarded with bloody deaths. Nor was he more mild or respectful in his behaviour towards the senate. Some who had held the highest offices in the government, he suffered to run by his litter in their togas for several miles together and to attend him at supper, sometimes at the head of his couch, sometimes at his feet, with napkins. Others, after he had secretly murdered them, he nevertheless continued to send for, as if they were still alive, and a few days later pretended that they had made away with themselves. The consuls having forgotten to give public notice of his birthday, he deprived them of their magistracy; and the republic was three days without any one in that high office. A quaestor who was said to be concerned in a conspiracy against him, he scourged severely, having first stripped off his clothes and spread them under the feet of the soldiers employed in the work, that they might stand the more firm while whipping him. He handled the other orders with like haughtiness and violence. Being disquieted by the noise of people taking their places at midnight in the circus, as they were to have free admission, he drove them all away with clubs; in which tumult above twenty Roman knights and as many matrons were trampled and crushed to death, besides an infinite number of the common people. At the stage plays, in order to sow discord and occasion disputes between the people and the knights, he distributed the money tickets sooner than usual, that the seats assigned to the knights might be all occupied by the crowd. In the spectacles of gladiators, sometimes, when the sun was parching hot, he would order the curtains which covered the amphitheatre, to be drawn aside, and forbad any person to be let out; withdrawing at the same time the usual apparatus for the entertainment, and presenting wild beasts almost dead and very lean, the most sorry gladiators, decrepit with age, and fit only to work the machinery, and decent householders who were noted for some special feebleness or imperfection of body. Sometimes he contrived temporary famine by shutting up the public granaries.

## 27

The cruelty of his nature is evinced chiefly by the following examples. When flesh for the feeding of the wild beasts reserved for public spectacles grew very high in price, he ordered that criminals should be given them to be devoured; and upon inspecting them in a row, while he stood in the middle of the portico, without troubling himself to examine their cases, he commanded that they be dragged away, 'from bald pate to bald pate', he having espied two wholly devoid of hair who stood at some distance from one another. Of one person who had made a vow for his recovery to combat with a gladiator, he exacted its performance; nor would he allow him to desist until he came off conqueror, and after many entreaties. Another, having vowed to give his life for the same cause, and not being very eager to pay his vow, he delivered, decked as a victim for the sacrifice, with garlands and fillets, to young boys who were to drive him through the streets, calling on him to fulfil his vow, until he was thrown headlong from the ramparts. After disfiguring many persons of honourable degree, by branding them in the face with irons, he condemned them to the mines, to work in repairing the highways, or to fight with wild beasts; or, tying them by the neck and heels, in the manner of beasts carried to slaughter, he would shut them up in cages, or saw them asunder. Nor were these atrocities visited only on those guilty of great crimes; it sufficed if they had but passed remarks on his public games, or failed to swear by the genius of the emperor. He forced parents to witness the execution of their children; and to one father, who pleaded indisposition, he sent his own litter. Another he invited to his table immediately after he had seen his son executed, and challenged him, by all manner of provocation, to jest and be merry. He ordered the overseer of the spectacles and wild beasts to be scourged in fetters, during several days successively, in his own presence, and did not put him to death until he was disgusted with the stench of his putrefied brain. He burned alive, in the centre of the arena of the amphitheatre, the author of a farce, for writing some witty verses which had a double meaning. A Roman knight, who had been cast before the wild beasts, crying out that he was innocent, he commanded him to be brought back; and having had his tongue cut out, remanded him to the arena.

## 28

Having recalled a certain person from a long exile, he asked of him how he used to spend his time; who answered, in a flattering vein: 'I was always praying the gods for what has happened, that Tiberius might die, and you be emperor.' Caligula, therefore, concluding that those he had himself banished prayed likewise for his death, sent orders to the various islands on which they were exiled to have them all put to death. Being very desirous to have a senator torn to pieces, he employed some persons to call him a public enemy, fall upon him as he entered the senate-house, stab him with their styles, and deliver him to the rest to tear asunder. Nor was he satisfied, until he saw the man's limbs, joints, and bowels drawn along the streets, and piled up in a heap before him.

## 29

His deeds, horrible as they were, he augmented with words equally outrageous. 'There is nothing in my nature,' he would say, 'that I commend or approve so much, as my inflexible rigour.' When his grandmother Antonia gave him some advice, he said to her (as though it were not enough to disregard it), 'Remember that all things are lawful for me.' When about to murder his brother, whom he suspected of taking antidotes against poison, he said, 'See then, an antidote against Caesar!' And when he banished his sisters, he told them in a menacing tone that he had not only islands at command, but likewise swords. One of praetorian rank having sent several times from Anticyra, whither he had gone for his health, to have his leave of absence prolonged, he ordered him to be put to death; adding these words: 'Bleeding is necessary for one that has taken hellebore so long, and found no benefit.' It was his custom every tenth day to sign the lists of prisoners appointed for execution; and this he called 'clearing his accounts'. And having condemned several Gauls and Greeks at one time, he boasted that he had subdued Gallograecia.

## 30

He would not permit any to die quickly, but only after many strokes, and those dealt softly, this being his well known and constant order: 'Strike so that he may feel that he is dying.' He once executed a person whom he had not appointed to die, by mistaking him for the one condemned; 'But it makes no difference,' said he, 'this one deserved it quite as much.' He had many times upon his tongue these words of the tragedian,

*Oderint dum metuant*

I scorn their hatred, if they do but fear me.

Many a time he inveighed bitterly against all the senators at once, as clients of Sejanus, and informers against his mother and brothers, producing the memorials which he had pretended to burn, and excusing the cruelty of Tiberius as necessary, since it was impossible to question the veracity of such a number of accusers. He continually reproached the whole equestrian order, as devoting themselves to nothing but acting on the stage, and fighting as gladiators. Being highly displeased at the people's applauding a party at the Circensian games in opposition to him, he exclaimed, 'Would God that the Roman people had but one neck!' When Tetrinius, the highwayman, was denounced, he said his persecutors too were all Tetriniuses. Five Retiarii, in tunics, fighting in a company, yielded without a struggle to the same number of Secutores; and being ordered by the people to be slain, one of them taking up his lance again, killed all the conquerors. This he lamented in a proclamation as a *most* cruel butchery, and cursed all those who had borne the sight

## 31

He was wont moreover to complain openly of the condition of the times wherein he lived, as not being renowned by any public calamities; whereas the reign of Augustus was memorable for the overthrow of Varus, and that of Tiberius ennobled by the fall of scaffolds in the theatre at Fidenae. As for himself, he was likely to pass into oblivion, such was the prosperity of his days. And, at times, he wished for some terrible carnage of his armies, a famine, a pestilence, conflagrations, or an earthquake.

## 32

Even in the midst of his recreations, while gaming or feasting, his cruelty of word and deed was never mitigated one whit. Often as he sat at dinner, persons were put to the torture in his presence; and a soldier, who was skilled in the art of beheading, used at such times to take off the heads of prisoners who were brought in for that purpose. At Puteoli, when he dedicated the bridge which he planned, as already described, he invited a number of people to come to him from the shore, and then suddenly flung them headlong from the bridge into the water; thrusting down with poles and oars those who, to save themselves, caught at the rudders of the ships. At a public feast in Rome, when a slave stole some thin plates of silver with which the couches were inlaid, he delivered him at once to an executioner, with orders to cut off his hands, hang them from his neck over his breast, together with a written placard declaring the cause of his punishment; and so led around the company as they sat at the board. A gladiator who was practising with him, and voluntarily threw himself at his feet, he stabbed with a poniard, and then ran about with a palm branch in his hand, after the manner of those who are victorious in the games. When a victim was to be offered upon an altar he, clad in the habit of the Popae, and holding the axe aloft for a while, at last slaughtered, instead of the animal, an officer who attended to cut up the sacrifice. And at a sumptuous entertainment, he suddenly burst into immoderate laughter, and upon the consuls, who reclined next to him, respectfully asking him the occasion: 'At what else,' he retorted, 'but this, that upon a single nod of my head, you might both have your throats cut.'

## 33

Among many other jests and merry conceits of his, as he stood once by the statue of Jupiter, he asked Apelles, the tragedian, which of them he considered the greater, Jupiter or himself. And upon his hesitating somewhat in his reply, he lashed him most severely, now and then commending his voice, while he cried out for mercy, as being well modulated and pleasant even when raised in supplication. As often as he kissed the neck of his wife or concubine, he would murmur, 'As fair and lovely a neck as this is, off it shall go if I do but give the word'; and now and then he would threaten to put his dear Caesonia to the torture, that he might discover why he loved her so entirely; as if it had entered his mind that she had administered love philtres to him.

## 34

In his manner towards men of almost all ages, he manifested a degree of jealousy and malice equal to that of his cruelty and pride. He so demolished and dispersed the statues of several illustrious persons, which had been removed by Augustus, for want of room, from the court of the Capitol into the Campus Martius, that it was impossible to set them up again with their inscriptions entire. And for the future he forbad any statue whatever to be erected without his knowledge and leave. He had thoughts too of suppressing Homer's poems: 'For why,' said he, 'may not I do what Plato has done before me, who excluded him from his commonwealth?' He was likewise very near banishing the writings and the busts of Virgil and Livy from all libraries; censuring one of them as 'a man of no genius and very little learning'; and the other as 'a verbose and careless historian'. He often talked of the lawyers as if he intended to abolish their profession. 'By Hercules!' he would say, 'I shall put it out of their power to answer any questions in law, otherwise than by referring them to me!'

## 35

He took from the noblest persons in the city the ancient marks of distinction used by their families; as the collar from Torquatus; from Cincinnatus the curl of hair; and from Cnaeus Pompey, the surname of Great, belonging to that ancient family. Ptolemy, mentioned before, whom he invited from his kingdom and received with great honours, he suddenly put to death, for no reason but because he observed that upon entering the theatre, at a public exhibition, he drew the glances of all the spectators, by the splendour of his purple robe. As often as he met with well favoured men, who had fine heads of hair, he would order the back of their heads to be shaved, to make them appear ridiculous. There was one Aesius Proculus, the son of a centurion of the first rank, who, for his great stature and fine proportions, was called 'Colosseros'. Him he ordered to be dragged from his seat in the arena and matched with a gladiator in light armour, and afterwards with another completely armed; and upon his overcoming them both, commanded him forthwith to be bound, to be led clothed in rags up and down the streets of the city, and, after being exhibited in that plight to the women, to be then butchered. There was none of so base and abject condition that he did not envy whatever excellency they enjoyed. The Rex Nemorensis having many years enjoyed his sacerdotal dignity, he procured a still stronger antagonist to oppose him. One Porius, who fought in a chariot, having been victorious in an exhibition, and in his joy given freedom to a slave, was applauded so vehemently, that Caligula rose from his seat in such haste that, treading upon the hem of his toga, he tumbled down the steps, full of indignation, and crying out, 'A people who are masters of the world pay greater respect to a gladiator for a trifle, than to princes admitted among the gods, or to my own majesty here present among them.'

## 36

He never had the least regard for chastity, either in himself or in others. He is said to have entertained an unnatural passion for Marcus Lepidus Mnester, an actor in pantomimes, and for certain hostages; and to have engaged with them in the practice of mutual pollution. Valerius Catullus, a young man of a consular family, complained aloud in public that he had been exhausted by him in that abominable commerce. Besides his incest with his sisters and his notorious passion for Pyrallis, a common prostitute, there was hardly any lady of distinction with whom he did not make free. He used commonly to invite them with their husbands to supper, and as they passed by the couch on which he reclined, consider them curiously, in the leisurely manner of those who traffic in slaves; and if anyone from modesty held down her face, he raised it up with his hand. Afterwards, as often as he was in the humour, he would quit the refection room, send for her he fancied most, and in a short time return, while the marks of their wanton conduct were still evident. He would then either praise or disparage her in the presence of the company, recounting the charms or flaws of her person and behaviour in private. To some he sent a bill of divorce in the name of their absent husbands, and ordered it to be registered in the public acts.

## 37

In riotous and extraordinary expenditure, he surpassed the wits and inventions of all the prodigals that ever lived; devising a new kind of bath, with strange dishes and suppers, washing in precious unguents, both warm and cold, drinking pearls of immense value dissolved in vinegar, and serving up for his guests loaves and other victuals modelled in gold, often saying, 'that a man ought either to be parsimonious or Caesar'. Besides, he scattered money of no mean value among the people, from the top of the Julian Basilica, during several days successively. He built two ships with ten banks of oars, after the Liburnian fashion, the poops of which blazed with jewels, and the sails were of various parti-colours. They were fitted up with ample baths, galleries, and saloons, and supplied with a great variety of vines and other fruit trees. In these he would sail in the daytime along the coast of Campania, feasting amid dancing and concerts of music. In building his palaces and villas, there was nothing he desired to effect so much, in defiance of all reason, as what was considered impossible. Accordingly, moles were formed in the deep and raging sea, rocks of the hardest stone cut away, plains raised to the height of mountains with a vast mass of earth, and the tops of mountains levelled by digging; and all these were to be executed with incredible celerity, for the least default was punishable with death. To sum up, not reckoning particulars, he spent enormous sums and the whole treasures which had been amassed by Tiberius Caesar, amounting to two thousand seven hundred millions of sesterces, within less than a year.

## 38

Having therefore quite exhausted these funds, and being in want of money, he turned his mind to plundering the people, by every nicety of false accusation, confiscation, and taxation that could be invented. He affirmed plainly that no one had any right to the freedom of Rome, although their ancestors had acquired it for themselves and their posterity, unless they were sons; for that none beyond that degree ought to be considered as *posterity*. When the grants of the Divine Julius and Augustus were produced to him, he only said that he was very sorry they were obsolete and invalid. He also charged all those with making false returns, who, after the taking of the census, had by any means whatever increased their property. He annulled the wills of all who had been centurions of the first rank, as testimonies of their base ingratitude, if from the beginning of Tiberius' reign they had not left either that prince or himself their heir. He also set aside the wills of all others, if any person only pretended to say that they designed at their death to leave Caesar their heir. The public becoming terrified at this proceeding, he was now appointed joint heir with their friends, and in the case of parents with their children, by persons unknown to him. Those who lived any considerable time after making such a will, he said were only making sport of him; and accordingly he sent many of them poisoned cakes. He used to try such causes himself; fixing previously the sum he proposed to raise during the sitting and, after he had secured it, quitting the tribunal. Impatient of the least delay, he condemned by a single sentence forty persons, against whom there were different charges; bragging to

Caesonia when she awoke, 'how much business he had dispatched while she was taking her mid-day sleep'. He exposed to sale by auction the remains of the apparatus used in the public spectacles; and exacted such biddings, and raised the prices so high, that some of the purchasers were ruined and bled themselves to death. There is a well-known story told of Aponius Saturninus, who, happening to fall asleep as he sat on a bench at the sale, Caius called out to the auctioneer not to overlook the venerable personage who nodded to him so often; and accordingly the auctioneer addressed the bids to him, raising the price at each nod, as if he thereby received assent, the while the luckless individual remained in total unconsciousness of what was going on, until there were fastened upon him thirteen gladiators at the sum of nine millions of sesterces.

## 39

Having also sold in Gaul all the jewels, apparel, furniture, slaves, and even freedmen belonging to his sisters, at prodigious prices, after their condemnation, he was so much delighted with his gains that he sent to Rome for all the furniture of the old palace; pressing for its conveyance all the carriages let to hire in the city, with the horses and mules belonging to the bakers, so that they often wanted bread at Rome; and many who had suits at law in progress, lost their causes, because they could not make their appearance in due time according to their recognisances. In the selling of this furniture, there was no fraud, no guile, no impudent imposture that he would not employ. Sometimes he would rail at the bidders for being niggardly, and ask them 'if they were not ashamed to be richer than he was'; at another, he would affect to be sorry that the property of princes should be passing into the hands of private persons. He had received intelligence that a rich provincial had given two hundred thousand sesterces to his chamberlains for arranging that by some subtle shift he might be admitted among the guests of his table; and he was not displeased to find that the honour of supping with him was rated so highly. The next day, as the same person was sitting at the sale, he sent him some frivolous trifle (I know not precisely what), for which he told him he must pay two hundred thousand sesterces, and 'that he should sup with Caesar upon his own invitation.'

## 40

He levied new taxes, and such as were never before known, at first by the publicans, but afterwards, because their profit was enormous, by centurions and tribunes of the praetorian guards; no kind of property or persons being exempted from some form of tribute or other. For all eatables brought into the city, a certain excise was collected: for all law-suits or trials in whatever court, the fortieth part of the sum in dispute; and such as were convicted of compromising litigations were made liable to a penalty. Out of the daily wages of the porters, he received an eighth, and from the gains of common strumpets, what they received for one service. There was a clause in the law that all bawds who kept women for prostitution or sale should be liable to tribute, and that marriage itself should not be exempted.

## 41

These taxes being imposed, but the act by which they were levied never submitted to public inspection, great grievances were experienced from the want of sufficient knowledge of the law. At length, on the urgent demands of the Roman people, he published the law, but it was written in a very small hand and posted up in a corner, so that no one could make a copy of it. To leave no sort of gains untried, he opened brothels in the Palatium, with a number of cells, furnished suitably to the dignity of the place, in which married women and freeborn youths were ready for the reception of customers. He likewise sent his nomenclators about the Forums and courts, to invite by name young men and old to come thither and satisfy their lusts. He was ready to lend money for this purpose upon interest, and had clerks in attendance to take down their names in public, as good friends who contributed to the emperor's revenue. Another method of acquiring money, which he did not disdain, was gaming; which, by the help of lying and perjury, he turned to considerable account. Leaving once the management of his play to his partner in the game, he stepped into the court, and observing two wealthy Roman knights passing by he commanded them to be apprehended at once, and their estates confiscated; which being done, he returned to the game, leaping for joy, and boasting that he had never had a luckier hand at dice.

## 42

Upon the birth of his daughter, complaining of his poverty and the heavy burdens that lay upon him not only as an emperor but a father, he meekly accepted the voluntary contributions of all men toward the girl's maintenance and fortune. He declared also by an edict, that he would receive New Year's gifts on the kalends of January following; and accordingly stood in the vestibule of his house, to take the presents which people of all ranks threw down before him by the handful and lapful. Finally, being seized with an uncontrollable desire of feeling money, he would often take off his slippers, and walk barefoot over great heaps of it spread upon the spacious floor, and then, laying himself down, wallow bodily among the gold pieces.

## 43

Only once in his life did he take an active part in military affairs, and then not from any set purpose, but during his journey to Mevania to see the grove and river of Clitumnus. Being recommended to recruit a body of Batavians, who attended him, he resolved upon an expedition into Germany. Immediately he drew together several legions and auxiliary forces from all quarters, and made everywhere new levies with the utmost rigour. Collecting supplies of all kinds, such as never had been assembled upon the like occasion, he set forward on his march, and pursued it sometimes with so much haste and precipitation that the praetorian cohorts were obliged, contrary to custom, to pack their standards on horses or mules and so follow him. At other times, he would march so slowly and luxuriously that he was carried in a litter by eight men; ordering the roads to be swept by the people of the neighbouring towns and sprinkled with water to lay the dust.

## 44

On arriving at the camp, in order to show himself an active general and severe disciplinarian, he cashiered the lieutenants who came up late with the auxiliary forces from different quarters. In reviewing the army, he deprived of their companies most of the centurions of the first rank, who had now served their legal time in the wars, and some whose time would have expired in a few days; alleging against them their age and infirmity; and railing at the covetous disposition of the rest of them, he reduced the bounty due to those who had served out their time to the sum of six thousand sesterces. Though he only received the submission of Adminius, the son of Cunobeline, a British king, who being driven from his native country by his father, came over to him with a small body of troops; yet, as if the whole island had been surrendered to him, he dispatched magnificent letters to Rome, ordering the bearers to proceed in their carriages directly up to the Forum and the senate house, and not to deliver the letters but to the consuls in the temple of Mars, and in the presence of a full assembly of the senators.

## 45

Soon after this, there being no hostilities, he ordered a few Germans of his guard to be carried over and placed in concealment on the other side of the Rhine, and word to be brought him after dinner that an enemy was advancing with great impetuosity. This being accordingly done, he immediately threw himself, with his friends and a party of the praetorian knights, into the adjoining wood where, lopping branches from the trees, and forming trophies of them, he returned by torchlight, upbraiding those who did not follow him with timorousness and cowardice; but he presented the companions and sharers of his victory with crowns of a new form, and under a new name, having the sun, moon, and stars represented on them, and which he called *Exploratoriae*. Again, some hostages were by his order taken from the school, and privately sent off; upon notice of which he immediately rose from table, pursued them with the cavalry, as if they had run away, and coming up with them, brought them back in fetters; proceeding to an intemperate pitch of ostentation likewise in this military comedy. Upon his again sitting down to table, it being reported to him that the troops were all reassembled, he ordered them to sit down as they were, in their armour, animating them in the words of that well known verse of Virgil:

*Durate, et vosmet rebus servate secundis —*

Bear up, and save yourselves for better days.

In the meantime, he sharply rebuked the senate and people of Rome, in a proclamation, 'For revelling and frequenting the diversions of the circus and theatre, and enjoying themselves at their villas, while their emperor fought battles and exposed himself to so many perils.'

## 46

At last, as if he meant to make war in earnest, he drew up his army upon the shore of the ocean, with his ballistas and other engines of war, and while no one could imagine what he intended to do, on a sudden commanded them to gather up the sea shells, and fill their helmets as well as the folds of their dress with them, which he termed 'the spoils of the ocean due to the Capitol and the Palatium'. In commemoration of this brave victory, he raised a lofty tower, upon which, as at Pharos, he ordered lights to be burnt in the night time, for the direction of ships at sea; and then promising the soldiers a donative of a hundred denarii a man, as if he had surpassed all former precedents of liberality, 'Go your ways,' said he, 'and be merry: go, ye are rich.'

## 47

Turning his mind now to preparations for his triumph, he selected, over and above the prisoners and deserters from the barbarian armies, the men of greatest stature that were to be found in Gaul, such as he said were fittest to grace a triumph, with some of the chiefs, and reserved them to appear in the procession; obliging them not only to dye their hair yellow, and let it grow long, but to learn the German language and assume the names commonly used in that country. He ordered likewise the galleys in which he had entered the ocean to be conveyed to Rome a great part of the way by land; and wrote to his procurators and officers in the city, 'to make preparations for a triumph against his arrival, at as small expense as might be; but on a scale such as had never been seen before, since they had full power over all men's property.'

# 48

Before he quitted the province, he planned the execution of a most horrible outrage: to massacre the legions which had long ago mutinied upon the death of Augustus, because they had seized and detained by force his father, Germanicus, their commander, and himself, then an infant, in the camp. And though he was with great difficulty dissuaded from this rash attempt, yet neither the most urgent entreaties nor representations could prevent him from persisting in the design of decimating these legions. Accordingly, he ordered them to assemble unarmed, without so much as their swords; and then surrounded them with armed horse. But finding that many of them, suspecting that violence was intended, were making off, to arm in their own defence, he abandoned the assembly and fled to Rome, diverting all his bitterness and cruelty toward the senate, whom he publicly threatened, to avert from himself the odious rumours excited by his villainous conduct. Among other pretexts of offence, he complained that he was defrauded of a triumph, which was his just due, though he had just before forbidden, upon pain of death, any honour to be decreed him.

# 49

In his march, he was waited upon by deputies from the senatorian order, entreating him to hasten his return. He replied to them, 'I will come, I will come, and this with me,' striking at the same time the hilt of his sword. He issued likewise this proclamation: 'I am coming, but for those only who wish for me, the equestrian order and the people; for I shall no longer treat the senate as their fellow citizen or prince.' He forbad any of the senators to come to meet him; and either abandoning or deferring his triumph, he entered the city in ovation on his birthday. Within four months from this period he was slain, after he had perpetrated monstrous crimes, and while he was plotting still greater. He had entertained the design of removing to Antium, but only after having first massacred the most honourable and important persons of the equestrian and senatorian orders. And to remove all doubt that he intended to execute this plan, there were found in his secret cabinet two books bearing different titles; one being called *The Sword,* and the other, *The Dagger.* They both contained private marks, and the names of those who were appointed to die. There was found also a large chest, filled with a variety of poisons which being afterwards thrown into the sea by order of Claudius are said to have so infected the waters that swarms of dead fishes were cast by the tide upon the neighbouring shores.

## 50

He was very tall in stature, of a pale complexion, ill-shaped, with very slender neck and legs, sunken eyes and hollow temples, a broad and furrowed forehead, his hair thin, and the crown of the head bald. The other parts of his body were very hairy. On this account, it was reckoned a capital crime for any person to look down from above, as he was passing by, or so much as name a *goat.* His countenance, which was naturally stern and frightful, he purposely made more so, composing it before a mirror into the most horrible contortions. He was neither healthful in body nor sound in mind, being subject, as a child, to the falling sickness. When he arrived at the age of manhood, he endured fatigue tolerably well; but still, occasionally, he was liable to a faintness, during which he remained incapable of any exertion. He was not insensible to the infirmity of his mind, and sometimes had thoughts of retiring to Anticyra to clear his brain. It is believed that his wife Caesonia administered to him a love potion which threw him into a frenzy. What most of all troubled him was want of sleep, for he seldom had more than three or four hours' rest in a night; and even then his repose was not sound, but haunted by strange dreams; he fancied, among other things, that a form representing the ocean spoke to him. Being therefore often weary with lying awake so long, sometimes he sat up in his bed; at others, he walked in the longest porticos about the house, and from time to time invoked, and looked out for, the approach of daylight.

## 51

To this crazy constitution of his mind, I think I may properly attribute two faults which he had, of a nature opposed one to the other; namely, an excessive confidence and the most abject timidity. For he, who affected so much to despise the gods, was ready to shut his eyes, and wrap up his head in his cloak at the least thunder and lightning; and if it became violent, he got up and hid himself under his bed. In his visit to Sicily, after ridiculing many strange objects which that country affords, he ran away suddenly in the night from Messini, so frightened was he by the smoke and rumbling at the summit of Mount Aetna. And though he was so full of threats and menaces against the barbarians, yet upon passing a narrow defile in Germany in his light car, surrounded by a strong body of his troops, when someone chanced to remark, 'There would be no small confusion among us, if an enemy were to appear,' he immediately mounted his horse, and rode towards the bridges in great haste; but finding them blocked up with camp followers and baggage waggons, he was in such a hurry, that he caused himself to be carried in men's hands over the heads of the crowd. Soon afterwards, upon hearing that the Germans were again in rebellion, he prepared to quit Rome, and equipped a fleet; comforting himself with this consideration, that if the enemy should prove victorious and possess themselves of the heights of the Alps, as the Cimbri had done, or of the city, as the Senones formerly did, he should still have in reserve the transmarine provinces. Hence it was, I suppose, that it occurred to his assassins to invent the story, intended to pacify the troops who mutinied at his death, that he had laid violent hands upon himself, in a fit of terror occasioned by the news brought him of the defeat of his army.

## 52

His apparel not only did not conform to any national or civil fashion: it was not even peculiar to the male sex, or appropriate to mere mortals. He often went abroad clad in a short coat of stout cloth, richly embroidered in many colours, and studded with gems, in a tunic with long sleeves, and wearing bracelets. Sometimes he was seen all in silks and habited like a woman; at other times in the crepidae or buskins; sometimes in the sort of shoes worn by the light-armed soldiers, or in the sock used by women, and commonly with a golden beard fixed to his chin, holding in his hand a thunderbolt, a trident, or a caduceus, marks of distinction belonging to the gods only. Some-times he even appeared in the costume of Venus. He constantly wore the triumphal ornaments, even before his expedition, and sometimes the breastplate of Alexander the Great, taken out of his coffin.

## 53

Of all the liberal sciences, he applied himself least to profound literature and sound learning, and most to eloquence; being indeed by nature of a fluent and ready tongue; and in his perorations, when he was moved to anger, there was an abundant flow of words and periods. In speaking, his action was vehement and his voice so strong, that he was heard at a great distance. When concluding an address, he would threaten to draw 'the sword of his lucubration', holding a milder and freer style in such contempt, that he said of Seneca, who was then much admired, that he 'wrote only detached essays', and that 'his language was nothing but sand without lime'. He often composed answers to the speeches of successful orators; and employed himself in devising accusations or vindications of eminent persons who were impeached before the senate; and gave his vote for or against the party accused, according to his success in speaking, inviting the equestrian order, by proclamation, to hear him.

## 54

By diligent practice, he also acquired a mastery of several other arts of different kinds, such as fencing, charioteering, singing and dancing. In fencing, he practised with the weapons used in war; and he drove the chariot in circuses built in several places. He responded so passionately to singing and dancing, that he could not refrain, in the theatre, from singing with the tragedians and imitating the gestures of the actors, either by way of approval or correction. A night exhibition which he had ordered the day he was slain, was thought to be intended for no other reason than to take the opportunity afforded by the licentiousness of the season to make his first appearance upon the stage. Sometimes, also, he danced in the night. Summoning once to the Palatium, in the second watch of the night, three men of consular rank, who feared the words of the message, he placed them on the proscenium of the stage, and then suddenly came bursting out, with a loud noise of flutes and castanets, dressed in a mantle and tunic reaching down to his heels. Having danced out a song, he retired. Yet he who had acquired such dexterity in other exercises, never learnt to swim.

## 55

Those for whom he once conceived a fondness, he favoured beyond all reason. He used to kiss Mnester, the pantomimic actor, publicly in the theatre; and if any person made the least noise while he was performing, he would order him to be dragged from his seat, and scourged him with his own hand. A Roman knight once chanced to make a slight stir, whereupon he sent him, by a centurion, an order to depart immediately for Ostia, and carry a letter from him to King Ptolemy in Mauritania. The letter was couched in these words: 'Do neither good nor harm to the bearer.' He made certain gladiators captains of his German guards. Those called Murmillones, he deprived of some of their arms. One Columbus coming off with victory in a combat, but being slightly wounded, he ordered some poison to be poured in the wound, which he thence called Columbinum. For thus it was certainly named with his own hand in a list of other poisons. He was so greatly devoted to the faction of charioteers whose colours were green that he supped and lodged for some time constantly in the stable where their horses were kept. At a certain revel, he made a present of two millions of sesterces to one Cythicus, a driver of a chariot. The day before the Circensian games, he used to send his soldiers to enjoin silence in the neighbourhood, that the repose of his horse *Incitatus* might not be disturbed. For this favourite animal, besides a marble stable, an ivory manger, purple housings, and a jewelled frontlet, he appointed a house, with a retinue of slaves, and fine furniture, for the reception of such as were invited in the horse's name to sup with him. It is even said that he intended to appoint him consul.

## 56

In this mad and riotous career, there were many persons who lacked neither the will nor the courage to assassinate him; but one or two conspiracies being detected, and others postponed for want of opportunity, at last two men concerted a plan together and accomplished their purpose, not without the privity of some of the greatest favourites among his freedmen, and the prefects of the praetorian guards; because having been named, though falsely, as accessories in one conspiracy against him, they perceived that they were suspected and become objects of his hatred. For he had immediately endeavoured to render them odious to the sóldiery, by drawing his sword and protesting that he would die by his own hand, 'if they also thought him worthy of death'; and even afterward he was continually accusing them to one another, and setting them all mutually at variance. The conspirators having agreed to fall upon him as he returned at noon from the Palatine games, Cassius Chaerea, tribune of the praetorian guards, claimed the privilege of making the onset. This Chaerea was now an elderly man, and had been often reproached by Caius for effeminacy. When he came for the watchword, Caius would give 'Priapus', or 'Venus'; and if on any occasion he returned thanks, would offer him his hand to kiss, making with his fingers a gesture of obscene significance.

## 57

Many prodigies were observed, presaging his eventual murder. The statue of Jupiter at Olympia, which he had ordered to be taken down and brought to Rome, suddenly burst out into such a violent fit of laughter, that, the machines employed in the work giving way, the workmen took to their heels. When this accident took place, there came up a man named Cassius, who said that he was commanded in a dream to sacrifice a bull to Jupiter. The Capitol at Capua was struck with lightning upon the ides of March; as was also, at Rome, the apartment of the chief porter of the Palatium. Some construed the latter as an omen that the master of the place was in danger from his own guards; and the other they regarded as a sign that an illustrious person would be cut off, as had happened before on that day. Sylla, the astrologer, being consulted by him respecting his nativity, assured him, 'That death would unavoidably and speedily befall him.' The oracle of Fortune at Antium likewise forewarned him of Cassius; on which account he had given orders for putting to death Cassius Longinus, at that time proconsul of Asia, not considering that Chaerea also bore that name. The day preceding his death, he dreamt that he was standing in heaven near the throne of Jupiter, who spurned him with the great toe of his right foot and threw him headlong down to earth. Some things which happened the very day of his death, and only a little before it, were likewise considered as ominous presages of that event. While offering sacrifice, he was besprinkled with the blood of a flamingo. And Mnester, the pantomimic actor, performed in a play which the tragedian Neoptolemus had formerly acted at the games in which Philip, the king of Macedon, was slain. And in the piece called Laureolus, in which the principal actor, running out in a hurry, and falling, vomited blood, several of the inferior actors vying with each other to give the best specimen of their art, made the whole stage flow with blood. A spectacle had been intended to be performed that night, in which the fables of the infernal regions were to be represented by Egyptians and Ethiopians.

## 58                                    A.U.C. 794

On the ninth of the kalends of February and about the seventh hour of the day, after debating with himself whether he should rise to dinner, (as his stomach was disordered by an excess of food eaten the day before), at last, by the advice of his friends, he came forth. In the vaulted passage through which he had to pass, some boys of noble extraction, who had been brought from Asia to act upon the stage, were waiting for him in a private corridor, and he stopped to see and speak to them; and had not the leader of the party said that he was suffering from cold, he would have gone back and made them perform immediately. Respecting what followed, two different accounts are given. Some say, that while he was speaking to the boys, Chaerea came behind him, and gave him a heavy blow on the neck with his sword, first crying out: 'Take this'; and then a tribune, by name Cornelius Sabinus, another of the conspirators, ran him through the breast. Others say, that the crowd being kept at a distance by some centurions who were in the plot, Sabinus came, according to custom, for the word, and that Caius gave him 'Jupiter', upon which Chaerea cried out, 'Be it so!' and then, on his looking round, clove one of his jaws with a blow. As he lay on the ground, crying out that he was still alive, the rest dispatched him with thirty wounds. For the word agreed upon among them all was 'Strike again'. Some likewise ran their swords through his private parts. Upon the first noise and outcry, the litter bearers came running in with their poles to defend him, and, immediately afterwards, his German body guards, who killed some of the assassins, and also some senators who had no concern in the affair.

## 59

He lived twenty-nine years, and reigned three years, ten months, and eight days. His body was conveyed secretly into the Lamian Gardens, where it was half burnt upon a funeral pile hastily raised, and then covered with some clots of earth carelessly cast over it. It was afterwards disinterred by his sisters, on their return from exile, burnt to ashes, and buried. Before this was done, it is well known that the keepers of the gardens were greatly disturbed by apparitions; and that not a night passed without some terrible alarm or other in the house where he was slain, until it was consumed with fire. His wife Caesonia was killed with him, being stabbed by a centurion; and his daughter had her brains knocked out against a wall.

## 60

What the condition of the republic was in those days, any one may gather from the following particulars. When his death was made public, the news was not immediately credited; and there went forth a rumour that a report of his being killed had been contrived and spread by himself, with the view of discovering how they stood affected towards him. Nor had the conspirators fixed upon anyone to succeed him. The senators were so unanimous in their resolution to assert the liberty of their country, that the consuls assembled them at first, not in the usual place of meeting, because it was named after Julius Caesar, but in the Capitol. Some proposed to abolish the memory of the Caesars, and level their temples with the ground. It was particularly remarked on this occasion that all the Caesars who had the praenomen of Caius died by the sword, from the Caius Caesar who was slain in the times of Cinna.

# Tiberius Claudius Drusus Caesar

Livia, having married Augustus when she was with child, gave birth within three months to Drusus, the father of Claudius Caesar, who had at first the praenomen of Decimus, but afterwards that of Nero; and it was suspected that this Drusus was begotten in adultery by Augustus, his supposed father-in-law. After his birth, the following verse was immediately in every one's mouth:

> Nine months for common births the fates decree;
> But, for the great, reduce the term to three.

Drusus, during the period when he was quaestor and praetor, commanded in the Rhaetian and German wars, and was the first of all the Roman generals who navigated the Northern Ocean; and on the farther side of the Rhine, he made some prodigious trenches, which to this day are called by his name. He overthrew the enemy in several battles, and drove them far back into the depths of the desert. Nor did he desist from pursuing them, until an apparition, in the likeness of a barbarian woman of more than human proportions, forbad him, in the Latin tongue, to advance any farther. For these achievements, he had the honour of an ovation, and the triumphal ornaments. After his praetorship, he immediately entered on the office of consul, and returning again to Germany, died of disease, in the summer encampment, which thence obtained the name of 'The Unlucky Camp'. His corpse was conveyed to Rome by the principal persons of the several municipalities and colonies upon the road, being met and received by the recorders of each place, and buried in the Campus Martius. In honour of him, the army erected a monument, round which the soldiers used, annually, upon a certain day, to march in solemn procession, and persons deputed from the several cities of Gaul performed religious rites. The senate, likewise, decreed for him, among other honours, a triumphal arch of marble with trophies, in the Appian Way, and gave the cognomen of Germanicus to him and his posterity. In him the civil and military virtues were equally balanced; for, beside his victories, he gained from the enemy the *Spolia Optima*, and frequently marked out the German chiefs in the midst of their army and encountered them in single combat, at the utmost hazard of his life. He likewise often declared that he would, some time or other, if possible, restore the ancient government. On this account, I suppose, some have ventured to affirm that Augustus was jealous of him and recalled him; and, because he made no haste to comply with the order, made away with him by poison. This I mention, that I may not be guilty of any omission, more than because I think it either true or probable; considering that Augustus loved him so much when living, that he always, in his wills, made him joint heir with his sons, as he once declared in the senate; and upon his decease, extolled him in a speech to the people to that degree that he prayed the gods 'to make his Caesars like him, and to grant himself as honourable an exit out of this world as they had given him'. And, not content with inscribing upon his tomb an epitaph in verse composed by himself, he wrote likewise the history of his life in prose. He had by the younger Antonia several children, but left behind him at his death only three, namely, Germanicus, Livilla, and Claudius.

2

A.U.C. 744

This Claudius was born at Lyons, in the consulship of Julius Antonius and Fabius Africanus, upon the first of August, the very day upon which an altar was first dedicated there to Augustus. He was named Tiberius Claudius Drusus, but soon afterwards, upon the adoption of his elder brother in the Julian family, he assumed the cognomen of Germanicus. He was left an infant by his father, and during his whole childhood and part of his youth, he was assailed by a variety of obstinate disorders, insomuch that his mind and body being greatly enfeebled, he was, even after his arrival at the age of manhood, never thought sufficiently qualified for any public or private employment. He was, therefore, during a long time, and even after the expiration of his minority, under the direction of a pedagogue, who, he complains in a certain memoir, 'was a barbarous wretch, and formerly superintendent of the mule drivers, who was selected for his governor on purpose to correct him cruelly on every trifling pretext'. On account of this crazy constitution of body and mind, at the spectacle of gladiators, which he gave the people jointly with his brother, in honour of his father's memory, he presided, wrapped up in a pallium, which was not the accustomed fashion. When he assumed his virile gown, he was carried in a litter at midnight to the Capitol, without the usual ceremony.

## 3

Nevertheless, from his very childhood he applied himself most diligently to the study of the liberal sciences, and often published specimens of his skill in each of them. But he could never, despite his efforts, attain to any post of dignity in the government, or afford any hope of arriving at distinction thereafter. His mother, Antonia, frequently called him 'an abortion of a man, that had been only begun, but never finished, by nature'. And when she reproved anyone for his foolishness, she would say, 'that he was more sottish than her son Claudius'. His grandmother, Augusta, always treated him with the utmost contempt, spoke to him but rarely, and when she did admonish him upon any occasion, it was in writing, very curt and sharp, or by messengers. His sister Livilla, upon hearing that he was about to be made emperor, openly and in a loud voice expressed her indignation that the Roman people should experience a fate so hard and so much below their grandeur. To exhibit the opinion, both favourable and otherwise, entertained concerning him by Augustus, his great uncle, I have here set down some extracts from the letters of that emperor:

## 4

'I have had some conversation with Tiberius, according to your desire, my dear Livia, as to what must be done with your grandson, Claudius, at the games of Mars. We are both agreed in this, that once for all we ought to determine what course to take with him. For if he be really sound and, so to speak, quite right in his intellects, why should we hesitate to promote him by the same steps and degrees as we did his brother? But if we find him below par, and deficient both in body and mind, we must beware of giving occasion for him and ourselves to be laughed at by the world, which is ready enough to make such matters the subject of mirth and derision. For we never shall be easy, if we are always to be debating upon every occasion of this kind, without settling, in the first instance, whether he be really capable of public offices or not. Concerning the things about which you consult me at the present moment, I am not averse to his taking charge of the priests' dining chamber, in the games of Mars, if he will suffer himself to be governed by his kinsman, Silanus's son, that he may do nothing to make the people stare, and deride him. But I do not approve of his witnessing the Circensian games from the Pulvinar. He will be there exposed to view in the very front of the theatre. Nor do I like that he should go to the Alban Mount, or be at Rome during the Latin festival. For if he be capable of attending his brother to the mount, why is he not made prefect of the city? Thus, my dear Livia, you have my thoughts upon the matter. In my opinion, we ought to settle this affair once for all, that we may not be always in suspense between hope and fear. You may, if you think proper, give your kinsman Antonia this part of my letter to read.'

In another letter, he writes: 'I shall invite the youth, Tiberius, every day during your absence, to supper, that he may not sup alone with his friends Sulpicius and Athenodorus. I wish the poor creature were more cautious and attentive in the choice of someone, whose manners, air, and gait might be proper for his imitation: "In things of consequence he sadly fails." Where his mind does not run astray, he discovers a noble disposition.' In a third letter, he says, 'Let me die, my dear Livia, if I am not astonished that the declamation of your grandson, Claudius, should please me; for how he who talks so ill, should be able to declaim so clearly and properly, I cannot imagine.' There is no doubt but that Augustus, after this, came to a resolution upon the subject, and accordingly left him invested with no other honour than that of the Augural priesthood; naming him among the heirs of the third degree who were but distantly allied to his family, for a sixth part of his estate only, with a legacy of no more than eight hundred thousand sesterces.

# 5

Upon his requesting some office in the state, Tiberius granted him the honorary appendages of the consulship, and when he pressed for a legitimate appointment, the emperor wrote word back that 'he sent him forty gold pieces for his expenses, during the festivals of the Saturnalia and Sigillarea.' Upon this, laying aside all hope of advancement, he resigned himself entirely to a life of ease and pleasure; living in great seclusion, one while in his gardens, or a villa which he had near the city; another while in Campania, where he passed his time in the lowest society; by which means he incurred, besides the old infamous note of dullness and sluggishness, an ill name for drunkenness and gaming.

# 6

Notwithstanding this manner of living, much respect was shown him both in public and private. The equestrian order twice made choice of him to intercede on their behalf; once to obtain from the consuls the favour of bearing on their shoulders the corpse of Augustus to Rome, and a second time to congratulate him upon the death of Sejanus. When he entered the theatre, they used to rise and put off their cloaks. The senate likewise decreed that he should be added to the number of the Augustal college of priests, who were chosen by lot; and soon afterwards, when his house was burnt down, that it should be rebuilt at the public charge; and that he should have the privilege of giving his vote among the men of consular rank. This decree was, however, repealed; Tiberius insisting that he be excused on account of his imbecility, and promising to make good the loss out of his own purse. But at his death, he named him in his will, among his heirs, for a third part of his estate, leaving him besides a legacy of two millions of sesterces, and expressly recommending him to the armies, the senate and people of Rome, among his other relations.

## 7

At length Caius Caligula, his brother's son, upon his advancement to the empire, endeavouring to gain the affections of the public by all manner of blandishment, Claudius also was admitted to public offices, and held the consulship jointly with his nephew for two months. As he was entering the Forum for the first time with the fasces, an eagle which was flying that way, alighted upon his right shoulder. A second consulship was also allotted him to commence at the expiration of the fourth year. He sometimes presided at the public spectacles, as the representative of Caius; being always, on those occasions, complimented with the acclamations of the people, wishing him all good fortune, sometimes under the title of the emperor's uncle, and sometimes under that of Germanicus' brother.

## 8

Yet he still lived subject to the contumelious reproaches of the world. If at any time he came in late to supper, no one stirred to make room for him, until he had walked round the room some time to find a place; likewise, whenever he fell asleep after eating, which was habitual with him, the company used to throw olive stones and date stones at him. And the buffoons who attended would wake him, as if it were only in jest, with a cane or a whip. Sometimes they would put slippers upon his hands, as he lay snoring, that he might, upon suddenly awaking, rub his face therewith.

## 9

He sometimes was threatened with considerable danger; first, in his consulship; for, having been too remiss in providing and erecting the statues of Caius's brothers, Nero and Drusus, he was very near being deprived of his office; and afterwards he was continually harassed with informations against him by one or the other, sometimes even by his own domestics. When the conspiracy of Lepidus and Gaetulicus was discovered, being sent with some other deputies into Germany to congratulate the emperor upon the occasion, he was in danger of his life; Caius being greatly enraged, and loudly complaining that his uncle was sent to him, as if he was a boy who wanted a governor. Some even say that he was thrown into a river in his travelling dress. From this period, he voted in the senate always the last of the members of consular rank; being called upon after the rest, on purpose to humiliate him. A charge for the forgery of a will was also allowed to be prosecuted, though he had only signed it as a witness. At last, being obliged to pay eight millions of sesterces on entering upon a new office of priesthood, he was driven to such straits in his private affairs, that in order to discharge his bond to the treasury, he was under the necessity of exposing to sale his whole estate, by an order of the prefects.

IO                    A.U.C. 794

Having spent the greater part of his life in passing through these and similar troubles, he came at last, in the fiftieth year of his age, to the empire, and that by a very strange and surprising trick of fortune. Being among others prevented from approaching Caius by the conspirators, who dispersed the crowd, he retired into an apartment called the Hermaeum, under colour of a desire for privacy; and soon afterwards, being terrified by the rumour of Caius's murder, he crept into an adjoining balcony, where he hid himself behind the hangings of the door. A common soldier, who happened to pass that way, espied his feet, and desirous of knowing who he was, pulled him out; when, immediately recognizing him, he threw himself in a great fright at his feet, and saluted him by the title of emperor. He then conducted him to his fellow soldiers, who were all in a great rage, and irresolute what they should do. They put him into a litter, and as the slaves of the palace had all fled, took their turns in carrying him on their shoulders, and so brought him into the camp, amazed and trembling; the people who met him on the way pitying his situation, as if he were some poor innocent being haled to execution. Being received within the ramparts, he continued all night with the sentries on guard, and recovered somewhat from his fright, but in no great hopes of the succession. For the consuls, with the senate and civic troops, had possessed themselves of the Forum and Capitol, with the purpose of restoring the public liberty; and he being sent for likewise, by a tribune of the people, to the senate house to give his advice upon the present juncture of affairs, returned answer: 'I am under constraint, and cannot possibly come.' The day afterwards, the senate being dilatory in their proceedings and worn out by divisions among themselves, while the people who surrounded the senate house shouted that they would have one master, naming Claudius, he suffered the soldiers assembled under arms to swear allegiance to him, promising them fifteen thousand sesterces a man; he being the first of the Caesars who purchased the submission of the soldiers with money.

## II

Having thus established himself in power, his first object was to abolish all remembrance of the two preceding days, in which a revolution in the state had been canvassed. Accordingly, he passed an act of perpetual oblivion and pardon for everything said or done during that time; and this he faithfully observed, with the exception only of putting to death a few tribunes and centurions concerned in the conspiracy against Caius, both as an example, and because he had intelligence that they had also planned his own murder. He now turned his mind to the duties of piety and respect towards the memory of his relations. His most solemn and customary oath was, 'By Augustus'. He prevailed upon the senate to decree divine honours to his grandmother Livia, with a chariot in the Circensian procession drawn by elephants, as had been appointed for Augustus; and public offerings to the shades of his parents. Besides which, he instituted Circensian games for his father, to be celebrated every year, upon his birthday, and, for his mother, a chariot to be drawn through the circus; with the title of Augusta, which had been refused by his grandmother. To the memory of his brother, Germanicus, to which, upon all occasions, he showed a great regard, he gave a Greek comedy, to be exhibited in the public diversions at Naples, and awarded the crown for it, according to the sentence of the judges in that solemnity. Nor did he omit to make honourable and grateful mention of Mark Antony; declaring by a proclamation, 'That he the more earnestly insisted upon the observation of his father Drusus's birthday, because it was likewise that of his grand-father Antony.' He completed the marble arch near Pompey's theatre, which had formerly been decreed by the senate in honour of Tiberius, his uncle, but which had been neglected. And though he cancelled all the acts of Caius, yet he forbad the day of his assassination, notwithstanding it was that of his own accession to the empire, to be reckoned among the festivals.

## 12

But in taking honours upon himself he was sparing, setting aside the title of emperor, and refusing all excessive honours. He celebrated the marriage of his daughter and the birthday of a grandson with great privacy, at home. He recalled no banished person, without a decree of the senate: and requested of them permission for the prefect of the military tribunes and praetorian guards to attend him in the senate house, and also that they would be pleased to bestow upon his procurators judicial authority in the provinces. He asked of the consuls likewise the privilege of holding fairs upon his private estate. He frequently assisted the magistrates in the trial of causes, as one of their assessors. And when they gave public spectacles, he would rise up with the rest of the spectators, and salute them both by words and gestures. When the tribunes of the people came to him while he was on the tribunal, he excused himself, because, on account of the crowd, he could not hear them unless they stood. In a short time, he succeeded, by these means, in so ingratiating himself into the love and favour of the people, that when, upon his going to Ostia, a report was spread in the city that he had been waylaid and slain, the people never ceased cursing the soldiers for traitors and the senate as parricides, until one or two persons, and presently several others, were brought by the magistrates upon the rostra, who assured them that he was alive, and not far from the city, on his way home.

## 13

Yet these manifestations did not secure him from danger. Conspiracies were formed against him, not only by individuals separately, but by a faction; and at last his government was disturbed by a civil war. A low fellow was captured with a poniard about him, near his bedchamber, at midnight. Two men of the equestrian order were discovered waiting for him in the streets, armed with a tuck and a huntsman's dagger; one of them intending to attack him as he came out of the theatre, and the other as he was sacrificing in the temple of Mars. Gallus Asinius and Statilius Corvinus, grandsons of the famous orators, Pollio and Messala, formed a conspiracy against him, in which they engaged many of his freedmen and slaves. Furius Camillus Scribonianus, his lieutenant in Dalmatia, broke into rebellion, but was reduced in the space of five days; the legions which he had seduced from their oath of fidelity abandoning their purpose, upon alarm occasioned by unfavourable omens. For when orders were given them to march, to meet their new emperor, whether it was by accident, or a divine warning, the eagles could not be decorated, nor the standards pulled out of the ground.

## 14

Besides his former consulship, he held the office afterwards four times; the first two successively, but the following after an interval of four years each; the last for six months, the others for two; and the third, upon his being chosen in the room of a consul who died; which had never been done by any of the emperors before him. Whether he was consul or out of office, he was constant in his attendance at the courts for the administration of justice, even upon such days as were solemnly observed as days of rejoicing in his family, or by his friends; and sometimes upon the public festivals of ancient institution. Nor did he always adhere strictly to the letter of the laws, but overruled the rigour or lenity of many of their enactments, according to his sentiments of justice and equity. For where persons lost their suits by insisting upon more than appeared to be their due, before the judges of private causes he granted them the indulgence of a second trial. And in cases of those that were convicted of any great delinquency, he condemned them to be cast before the wild beasts: exceeding therein the ordinary punishment appointed by law.

## 15

But in the examination and conducting of causes, he was extremely variable; being at one time circumspect, wary and sagacious, at another inconsiderate and rash, sometimes frivolous, and like one bereft of reason. In correcting the roll of judges, he struck off the name of one who, concealing the privilege his children gave him to be excused from serving, had answered to his name, as too eager for the office. Another who was summoned before him in a cause of his own, and alleged that the affair did not properly come under the emperor's cognisance, but that of the ordinary judges, he ordered to plead the cause himself immediately before him, and show in a case of his own, how equitable a judge he would prove in that of other persons. When a woman was brought before him, who refused to acknowledge her own son, and there being no clear proof on either side, he ordered her to marry the young man; and so forced her to confess the truth and to take him as her child. He was much inclined to decide causes in favour of the parties who appeared, and against those who did not, without considering whether their absence was occasioned by their own fault, or by real necessity. On proclamation of a man's being convicted of forgery, and that he ought to have his hand cut off, he insisted that an executioner should be immediately sent for, with a Spanish sword and a block. A person who was a foreigner being prosecuted for falsely assuming the freedom of Rome, and a frivolous dispute arising between the advocates in the cause, whether he ought to make his appearance in the Roman or Grecian dress, to show his impartiality he commanded him to change his clothes several times according to the character he assumed in the accusation or defence. An anecdote is related of him, and believed to be true, that, in a particular cause, he delivered this preposterous sentence in writing: 'I am in favour of those who have spoken the truth', as if there were any sure means of determining truth except by carefully weighing the evidence. For these unbecoming pranks he suffered so much in the opinion of the world, that he was everywhere held in contempt. A person making an excuse for the non-appearance of a witness whom he had sent for from the provinces, declared it was impossible for him to appear, dissimulating the cause for some time: at last, after several demands as to what the reason might be, he answered: 'The man is dead'; to which Claudius replied: 'I think that is a sufficient excuse.' Another, thanking him for suffering a person who was prosecuted to make his defence by counsel, added: 'And yet it is no more than what is usual.' I have likewise heard some old men say that the advocates used to abuse his patience so grossly, that as he was going down from the tribunal, they would not only call him back, but also take hold of the cap of his coat, and sometimes catch him by the heels, to make him stay. That such behaviour, however strange, is not incredible, will appear from this anecdote. Some obscure Greek, who was a litigant, in the course of an altercation with him, let fall these words: 'You are an old fool.' It is certain that a Roman knight, who was prosecuted falsely by powerful enemies, on a charge of unnatural abuse of women, when he saw that common strumpets were summoned against him and allowed to give evidence, flung his writing style, and some books which he held, in his face, with such violence as to wound him severely in the cheek; at the same time upbraiding him in very harsh and offensive terms with his folly and cruelty.

## 16

He likewise assumed the censorship, which had been discontinued since the time that Paulus and Plancus had jointly held it; but this office also he held with an uneven hand and a variable mind. In his review of the knights, he dismissed without shame or disgrace a young man charged with many infamous villainies, only because his father testified of him in favourable terms; 'for,' said he, 'his father is his proper censor.' Another, who had a very bad name for despoiling maidens and for adulterous practices, he only admonished 'to indulge his youthful impulses more sparingly, or at least more cautiously'; adding, 'why must I know what wench you keep?' When, at the request of his friends, he had taken off a mark of infamy which he had set upon one knight's name, he said, 'Let the blot, however, remain.' He not only struck out of the list of judges, but likewise deprived of the freedom of Rome, an illustrious man of the highest provincial rank in Rome, only because he was ignorant of the Latin language. Nor in this review did he suffer any one to give an account of his conduct by an advocate, but obliged each man to speak for himself in the best way he could. He disgraced many, and some that little expected it, for a reason entirely without precedent, namely, for going out of Italy without his license; and one likewise, for having in his province been the familiar companion of a king; observing that, in former times, Rabirius Postumus had been prosecuted for treason, although he only went after Ptolemy to Alexandria for the purpose of securing payment of a debt. Having tried to inflict disgrace upon several others, he, to his own greater shame, found them generally innocent, such was the negligence of the inquisitors he had employed; those whom he charged with living in celibacy, with want of children, or estate, proving themselves to be husbands, fathers, and in affluent circumstances. One of the knights who was charged with stabbing himself, laid his bosom bare, to show that there was not the least mark of violence upon his body. The following incidents were remarkable in his censorship. He ordered a car, plated with silver and of very sumptuous workmanship, which was exposed for sale in the Sigillaria, to be purchased and broken in pieces before his eyes. He published twenty proclamations in one day, in one of which he advised the people, 'since the vintage was very plentiful, to have their casks well secured at the bung with pitch': and in another, he gave them to understand, 'that nothing would sooner cure the bite of a viper, than the sap of the yew tree'.

## 17                                    A.U.C. 797

He undertook only one expedition, and that was of short duration. The triumphal ornaments decreed him by the senate, he considered as beneath the majesty of an emperor, and was therefore resolved to have the honour of a real triumph. For this purpose, he selected Britain, which had never been attempted by any one since Julius Caesar, and was then chafing with rage, because the Romans would not give up some deserters. Accordingly, he set sail from Ostia, but was twice very near being wrecked by the boisterous wind called Circius, upon the coast of Liguria, and near the islands called Stoechades. Having travelled by land from Marseilles to Gessoriachum, he thence passed over to Britain; and within a few days after his arrival, without battle or bloodshed, part of the island submitted to him. So, in the sixth month after his departure, he returned to Rome, and triumphed in the most pompous manner; to witness which, he not only gave leave to governors of provinces to come to Rome, but even to some of the exiles. Among the spoils taken from the enemy, he fixed upon the pediment of his house in the Palatium a naval crown, in token of his having passed, and, as it were, conquered the ocean, and had it suspended near the civic crown which was there before. Messalina, his wife, followed his chariot in a covered litter. Those who had attained the honour of triumphal ornaments in the same war rode behind; the rest followed on foot, wearing the robe with the broad stripes. Crassus Frugi was mounted upon a horse richly caparisoned, in a robe embroidered with palm leaves, because this was the second time of his obtaining that honour.

## 18/19

He was at all times most solicitous that the city be well supplied with provisions. A dreadful fire breaking out in the Aemiliana, which lasted some time, he passed two nights in the Diribitorium, and the soldiers and gladiators not being in sufficient numbers to get it under control, he caused the magistrates to summon the people out of all the streets in the city to their assistance. Placing bags of money before him, he exhorted them to do their utmost towards quenching the fire, and promised to reward every one on the spot, according to their exertions. During a scarcity of corn and other provisions, caused by unseasonable weather which affected the crops for several successive years, he was stopped in the middle of the Forum by a mob, who so abused him, pelting him no less with reviling words than with fragments of broken bread, that he had some difficulty in escaping into the palace by a back door. He therefore resorted to all possible devices to bring provisions to the city, even in the winter. For he not only proposed sure profits to the merchants by indemnifying them against any loss that might befall them by storms at sea; but granted great privileges to those who built ships for that traffic. To a citizen of Rome he gave an exemption from the penalty of the Papia-Poppaean law; to one who had only the privilege of Latium, the freedom of the city; and to women, the rights which by law belonged to those who had four children: which enactments are in force to this day.

## 20

He completed some important public works, which, though not numerous, were very beneficial. The principal ones were: an aqueduct which had been begun by Caius; an emissary for the discharge of the waters of the Fucine lake, and the harbour of Ostia — although he knew that Augustus had refused to comply with the repeated application of the Marsians for one of these, and that the other had been several times intended by Julius Caesar, but as often abandoned on account of the difficulty of its execution. He brought to the city the cool and plentiful springs of the Claudian water, one of which is called Caeruleus, and the other Curtius and Albudinus, as likewise the river of the New Anio, in a stone canal; and distributed them into many beautiful reservoirs. The canal from the Fucine lake was undertaken as much for the sake of profit, as for the honour of the enterprise; for there were parties who offered to drain it at their own expense on condition of their having a grant of the land laid dry. With great difficulty, he completed a canal three miles in length, partly by cutting through, and partly by tunnelling, a mountain; thirty thousand men being regularly employed in the work for eleven years. He formed the harbour at Ostia by carrying out circular piers on the right and on the left, with a mole protecting, in deep water, the entrance of the port. For the surer foundation of this mole, he sunk the vessel in which the great obelisk had been brought from Egypt; and built upon piles a very lofty tower, in imitation of the Pharos at Alexandria, on which lights were kept burning to direct mariners in the night.

21

He often distributed largesses of corn and money among the people; and for their entertainment likewise he exhibited a great variety of magnificent spectacles, not only such as were familiar, and in the accustomed places, but some that had been newly planned, and others revived from ancient models, and these he sometimes set forth in places where nothing of the kind had been ever before attempted. In the games which he presented at the dedication of Pompey's theatre, which had been burnt down, and rebuilt by him, he presided upon a tribunal erected for him in the orchestra; having first paid his devotions, in the temple above, and then coming down through the centre of the circle, while all the people kept their seats in unbroken silence, contrary to the usual custom which was to greet the emperor with loud applause. He likewise exhibited the secular games, giving out that Augustus had anticipated the appropriate period; though he himself says in his history, 'that they had been omitted before the age of Augustus, who had calculated the years with great exactness and again brought them to their regular period'. By reason thereof, the crier was laughed at when he called the people in the usual form, 'to games which no person had ever before seen, nor ever would again'; whereas there survived many who had already seen them; and some of the performers who had once acted in them were now again brought upon the stage. He likewise frequently celebrated the Circensian games in the Vatican, in the circus which he had himself built, sometimes exhibiting a hunt of wild beasts, after every five courses. He embellished the Circus Maximus with marble barriers, and gilded goals, which before were of common stone and wood, and assigned proper places for the senators, who were used to sit promiscuously with the other spectators. Beside the chariot races, he exhibited there the Trojan game, and wild beasts from Africa, which were encountered by a troop of praetorian knights, with their tribunes, and even the prefect at the head of them; besides Thessalian horse, who drive fierce bulls round the circus, leap upon their backs when they have exhausted their fury, and drag them by the horns to the ground. He gave exhibitions of gladiators in several places, and of various kinds; one yearly on the anniversary of his accession in the praetorian camp, but without any hunting, or the usual apparatus; another in the Saepta as usual; and in the same place, another out of the common way, and of a few days' continuance only, which he called *Sportula;* because when he was going to present it, he informed the people by proclamation, 'that he invited them to a late supper, got up in haste, and without ceremony'. Nor did he lend himself to any kind of public diversion with more freedom and hilarity; insomuch that he would hold out his left hand, and joined by the common people, count upon his fingers aloud the gold pieces presented to those who came off conquerors. He would earnestly invite the company to be merry; sometimes calling them his 'masters', with a mixture of insipid, far-fetched jests. Thus, when the people called for Palumbus, (which name signifies a wood pigeon), he said, 'he would give them one when he could catch it'. The following, however, was said to good purpose and in good season; having, amidst great applause, spared a gladiator, on the intercession of his four sons, he sent a billet immediately round the theatre, to remind the people, 'how much it behoved them to get children, since they had before them an example of how useful they had been in procuring favour and security for a gladiator'. He likewise represented in the Campus Martius the assault and sacking of a town, and the surrender of the British kings, presiding in his general's cloak. Immediately before he drew off the waters from the Fucine lake, he exhibited upon it a naval fight. But the combatants on board the fleets crying out, 'Health attend you, noble emperor! We, who are about to peril our lives, salute you'; and he replying, 'Health attend you too', they all refused to fight, as if by that response he pardoned them from the skirmish. Upon this, he hesitated for a time, whether he should not destroy them all with fire and sword. At last, leaping from his seat, and running along the shore of the lake with tottering steps, (the result of his foul excesses), he, partly by fair words, and partly by threats, persuaded them to engage. This spectacle represented an encounter between the fleets of Sicily and Rhodes; consisting each of twelve ships of war, and of three banks of oars. The signal for the encounter was given by a silver Triton, raised by machinery from the middle of the lake.

## 22

Concerning religious ceremonies, the administration of affairs both civil and military, and the condition of all orders of the people at home and abroad, some practices he reformed, others which had been laid aside he revived; and certain regulations he introduced which were entirely new. In appointing new priests for the several colleges, he made no appointments without being sworn. When an earthquake shook the city, he never failed to summon the people together by the praetor, and appoint holidays for sacred rites. And upon the sight of an ominous bird in the City or Capitol, he issued an order for supplication, the words of which, by virtue of his office of high priest, after an exhortation from the rostra, he recited in the presence of the people, who repeated them after him, all workmen and slaves being first ordered to withdraw.

## 23

The courts of judicature, whose sittings had been formerly divided between the summer and winter months, he ordered for the dispatch of business to sit the whole year round. The jurisdiction in matters of trust, which used to be granted annually by special commission to certain magistrates, and in the city only, he made permanent, and extended to the provincial judges likewise. He altered a clause added by Tiberius to the Papia-Poppaean law, which implied that men of sixty years of age were incapable of begetting children. He ordered

that, out of the ordinary course of proceeding, orphans might have
guardians appointed them by the consuls; and that those who were
banished from any province by the chief magistrate should be
debarred from coming into the City, or any part of Italy. He inflicted
on certain persons a new sort of banishment by forbidding them to
depart further than three miles from Rome. When any affair of
importance came before the senate, he used to sit between the two
consuls upon the seats of the tribunes. He reserved to himself the
power of granting licences to travel out of Italy, which before had
belonged to the senate.

## 24

He likewise granted the consular ornaments to his Ducenarian
procurators. Those who declined the senatorian dignity, he deprived
also of the equestrian degree. Although he had in the beginning of his
reign declared that he would admit no man into the senate who was
not the great-grandson of a Roman citizen, yet he gave the 'broad
hem' to the son of a freedman on condition that he should be
adopted by a Roman knight. Fearing, however, that he would be
rebuked for such an act, he informed the public that his ancestor
Appius Caecus, the censor, had elected the sons of freedmen into the
senate; ignorant as he was that in the times of Appius, and a long
while afterwards, persons manumitted were not called freedmen, but
only their sons who were freeborn. He ordered the college of
quaestors to exhibit a game of gladiators, instead of incurring the
expense of paving the highways; and in lieu of the provinces of Ostia
and Cisalpine Gaul, which he took from them, he reinstated them in
the charge of the treasury, which, since they had been relieved of it,
had been managed by the praetors, or those who had formerly filled
that office. To Silanus, who was betrothed to his daughter, he gave
the triumphal ornaments, though he was under age; and in other
cases, he bestowed them on so many, and with so little reserve, that
there is extant a letter unanimously addressed to him by all the
legions, begging him 'to grant his consular lieutenants the triumphal
ornaments at the time of their appointment to commands, in order to
prevent their seeking occasion to engage in needless wars'. He
decreed to Aulus Plautius the honour of an ovation, for his able
services as commander of the army in Britain; going to meet him at

his entering the city, and walking with him in the procession to the Capitol and back, during which he took the left side, giving him the post of honour. He allowed Gabinius Secundus, upon his conquest of the Chauci, a German tribe, to assume the cognomen of Chaucius.

## 25

His military organisation of the equestrian order was this. After having the command of a cohort, they were promoted to a wing of auxiliary horse, and subsequently received the commission of tribune of a legion. He raised a body of militia, called Supernumeraries, who, though they were a sort of soldier, and kept in reserve, yet received pay. He procured an act of the senate to prohibit all soldiers from attending senators at their houses, in the way of respect and compliment. He confiscated the estates of all freedmen who presumed to take upon themselves the equestrian rank. Such of them as were ungrateful to their patrons, and the subject of complaint, he reduced to their former condition of slavery; and declared to their advocates that he would always give judgment against the freedmen, in any suit at law which the masters might happen to have with them. Some persons having exposed their sick slaves, in a languishing condition, on the island of Aesculapius, because of the tediousness of their cure at home, he declared all who were so exposed perfectly free, never more to return, if they should recover, to their former servitude; and that if any one chose to kill outright, rather than expose, a slave, he should be liable for murder. He published a proclamation, forbidding all travellers to pass through the towns of Italy otherwise than on foot, or in a litter or chair. In Puteoli and in Ostia he stationed several cohorts of soldiers, to be in readiness against any accidents from fire. He prohibited foreigners from adopting Roman names, especially those which belonged to families. Those who usurped the freedom of Rome, he beheaded on the Esquiline. He gave up to the senate the provinces of Achaia and Macedonia, which Tiberius had transferred to his own administration. He deprived the Lycians of their liberties, as a punishment for their fatal dissensions; but restored to the Rhodians their freedom, upon their repentance of their former misdemeanours. He exonerated forever the people of Ilium from the payment of taxes, as being the founders of the Roman race; reciting upon the occasion a letter in Greek from the senate and people of Rome to king Seleucus, on which they promised him their friendship and alliance, provided that he would grant their kinsmen, the Iliensians, immunity from all burdens.

He banished from Rome all the Jews, who were continually making disturbances at the instigation of one Chrestus. The ambassadors of the Germans he allowed to sit in the seats assigned to the senators at the public spectacles, being induced to grant them favours by their frank and honourable conduct; for, having been seated in the rows of benches which were common to the people, on observing the Parthian and Armenian ambassadors sitting among the senators, they took upon themselves to cross over into the same seats, as being, they said, no way inferior to the others, in point either of merit or rank. The religious rites of the Druids, solemnised with such horrible cruelties, which had only been forbidden the citizens of Rome during the reign of Augustus, he utterly abolished among the Gauls. On the other hand, he attempted to transfer the Eleusinian mysteries from Attica to Rome. He likewise ordered the temple of Venus Erycina in Sicily, which was old and in a ruinous condition, to be repaired at the expense of the Roman people. He concluded treaties with foreign princes in the Forum, with the sacrifice of a sow, and the form of words used by the heralds in former times. But in these and other affairs, and indeed the greater part of his administration, he was directed not so much by his own judgment, as by the influence of his wives and freedmen; for the most part acting in conformity to what their interest or pleasure dictated.

## 26

In his early youth he was twice married, first to Aemilia Lepida, the granddaughter of Augustus, and afterwards to Livia Medullina, who had the cognomen of Camilla, and was descended from the old dictator Camillus. The former of these, because her parents had incurred the displeasure of Augustus, he divorced while still a virgin; and the latter he lost by sickness upon the very day appointed for the marriage. He next married Plautia Urgulanilla, whose father had enjoyed the honour of a triumph; and soon afterwards, Aelia Paetina, the daughter of a man of consular rank. Both of these he divorced: Paetina, upon some light cause of offence; and Urgulanilla, for filthy conduct and the suspicion of murder. After these, he took in marriage

Valeria Messalina, the daughter of Barbatus Messala, his cousin. But finding that, besides her other abominable vices and debaucheries, she had even gone so far as to marry in his absence Caius Silius, the settlement of her dowry being formally signed in the presence of the augurs, he put her to death. And in a speech that he made before his praetorians, he avowed that because his marriages had been so unhappy, he resolved to remain unmarried for all future time, and if he did not continue so, he would not resist being stabbed by their hands. He was, however, unable to remain true to this oath; for he began immediately to think of another wife, and even of taking back Paetina, whom he had divorced: he thought also of Lollia Paulina, who had been married to Caius Caesar. But through the enticing allurements of Agrippina, the daughter of his brother Germanicus, who made full use of the kisses and endearments which their near relationship sanctioned to draw him into love with her, he was completely won; and he got someone to propose at the next meeting of the senate that they should oblige the emperor to marry Agrippina, as a measure highly conducive to the public interest; and that in future liberty should be given for such unions, which until that time had been considered incestuous. In less than twenty-four hours after this, he married her; but none were found that followed the precedent, except one freedman and a centurion of the first rank, at the solemnisation of whose nuptials both he and Agrippina attended.

## 27                                        A.U.C. 773

He had children by three of his wives: by Urgulanilla, Drusus and Claudia; by Paetina, Antonia; and by Messalina, Octavia, and also a son, whom at first he called Germanicus, but afterwards Britannicus. He lost Drusus at Pompeii, when he was very young; he being choked with a pear, which in his play he tossed up and caught in his mouth. Only a few days before, he had betrothed him to one of Sejanus's daughters; and I am therefore surprised that some authors should write that he lost his life by the treachery of Sejanus. Claudia, who was, in truth, the daughter of Boter his freedman, though she was born five months before his divorce, he ordered to be thrown naked at her mother's door. He gave Antonia in marriage to Cnaeus Pompey the Great, and afterwards to Faustus Sulla, both youths of very noble parentage; Octavia to his stepson Nero, after she had been contracted to Silanus. Britannicus was born upon the twentieth day of his reign, and in his second consulship. He often earnestly commended him to the soldiers, dandling him in his own hands before their ranks; and would likewise show him to the people in the theatre, setting him upon his lap, or holding him out, while he was still a babe; and was sure to receive their acclamations and good wishes on his behalf. Of his sons-in-law, he adopted Nero; while Pompey and Silanus he not only dismissed from his favour but put to death.

## 28

Of all his freedmen he esteemed especially Posides, the eunuch, whom, in his British triumph, he presented with the pointless spear, classing him among the military men. Next to him, if not equal, in favour was Felix, whom he not only preferred to commands both of cohorts and troops, but to the government of the province of Judaea; and he became, in consequence of his elevation, the husband of three queens. Another favourite was Harpocras, to whom he granted the privilege of being carried in a litter within the city, and of holding public spectacles for the entertainment of the people. In this class was likewise Polybius, who assisted him in his studies, and had often the honour of walking between the two consuls. But above all these in his affections were Narcissus, his secretary, and Pallas, the comptroller of his accounts; whom, by virtue of a decree of the senate, he suffered to receive not only rich presents, but also the decoration of the quaestorian and praetorian ensigns of honour. So much did he indulge them in amassing wealth and plundering the public that, upon his complaining once of the lowness of his exchequer, someone said, not absurdly, that he would have store enough, and to spare, if those two freedmen of his would but take him into partnership.

## 29

Being entirely enthralled by these freedmen and, as I have already said, by his wives, he bore himself rather as the servitor of others than as an absolute prince. He distributed offices or the command of armies, pardoned or punished, according as it suited their interests, their passions, or their caprice; and for the most part, without knowing, or being sensible of what he did. Not to enter into minute details relative to the revocation of grants, the reversal of judicial decisions, obtaining his signature to fictitious appointments, or the barefaced alteration of them after signing: he put to death Appius Silanus, the father of his son-in-law, and the two Julias, the daughters of Drusus and Germanicus, without any positive proof of the crimes with which they were charged, or so much as permitting them to make any defence. He also cut off Cnaeus Pompey, the husband of his eldest daughter; and Lucius Silanus, who was betrothed to the younger; Pompey was stabbed as he lay in bed with a beloved paramour, and Silanus was obliged to quit the office of praetor upon the fourth of the kalends of January, and to kill himself on New Year's Day following, the very same on which Claudius and Agrippina were married. He condemned to death five and thirty senators and above three hundred Roman knights, with so little attention to what he did, that when a centurion brought him word of the execution of a man of consular rank, who was one of the number, and told him he had carried out his order, he declared that 'he had ordered no such thing, but he approved of it'; because his freedmen, it seems, had said that the soldiers did nothing more than their duty, in dispatching the emperor's enemies without waiting for a warrant. But it is beyond all belief that he himself, at the marriage of Messalina with the adulterous Silius, should actually sign the writings relative to her dowry; induced, as it is pretended, by the design of diverting from himself and transferring upon another the danger with which some omens seemed to threaten him.

30

He was most personable, with a graceful and majestic aspect whether he sat or stood, but especially when he lay in repose; for he was tall, but not thin. His countenance was lively, his grey hair becoming, and he had a round full neck. But his knees were feeble and failed him in walking, so that his gait was unsteady, both when he assumed state and when he was taking diversion. He was indecent and unseemly in his mirth, and especially so in his anger, under the influence of which he foamed at the mouth and discharged from his nostrils. He also stammered in his speech, and had a tremulous motion of the head at all times, but particularly when he was engaged in any business, however trifling.

## 31

Concerning his bodily health, though it had been very poor during the first part of his life, yet after he became emperor, it improved mightily and continued good, except only that he was subject to a pain of the stomach. In a fit of this complaint, he said he had thoughts of killing himself.

## 32

He gave banquets that were as frequent as they were sumptuous; and generally in such spacious surroundings, that very often six hundred guests sat down together. At a feast he gave on the banks of the canal for draining the Fucine Lake, he narrowly escaped being drowned, the water at its discharge rushing out with such violence that it overflowed the conduit. At supper he always had his own children, with those of several of the nobility who, according to an ancient custom, sat at the feet of the couches. One of his guests having been suspected of purloining a golden cup, he invited him again the next day, and set before him a porcelain jug. It is said, too, that he intended to publish an edict, 'allowing to all people the liberty of giving vent at table to any distension occasioned by flatulence', upon hearing of a person whose modesty, causing him to restrain himself, had endangered his life.

## 33

His appetite for meat and drink was always ready at any time or in any place. One day, as he was hearing causes in the Forum of Augustus, he smelt the dinner which was preparing for the Salii, in the temple of Mars adjoining, whereupon he quitted the tribunal and went to partake of the feast with the priests. He scarcely ever left the table until he had thoroughly crammed himself and drank to intoxication; and then he would immediately fall asleep, lying upon his back with his mouth open. While in this condition, a feather would ordinarily be put down his throat, to make him throw up the contents of his stomach. His sleep was made up of short naps, and he usually awoke before midnight; but he would sometimes sleep in the daytime, and that even when he was upon the tribunal; so that the advocates cultivated very loud voices, but even so, often failed to rouse him. He was excessively given to the wanton love of women, but was wholly unacquainted with unnatural desires toward his own sex. He was much addicted to gaming, and published a book upon the subject; he even used to play as he rode in his chariot, having the tables so fitted that the game was not disturbed by the motion of the carriage.

## 34

His disposition towards cruelty and bloodshed appeared upon great as well as trivial occasions. When any person was to be put to the torture, or a criminal punished for parricide, he was impatient for the execution and would have it performed in his own presence. When he was at Tibur, being desirous of seeing an example of the old way of putting malefactors to death, some were immediately bound to a stake for the purpose; but there being no executioner to be had at the place, he sent for one from Rome, and waited for his coming until night. In any exhibition of gladiators, presented either by himself or others, if any of the combatants chanced to fall, he ordered them to be butchered, especially the Retiarii: and why! – because he wanted to see their faces as they lay gasping and yielding up their breath. Two gladiators happening to kill each other, he immediately ordered some little knives to be made of their swords for his own use. He took such pleasure in seeing men fight wild beasts (which ordinarily took place in the morning) and also the combatants who appeared on the stage at noon, that he would come to the theatre at break of day; and at noon, dismissing the people to dinner, would continue sitting himself to see the later show; and besides those who were devoted to that hazardous profession, he would match others with the beasts, upon slight or sudden occasions: as, for instance, the carpenters and their assistants, and people of that sort, if a machine, or any piece of work in which they had been employed about the theatre did not answer the purpose for which it had been intended. To this desperate kind of encounter he forced one of his nomenclators, even encumbered as he was by wearing the toga.

## 35

But distrust and fear came before all his other qualities. At the beginning of his reign, though he much affected a modest and humble behaviour, as has been said before, yet he dared not venture to appear at an entertainment without being attended by a guard of spearmen, and he made soldiers wait upon him at table instead of servants. He never visited a sick person, until the chamber had been first searched, and the bed and bedding thoroughly examined. At other times, all persons who came to pay their court to him were strictly searched by officers appointed for that purpose; nor was it until after a long time, and with much difficulty, that he was prevailed upon to excuse women, boys, and girls from such rude handling, or suffer their attendants or writing masters to retain their cases for pens and styles. In a civil commotion, when Camillus, doubting not that his timidity could be worked upon without a war, wrote him a scurrilous, petulant, and threatening letter, demanding that he resign the government, and betake himself to a life of privacy: he called his nobles and principal persons about him, to take counsel with them as to whether it would be best to comply with these demands, or not.

## 36

At the groundless report of some conspiracies that were being formed against him, he was so terrified that he immediately contemplated abdicating his imperial dignity. And when, as I have before related, a man armed with a dagger was discovered near him while he was sacrificing, he instantly ordered the heralds to convoke the senate, and with tears and dismal exclamations, lamented that such was his condition that he was safe nowhere; and for a long time afterwards he abstained from appearing in public. His ardent love for Messalina he renounced and cast from him, not so much on account of her dishonourable behaviour, as from apprehension of danger; for he was fully persuaded that she plotted to bring the empire into the hands of Silius, her partner in adultery, to share it with him. Upon this occasion, he ran in a great fright, and a very shameful manner, to the camp, asking all along the way, 'if the empire were indeed safely his?'

# 37

There arose no suspicion too absurd, no person on whom it rested too contemptible, to throw him into a panic, induce him to take precautions for his safety, and meditate revenge. A man engaged in a litigation before his tribunal, having saluted him, drew him aside, and told him he had dreamt that he saw him murdered; and shortly afterwards, when his adversary came to deliver his plea to the emperor, the plaintiff, pretending to have discovered the murderer, pointed to him as the man he had seen in his dream; whereupon, as if he had been taken in the act, he was hurried away to execution. We are informed that Appius Silanus was got rid of in the same manner, by a contrivance betwixt Messalina and Narcissus in which they had their several parts assigned them. Narcissus therefore burst into his lord's chamber before daylight, apparently in great fright, and told him that he had dreamt that Appius Silanus had murdered him. The empress, upon this, as if greatly amazed, reported that she had likewise seen the same vision for several nights successively. Not long after this, word came, as it had been agreed on, that Appius was come, he having, indeed, received orders the preceding day to be there at that time; and, as if the truth of the dream was sufficiently confirmed by his appearance at that juncture, he was ordered to be indicted, arraigned, and to suffer death. The day following, Claudius related the whole affair to the senate, and acknowledged his great obligation to his freedman for watching over him even in his sleep.

# 38

Conscious of his tendency towards passionate anger and resentment, he excused both faults in an edict, assuring the public that 'the former should be short and harmless, and the latter never without good cause'. Having sharply rebuked the people of Ostia for not sending some boats to meet him upon his entering the mouth of the Tiber, and in such terms as might expose them to the public resentment, he wrote to Rome that he had been treated as a private person; yet immediately afterwards he pardoned them, and that in a way which had the appearance of making them satisfaction, or begging pardon for some injury he had done them. Some persons who addressed him unseasonably in public, he pushed away with his own hand. He likewise banished one who had been secretary to a quaestor, and even a senator who had filled the office of praetor, without a hearing, although they were innocent: the former only because he had treated him with rudeness while he was in a private station, and the other, because in his aedileship he had fined some tenants of his for selling cooked victuals contrary to law, and had ordered his steward, who interfered, to be whipped. On this account, likewise, he took from the aediles the jurisdiction they had over cooks' shops. He did not conceal his own absurdities, but on the contrary openly referred to them in some short speeches which he published, and gave out that he had only feigned imbecility in the reign of Caius, because otherwise it would have been impossible for him to have escaped and arrived at the station he had then attained. He could not, however, gain credit for this assertion; for a short time afterwards, a book was published under the title of *The Resurrection of Fools*, the purpose of which was to show 'that nobody ever counterfeited folly'.

## 39

Among other things, people wondered at him for his strange obliviousness and unconcern. After Messalina was, by his own command, put to death, he sat down in his dining parlour, and inquired why his lady came not. Many of those he had condemned to death, he ordered the next day to be invited to his table, and to game with him; and even sent messengers to reprimand them as drowsy and sluggish fellows for not coming with greater promptitude. While he was meditating his incestuous marriage with Agrippina, he was perpetually calling her 'his daughter, his nursling, brought up on his knee'. And when he was going to adopt Nero, as if there was little cause for censure in his adopting a son-in-law, when he had a son of his own arrived at years of maturity, he continually gave out in public, 'that no one had ever been admitted by adoption into the Claudian family'.

## 40

He oftentimes showed such great negligence and carelessness in what he said or did, that it was believed he never reflected who he himself was, or among whom, or at what time, or in what place, he spoke. In a debate in the senate relative to the butchers and vintners, he cried out, 'I ask you, who can live without a bit of meat?' – and mentioned the great plenty of old taverns, from which he himself used formerly to have his wine. Among other reasons for his supporting a certain person who was candidate for the quaestorship, he gave this: 'His father,' said he, 'once gave me, very seasonably, a draught of cold water when I was sick.' Upon his bringing a woman as a witness in some cause before the senate, he said, 'this woman was my mother's freedwoman and dresser, but she always considered me as her master; and this I say, because there are some still in my family that do not look upon me as such.' The people of Ostia addressing him in open court with a petition, he flew into a rage at them, and said, 'There is no reason why I should oblige you: if any one else is free to act as he pleases, surely I am.' The following expressions he had in his mouth every day, and at all hours and seasons: 'What! do you take me for a Theogonius?' – which was a byword for a fool. And in Greek, 'Speak, but do not touch me'; besides many other foolish sentences below the dignity of a private person, much more of an emperor, who was not deficient either in eloquence or learning, and had been a great student of the liberal sciences.

## 41

In his youth, he attempted to write a history, being encouraged to the task by Titus Livius, and having the assistance of Sulpicius Flavus. And having called together a numerous auditory, to hear and give their judgment upon it, he read it over with much difficulty, frequently interrupting himself. For after he had begun, a great laugh was raised among the company, by the breaking of several benches from the weight of a very fat man; and even when order was restored, he could not forbear bursting out into violent fits of laughter, at the remembrance of the accident. After he became emperor, likewise, he wrote several things which he was careful to have recited to his friends by a reader. He commenced his history from the death of the dictator Caesar; but afterwards he took a later period, and began at the conclusion of the civil wars; because he found he could not speak with freedom, and a due regard to truth, concerning the former period, having been often taken to task both by his mother and grandmother. Of the earlier history he left only two books, but of the latter, one and forty. He compiled likewise the *History of his Own Life*, in eight books, full of absurdities, but in no bad style; also, *A Defence of Cicero against the Books of Asinius Gallus*, which exhibited a considerable degree of learning. He besides invented three new letters, and added them to the former alphabet, as highly necessary. He published a book to recommend them while he was yet only a private person; but on his elevation to imperial power he had little difficulty in introducing them into common use; and these letters are still extant in a variety of books, registers, and inscriptions upon buildings.

## 42

He applied himself with no less diligence to the study of Greek literature, professing upon all occasions his love of that language, and its surpassing excellency. A stranger once holding a discourse both in Greek and Latin, he addressed him thus: 'Since you are skilled in both our tongues — '. And recommending Achaia to the favour of the senate, he said, 'I have a particular attachment to that province, on account of our common studies.' In the senate he often made long replies to ambassadors in that language. On the tribunal he frequently quoted the verses of Homer. When at any time he had taken vengeance on an enemy or a conspirator, he scarcely ever gave to the tribune on guard who, according to custom, came for the word, any other than this:

'Tis time to strike when wrong demands the blow.

To conclude, he wrote some histories likewise in Greek, namely, twenty books on Tuscan affairs, and eight on the Carthaginian; in consequence of which, another museum was founded at Alexandria, in addition to the old one, and called after his name; and it was ordered that, upon certain days in every year, his Tuscan history should be read over in one of these, and his Carthaginian in the other, as in a school; each history being read through by persons who took it in turn.

## 43

Towards the end of his life, he gave certain indications, and those evident enough, that he repented both his marriage with Agrippina, and his adoption of Nero. For some of his freedmen, making favourable mention of his having condemned, the day before, a woman accused of adultery, he remarked: 'Destiny has ordained that my wives should be unfaithful to my bed; but they did not go unpunished.' Often, when he happened to meet Britannicus, he would embrace him tenderly, and charge him 'to grow apace, and take account of me for all that I have done'; using the Greek quotation, 'He who has wounded will also heal.' And intending to give him his virile robe, while he was yet under age and a tender youth, because his growth would permit it, he added: 'I do so, that the people of Rome may at last have a true Caesar'; that is, Caesar by birth and not by adoption.

## 44

And not long after this he made his will and had it signed by all the magistrates as witnesses; whereupon, before he could proceed any further he was prevented by Agrippina, who was accused by informers, among other crimes, of taking him off by poison; but where, and by whom it was administered, remains uncertain. Some write that it was given him as he was feasting with the priests in the Capitol, by the eunuch Halotus, his taster. Others say by Agrippina, at his own table, in mushrooms, a dish of which he was very fond. The accounts of what ensued are likewise variable. Some relate that he instantly became speechless, was seized with pain through the night, and died about daybreak; others, that at the first he fell into a sound sleep, and afterwards, his food rising, he threw up the whole, but had another dose given him; whether in water–gruel, under pretence of refreshment after his exhaustion, or in a clyster, as if designed to relieve his bowels, is also uncertain.

## 45

His death was kept secret until all things were set in order relative to his successor. Accordingly, vows were made for his recovery, and comedians were called to amuse him, as it was pretended, by his own desire. He died upon the third of the ides of October, in the consulship of Asinius Marcellus and Acilius Aviola, in the sixty-fourth year of his age, and the fourteenth of his reign. His funeral was celebrated with the customary imperial pomp, and he was ranked among the gods; which honour, being taken from him by Nero, was afterwards restored by Vespasian.

## 46

There occurred significant tokens presaging his death, to wit: the appearance of a comet; the blasting of his father Drusus's monument by lightning; and the death, during that year, of most of the principal magistrates. It would seem from several circumstances that he was sensible of his approaching dissolution, and made no secret of it. For when he nominated the consuls, he appointed no one to fill the office beyond the month in which he died. At the last assembly of the senate in which he made his appearance, he earnestly exhorted his two sons to unity with each other, and with earnest entreaties commended to the fathers the care of their tender years. And in the last cause he heard from the tribunal, he repeatedly declared in open court, 'that he was now arrived at the last stage of mortal existence'; while all who heard him, grieved by such ominous words, prayed the gods to avert the doom.

# Nero Claudius Caesar

From the Domitian stock sprung two famous families, to wit, the Calvini and the Ahenobarbi. The Ahenobarbi derive both their extraction and their cognomen from one Lucius Domitius, of whom it is related that, as he was returning out of the country to Rome, he was met by two young men of awe-inspiring presence, who desired him to carry to the senate and people news of a victory, of which no certain intelligence had yet reached the city; and for the better assurance of their divine estate, they stroked his cheeks and thereby changed his hair, which had been black, to a bright colour, resembling that of brass. This mark of honour descended to his posterity, for they had generally red beards. This family had the honour of seven consulships, one triumph, and two censorships; and being admitted into the patrician order, they continued the use of the same cognomen, with no other prenomina than those of Cnaeus and Lucius. These, however, they assumed with singular irregularity; three persons in succession sometimes adhering to one of them, and then they were changed alternately. For the first, second, and third of the Ahenobarbi had the prenomen of Lucius and again the three following, successively, that of Cnaeus, while those who came after were called, by turns, Lucius and Cnaeus. That many persons of this house should be here described, seems to me pertinent and material, to show that Nero so far degenerated from the noble qualities of his ancestors, that he retained only their vices, as if those alone had been transmitted to him by his descent.

To begin, therefore, at a remote date, his great grandfather's grandfather, Cnaeus Domitius, when he was tribune of the people, being offended with the high priests for electing another than himself in the room of his father, obtained the transfer of the right of election from the colleges of the priests to the people. In his consulship, having conquered the Allobroges and the Arverni, he rode through his province, mounted upon an elephant, with a body of soldiers attending him in the manner of a solemn triumph. It was he of whom the orator Licinius Crassus said that it was no marvel he had a brazen beard, who had a face of iron and a heart of lead. His son, during his praetorship, was the man who proposed that Cnaeus Caesar, upon the expiration of his consulship, should be called to account before the senate for his administration of that office, which was supposed to be contrary both to the omens and the laws. Afterwards, when he was himself consul, he tried to deprive Cnaeus of the command of the army, and having been, by intrigue and cabal, appointed his successor, he was made prisoner at Corsinium, in the beginning of the civil war. Being set at liberty, he went to Marseilles, which was then besieged; where having, by his presence, animated the people to hold out, he suddenly deserted them, and at last was slain in the battle of Pharsalia. He was a man neither constant nor resolute, and of a savage nature. Being driven by utter despair to swallow poison, he repented instantly, and in terror at the thought of death, took a vomit to cast it up again. He even enfranchised his physician for having, with great wisdom and forethought, tempered the dose so as to do him no great harm. When Cnaeus Pompey was consulting with his friends in what manner he should treat those neutrals who regarded indifferently both sides in the contest, he was the only one who proposed that they should be reckoned as enemies and proceeded against accordingly.

He left behind him a son, worthy beyond question and to be preferred before all others of his name and lineage. This man was among those who were condemned by the Pedian law as members of the conspiracy against Caesar, although he himself was guiltless.

Upon this, he went over to Brutus and Cassius his near relations; and, after their death, not only kept together the fleet, the command of which had been given him some time before, but even increased it. At last, when the party had everywhere been defeated, he voluntarily surrendered it to Mark Antony; considering it as a piece of service for which the latter owed him no small obligation. Of all those who were condemned by the law above mentioned, he was the only man who was restored to his country, and filled the highest offices. When civil dissension was rekindled, he was appointed lieutenant under the same Antony, and offered the chief command by those who were ashamed of Cleopatra; but not daring, on account of a sudden illness which assailed him, either to accept or decline it, he went over to Augustus, and died a few days later, not without incurring a note of infamy; for Antony gave out that he was induced to change sides by his impatience to be with his mistress, one Servilia Nais.

## 4

This Cnaeus had a son, named Domitius, who was afterwards well known as the nominal purchaser of the family property left by Augustus' will; and no less famous in his youth for his skill in chariot-driving, than he was afterwards for the triumphal ornaments which he obtained in the German war; but arrogant of spirit, wasteful in his habits, and cruel withal. When he was aedile, he forced Lucius Plancus, the censor, to give him the way; and in his praetorship and consulship, he made Roman knights and married women perform upon the stage. He gave hunts of wild beasts, both in the Circus and in all the wards of the city; as also a show of gladiators; but with such barbarity, that Augustus, after privately reprimanding him, to no purpose, was obliged to restrain him by a public edict.

## 5

By the elder Antonia he begat Nero's father, a man of ungracious and despicable character. During his attendance upon Caius Caesar in the East, he killed a freedman of his own for refusing to drink as much as he ordered him. Being dismissed for this from Caesar's cohort, he did not conduct himself one whit more modestly; for, in a village upon the Appian road, he suddenly put his horses to a gallop and drove his

chariot, not unwittingly, over a little child, crushing him to death. At
Rome, he struck out the eye of a Roman knight in the Forum,
because he had addressed him in bold terms during a dispute between
them. He was likewise so unscrupulous and dishonest, that he not
only defrauded some silversmiths of the price of goods he had bought
of them, but, during his praetorship, withheld from the owners of
chariots in the Circensian games the prizes due to them for their
victory. For this prank, he was reproved ironically by his sister,
Lepida, and upon complaint being made by the leaders of the several
parties, he agreed to sanction a law, 'that, for the future, the prizes
should be immediately paid'. A little before the death of Tiberius, he
was prosecuted for treason and for incest with his sister Lepida, but
escaped in the timely change of affairs, and died of a dropsy, at Pyrgi;
leaving behind him his son, Nero, whom he had by Agrippina, the
daughter of Germanicus.

# 6

Nero was born at Antium, nine months after the death of Tiberius,
upon the eighteenth of the kalends of January, just as the sun rose so
that its beams touched him before they could well reach the earth.
While many fearful conjectures, in respect to his future fortune, were
essayed by various persons, from the circumstances of his nativity, a
saying of his father Domitius was regarded as an ill presage. When his
friends offered their congratulations upon the birth of a son, he said,
'that nothing but what was accursed, detestable, and pernicious to the
public weal, could ever proceed from him and Agrippina.' Another
manifest prognostic of his future infelicity occurred upon his lustration
day. For Caius Caesar, being requested by his sister to give the child
what name he would, looking wistfully at his uncle, Claudius, who
afterwards, when emperor, adopted Nero, he gave him his; speaking
not seriously, but only in jest; and Agrippina scorned it, because
Claudius at that time was considered a fool, and was the laughing-
stock of the court.

At three years of age, he became fatherless; and being heir but of
one third part, he could not even touch that, because his co-heir,
Caius, seized the whole. His mother being soon after banished, he
lived with his aunt Lepida, in a very necessitous condition, under the
care of two tutors, a dancing master and a barber. But when Claudius

came to the empire, he not only recovered his father's estate, but was enriched with the additional inheritance of that of his stepfather, Crispus Passienus. Upon his mother's recall from banishment, he was advanced to such favour and became so powerful, that a rumour went abroad that Messalina, the wife of Claudius, sent assassins to strangle him in his noonday sleep, as the rival of Britannicus, her son. To this tale was added the report that the conspirators were frightened by a serpent that issued from his pillow, and fled from the scene. The anecdote arose upon the occasion of finding on his couch, near the pillow, the skin of a snake, which, by his mother's order, he wore for some time upon his right arm, enclosed in a bracelet of gold. This amulet, at last, he laid aside, in disgust of any memorial of her; but afterwards, in a time of extremity, he sought for it again in vain.

# 7

While yet a child of tender age, he performed his part in the Trojan play during the Circensian games, with a degree of spirit and resolution that gained him great applause from the people. In his eleventh year, he was adopted by Claudius, and placed under the tuition of Annaeus Seneca, the renowned writer, who had been made a senator. It is said that Seneca dreamt the night after that he was giving a lesson to Caligula; and shortly after Nero proved his dream true, by betraying in every way the cruelty and cunning of that prince. For when his brother Britannicus saluted him, after his adoption, by the customary name of Ahenobarbus, he tried to persuade his father that his brother was nothing but a changeling, and no son of his, as was reputed. When his aunt Lepida was brought to trial, he appeared in court as a witness against her, to gratify his mother who persecuted the accused. On his introduction into the Forum, at the age of manhood, he gave a largesse to the people and a donative to the soldiers; for the praetorian cohorts he appointed a solemn procession under arms, and marched at the head of them with a shield in his hand; after which he went to return thanks to his father in the senate. Before Claudius, likewise, at the time he was consul, he made a speech for the Bolognese, in Latin, and for the Rhodians and people of Ilium, in Greek. He had the jurisdiction of prefect of the city, for the first time, during the Latin festival; during which the most celebrated advocates brought before him, not short and trifling causes, as is usual in that case, but trials of importance, notwithstanding they had instructions from Claudius himself to the contrary. Not long after, he married Octavia; and in honour of Claudius exhibited the Circensian games, and the hunting of wild beasts.

## 8

He was seventeen years old at the death of Claudius, and as soon as that event was made public, he went out to the cohort on guard between the hours of six and seven; for the signs were so ominous, that no earlier time of the day was deemed auspicious to enter upon the Empire. On the steps before the palace gate, he was unanimously saluted by the soldiers as their emperor, and then carried in a litter to the camp; thence, after making a short speech to the troops, into the senate-house, where he continued until the evening; of all the many high honours which were heaped upon him, he refused only the title of Father of his Country, by reason of his youth.

## 9

Beginning his reign with a great show of piety and respect at the funeral of Claudius, which was most sumptuously performed, he pronounced the oration himself, and then had him enrolled among the gods. He likewise paid the highest honours to the memory of his father Domitius. The management of affairs, both public and private, he left to his mother. The first day of his rule, when the tribune on guard asked him for a watchword, he gave him 'The Best of Mothers', and afterwards she frequently accompanied him through the streets, in his own litter. He settled a colony at Antium, in which he placed the veteran soldiers belonging to the guards; and obliged several of the richest centurions of the first rank to transfer their residence to that place; where also he made a noble harbour, a most magnificent piece of work.

## 10

To show still further proof of his attitude, he made profession that he would govern the empire according to the rule of Augustus; and omitted no occasion to exhibit his bountifulness, clemency, and complaisance. The more burdensome taxes he either entirely abolished, or lowered. The rewards appointed for informers by the Papian law, he reduced to a fourth part, and distributed to the people four hundred sesterces a man. To the noblest of the senators who were much reduced in their circumstances, he granted annual allowances, in some cases as much as five hundred thousand sesterces; and to the praetorian cohorts a monthly allowance of corn gratis. When called upon to subscribe the sentence, according to custom, of a criminal condemned to die, he would say, 'Would that I had never learnt to read and write.' Many times he saluted people of the several orders by name, without a prompter. When the senate returned him their thanks for his good government, his answer was, 'It will be time enough to do so when I shall have deserved it.' He admitted the common people to his exercises in the Campus Martius. He also frequently declaimed in public, and recited verses of his own, not only at home, but in the theatre; and that with so much general joy to those who heard him, that public prayers were appointed to be put up to the gods upon that account; and the verses were, after being written in gold letters, dedicated to Jupiter Capitolinus.

## 11

He set forth a great number and variety of shows, as the Juvenal and Circensian games, stage plays, and an exhibition of gladiators. In the Juvenal, he even permitted senators and aged matrons to disport themselves. At the Circensian games, he assigned the equestrian order seats apart from the rest of the people, and had races performed by chariots drawn each by four camels. In the games which he instituted for the eternal duration of the empire, and therefore ordered to be called Maximi, many of the senatorian and equestrian order, of both sexes, performed. A distinguished Roman knight descended on the stage by a rope, mounted on an elephant. A Roman play, likewise, composed by Afranius, was brought upon the stage. It was entitled

*The Fire*; and in it the performers were allowed to carry off, and to keep to themselves, the furniture of the house which, as the plot of the play required, was burnt down in the theatre. Every day, during the solemnity, many thousand articles of all descriptions were thrown among the people to be caught up and carried off; such as fowls of different kinds, tickets for corn, clothes, gold, silver, gems, pearls, pictures, slaves, beasts of burden, wild beasts that had been tamed; at last, ships, lots of houses, and lands, were offered as prizes in a lottery.

## 12                                                A.U.C. 810

These games he beheld from the front of the proscenium. In the show of gladiators, which he exhibited in a wooden amphitheatre, built within a year in the district of the Campus Martius, he ordered that none should be slain, not even the condemned criminals employed in the combats. He secured four hundred senators, and six hundred Roman knights, among whom were some of unbroken fortunes and blameless reputation, to perform as gladiators, to fight wild beasts, and attend to various other matters in the theatre. He presented the people with the spectacle of a mock sea fight, upon salt water, with great fishes swimming therein; as also with the Pyrrhic dance, executed by certain youths, to each of whom, after the performance was over, he granted the freedom of Rome. During this diversion, it was arranged that a bull should leap Pasiphae, concealed within a wooden statue of a cow; and the action was so lively that many of the people were deceived. Icarus, upon his first attempt to fly, fell on the stage close to the emperor's pavilion, and bespattered him with blood. For he very seldom presided in the games, but used to view them reclining on a couch, at first through some narrow apertures, but afterwards with the podium quite open. He was the first who instituted at Rome, in the Greek fashion, a trial of skill in the three several exercises of music, wrestling, and horse-racing, to be performed at Rome every five years, and which he called Neronia. Upon the dedication of his bath and gymnasium, he furnished the senate and the equestrian order with oil. He appointed as judges of the trial men of consular rank, chosen by lot, who sat with the praetors; and he came down himself into the orchestra among the senators, and received the crown for the best composition in Latin prose and verse, for which several persons of the highest merit contended, but which was unanimously yielded to him.

The harp which was presented to him by the judges he received with joy and fervour, and commanded that it be carried to the statue of Augustus. In the gymnastic exercises, which he presented in the Saepta, while they were preparing the great sacrifice of an ox, he shaved his beard for the first time, and placing it in a golden casket studded with precious pearls, consecrated it to Jupiter Capitolinus. He invited the Vestal Virgins to see the show of wrestlers, because, at Olympia, the priestesses of Ceres are allowed the privilege of witnessing that exhibition.

## 13                                    A.U.C. 819

I may include, with good reason, among the spectacles presented by him, the entrance into Rome of Tiridates, king of Armenia, whom he invited by very enticing promises. When the day appointed by edict for showing him to the people dawned cloudy and unfavourable, he brought him forward upon the first opportune day that followed; several cohorts being drawn up under arms, about the temples in the Forum, while he was seated on a curule chair on the rostra, in a triumphal dress, amidst the military standards and ensigns. Upon Tiridates advancing towards him by the ascent of the steep pulpit, he suffered him to throw himself at his feet, but quickly raised him with his right hand, and kissed him. The emperor then, at the king's request, took the turban from his head, and replaced it by a crown, while one of praetorian rank proclaimed in Latin the words in which the prince addressed the emperor. After this ceremony, the king was conducted to the theatre where, after renewing his obeisance, Nero seated him on his right hand. Being then greeted by universal acclamation with the title of Emperor, and sending his laurel crown to the Capitol, Nero shut the temple of the two-faced Janus, as though there now existed no war throughout the Roman empire.

## 14

He bore four consulships; the first for two months, the second and last for six, and the third for four; the two intermediate ones he held successively, but the others after an interval of some years between them.

## 15

In his ordinary jurisdiction, he rarely gave his decision on the pleadings before the next day, and then in writing. His manner of hearing causes was not to allow any adjournment, but to dispatch them in order as they stood. When he withdrew to consult his assessors, he did not debate the matter openly with them; but silently and privately reading over their opinions, which they gave separately in writing, he pronounced sentence from the tribunal according to his own view of the case, as if it was the opinion of the majority. For a long time he would not admit the sons of freedmen into the senate; and those who had been admitted by former princes, he excluded from all public offices. To supernumerary candidates, in order to comfort them under the delay of their hopes, he gave command in the legions. The consulship he commonly conferred for six months; and if one of the consuls died about the kalends of January, he substituted no one in his place; disliking what had been formerly done for Caninius Rebilus on such an occasion, who was consul for one day only. Triumphal honours he bestowed, without regard to military service, only to those who were of quaestorian rank, and to some of the equestrian order. His addresses, which he sent to the senate on certain matters, he ordered for the most part to be read by the consuls, instead of the quaestors, whose office it properly was.

## 16

He devised a new style of building in the city, namely, the erection of piazzas before all houses, both in the streets and detached, to give facilities from their terraces, in case of fire, for preventing it from spreading; and these he built at his own expense. He likewise had a design to extend the city walls as far as Ostia, and bring the sea from thence by a canal into the old city. Many severe regulations and new orders were made in his time. A sumptuary law was enacted. Public suppers were limited to the Sportulae; and victualling-houses restrained from selling any dressed viands, except pulse and herbs, whereas before they sold all kinds of meat. Christians, a sect given to a new, wicked and mischievous superstition, were put to death with grievous torments. The sports of the charioteers, who from old time had been allowed to range up and down to beguile folk, to pilfer and spoil in merriment, were prohibited. The partisans of the rival theatrical performers were banished as well as the actors themselves.

## 17

To prevent forgery, a method was then first introduced of having writings bored, run through three times with a thread, and then sealed. It was likewise provided that in wills, the first two pages, with only the testator's name upon them, should be presented blank to those who were to sign them as witnesses; and that no one who wrote a will for another should insert any legacy for himself. It was ordained that clients should pay their advocates a certain reasonable fee, but nothing for the court, which was to be gratuitous, the charges for it being paid out of the public treasury; that causes, the cognisance of which before belonged to the judges of the exchequer, should be transferred to the Forum, and the ordinary tribunals; and that all appeals from the judges should be made to the senate.

## 18

Having no desire or aspiration at any time to propagate and enlarge the empire, he even considered withdrawing the troops from Britain; and only abandoned that design from the fear of appearing to detract from the glory of his father (Claudius). All that he did was to reduce the kingdom of Pontus, which was ceded to him by Polemon, and also the Alps, upon the death of Cottius, to the form of a province.

## 19

Twice only he undertook any foreign expeditions, one to Alexandria, and the other to Achaia. But his journey to Alexandria he gave up on the very day fixed for his departure, by reason both of disquieting omens and the perilous nature of the voyage. For while he was making the circuit of the temples, having seated himself in that of Vesta, when he attempted to rise, the hem of his robe stuck fast, and there arose such a dark mist before his eyes that he could see nothing about him. In Achaia, he attempted to make a cut through the Isthmus; and, having made a speech encouraging his praetorians to set about the work, on a signal given by sound of trumpet, he first broke ground with a spade, and carried off a basket full of earth upon his shoulders. He prepared also for an expedition to the Pass of the Caspian mountains; forming a new legion out of his late levies in Italy, of men all six feet high, which he called the phalanx of Alexander the Great.

Premising my account with these particulars, in part deserving no blame, and in part worthy even of no small praise, which I have collected with the view of distinguishing them from his villainies, I now proceed to make report of the darker side of his conduct.

## 20

Among the other liberal arts which he was taught in his youth, he was instructed in music; and no sooner had he attained to the empire, but he sent for Terpnus, a performer upon the harp, who was renowned in those days for his great skill. Sitting with him as he played and sang after supper until far in the night, he began little by little to practise upon the instrument himself; nor did he omit any of those means by which artists in music safeguard and fortify their voices. He would lie upon his back with a sheet of lead upon his breast, purge himself thoroughly by vomits and clysters, and abstain from the eating of fruits, or other food prejudicial to the voice. Becoming sure of himself through his daily trials, though he had but a small and slightly shrill voice, he was desirous of appearing upon the stage, having among his companions this Greek proverb continually in his mouth, 'that hidden music was worth nothing'. The first time that he mounted the stage was at Naples, at which time he did not cease singing (although the theatre was shaken, and ready to fall, from a sudden earthquake) until he had finished the piece of music he had begun. He sang in the same place several times, and for many days together; pausing only now and then to refresh his voice. As if impatient of retirement, he would pass directly from the bath to the theatre; and after dining in the orchestra, amid a crowded assembly of the people, he promised them in the Greek tongue, 'that after he had sipped a little, he would give them some notes of greater richness and volume'. Being much delighted with the songs that were sung in his praise by some Alexandrians belonging to the fleet just arrived at Naples, he sent for more of the like singers from Alexandria. At the same time, he chose young men of the equestrian order, and above five thousand robust young fellows from the common people, on purpose to learn various kinds of shouts and applause, called *bombi*, from the humming of bees, *imbrices*, from the rattling of rain or hail on the roofs, and *testae*, from the tinkling of porcelain vessels when clashed together; and those boys that were most deft and trim, and had the finest heads of hair, the most excellent apparel, and rings upon their left hands, were engaged to give their attendance upon him whenever he sang. They were divided into several parties, and their leaders received as their stipend forty thousand sesterces.

## 21

At Rome also, being extremely proud of his singing, he ordered the games called Neronia to be celebrated before the time fixed for their return. And when all the people called upon him to let them hear 'his celestial voice', he answered 'that he would willingly do them that pleasure (being as desirous to sing as they were to listen), but it should be at the gardens'. However, when the soldiers then on guard seconded the voice of the people, he promised to comply with their request immediately, and with all his heart. He instantly ordered his name to be entered upon the list of musicians who proposed to contend, and having thrown his lot into the urn with the rest, took his turn, and entered the stage, attended by the prefects of the praetorian cohorts bearing his harp, and followed by the military tribunes and several of his intimate friends. After he had taken his station and made the usual prelude, he commanded Cluvius Rufus, a man of consular rank, to proclaim in the theatre that he would sing and act the story of Niobe. This he accordingly did, and continued it until nearly ten o'clock, but deferred the disposal of the crown, and the remaining part of the solemnity, until the next year, that he might have more frequent opportunities of performing. But bethinking himself that the time was long, he could not refrain from often appearing as a public performer in the interval. He did not disdain to appear on the stage, even in shows presented to the people by private persons; and was offered by one of the praetors no less than a million of sesterces for his services. Moreover he sang tragedies, in disguise; the visors of the heroes and gods, as also of the heroines and goddesses, being formed into a resemblance of his own face, and that of any woman whom he fancied. Among the rest, he sang *Canace in Childbirth*, *Orestes the Murderer of his Mother*, *Oedipus Blinded*, and *Hercules Mad*. In the last tragedy, it is said that a young sentinel, posted at the entrance of the stage, seeing him in a prison dress and bound with chains, as the fable of the play required, ran with all haste to his assistance.

## 22

Even as a boy he delighted greatly in horsemanship; and he talked constantly of the Circensian races, although he was forbidden to attend. One time as he was bewailing among his fellow pupils the case of a charioteer of the green party, who was dragged round the circus at the tail of his chariot, and being chided therefore by his tutor, he had a lie ready and said that he was speaking of Hector. In the beginning of his reign, his custom every day was to play upon a chessboard with four horses, fashioned in ivory, and drawing chariots; and he used to resort to all the Circensian games, even the lesser ones, at first secretly, but at last in the sight of all men; so that nobody ever doubted of his presence on any particular day. Neither did he dissimulate his desire to have the number of the prizes doubled; so that the races being increased accordingly, the diversion continued until a late hour; the leaders of parties refusing now to bring out their companies for any time less than the whole day, with a view of greater gain. Soon after, he also took a fancy for the exercise, and was often seen driving a chariot in public. And when he had made tests of his skill at first in the gardens, amid crowds of slaves and other rabble, he at length proceeded to show himself in this manner in the Circus Maximus, appointing one of his freedmen to drop a white towel for a signal, from the place where the magistrates were wont to give it. But not content with having given good proof of his prowess in this game at Rome, he went over to Achaia, as has already been said, principally for this purpose. The several cities, in which solemn trials of musical talent used to be publicly held, had resolved to send him the crowns belonging to those who bore away the prize. These he accepted so kindly, that he not only admitted at once to his presence the ambassadors who brought them, but also invited them to his table among his intimates. And being requested by some of them to sing at supper, and highly praised with excessive applause, he said, 'that the

Greeks were the only people who had an ear for music, and the only auditors worthy of his efforts'.

Without delay he commenced his journey, and on his arrival at Cassiope, in Corcyra, he began to sing there at the altar of Jupiter Cassius.

## 23

After this, he appeared at all the public games in Greece: for such as fell in different years, he brought within the compass of one, and some he ordered to be celebrated a second time in the same year. At Olympia, likewise, contrary to custom, he appointed a public performance in music. And that he might meet with no interruption while he was busied about these matters, when his freedman Helius informed him that affairs at Rome required his presence, he wrote to him in these words: 'Though now all your hopes and wishes are for my speedy return, yet you ought rather to advise and pray that I may come back with a character worthy of Nero.' All the while he was singing, it was not lawful that any person should depart from the theatre, were the cause never so urgent. Whereupon it is said that some women with child fell into travail and were delivered there; and many men besides, wearied of hearing and praising him, because the town gates were shut, either leaped from the walls by stealth, or counterfeiting themselves dead, were carried forth as corpses to be buried. But how timorously, with what fear and awe of the judges, he strove for the mastery in these contests, is almost incredible. His manner was to deal with his adversaries as if they were his equals in condition; and he would observe them narrowly, watch for occasions to defame them, rail at them in harsh terms upon meeting them; or bribe such as excelled him in the art. He would address the judges with all reverence before he began to sing, telling them, 'he had done all things that were necessary, by way of preparation, but that the issue of the approaching trial was in the hand of fortune; and that they, as wise and experienced men, ought to exclude from their judgment things merely accidental.' Upon their exhortation to him to be of good heart, he would go away with more confidence, but not entirely eased in his mind; construing the silence and modesty of some of them as sourness and ill-content, and saying that he was suspicious of them.

## 24

In these contests, he strictly obeyed the rules, and never dared spit, nor dry the sweat of his forehead in any other way than with his sleeve. Once in the performance of a tragedy, when he happened to let fall his sceptre, and not quickly recovering it, he was in great fear and dismay, lest for that delinquency he should be set aside; and he could not take heart again, until an actor who stood by swore that it was not noticed in the midst of the shouts and acclamations of the people beneath. Whenever the prize was awarded to him, he used to proclaim it himself; and even entered the lists with the heralds. In order that no memorial or token of any other victor might remain extant, he commanded all their statues and pictures to be pulled down, and flung into the common sewers. Furthermore, he drove the chariot with various numbers of horses and at the Olympic games with no fewer than ten; notwithstanding he had reproved Mithridates for that exploit in some verses of his own making. But being thrown out of his chariot and finding that he was not able to hold out when replaced therein, he was obliged to give up, before he reached the goal; yet he was crowned nevertheless. On his departure, he enfranchised the whole province throughout, and conferred upon the judges in the several games the freedom of Rome, with large sums of money. All these benefits he proclaimed himself with his own voice, from the middle of the stadium, during the solemnity of the Isthmian games.

## 25

On his return from Greece, he entered Naples in a chariot drawn by white horses through a breach in the city wall, in the manner of those who were victorious in the sacred Grecian games; because it was in that city that he had first professed his musical skill. In like manner he entered Antium, Alba, and Rome. He rode into Rome in the same chariot in which Augustus had triumphed, in a purple tunic, and a cloak embroidered with golden stars, having on his head the crown won at Olympia, and in his right hand that which was awarded him at the Parthian games: the rest being carried in a procession before him, with inscriptions denoting the places where they had been won, from whom, and in what plays or musical performances; while a train followed him with loud acclamations, crying out that 'they were the emperor's attendants, and the soldiers of his triumph'. Having then caused an arch of the Circus Maximus to be taken down, he passed through the breach, as also through the Velabrum and the Forum, to the Palatine hill and the temple of Apollo. To do him honour at every step of his progress, sacrifices were offered, while the streets were strewn with saffron, and birds, chaplets, and sweetmeats scattered abroad. He hung the sacred crowns in his chamber, about his bed, and caused statues of himself to be erected in the attire of a harper, and had his likeness in that guise stamped upon the coin. And after all this, so far was he from abating anything of his ardour for the study of music that, for the preservation of his voice, he never addressed the soldiers but by messages, or with some person to deliver his speeches for him, when he thought fit to make his appearance among them. Nor did he ever do anything either in jest or earnest, without a voice master standing by him to caution him against taxing his vocal organs, and to hold a handkerchief to his mouth when he did. And he offered his friendship, or avowed open enmity to many, according as they were lavish or meagre in giving him praise.

## 26

His unruly whims, lewdness, riotousness, avarice, and cruelty he indulged at first in private and with caution, as if they were the tricks of youthful folly; but, even then, men were of opinion that they were the inbred vices of nature, and not the waywardness of youth. No sooner did twilight set in than he would catch up a cap or a wig, and so disguised, enter the taverns, and walk about the streets in sport which was not void of mischief. For he used to fall upon those that came late from supper and knock them soundly; and, if they struggled and made resistance, would wound them, and throw them into the common sewer. He broke into shops, and rifled them; for he had set up an auction at home for selling his booty. But many a time in these brawls and scuffles, he endangered his eyes, and even his life; being once beaten nearly to death by a certain young gentleman of senatorial degree, whose wife he had misused with unclean handling. After this, he never again ventured abroad at that hour of the night, without his military tribunes following him at a little distance. In the daytime he would be carried to the theatre incognito in a litter, placing himself upon the upper part of the proscenium, where he not only witnessed the quarrels which arose on account of the performances, but also encouraged them. When they came to blows, and stones and pieces of broken benches began to fly about, he threw them plentifully among the people, and once even broke a praetor's head.

## 27

But as his vices gained strength by degrees, he laid aside these wild tricks, and all attempt at secrecy, and without the least dissimulation, he broke out into greater outrages. His banquets he drew out at length, eating and drinking from noon to midnight, frequently refreshing himself by warm baths, and, in the summer season, having the water cooled with snow. He often supped in public, in the Naumachia, with the sluices shut, or in the Campus Martius, or the Circus Maximus, being waited upon at table by common prostitutes of the town, Syrian strumpets, and glee girls. As often as he went down the Tiber to Ostia, or coasted through the gulf of Baiae, booths furnished as brothels and eating-houses were erected along the shore and river banks; where stood matrons, who, like bawds and hostesses, allured the company to land and turn in to them. It was also his habit to invite himself to supper with his friends; at one of which was expended no less than four millions of sesterces in chaplets, and at another a good deal more in rose water and aromatic oils.

## 28

Besides the unnatural abuse of freeborn boys, and the dishonouring of married women, he committed a rape upon Rubria, a Vestal Virgin. He very nearly took Acte, a freedwoman, as his lawful wife, having suborned some men of consular rank to swear that she was of royal blood. There was a certain boy named Sporus, whose genitories he cut out, and endeavoured to transform him thereby into a woman. He even caused him to be brought to him as a bride, with a marriage settlement, and in a rose-coloured nuptial veil; and he invited a numerous company to attend the ceremony. Afterwards, he had him brought to his own house, and there treated him as his wife. It was upon this occasion that there went forth a quip made by some wag, 'that it would have been well for the world, if his father Domitius had wedded such a wife'. This Sporus, decked with the rich ornaments and apparel of an empress, he carried about with him in a litter round the solemn assemblies and fairs of Greece, and afterwards at Rome through the Sigillaria; kissing him sweetly from time to time as they rode together. That he had an incestuous passion for his own mother, but was deterred from it by some enemies of hers, for fear that this proud and overbearing woman should, by this kind of favour, wax too powerful, no one ever doubted; especially after he had introduced among his concubines a strumpet, who was reported to bear a strong resemblance to Agrippina. It is said moreover, that so often as he rode in a litter with his mother, he played the wanton and was betrayed by the marks appearing on her garments.

## 29

As for his own body, it is known that he dishonoured it to such a degree, that after he had defiled every portion of it with some unnatural pollution, he at last devised a new kind of sport; that, being covered all over with a wild beast's skin, he should be let loose from a cage, and then assault the private parts both of men and women, while they stood tied to stakes. And when he had vented his furious passion upon them, he finished the game in the embraces of his freedman Doryphorus, to whom he was married in the same way that Sporus had been married to himself; insomuch that he counterfeited the noise and cries of maidens, when they are forced to suffer deflowering. I have heard from various sources that he firmly believed no man or woman was chaste, or in any part of their bodies pure and clean, but that most of them dissimulated their uncleanness, and craftily kept it secret. To those, therefore, who frankly owned their obscene practices, he forgave all other faults and crimes.

## 30

The use of riches, as he saw it, was lavish expenditure. He regarded as niggardly pinchpennies those who kept any account or regulated their financial affairs; and praised those as truly magnificent, who squandered all they possessed. He praised and admired his uncle Caius in nothing more than that he had consumed in a short space the huge mass of wealth left him by Tiberius. He kept, therefore, to no limit, but was prodigal in all things. He allowed Tiridates eight hundred thousand sesterces a day (a thing almost incredible) for his expenses; and at his departure bestowed upon him upwards of a million. He likewise conferred upon Menecrates, the harper, and Spicillus, a gladiator, the estates and houses of men who had received the honour of a triumph. Cercopithecus Panerotes, whom he had enriched with estates both in town and country, he further honoured with a funeral, little inferior in pomp and magnificence to that of princes. He never wore the same garment twice. At games of chance, he ventured no less than four hundred thousand sesterces on a throw of the dice. He fished with a golden net, drawn by silken cords of purple and scarlet. It is said that he never travelled with less than a thousand baggage carts; the mules being all shod with silver, and the drivers dressed in scarlet jackets of the finest Canusian cloth, with a numerous train of footmen, and troops of Mazacans, with bracelets on their arms, and mounted upon horses in splendid trappings.

## 31

In no one thing was he more prodigal than in his buildings. He completed his palace by continuing it from the Palatine to the Esquiline hill, and called it at first only 'The Passage', but, after it was burnt down and rebuilt, 'The Golden House'. Of its dimensions and furniture, it may be sufficient to say thus much: the porch was so high that there stood in it a colossal statue of himself a hundred and twenty feet in height; and the space included in it was so ample, that it had triple porticos a mile in length, and a lake like a sea, surrounded with buildings which had the appearance of a city. Within its area were corn fields, vineyards, pastures, and woods, containing a vast number of animals of various kinds, both wild and tame. In other parts it was entirely overlaid with gold and adorned with jewels and mother-of-pearl. The supper rooms were vaulted, and compartments of the ceilings, inlaid with ivory, were made to revolve, and scatter flowers; while a device of pipes sprinkled sweet oils upon the guests. But of all these rooms, the principal banquet chamber was the finest, being made circular, and revolving perpetually, both night and day, in the manner of the celestial bodies. The baths flowed with salt water derived from the sea and the Albula. Upon the dedication of this stupendous edifice, all he said in approval of it was, 'that he had now a dwelling fit for a man'. He commenced making a pond for the reception of all the hot streams from Baiae, which he designed to have continued from Misenum to the Avernian lake, in a conduit, enclosed in galleries; and also a canal from Avernum to Ostia, that ships might pass from one to the other, without a sea voyage. The length of the proposed canal was one hundred and sixty miles; and it was intended to be of breadth sufficient to permit ships with five banks of oars to pass each other. For the execution of these designs, he ordered all prisoners, in every part of the empire, to be brought to Italy, and that even those who were convicted of the most heinous crimes, in lieu of any other sentence, should be condemned to work at them.

To these outrageous expenditures he was stimulated, both by the great revenue of the empire, and by the sudden honour given him of an immense hidden treasure, which queen Dido, upon her flight from Tyre, had brought with her to Africa. This, a Roman knight assured him upon his knowledge, was still hidden there in some huge and deep caverns, and might with a little labour be recovered.

## 32

But when this hope failed him and came to nothing, being now altogether destitute and obliged even to defer paying his troops and the rewards due to veterans, he bent his mind to raising money by means of false accusations and plunder. First he ordered that if any freedman, without sufficient reason, bore the name of the family to which he belonged, that five-sixths, instead of a half, of his estate should be brought into the exchequer at his decease: also that the estates of all such persons as had not in their wills been mindful of their prince should be confiscated; and that the lawyers who had drawn and dictated such wills should be liable to a fine. He ordained likewise, that all words and actions, upon which any informer could ground a prosecution, should be deemed treason. He demanded an equivalent for the crowns which the cities of Greece had at any time offered him in the solemn games. Having forbad anyone to use the colours of amethyst and Tyrian purple, he privately sent a person to sell a few ounces of them upon the day of the Nundinae, and then shut up all the merchants' shops on the pretext that his edict had been violated. It is said that, as he was playing and singing in the theatre, observing a married lady dressed in the purple which he had prohibited, he pointed her out to his procurators; upon which she was immediately dragged out of her seat, and not only stripped of her clothes, but her property. He never assigned a person to any office without making use of these words: 'You know what I want, and let us take care that nobody has anything he can call his own.' At last he rifled many temples of the rich offerings with which they were stored, and melted down all the gold and silver statues; and among the rest, those of the tutelary gods, which Galba afterwards restored.

## 33

His parricides and murders he began with Claudius himself; for although he was not the contriver of his death, he was privy to the plot. Nor did he dissimulate his complicity, but used frequently to quote a Greek proverb, in which he praised mushrooms as food fit for the gods, because Claudius had been poisoned with them. It is certain that he abused his memory in a most spiteful and atrocious manner, both in word and deed; charging him at one time with folly, at another while with cruelty. For he used to say in scoffing tone, that he had ceased *morari* among men, pronouncing the first syllable long; and treated as null many of his decrees and ordinances, as made by a doting and incompetent old man. He enclosed the place where his body was burnt with only a low wall of rough masonry. As for Britannicus, he attempted to poison him, not so much out of envy because he had a sweeter and pleasanter voice than himself, as from fear that he should be more gracious than himself among men, by reason of the respect which was inspired by the memory of his father. He employed for this purpose a woman named Locusta, who had been a witness against some persons guilty of like practices. But the poison she gave him, working more slowly than he expected, and only causing a purge, he sent for the woman, and beat her with his own hand, charging her with administering an antidote instead of poison. When she alleged in excuse that she had given Britannicus but a gentle mixture in order to prevent suspicion, 'Think you,' said he, 'that I am afraid of the Julian law!' And he forced her to compound, before his face in his own bedchamber, a poison as quick and strong as possible. This he tried upon a kid; but the animal lingering for five hours before it died, he ordered her to go to work again; and when she had boiled it many times more, he gave it to a pig, which died immediately. He then commanded the potion to be brought into the eating room and given to Britannicus, while he was at supper with him. The prince had no sooner tasted it than he fell to the floor. Nero readily pretended to the guests that it was only a fit of the falling sickness, to which, he said, he was subject. He buried him the following day, in a mean and hurried manner, during wild storms of rain. Locusta he pardoned, rewarding her with a great estate in land, and placing some disciples with her, to be trained up for like feats.

## 34

His mother being used to make strict inquiry into what he said or did, and to reprimand him with the freedom of a parent, he was so much offended, that he endeavoured to make her odious to the world by frequently pretending that he was about to quit the government and retire to Rhodes. Soon after, he deprived her of all honour, dignity, and authority, and removing from about her the guard of Roman and German soldiers, banished her from the palace and from his society, and persecuted her in every way he could; suborning some persons to harass her when at Rome with lawsuits, and to disturb her in her retirement from town with the most scurrilous and abusive language, following her about by land and sea. But being terrified by her threats and violent spirit, he determined to kill her, and thrice attempted to do so by poison. Perceiving that she was defended with antidotes and preservatives, he contrived machinery, by which the floor over her bedchamber might be made to fall upon her while she was asleep in the night. This design failing also, through the little caution used by those who were privy thereto, he next constructed a ship, so made that it would very suddenly cleave asunder, in the hope of destroying her either by drowning, or by the deck above her cabin crushing her in its fall. And so, under colour of a reconciliation, he wrote her an extremely affectionate letter, inviting her to Baiae, to celebrate with him the festival of Minerva. And having given order beforehand to the captains of the galleys which were to attend her, to split the ship wherein she was embarked, by falling foul of it, as if by chance, he came late to the feast, and prolonged it for the better execution of the plot in the night time. At her return for Bauli, instead of the old ship which had conveyed her to Baiae, he put her into that one which was cunningly devised to fall easily apart; and so, with a cheerful countenance, accompanied her to the waterfront, and at the parting kissed her breasts; after which, he sat up very late in the night, waiting with great anxiety to learn the issue of the enterprise. But when he understood that all had fallen out contrary to his wishes, and that she had saved herself by swimming to land: not knowing what course to take, upon her freedman, Lucius Agerinus bringing word, with great joy, that she was safe and well, he privately dropped a poniard by him. He then commanded the freedman to be seized and put in chains, under pretence of his having been hired by his mother to murder him; at the same time ordering her to be put to death, and giving out, that, to avoid punishment for her intended crime, she had voluntarily made away with herself.

Other circumstances, still more horrible, are related on good authority; as that he went to view her corpse and handled every portion of it, finding fault with some, commending others; and that, growing thirsty during the survey, he called for drink. Yet notwithstanding that he was heartened by the joyous congratulations of the soldiers, senate, and people, he could never afterwards bear the stings of his own conscience for this foul act. He confessed many times that he was haunted by his mother's ghost; and tormented also with the scourgings and burning torches of the Furies. Nay, he attempted by magical rites to bring up her ghost from below and soften her rage against him. When he was in Greece, he dared not attend the celebration of the Eleusinian mysteries, at the initiation of which, impious and wicked persons are debarred by the voice of the herald from approaching the rites.

Besides the murder of his mother, he was guilty also of that of his aunt; for once when he visited her, lying sick of a complaint in her bowels, and she, being then advanced in years, stroked his downy chin, and said, by way of pleasing and affectionate speech, 'May I but live to touch this soft hair when it is first shaved, and I shall die content,' he turned to those about him, and said in a derisive manner that he would straight way cut it off for her sake; and ordered the physicians to give her more violent purgatives. Even before she had expired, he laid hands upon her estate and suppressed her will that he might enjoy the whole himself.

Besides Octavia, the daughter of Claudius, he had two other wives:
to wit, Poppaea Sabina, whose father, Titus Ossius, had borne the
office of quaestor, and who had been married before to a Roman
knight: and, after her, Statilia Messalina, great granddaughter of
Taurus, who was twice consul, and received the honour of a
triumph. To secure her, he put to death her husband, Atticus
Vestinus, who was then consul. He soon wearied of Octavia's
company and forsook her bed; and when some friends reproved him
for it, he answered, that the rank and appendages of his wife should
content her. Soon afterwards he attempted many times, but in vain,
to strangle her, and then divorced her on the pretext that she was
barren. But when the people, who greatly loved her, disapproved of
this divorce, and railed at him for it, he went the length of banishing
her. In the end he murdered her, under colour of divers adulteries,
which were charged so impudently and falsely, that when all those
who were examined by torture upon the point stoutly denied any
knowledge of it, he suborned his pedagogue Anicetus, to affirm that
he had gained access to her by wile and debauched her. The twelfth
day after the divorcement of Octavia, he married Poppaea, whom he
loved entirely; yet he killed her, also, by a kick which he gave her
when she was big with child and sickly withal, only because she had
complained of him for returning late from driving his chariot. By her
he had a daughter named Claudia Augusta, who died while still an
infant. There was no person in any way associated with him who did
not feel the weight of his deadly hand. He slew Antonia, the daughter
of Claudius, who refused to be his wife after the death of Poppaea,
under a pretence that she was engaged in a conspiracy against him. In
the same way, he destroyed all who were allied to him either by
blood or marriage, among whom was young Aulus Plautius, whose
body he first abused against his will, crying out: 'Let my mother
bestow her kisses now on my successor's sweet lips'; pretending that
he had been his mother's paramour, and by her set on to gape after
the Empire. His stepson, Rufinus Crispinus, Poppaea's son, who was
yet a youth under age, because he was reported to act among his
playfellows the part of a general or an emperor, he ordered to be
drowned in the sea by his own slaves, while he was fishing. He

banished Tuscus, his nurse's son, for presuming, when he was procurator of Egypt, to wash in the baths which had been constructed in expectation of his own coming. Seneca, his preceptor, he forced to kill himself; although he had sworn very solemnly, upon Seneca's request for leave to retire from court and yield up his estate into his hands, 'that there was no just cause to suspect him, and that he would rather lose his own life than do him any hurt'. Having promised Burrus, the praetorian prefect, a remedy for a swelling in his throat, he sent him poison. Some old rich freedmen of Claudius who had formerly not only promoted his adoption, but were also instrumental in his advancement in the empire, and had been his governors, he cut off by poison mixed with their meat or drink.

## 36

With no less cruelty he raged against strangers and foreigners. A blazing star, which is commonly thought to portend death to kings and princes, appeared many nights together. Being greatly troubled thereby, and being informed by Babilus the Astrologer that princes were wont to expiate such prodigious signs by some notable massacre, and so divert the danger from their own persons by bringing it upon the heads of their nobles, he thereupon projected the death of all the highest personages in the City. He was the more strongly drawn toward this, because he had some plausible pretence for contriving it, having discovered two conspiracies that were formed against him; the former and greater of which was that formed by Piso, and discovered at Rome; the other was that of Vinicius, at Beneventum. The conspirators were brought to their trials bound with triple fetters. Some confessed of their own accord, and others said moreover that he was beholden to them for the attempt, as it was impossible to cure in any way except by death a person dishonoured by so many hideous acts. The children of the condemned were expelled from the City and then dispatched with poison or starved to death. It is certainly known that some of them, with their tutors and the slaves who carried their satchels, were all poisoned together at one dinner; and others were restrained from seeking their daily bread.

## 37

After this, without respect to persons, or measure in his cruelty, he put to death all whom his caprice seized upon, and preferred the most frivolous charges against them. But not to make a tedious relation of all these events: he charged Salvidienus Orfitus with letting out three taverns attached to his house in the Forum to some cities for the use of their deputies at Rome. Against Cassius Longinus, a lawyer bereft of both his eyes, it was objected that he kept among the busts of his ancestors that of Caius Cassius, one of the assassins in the death of Julius Caesar. The only charge brought against Paetus Thrasea was that he had a stern and melancholy countenance, like a pedagogue. To those whom he forced to kill themselves, he allowed but one hour; and, to prevent delay, he sent them physicians 'to *cure* them immediately, if they lingered beyond that time'; for so he called bleeding them to death. There was at that time an Egyptian who was a great eater, and would feed on raw flesh, or whatsoever was given him. It was credibly reported that the emperor had a great desire to provide him with living men to tear and devour. Being puffed up with his great success in the perpetration of crimes, he declared 'that no prince before himself ever realised the extent of his power'; and he many times threw out strong intimations that he would not even spare the senators who survived, but would entirely extirpate that order and put the provinces and armies in the hands of the Roman knights and his own freedmen. It is certain that he never gave or vouchsafed to allow anyone the customary kiss, either on entering or departing, or even returned a salute. And at the inauguration of a work, the cut through the Isthmus, he prayed aloud before a large assembly, that 'the undertaking might speed well and turn out auspiciously for himself and the Roman people' – suppressing all mention of the senate.

## 38

Yet for all that, he spared not the people, nor the very walls and buildings of the City. When somebody, in conversation, chanced to quote: 'When I am dead let fire devour the world', 'Nay, rather,' said he, 'when I am living – ' and he acted accordingly; for, pretending to be offended with the ill-favoured houses, and the crooked and narrow streets, he set fire to Rome so openly, that many men of consular rank caught his own household servants on their property, armed with tow and torches, but dared not balk them. There being near his Golden House some granaries, the site of which he exceedingly coveted, they were battered as if with machines of war, and set on fire, the walls being built of stone. For six days and seven nights together this terrible havoc raged, driving the people to seek the tombs and monuments for lodging and shelter. During this time, a vast number of stately buildings, the houses of generals celebrated in former times, and even then still decorated with the spoils of war, were laid in ashes; as well as the temples of the gods, which had been vowed and dedicated by the kings of Rome, and afterwards in the Punic and Gallic wars: in short, whatsoever was memorable and worthy of seeing, and which time had spared, was consumed. This fire he beheld from a tower in the house of Maecenas and, taking great joy (as he himself said) in the beautiful effect of the flames, he chanted a poem on the ruin of Troy, in the tragic dress he used on the stage. And so that he might wring from this calamity all that he could by plunder and rapine, he promised to remove the bodies of those who had perished in the fire, and clear the rubbish at his own expense; suffering no one to meddle with the remains of their property. Finally, not only by receiving, but also by exacting contributions from all parts on account of the loss, he beggared the provinces and exhausted the wealth of private persons.

## 39

To these great and shameful misfortunes brought upon the people by their prince were added some that arose from other causes. Such were a pestilence by which, within the space of one autumn, there died no less than thirty thousand persons, as appeared from the registers in the temple of Libitina; a great disaster in Britain, where two of the principal towns belonging to the Romans were plundered, and a dreadful havoc made both among Roman soldiers and allies; and, finally, a shameful discomfiture of the army of the East where, in Armenia, the legions were obliged to pass under the yoke, and it was with great difficulty that Syria was retained. Amidst all these disasters, it was a wonder to see that he bore nothing more patiently than the scurrilous language and railing abuse which was in every one's mouth; and to none was he milder in his treatment than those who assailed him with harsh speeches, or opprobrious verses. Many infamous libels and defamatory words, both in Greek and Latin, were publicly written, such as these:

> Orestes and Alcmaeon – Nero too,
> The lustful Nero, worst of all the crew,
> Fresh from his bridal – their own mothers slew.

> Sprung from Aeneas, pious, wise and great,
> Who says that Nero is degenerate?
> Safe through the flames, one bore his sire; the other,
> To save himself, took off his loving mother.

> His lyre to harmony our Nero strings;
> His arrows o'er the plain the Parthian wings;
> Ours call the tuneful Paean – famed in war,
> The other Phoebus' name, the god who shoots afar.

> All Rome will be one house: to Veii fly,
> Should it not stretch to Veii, by and by.

But he made no search after the authors, and when some of them were convened before the senate, by the Appeacher, he would not suffer them to sustain any grievous punishment. As he passed along in the open street, Isidorus, the Cynic philosopher, said to him aloud: 'You chant the calamities of Nauplius well, but conduct yourself badly.' And Datus, a comic actor, when repeating these words in the piece 'Farewell, father! Farewell mother!', mimicked the gestures of persons drinking and swimming, in allusion to the deaths of Claudius and Agrippina: and on uttering the last clause,

> You stand this moment on the brink of Orcus;

he plainly referred to the senate. Yet Nero did no more than banish the actor and philosopher from the city and Italy; either because he was insensible to shame, or from fear that if he betrayed his vexation, still more pregnant wits might set to work upon him.

## 40

The world, having endured such an emperor for little less than fourteen years, at length forsook him. At first the Gallic revolted, headed by Julius Vindex, who at that time governed the province as propraetor. Nero had been formerly told by astrologers that it would be his fortune to be at last deserted by all the world; and this occasioned that celebrated saying of his, 'an artist can live in any country'; by which he meant to offer as an excuse for his practice of music that it was not only his amusement as a prince, but might be his support when reduced to a private station. Yet some of the astrologers promised him, in his forlorn estate, the rule of the East, and some in express words the kingdom of Jerusalem. But the greater part of them flattered him with assurances of his being restored to his former fortune. And being most inclined to believe the latter prediction, upon losing Britain and Armenia, he imagined he had run through all the misfortunes which the fates had decreed him. But when, upon consulting the oracle of Apollo at Delphi, he was advised to beware of the seventy-third year, as if he were not to die till then, never thinking of Galba's age, he conceived such hopes, not only of living to advanced years, but of constant and singular good fortune, that having lost some things of great value by shipwreck, he scrupled not to say among his friends, that 'the fishes would bring them back to him'. At Naples he was informed of the rebellion in Gaul, which fell out on the very same day of the year on which he had killed his mother. But he received the news with such unconcern as to create a suspicion that he was really glad of the event, as an occasion for plundering those wealthy provinces by the right of war; and going straightway to the gymnasium, he beheld with great earnestness and delight the exercise of the wrestlers. At supper-time, being interrupted with letters which apprised him of greater tumults, he expressed no hotter resentment than only to threaten the rebels. For eight days together he never attempted to answer any letters nor give any orders but buried the whole matter in profound silence.

## 41

At last, thoroughly aroused and nettled by the contumelious edicts of Vindex, coming thick and fast upon him, he exhorted the senate, in a letter, to avenge his wrongs and those of the republic; alleging, as an excuse for his non-appearance, that he had caught cold. In the midst of all this, nothing vexed him so much as to find himself railed at as an unskilled harper, and, instead of Nero, styled Ahenobarbus: which, being his family name and because he was twitted with it, he proclaimed that he would resume and lay aside the other that he had taken by adoption. All other reviling taunts and slanders he dismissed as wholly false, and earnestly refuted the charge of want of skill in an art upon which he had bestowed so much pains and brought to perfection; and frequently asked those about him if they had ever known a more excellent musician than himself. But when messengers continued to pour in from Gaul, one after another, he returned in great fear to Rome. On the way his heart was lightened somewhat by a vain and foolish presage; for he observed a sculptured monument which depicted a Gaulish soldier vanquished by a Roman knight and dragged forward by the hair. At this sight he leaped for joy and worshipped the heavens. Even then he made no appeal either to the senate or people, but calling together some of the leading men at his own house he held a hasty consultation upon the present state of affairs; and then, during the remainder of the day, led them all about with him to view some musical instruments of a strange device, not hitherto known, which were played by water; showing all the parts minutely and discoursing upon the principles and intricacies of the workmanship. This contrivance, he promised them, would be brought forth into the theatre, 'if Vindex would give him leave'.

## 42

When he received word that Galba and the Spaniards had revolted, he fell down in a faint and, his heart and reason apparently having left him, he lay a good while speechless and as one dead. As soon as he came to himself again, he rent his clothes and beat his head, saying dolefully: 'I am utterly undone!' And when his nurse came to comfort him, telling him that like accidents had befallen other princes before him, he answered: 'I am afflicted beyond all others, for I have lost an empire while still living.' Yet he did not abate one whit his customary luxuriousness and slothfulness. Nay, when some inkling of better news came from the provinces as he sat at a most sumptuous banquet, he sang, with gestures like those of a player, some ridiculous verses set to lascivious measures, against the chieftains of the revolt, which were made public. Being conveyed secretly into the theatre, he sent word to a certain player who was acting his part to the great content and approval of the spectators, 'that he had it all his own way, now that he himself did not appear on the stage'.

## 43

At the first breaking out of these tumults, it is credibly thought that he intended to execute many further designs of a cruel and horrible nature, yet such as conformed well to his natural humour: namely, to send new governors and commanders to the provinces and the armies, and employ assassins to murder all the former governors and commanders, as men unanimously engaged in a conspiracy against him; to massacre the exiles in every quarter and all the Gaulish population in Rome; the former lest they should join the insurrection; the latter as privy to the designs of their countrymen, and ready to support them; to abandon Gaul itself, to be wasted and plundered by his armies; to poison the whole senate at a feast; to fire the city and then let loose the wild beasts upon the people, in order to impede their checking the destruction of the flames. But being deterred from these designs, not so much by remorse of conscience, as by despair of being able to effect them, and judging an expedition into Gaul necessary, he removed the consuls from office before the time of its expiration was arrived; and in their room assumed the consulship himself without a colleague, as if the destinies had so ordained, that Gaul could not be subdued but by a consul with the sole authority. Upon assuming the fasces, after an entertainment at the palace, as he walked out of the room leaning on the arms of some of his friends, he protested that as soon as he should arrive in the province, he would show himself unarmed before the armies and do nothing else but weep; and that, after he had brought them to repentance, he would sing merrily, on the day following, some songs of triumph, with those that rejoiced with him; 'Which songs,' he said, 'ought with all speed to be composed by me.'

## 44

In preparing for this expedition, his special care was to provide carriages for his musical instruments and machinery to be used upon the stage; to have the hair of the concubines he carried with him dressed in the fashion of men; and to supply them with battle axes, and Amazonian bucklers. This done, he summoned the city tribes to take the military oath; and when no qualified persons would answer to their names, he ordered all masters to send a certain number of slaves, the best they had, not excepting their stewards and secretaries. He commanded the several orders of the people to bring in a fixed proportion of their estates, as they stood in the censor's books; all tenants of houses and mansions to pay one year's rent forthwith into the exchequer; and, with unheard-of strictness, would receive only new coin of the purest silver and the finest gold; insomuch that most people openly refused to pay, and demanded by general consent that he recover from the informers the monies they had received for their tattling.

## 45

The hatred that was felt for him was heightened by the great scarcity of corn, and an occurrence connected with it. For, as it fell out at that time, there arrived from Alexandria a ship, said to be freighted with a kind of dust for the use of the emperor's wrestlers, and which was for strewing on the ground so that the wrestlers could roll in it when their bodies dripped with oil or perspiration. This kindled the public anger so much that there was no abuse or denunciation that was not heaped upon him. Upon the top of one of his statues was placed the figure of a chariot with a Greek inscription reading: 'Now indeed he has a race to run; let him be gone.' A little bag was tied about another with a ticket reading: 'Truly thou hast merited the sack,' – in allusion to the punishment prescribed for a parricide by the Roman law, namely that of being sewed up in a sack and thrown into the sea. Some person likewise wrote on the pillars in the Forum 'that he had even woke the *cocks* with his singing,' – for the word 'Gallos' signifies both cocks and Gauls. And many masters, finding fault with their servants, used to call for a Vindex, or vindicator.

## 46

Beside all this he was greatly frightened by the manifest portents, both old and new, arising from dreams, auspices, and omens. Whereas before the murder of his mother he had never been wont to dream, after that event he saw in his sleep the rudder of a ship forced from his hand as he was steering; and he dreamed that his wife Octavia dragged him into a prodigiously dark place where he was one time covered over with a great swarm of winged ants, and at another surrounded by the national images which were set up near Pompey's theatre and hindered from going farther; that a Spanish jennet he was fond of had his hinder parts so changed as to resemble those of an ape and, having his head only left unaltered, neighed in a loud shrill voice. The doors of the mausoleum of Augustus flying open of their own accord, a voice was heard calling for him by name. Upon the kalends of January, the lares, being adorned with fresh garlands, fell down during the preparations for sacrificing to them. While he was taking the omens, Sporus presented him with a ring, the stone of which had carved upon it the Rape of Proserpine. When a great multitude of the several orders had assembled to attend at the solemnity of making vows to the gods, it was a long time before the keys of the Capitol could be found. And when, in a speech of his to the senate against Vindex, these words were read: 'That the miscreants should be punished, and soon *make* the end they merited,' they all cried out, 'You will do it, Augustus.' It was likewise observed that the last tragic piece he sung was *Oedipus in Exile,* and that he fell down just as he pronounced this line:

> Wife, mother, father, force me to my mind.

## 47

Meanwhile, when news came that all the other armies also rebelled, he tore to pieces the letters which were delivered to him as he sat at dinner, overthrew the table and dashed violently against the paved floor two favourite cups of crystal (which he called Homer's because

some of that poet's verses were cut upon them). Then, taking from
Locusta a dose of poison which he put up in a golden box, he went
into the Servilian gardens, and thence dispatching a trusty freedman to
Ostia, with orders to make ready a fleet, he endeavoured to prevail
upon some tribunes and centurions of the praetorian guards to attend
him in his flight; but part of them showing no great inclination to
comply, while others absolutely refused, and one even cried out aloud:

*Usque adeone mori miserum est?*

Say, is it then so sad a thing to die? —

he cast about in his mind for some plan of action: whether he should
go as a suppliant to the Parthians, or appear before the people arrayed
all in black and there upon the rostra, in most humble and piteous
accents, crave pardon for all that was passed and, if he could not move
their hearts to accept him again as emperor, sue at least for the
government of Egypt. There was afterwards found in his cabinet a
speech penned to this purpose. But it is thought that he was
discouraged from this enterprise by the fear that he should be torn to
pieces before he could gain the Forum. Thus, putting off all further
cogitation of this matter until the next day, he was startled out of his
sleep about midnight and, finding the guards dispersed, he sent about
for his friends. But when none of them came or sent any word in
response he went with a few attendants to their houses; where,
finding all doors shut and nobody appearing in answer to the
summons, he returned to his bedchamber. By this time those in
charge had slipped away, after taking the bedding and even the box of
poison which he had procured. He then sought Spicillus, the
gladiator, or someone to kill him; but finding none, 'What!' said he,
'have I then neither a friend or a foe?' And he immediately ran out as
if he would throw himself into the Tiber.

## 48

But recovering from this violent mood, he desired some secret
hiding-place where he might recall his wits. And when his freedman
Phaon offered him his country house, between the Salarian and
Nomentan roads, about four miles from the city, he mounted a
horse, barefoot as he was and in his tunic, only slipping over it an old

soiled cloak; and so he rode, holding a handkerchief before his face, and with only four persons to attend him of which Sporus was one. Once he was terrified by a sudden earthquake, and again by a flash of lightning which flashed against his face; and he heard from the neighbouring camp the shouts of the soldiers, wishing his destruction and prosperity to Galba. He heard, too, a traveller encountered on the road call out, 'They are in pursuit of Nero'; and another ask, 'Is there any news in the city about Nero?' His horse starting from his path at the scent of a carcass which lay in the road, his face was uncovered, and he was recognised by one Missicius, a praetorian soldier, who saluted him by name. When they reached the lane which turned up to the house, they quitted their horses, and with much difficulty he wound among bushes and briars and along a track through a bed of rushes, over which they spread their cloaks for him to tread on. Having reached a wall at the back of the villa, Phaon advised him to hide himself awhile in a sand pit. 'Nay,' he replied, 'I will not go under ground alive.' Staying there some little time, while preparations were made for bringing him secretly into the villa, he took up some water out of a neighbouring tank with his hand, saying as he drank, 'This is Nero's distilled water.' Then his cloak having been torn by the brambles, he pulled out the thorns that adhered to it; and so, creeping upon all fours through a narrow hole made for him in the wall, he gained the house, and laid himself down in the first room he came to, upon a miserable pallet, with an old and worn coverlet thrown over it. When hunger assailed him, and thirst too made itself felt, he refused the coarse brown bread which was offered to him, but drank a little warm water.

## 49

When all those about him pressed him to deliver himself from the indignities which were threatening him, he ordered a grave to be dug before his eyes, according to the proportions of his body, and the bottom to be covered with pieces of marble put together, if any could be found about the house; and water and wood to be got ready for immediate use about his corpse; weeping at every word he spoke, and inserting often this pitiful speech: 'What an artist is now about to perish!' Meanwhile, letters being brought in by a servant belonging to Phaon, he snatched them out of his hand, and therein read that he had been pronounced an enemy by the senate, and that search was being made for him that he might be punished according to the ancient custom of the Romans. He thereupon inquired what kind of punishment that was; and being told that the condemned man should be stripped naked, and scourged to death, while his neck was fastened within a forked stake, he was so terrified that he caught up two daggers which he had brought with him, and after feeling the points of both, put them up again saying, 'The fatal hour is not yet come.' One while he begged of Sporus to begin to wail and lament; another while, he entreated that one of them should set him an example by killing himself first; and then again, he lamented his own timorousness in these words: 'I yet live to my shame and disgrace: this is not becoming for Nero. In such a time as this, thou oughtest to be of stout heart. Rouse thyself, man!' Now, by this time, there had approached the house the horsemen who had a warrant to bring him alive. When he perceived this, and after he had in trembling tones uttered this verse:

The trampling noise of horses swift resoundeth in mine ears,

he set a dagger to his throat, being assisted in the act by Epaphroditus, his secretary. While he was yet but half-dead, a centurion broke in, and putting his cloak to the wound, pretending that he was come to his assistance, he made no other reply but this, ' 'Tis too late'; and 'Is this your loyalty?' No sooner had he pronounced these words than he expired, with his eyes staring and starting out of his head, to the great fear and horror of all that were present. He had requested of his attendants, as a favour of the first importance, that they would let no one sever his head from his body, which he implored might be burnt entire. And Icelus, Galba's freedman, who had but a little before been discharged from the prison into which he had been thrown at the beginning of the disturbances, permitted so much.

## 50

His funeral was performed at an expense of two hundred thousand sesterces; his body being carried forth to the pile upon a bed covered with the white robes, interwoven with gold, which he had worn upon the kalends of January preceding. His nurses, Ecloge and Alexandra, with his concubine Acte, deposited his remains in the tomb belonging to the family of the Domitii, which stands upon the top of the Hill of the Gardens, and is to be seen from the Campus Martius. In that monument a coffin of porphyry, with an altar of marble of Luna over it, is enclosed by a wall built of stone brought from Thasos.

## 51

In stature he was a little under the average height, his body full of spots and freckles and foul of skin besides. His hair was yellowish; his countenance fairly agreeable but not handsome; his eyes grey and dull, his neck thick, his belly prominent, his legs very slender, and his health excellent. For, intemperate as he was, and given to riotous living, he suffered, in the space of fourteen years, only three attacks of illness; and these so slight, that he neither forbore the use of wine, nor modified his usual diet. In his dress and grooming, he was so indifferent that he had his hair cut in rings, one above another; and when in Achaia, he let it grow long behind. He generally appeared in public in the loose and effeminate garment he wore at table, with a fine lawn handkerchief about his neck, and wearing neither a girdle nor shoes.

## 52

While still but a boy, he had a taste for almost all the liberal sciences; but his mother turned his mind from the study of philosophy, as unsuited to one destined to be a sovereign; and his preceptor, Seneca, discouraged him from acquiring a knowledge of the ancient orators, that he might longer hold his admiration of himself. Therefore, as he inclined readily toward poetry, he composed verses both with pleasure and ease; nor did he, as some think, publish those of other writers as his own. There have come into my hands several little writing tablets and loose sheets, containing verses very widely known, written in his own hand and in such a manner that it was very evident, from the blotting and interlining, that they had not been transcribed from a copy, nor dictated by another, but had been put down as they came out of his own head.

## 53

In drawing and painting, as well as in moulding statues in plaster, he also took no small delight. But above all, he yearned for the applause of the people; and desired to rival any man who won popularity with them, by whatsoever means. It was the general opinion that, after the crowns gained by his musical performances on the stage, he would at the next lustrum have competed among the wrestlers at the Olympic games. For he was continually practising that art; nor did he witness the gymnastic games in any part of Greece otherwise than sitting upon the ground in the stadium, as the umpires do. And if a pair of wrestlers happened to break the bounds, he would with his own hands drag them back into the centre of the circle. He had intended moreover (since he was reputed to equal Apollo in singing, and the sun in charioting) to imitate also the achievements of Hercules. And they say that a lion was got ready for him to kill, either with a club, or with a strangle clutch, in view of the people in the amphitheatre; which feat he was to perform naked.

## 54

Certainly, a little before the end of his life, he had publicly vowed that if he continued in power in the state, he would exhibit in his own person, at the games which would be held in honour of his success, a performance upon the organ, as well as upon flutes and bagpipes; and, on the last day of the games, would act in the play and take the part of Turnus, as we find it in Virgil. And some say that the actor Paris was put to death by him, as one who threatened his supremacy.

## 55

He had an insatiable desire for perpetual fame, which he strove to secure by foolish and inconsiderate acts. He abolished the old names of many things and places and gave them new names derived from his own. The month of April he called Neroneus; and had the design to change the name of Rome to Neropolis.

## 56

All religious rites of whatever kind he held in contempt, except those of the Syrian Goddess; but at last he became so indifferent to her that he polluted her image with urine; being now absorbed in another superstition, wherein alone he persevered most constantly. For having received from some obscure plebeian a little puppet representing a girl, as a preservative against plots, and chancing to discover a conspiracy immediately thereafter, he worshipped her as the sovereign deity, honouring her with three sacrifices daily ever afterwards. Nay, he would have it believed that he received prophetic warnings from her as to future events. A few months before he died, he attended a sacrifice, and took the omens by prying into beasts' entrails; but though he carefully observed the rites, he did not gain thereby the favour of the gods.

## 57                                    A.U.C. 821

He died in the thirty-second year of his age, and upon the same day of the year on which he had murdered his wife Octavia. His death brought such great joy to the people that they ran about the city with caps upon their heads, to testify to their regained freedom. Yet there were not wanting some who, for a long time after, decked his tomb with the gay flowers that spring and summer afford, and who sometimes placed his image upon the rostra, dressed in purple robes of state; at other times they published proclamations in his name, as if he were still alive, and would shortly return to Rome to work great mischief among his enemies. Moreover, Vologaesus, king of the Parthians, when he sent ambassadors to the senate to renew his alliance with the Roman people, earnestly requested that due honour should be paid to the memory of Nero; and, to conclude, when, twenty years later, at which time I was a young man, some person arose among them (no one knew from whence, nor of what condition) who gave out that he was Nero, so gracious was the name among the Parthians, that he was very strongly supported, and not delivered up again without great reluctance.

# Servius Sulpicius Galba

## I

The line of the Caesars ended in Nero; that it would so come to pass was made evident by various signs, of which two were particularly significant. When Livia, after her marriage with Augustus, was making a visit to her villa at Veii, it happened that an eagle soaring over her head let fall into her lap a white hen, holding in her bill a laurel branch, just as she had caught it up. Livia thought it well to have the hen taken care of, and the laurel planted; and behold! there proceeded from the hen such a fine brood of chickens, all white, that the villa, to this day, is called The Villa of the Hens; while from the laurel sprung so fair a row of trees that the Caesars procured thence the boughs and crowns they bore at their triumphs. It was also their constant custom to plant others on the same spot, immediately after a triumph; and it was observed that, a little before the death of each prince, the tree which had been set by him withered away. In the last year of Nero, however, not only the whole grove of trees perished to the very roots, but all the hens sickened and died. About the same time, the temple of the Caesars being struck with lightning, the heads of all the statues there fell off at once, and the sceptre of Augustus was shaken out of his hands.

2

Nero was succeeded by Galba, who was in no degree allied to the house of the Caesars, but was, without question, of a very noble race, being descended from a great and ancient family; for he always used to put among his other titles, upon the bases of his statues, that of great-grandson to Q. Catulus Capitolinus. And when he came to be emperor, he set up the images of his ancestors in the hall of the palace; and it appeared, from the inscriptions, that he derived his descent on his father's side from Jupiter, and by his mother from Pasiphae, the wife of Minos.

## 3

To touch upon the whole of his lineage would be a lengthy recital; and I will only recount briefly the members of his immediate family. Why or whence the first of the Sulpicii who had the cognomen of Galba was so called, is uncertain. Some are of opinion that it was because he set fire to a city in Spain, after he had a long time assaulted it vainly, with torches dipped in the gum called Galbanum: others, that he was so named because, in a lingering sickness, he had continual recourse to this extract, wrapped up in wool, as a remedy: still others, that it was because he was very fat, such a one being called, in the language of the Gauls, Galba; or, on the contrary, because he was of a slender habit of body, like those insects which breed in a kind of oak and are called Galbae. Servius Galba, who had been consul with L. Aurelius Cotta, and was the most eloquent man of his time, shed glory upon the line. It is reported that when he was propraetor of Spain, he treacherously put to the sword thirty thousand Lusitanians, and by that means gave occasion to the war of Viriatus. His grandson being incensed against Julius Caesar, whose lieutenant he had been in Gaul, because he was through him disappointed of the consulship, joined with Cassius and Brutus in the conspiracy against him, for which he was condemned by the Pedian law. From him were descended the grandfather and father of the emperor Galba. The grandfather was more famed for his scholarly learning than for any political dignity that he ever attained. For he rose no higher than the praetorship, but he wrote many histories, and those of no slight proportions and merit. His father attained to the consulship; he was a man of low stature and humpbacked, and although no great orator, he used to plead cases industriously. He was twice married: the first of his wives was Mummia Achaica, daughter of Catulus, and great-granddaughter of Lucius Mummius, who sacked Corinth; and the other, Livia Ocellina, an exceedingly wealthy and beautiful woman, by whom it is supposed he was courted for the nobleness of his descent. It is said, too, that she pursued him only the more hotly, after he had, (by reason of her importunate suit), stripped himself once when alone with her, to show the imperfections of his body, because he did not wish her to be deceived. By Achaica he had two sons, Caius and Servius. The elder, Caius, having wasted his estate, retired from Rome, and being prohibited by Tiberius from standing for a proconsulship in his year, put an end to his own life.

4                        A.U.C. 751

The emperor Servius Galba was born in the consulship of M. Valerius Messala and Cn. Lentulus, upon the ninth of the kalends of January, in a villa standing upon a hill, near Terracina, on the left-hand side of the road to Fundi. Being adopted by his stepmother, Livia Ocellina, he assumed the name of Livius, with the cognomen of Ocella, and changed his praenomen; for he afterwards used that of Lucius, instead of Servius, until he came to the empire. It is well known that Augustus, when Galba came to salute him, among other little boys, patted him on his pretty cheek, saying, 'and thou also, my child, shall have a taste one day of our sovereign rule.' Tiberius, likewise, being told that he would come to be emperor, but not before old age, said, 'Let him live, then, since that does not concern me!' When his grandfather was offering sacrifice to avert some ill omen from lightning, the entrails of the victim were snatched out of his hand by an eagle, and carried off into an oak tree loaded with acorns. Upon this, the soothsayers said that the family would come to be masters of the empire, but not until many years had passed: at which he, by way of jest, answered, 'Ay, when a mule shall bring forth a foal.' Afterwards, when Galba began to rebel against Nero and aspire to the empire, nothing heartened him so much in this design as a mule's happening at that time to have a foal. And while all others were shocked at the occurrence, as an evil omen, he alone regarded it as favourable, calling to mind the sacrifice and the speech of his grandfather. When he took upon him the virile gown, he dreamt that the goddess Fortune said to him how she stood before his door all weary, and unless she were let in speedily, she should become a prey to whomsoever she met. When he had awakened and opened the door of the house, he found, close to the threshold, a brazen statue of the goddess, about a cubit long: which he carried with him to Tusculum, where he used to pass the summer season, and having consecrated it in an apartment of his house, he ever after worshipped it with a monthly sacrifice and an anniversary vigil. And although he was but a very young man, he observed an ancient custom, no longer retained except in his own lineage; this was to have his freedmen and slaves appear in a body before him twice a day, morning and evening, to offer him the appropriate salutations.

## 5

Among the liberal sciences, he gave himself to the study of civil law. He married Lepida, by whom he had two sons; but the mother and children all dying, he remained a widower; nor could he be persuaded to marry again, not even Agrippina herself, at that time left a widow by the death of Domitius, who had tried by every means to allure him while he was still a married man; insomuch that Lepida's mother, when in company with several married women, took her to task for it, and even went so far as to shake her soundly. He honoured above all the empress Livia, wife of Augustus, through whose favour, while she lived, he became powerful, and by whose will he closely missed being enriched. For, among others whom she remembered with legacies, he had a special bequest of fifty millions of sesterces; but because the sum was written down in figures, and not in words at length, her heir Tiberius reduced it to one-half million; and even this he never received.

## 6

Having entered upon the great offices of state before the age stated by law, during his praetorship, at the celebration of games in honour of the goddess Flora, he presented the new spectacle of elephants walking upon ropes. After that, he governed the province Aquitania nearly a whole year, and soon afterwards took the consulship in the usual course, for the space of six months. It so happened that he succeeded L. Domitius, the father of Nero, and was succeeded by Salvius Otho, father of the emperor of that name; so that his holding it between the sons of these two men looked like a presage of his future triumph. Being appointed by Caius Caligula to supersede Gaetulicus in his command, the day after his joining the legions he put a stop to their plaudits in a public spectacle by issuing an order that they should keep their hands under their cloaks. Whereupon, this verse became a byword in the camp:

*Disce, miles, militare: Galba est, non Gaetulicus.*

Learn, soldier, now in arms to use your hands,
'Tis Galba, not Gaetulicus, commands.

With like severity, he would allow of no petitions for leave of absence from the camp. He hardened the soldiers, both veteran and raw, with constant work and exercise; and having repressed the barbarians, who had made violent inroads into Gaul, and hurled them back, he so far recommended himself and his army to Caius's approbation when that emperor came into Germany, that, among the innumerable troops drawn from all the provinces of the empire, none met with higher praise nor received greater rewards from him. He likewise distinguished himself by heading an escort, with a shield in his hand, and running at the side of the emperor's chariot twenty miles together.

## 7

When tidings came that Caius was murdered and many urged him to take the opportunity then offered, he preferred quiet and rest. Because of this, he stood in high favour with Claudius, and was admitted into the circle of his intimate friends; insomuch that when he was taken suddenly sick (though the ailment was not serious), the day appointed for the expedition to start for Britain was deferred. He governed Africa as proconsul for two years; being chosen out of the regular course to restore order in the province, which was in great tumult from civil dissensions and the alarms of the barbarians. This commission he discharged with great strictness and equity even in very small matters. A soldier upon some expedition being charged with selling, in a great scarcity of corn, a bushel of wheat, which was all he had left, for a hundred denarii, he forbad anyone to relieve him when he became in want of food, so that he died of hunger. When sitting in judgment, a cause being brought before him about some beast of burden, the ownership of which was claimed by two persons; the evidence being slight on both sides, and it being difficult to determine the truth, he ordered the beast to be led to a pond at which he had used to be watered, with his head muffled up; and the covering being there removed, that he should be the property of the one whom he followed voluntarily, after he had drunk.

## 8

For his brave exploits both at this time in Africa, and formerly in Germany, he received the triumphal ornaments, and three sacerdotal appointments, one among The Fifteen, another in the college of Titius, and a third among the Augustals; and from that time to the middle of Nero's reign, he lived for the most part in retirement. He never went abroad so much as to take the air without a carriage attending him, in which there was a million of sesterces in gold, ready at hand; until at last, at the time he was living in the town of Fundi, the province of Hispania Tarraconensis was offered him. And it chanced that after his arrival in the province, as he was sacrificing in a temple, a boy who attended with a censor became all on a sudden greyheaded. This incident was interpreted by some to mean that a change would take place in the government, and an old man would succeed a young one: that is, that he would succeed Nero. And not long after, a thunderbolt falling into a lake in Cantabria, twelve axes were found in it: a manifest token of the sovereign power.

## 9

For eight years he governed the province, with a somewhat variable and uneven hand. At first he was sharp, severe, and vigorous in administering justice. For a money-dealer having perpetrated a fraud in the way of his business, he cut off his hands and nailed them to his counter. Another, who had poisoned an orphan, to whom he was guardian and next heir to the estate, he crucified. On this delinquent imploring the protection of the law, and crying out that he was a Roman citizen, he affected to allay his punishment with some comfort and honour, and commanded that the cross already made should be changed, and another reared higher than usual and painted white. By little and little, however, he became slothful, idle, and careless, from the fear of giving Nero any occasion of jealousy, and because, as he used to say, 'nobody was obliged to render an account of their leisure hours'. He was holding a court of justice on the circuit at New Carthage when he received news that Gaul was in revolt; and while the lieutenant of Aquitania was soliciting his assistance, letters were brought from Vindex, requesting him 'to assert the rights of mankind, and put himself at their head to relieve them from the tyranny of Nero'. Without any long demur, he accepted the invitation, from a mixture of fear and hope. For he had discovered that private orders had been sent by Nero to his procurators in the province to get him dispatched; and he was confirmed and strengthened in the enterprise by several auspices and omens as well as by the prophecy of a young woman of good family. The more so, because the priest of Jupiter at Clunia, warned in a dream, had discovered in the recesses of the temple some verses similar to those in which she had delivered her prophecy. These had also been uttered by a girl under divine inspiration, about two hundred years before. The import of the verses was that one day there should arise out of Spain the sovereign lord of the whole world.

## 10

Taking his seat on the tribunal, therefore, as if with no other purpose than the manumitting of slaves, he had set up before him the effigies of a number of persons who had been condemned and put to death by Nero: while there stood also in his presence a boy of noble blood who had been banished and whom he had designedly sent for from one of the neighbouring Balearic isles: and he bewailed the state of the times. Whereupon, being with one accord saluted by the title of Emperor, he professed himself to be only the lieutenant of the senate and people of Rome. Then, proclaiming a cessation of judicial business for the time, he levied legions and auxiliary troops among the provincials, beside his veteran army consisting of one legion, two wings of horse, and three cohorts. Out of the military leaders most renowned for their wisdom, and superior in years, he formed a kind of senate, unto whom men should have recourse touching matters of importance, as need arose. He likewise chose several young men of the equestrian order, who were to be allowed the privilege of wearing the gold ring, and, being called 'The Reserve', should mount guard before his bedchamber, a post that had formerly belonged to the legionary soldiers. He issued proclamations throughout the provinces of the empire, exhorting all to rise in arms unanimously and aid the common cause by all the ways and means in their power. At about the same time, in fortifying a town which he had pitched upon for a military post, a ring of antique workmanship was found in the stone of which was engraved the goddess Victory, with a trophy. And soon after, a ship of Alexandria arrived at Dertosa, loaded with arms, and without pilot, mariner or passenger. Upon this marvellous event, nobody had the least doubt but that the war upon which they were embarking was just, honourable, and undertaken with the favour and approbation of the gods. But lo, in a manner sudden and unlooked for, the whole design was dashed to pieces. One of the two wings of horse, repenting of the violation of their oath to Nero, attempted to desert him upon approach to the camp, and were with some difficulty kept at their duty. And some slaves who had been presented to him by a freedman of Nero's, on purpose to murder him, attempted to kill him as he went through a narrow passage to the baths. They surely would have done so but that as they encouraged one another not to let the opportunity slip, they were overheard and called to an account concerning it; and being examined upon the occasion of their discourse, they were forced by torture to confess the truth.

## II

Following on the heels of these grave dangers came the death of Vindex, at which he felt so utterly disheartened, like a man quite deserted by fortune, that he meditated putting an end to his own life. But messengers coming from Rome with news that Nero was slain and that all had taken an oath to him as emperor, he laid aside the title of lieutenant, and took upon him that of Caesar. Putting himself upon his march, his general's cloak and a dagger hanging from his neck before his breast, he did not resume the toga until Nymphidius Sabinus, prefect of the praetorian guards at Rome, with the two lieutenants, Fonteius Capito in Germany, and Claudius Macer in Africa, who rose up in arms against him, were all put down.

## 12

A rumour had been raised before his arrival of his cruelty and avarice, in that he had punished some cities of Spain and Gaul for not joining him at once, by the imposition of heavy taxes, and some by levelling their walls; and had put to death the governors and procurators with their wives and children; likewise that he had melted down a golden crown, of fifteen pounds weight, taken out of the temple of Jupiter, with which he was presented by the people of Tarracona, and commanded that the three ounces which were wanting in the weight should be made good. This report of him was both confirmed and increased upon his entrance into the town. For when he would have compelled some seamen, who had been taken from the fleet and made full and lawful soldiers by Nero, to return to their former condition: and they obstinately refused to do so, as they clung to their eagles and standards, he not only dispersed them by a body of horse, but likewise decimated them. Likewise he disbanded a cohort of Germans which had been formed by the preceding emperors for their bodyguard, and by many good proofs found most trustworthy; and without rewarding them in any way for their service, he sent them back to their own country, pretending that they were more inclined to favour the advancement of Cnaeus Dolabella, near whose gardens they encamped, than his own. The following ridiculous stories were also told of him, but whether truly or falsely, I know not; such as, that when a more plentiful supper than usual was served up, he gave a great groan: that when one of the stewards presented him with an account of his expenses, he reached him a dish of legumes from his table as a reward for his care and diligence; and when Canus, the piper, had pleased him greatly by his playing, he bestowed prodigally upon him, with his own hand, five denarii from his private purse.

## 13

His advent in the City, therefore, was not highly welcome; and this appeared at the next public spectacle. For when the actors in a farce began a well-known song with this verse,

> *Venit, io, Simus a villa:*

> Lo! Clodpate from his village comes,

the spectators with one accord sung out the rest, repeating and acting the first verse several times over.

## 14

Thus he assumed the empire with more favour and authority than he administered it, although he gave many proofs of being an excellent prince; but these were not as acceptable to the people as his faults were offensive. He was ruled by three favourites who, because they lived in the palace, and were constantly at his elbow, were commonly called his pedagogues. These were Titus Vinius who had been his lieutenant in Spain, a man insatiably covetous; Cornelius Laco who, from an assessor to the prince, was advanced to be prefect of the praetorian guards, a person of intolerable arrogance and indolent as well; and his freedman Icelus, dignified a little before with the privilege of wearing the gold ring and the use of the cognomen Martianus, who looked now for the highest honour within the reach of any person of the equestrian order, namely the command of the praetorian guards. Unto these men, I say, playing their parts and committing outrages correspondent to their different vices, he yielded his will wholly, and this was so much abused by them that he followed no consistent line of conduct but was variable always; at one time he was more precise and parsimonious, at another, more remiss and extravagant than became a prince elected by the people, and so far advanced in years. Some men of the first rank in the senatorian and equestrian orders, he condemned upon the least suspicion and without a hearing. The freedom of the city he seldom granted to anyone. The privilege of immunity due to those who had three children, he gave only to one or two at the most; and that reluctantly and for a limited time. When the judges made suit to have a sixth decury added to their number, he not only denied them flatly, but abolished the vacation which had been granted them by Claudius.

## 15

It was thought that he also purposed to reduce the offices held by senators and men of the equestrian order to a term of two years' continuance; and to bestow them only on those who were unwilling to accept and had refused them. All the donations of Nero he revoked, saving only the tenth part of them. For this purpose he gave a commission to fifty Roman knights with orders that if players or wrestlers had sold what had been formerly given them, it should be exacted from the purchasers, since the others, having no doubt spent the money, were not in a position to pay. But on the other hand, he suffered his attendants and freedmen to sell or give away the revenue of the state, or immunities from taxes, and to punish the innocent, or pardon criminals, at their pleasure. Nay, when the Roman people called upon him, in the name of justice, to execute Halotus and Tigellinus, who of all the instruments of Nero had wrought the most mischief, he protected them, and even advanced Halotus to a most honourable procuratorship: and in the behalf of Tigellinus rebuked the people by proclamation for their cruelty to him.

## 16

Having thereby given offence and displeasure to all orders of the people, he incurred the especial hatred of the soldiery. For their commanders having promised them in his name a donative larger than usual upon their taking the oath to him before his arrival at Rome, he would not ratify and make it good, but frequently bragged that it was his custom to choose his soldiers, not buy them. By this means the troops in all quarters became incensed at him. He struck fear into the hearts of the praetorian guards by threats of danger and by offering them indignities: namely, by removing and displacing most of them one after another, as suspected persons, and adherents of Nymphidius. But the forces in Higher Germany grumbled and fumed most of all, for being defrauded of their rewards for services performed against the Gauls under Vindex. They were the first, therefore, to break out into open revolt, and upon New Year's Day refused to take any oath of allegiance except to the senate; and they immediately dispatched ambassadors to the praetorian troops to acquaint them with their displeasure with an emperor who had been set up in Spain, and their desire that they themselves should elect one whom all the armies in general might allow and approve.

## 17

When he received this news, supposing that he was held in contempt not so much on account of his advanced age as for his childless estate, he presently singled out of a thick throng of young persons of rank that came to salute him, Piso Frugi Licinianus, a youth of noble blood and excellent parts, for whom he had in the past conceived such an affectionate regard that he had appointed him in his will the heir both of his estate and name: him he now called son, presented to the praetorian camp and adopted before a large assembly. But of the aforesaid donative he vouchsafed not a word; and this circumstance ministered to the purpose of Marcus Salvius Otho by providing him with a better occasion to accomplish his enterprise, some days after the adoption.

## 18

Many marvellous prodigies, occurring continually from the very beginning of his reign, had given portent of the end that ensued. In every town through which he passed in his way from Spain to Rome, victims were slain on the right and left of the roads; and one of these, which was a bull, being maddened with the stroke of the axe, broke the rope with which it was tied and running straight against his chariot, with his forefeet elevated, bespattered him with blood. Likewise, as he was alighting, one of the guard, being pushed forward by the throng, had very nearly wounded him with his lance. As he entered into the city of Rome and passed on to the palace, he was greeted by an earthquake and a noise resembling the lowing of a beast. But there followed greater and more fearful prodigies still. Out of all his treasures he had selected a necklace of pearls and precious stones, to adorn his statue of Fortune at Tusculum. But it suddenly striking him that the jewel deserved a most stately and sacred place, he consecrated it to the Capitoline Venus; and next night, he dreamt that Fortune appeared to him, complaining that she had been defrauded of the present intended her and threatening to resume what she had given him. Terrified by this vision, at break of day he sent forward some persons to Tusculum, to make preparations for a sacrifice in expiation of his offence; and when he himself reached the place he found nothing but some hot embers upon the altar hearth and an old man in black standing by, holding a little incense in a glass and some wine in an earthen cup. It was observed, also, that while he was sacrificing upon the kalends of January, the crown fell from his head; and upon his consulting the pullets for omens, they flew away. Further, upon the day of his adopting Piso, when he was to address the soldiers, the seat which he used upon those occasions, through the neglect of his attendants, was not placed according to custom upon his tribunal; and in the senate house, his curule chair was set with the back forward.

## 19

As he was offering sacrifice on the morning of the day he was slain, the augur warned him from time to time to beware of danger, for murderers were not far off. Not long afterwards, he learned that Otho was in possession of the praetorian camp. And though most of his friends advised him to go thither with all speed, in order that he might, by his presence and authority, prevail over the rebels, he resolved to do no more than keep close within the palace and secure himself by guards of the legionary soldiers who were quartered in different parts about the city. He put on a linen coat of mail, however, although he acknowledged that it would avail him little against so many sword points. But being tempted out by false reports, which the conspirators had purposely spread to induce him to venture abroad, while some few about him rashly affirmed that all was dispatched, the rebels defeated, and the rest coming to congratulate him, ready to do all the obsequious service they could: he went forward to meet them with so much confidence, that upon a soldier's boasting that he had killed Otho, he asked him, 'By whose authority?' and proceeded as far as the Forum. There the knights appointed to kill him, making their way through the crowd of citizens, upon seeing him at a distance, halted a while; after which, galloping up to him, they slew him outright, forsaken as he was by all his followers.

## 20

Some report that upon their first approach, he cried out: 'What mean ye, my fellow soldiers? I am yours, and you are mine,' and withal promised to pay the donative. But many more have written that he himself offered his throat, saying, 'Do your work, and strike, since you have come for it.' It is a strange thing, that of all those who were at hand, not one attempted to help the emperor; and all who were sent for disregarded the summons except a troop of Germans. They, in remembrance of his late kindness in showing them particular attention during a sickness which raged in the camp, happened to the rescue, but too late; for, being not well acquainted with the town, they had taken a wrong turn and were retarded. He was slain near the Curtian Lake and there left, until a common soldier returning from the receipt of his allowance of corn, throwing down the load which he carried, cut off his head. Being unable to catch hold of it by the hair (for he was quite bald), he hid it in the bosom of his garment; and afterwards thrust his thumb into the mouth and so brought it to Otho, who gave it to the scullions, lackeys, and varlets that follow the camp; and they, sticking it upon a spear, carried it with scornful jests about the camp, crying out as they went along, 'Galba, thou lovely Cupid, take thy time, and make use of thy fresh and youthful years.' They were provoked to these pranks by a report spread a few days before that, upon some one's commending his person as still fair and vigorous, he made answer, 'My strength, as yet, has suffered no decay.' A freedman of Patrobius's, who himself had belonged to Nero's family, bought the head from them at the price of a hundred pieces of gold, and flung it into the very place where, by Galba's order, his patron had been executed. At length, (late though it was) his steward Argius buried it, with the trunk of his body, in his own gardens near the Aurelian Way.

## 21

He was of full stature, bald, with grey eyes, and an aquiline nose. His hands and feet, by reason of the gout, had grown exceedingly misshapen; insomuch that he could neither wear a shoe, nor turn over the leaves of a book nor even so much as hold it. He had likewise an excrescence in his right side, which hung down to that degree that it was with difficulty kept up by a bandage.

## 22

He is reported to have been a great eater. For in winter he used to eat before daylight; and at supper, to be served so plentifully, that he had the fragments which were left gathered together into heaps and distributed among those that stood in attendance. He was given much to an unnatural lust for the male sex and such of them, too, as were old. It is said that in Spain, when Icelus, an old catamite of his, brought him the news of Nero's death, he not only kissed him tenderly in the sight of all but entreated him to remove all impediments and then took him aside into a private apartment.

## 23

He died in the seventy-third year of his age and the seventh month of his reign. The senate, as soon as they could with safety, ordered a statue to be erected for him upon the naval column in that part of the Forum where he was slain; but Vespasian repealed the decree upon a suspicion that he had sent murderers out of Spain into Judaea to make away with him.

# Marcus Salvius Otho

## I

The ancestors of Otho derived their origin in the town of Ferentium, of an ancient and honourable family, indeed one of the noblest in Etruria. His grandfather, M. Salvius Otho (whose father was a Roman knight, but whose mother was of low birth, it being uncertain whether she was freeborn or no), by the favour of Livia Augusta, in whose house he had his education, was made a senator but never rose higher than the praetorship. His father, Lucius Otho, was by the mother's side of noble blood, allied to several great families and so dearly beloved by Tiberius, and so like him in features, that most people believed he was his son. He managed most severely, not only the city offices, but the proconsulship of Africa and some extraordinary commands in the army. He ventured so far as to put to death some soldiers in Illyricum, who, in the tumults engendered by Camillus, upon changing their minds, had put their generals to the sword, as authors of the revolt against Claudius. And this execution he ordered to take place under his own eyes, in the front of the camp; notwithstanding that he knew they had been advanced to higher ranks in the army by Claudius on that very account. By this action he grew in glory as he decreased in favour. And yet he soon recovered the latter, by discovering to Claudius a design upon his life, conceived by a Roman knight, which he had learnt from some of his slaves. For this the senate endowed him with an honour most rare and seldom accorded: to wit, that a statue of him should be erected in the palace; and Claudius admitted him to the patrician rank, praising him at the same time in the warmest terms and adding these words: 'He is a man than whom I would not wish, I assure you, to have better children of my own.' Of Albia Terentia, a very noble woman, he had two sons, namely, Lucius Titianus and a younger called Marcus, who had the same cognomen as himself. He had also a daughter, whom he contracted to Drusus, Germanicus' son, before she was of marriageable age.

2

A.U.C. 785

The emperor Otho was born upon the fourth of the kalends of May in the consulship of Camillus Arruntius and Domitius Ahenobarbus. From his earliest youth he was riotous, wild, and wanton; insomuch that his father often scourged him well and soundly for it. He was reported to run about in the night time and when he met anyone either feeble or drunk, to lay hold of him and toss him up in a blanket. After his father's death he paid court to a freedwoman about the palace who was in great favour and pretended to be in love with her, as the better means of winning her as his mistress, although she was old and almost decrepit. By her means winding himself into the favour of Nero, he easily became one of the principal favourites, such was the congruence of their humour and disposition; and, as some say, by the reciprocal practice of bodily pollution. He waxed so powerful at court that when a man of consular rank was condemned for bribery, he arranged with him, for a large sum of money, to procure his pardon; and who, before this was quite effected, scrupled not to introduce him into the senate to show his gratitude.

3

Being now, as he was, admitted to all the counsels and secret designs of Nero, he, to avert all manner of suspicion, upon the day which Nero had appointed for the murdering of his mother, entertained them both at supper in the kindest and most exquisite manner. Likewise, Poppaea Sabina, whom Nero had taken from her husband and committed in the meanwhile to him for safekeeping until he could put away Octavia, he received under colour of a marriage: and not content with alienating her heart from Nero and possessing himself of her body, he loved her so entirely that he could not endure Nero himself as his rival. It is certainly believed that he not only sent back those who were sent by Nero to fetch her, but also that he kept Nero himself without doors, standing there cooling his heels and mingling threats and prayers as he vainly demanded the return of that which had been entrusted to his keeping. The mock marriage, therefore, being dissolved, he was sent out of the way under pretence of an embassage to Lusitania. This punishment was thought sufficient, because harsher measures might have brought the whole comedy to light: notwithstanding this secrecy, it came out and was cast abroad in the following distich:

> You ask why Otho's banish'd? Know, the cause
> Comes not within the verge of vulgar laws.
> Against all rules of fashionable life,
> The rogue had dared to sleep with his own wife.

He governed the province in the quality of quaestor for ten years with singular moderation and equity.

## 4

As occasion and opportunity of revenge was offered at length, he was the first that combined with Galba in his attempts; and at the same time also conceived hope of the empire. To this he was much encouraged by the state of the times, but still more by the words of Seleucus the Astrologer who, having formerly told him that he would certainly outlive Nero, came to him at that juncture unexpectedly, promising him again that he should succeed to the empire and that in a very short time. He, therefore, omitted no kind of obsequious office that would minister to his power, even to the very meanest. As often as he entertained Galba at supper, he would deal out to every man of the cohort which attended the emperor on guard, a piece of gold; and no less careful was he to place under obligation to him one way or another the rest of the soldiers. Being chosen an arbitrator by one who had a dispute with his neighbour about a piece of land, he bought it and gave it him; so that now almost everybody thought and said that he was the only man worthy of succeeding to the empire.

## 5

Moreover he had fed himself with the hope of being adopted by Galba and looked for it daily; but finding himself disappointed, by Piso's being preferred before him, he turned his thoughts to gaining his purpose by violence; and to this he was driven not only by his resentment at Galba's conduct but by the fact that he was deeply in debt. For he did not conceal his conviction, 'that he could not stand his ground unless he became emperor, and that it signified nothing whether he fell by the hands of his enemies in the field, or his creditors in the Forum'. He had a few days before squeezed out of one of the emperor's slaves a million of sesterces for procuring him a stewardship; and this was the whole fund he had for carrying on so great an enterprise. At first the design was entrusted to only five of the guard, but afterwards to ten others, each of the five naming two. They had every one ten thousand sesterces paid down and were promised fifty thousand more. By these, others were drawn in, but not many; as if they had no doubt, but presumed confidently that when the matter came to the crisis, they should have enough to join them.

## 6

His first intention was, immediately after the departure of Piso, to seize the camp and fall upon Galba while he sat at supper in the palace; but out of regard for the cohort which at that time kept guard he restrained himself, lest he should bring too great odium upon it; because it happened that the same cohort was on guard before both when Caius was slain and Nero deserted. For some time afterwards, he was restrained also by scruples about the omens, and by the advice of Seleucus. Upon the day fixed at last for the enterprise, having given his accomplices notice to wait for him in the Forum near the temple of Saturn, at the gilded milestone, he went in the morning to pay his respects to Galba; and saluting him with a kiss as usual, he attended him at sacrifice and heard the predictions of the augur. A freedman of his then brought him word that the architects were come, which was the signal agreed upon, whereupon he withdrew as if it were to view a house upon sale and went out by a back door of the palace to the place appointed. Some say that he feigned an ague fit and ordered those about him to make that excuse for him, if he was inquired after. Being then quickly hidden in a woman's litter, he made the best of his way for the camp. But the bearers growing tired, he got out and began to run; his shoes becoming loose, he stopped again, but being immediately raised by his attendants upon their shoulders and unanimously saluted by the title of Emperor, he came

amidst auspicious acclamations and drawn swords into the Principia
of the camp; all who met him joining in the cavalcade, as if they had
been privy to the conspiracy. Upon this, after he had dispatched some
soldiers to kill both Galba and Piso, he said nothing else in his address
to the soldiers to win their hearts than these few words: 'I shall be
content with whatever ye think fit to leave me.'

## 7

As the day drew toward evening, he entered the senate, and briefly
laying before them an account of his proceeding, pretending that he
had been seized in the streets, and compelled to take the Empire
upon him, which he would administer according to their will and
pleasure, he retired to the palace. Besides other compliments which
he received from those who congratulated and flattered him, he was
called Nero by the mob, and gave no sign at all that he repudiated the
title. Nay, some authors relate that he used it in his official acts and
the first letters he sent to the governors of provinces. Certain it is, that
he suffered all his images and statues to be replaced, and restored his
procurators and freedmen to their former offices. And the first writing
which he signed as emperor was a promise of fifty millions of sesterces
to finish Nero's golden house. It is said that he was that night greatly
frightened in his sleep, and groaned loudly; and being found, by those
who came running in to see what ailed him, lying upon the floor
before his bed, he strove by every kind of atonement to appease the
ghost of Galba, by which he had been thrust out of bed. The next
day, as he was taking the omens, a great storm arose, whereupon he
took a grievous fall, and muttered to himself from time to time:

What business have I the long trumpets to sound!

## 8

About the same time, the armies in Germany took an oath of
allegiance to Vitellius as emperor. Upon hearing of this, he proposed
to the senate to send thither deputies, to inform them that a prince
had been already chosen and to exhort them to peace and a good
understanding; yet by letters and messages he offered Vitellius an
equal share in the Empire and his daughter in marriage. But a war

being now unavoidable and the generals and troops sent forward by Vitellius advancing, he had a proof of the attachment and fidelity of the praetorian guards, which had nearly proved fatal to the senatorian order. It had been decreed that some arms should be given out of the stores and conveyed to the fleet by the marine troops. While they were employed in fetching these from the camp in the night, some of the guards, suspecting treachery, raised a tumult; and suddenly the whole body, without any of their officers at their head, ran to the palace, demanding that the entire senate should be put to the sword; and having repulsed some of the tribunes who endeavoured to stop them, and slain others, they broke, all bloody as they were, into the banquet room, inquiring for the emperor; nor would they quit the place until they had seen him. He now entered upon his expedition against Vitellius with great alacrity, but with too great haste and without any care at all for the ominous portents. For the Ancilia had been taken out of the temple of Mars for the usual procession, and were not yet replaced; during which interval it had of old been looked upon as very unfortunate to embark upon any enterprise. He likewise set forward upon the very day when the worshippers of the Mother of the Gods begin their lamentations and wailing. Besides these, other unfavourable omens attended him. For, in a victim offered to Father Dis, he found the signs such as upon all other occasions are regarded as lucky; whereas, in that sacrifice, the contrary intimations are judged the most propitious. At his first setting forward he was stopped by inundations of the Tiber; and at twenty miles' distance from the city found the road blocked up by the fall of houses.

## 9

With equal rashness, though it was generally thought good policy to protract the war as the enemy were distressed as well by famine as by the straitness of their quarters, he yet resolved to hazard the fortune of the field with all speed; whether from impatience of prolonged uncertainty and in the hope of bringing matters to an issue before the arrival of Vitellius, or because he could not restrain his soldiers who were hot for battle. Yet he was not present at any conflict that ensued, but stayed behind at Brixellum. He was victorious in three slight skirmishes, near the Alps, about Placentia, and a place called

Castor's; but in the last and greatest battle, at Bedriacum, he lost the day, and was vanquished by a treacherous stratagem of the enemy; for, some hopes of a conference being given, and the soldiers being drawn up to hear the conditions of peace declared, very unexpectedly, and in the midst of their mutual salutations, they were obliged to stand to their arms. Upon this misfortune, he meditated making an end of himself straightway, rather from shame, as many think, and not without reason, at persisting in a struggle for the empire at so great a jeopardy to the state and so many lives, than from despair or distrust of his troops. For he had still in reserve and in full force those whom he had kept about him for a second trial of his fortune, and others were coming up from Dalmatia, Pannonia, and Moesia; nor were the troops lately defeated so far dejected as not to be ready, even of themselves, to undergo all risks in order to wipe out their recent discomfiture.

## 10

My father, Suetonius Lenis, served in this battle in the quality of an angusticlavian tribune in the thirteenth legion. He used frequently to say that Otho, before his advancement to the empire, had such an abhorrence of civil war that once, when some person related at the table the end of Cassius and Brutus, he fell a-quaking and trembling; and that he never would have interfered with Galba, but that he was confident of succeeding in his enterprise without a war; moreover, that he was then moved to a contempt of this life by the example of a common soldier who, having brought word of the overthrow of the army and finding that he met with no credit but was charged with lying and cowardice, as if he had run away from the field of battle, fell upon his sword at the emperor's feet; upon the sight of which, my father said that Otho cried out, 'that he would no more expose to danger such brave men, who had deserved so well at his hands'. Advising, therefore, his brother, his brother's son, and the rest of his friends, to provide for their security in the best manner they could, after he had embraced and kissed them, he sent them away; and then withdrawing into a private room by himself, he wrote a letter of consolation to his sister, and one also to Messalina, Nero's widow, whom he had intended to marry, committing to her the care of his relics and memory. He then burnt all the letters which he had by him to prevent the danger and mischief that might otherwise befall the writers from the conqueror. And that store of ready money which he had, he distributed among his domestics.

## II

Being now prepared and fully resolved to die, he was induced to delay dispatching himself, by reason of a great tumult which had broken out in the camp. Finding that some of the soldiers who had attempted to slip away had been seized and detained as traitors, 'Let us add,' said he, 'this night to our life.' These were his very words. He then gave orders that no violence should be offered to anyone; and keeping his chamber-door open until late at night, he allowed all who pleased the liberty to come and see him. At last, having allayed his thirst with a draught of cold water, he took up two poniards, and having tested the sharpness of both of them, put one under his pillow; and shutting his chamber door, slept very soundly, until, awaking about break of day, he stabbed himself under the left pap. At the first groan that he gave, some servants broke in, whereat he at one time covered and at another exposed his wound to the view of the bystanders, and thus yielded up his vital breath. His funeral was hastily performed according to his own order, in the thirty-eighth year of his age, and ninety-fifth day of his reign.

## 12

The person and aspect of Otho was not in agreement with the great spirit and courage which he displayed on this occasion; for he is said to have been of low stature, splayfooted, and bandylegged. In his attire he was, however, as nice as any woman; the hair on his body he plucked out by the roots; and because he was somewhat bald, he wore a kind of peruke, so perfectly fitted to his head that nobody could have known it for such. He used to shave every day and rub his face with soaked bread, the use of which he began when the down first appeared upon his chin, to prevent his having any beard. It is said, moreover, that he celebrated publicly the sacred rites of Isis, clad in a linen garment such as is used by the worshippers of that goddess. These things, I think likely, caused the world to wonder the more that his death was so little consonant with his life. Many of the soldiers who were present, kissing and bedewing with their tears his hands and feet as he lay dead, and commending him as 'a most gallant man, and an incomparable emperor', immediately put an end to their own lives upon the spot, not far from his funeral pile. Many of those likewise who were at a distance, upon hearing the news of his death, in the anguish of their hearts began fighting among themselves until they had slain one another. To conclude: most of those who, in his life time, had cursed and detested him, now that he was dead praised him highly; so that it came to be a common saying, 'that Galba was slain by him, not so much that he aspired to be sovereign ruler himself as because he desired to restore to the people of Rome the freedom they had lost'.

# *Aulus Vitellius*

## I

Concerning the origin of the Vitellian family, many different accounts are written; some report it to be ancient and noble, others recent and obscure, nay even base. These several reports, I am inclined to believe, were cast about by the flatterers and detractors of Vitellius, after he became emperor. There is extant a memoir addressed by Quintus Eulogius to Quintus Vitellius, quaestor to the Divine Augustus, in which it is said that the Vitellii were descended from Faunus, king of the aborigines, and Vitellia, who was worshipped in many places as a goddess, and that they reigned formerly over the whole of Latium: that all who were left of the family moved from the country of the Sabines to Rome, and were enrolled among the patricians; that some monuments of the family continued a long time, such as the Vitellian Way, reaching from the Janiculum to the sea, and likewise a colony of that name which, at a very remote period of time, they desired leave from the government to defend against the Aequicolae, with a force raised by their own family only: also that, in the time of the war with the Samnites, some of the Vitellii who went with the troops levied for the security of Apulia, settled at Nuceria, and their descendants, a long time afterwards, returned again to Rome, and were admitted into the patrician order.

On the other hand, the generality of writers say that the founder of the family was a freedman. Cassius Severus and some others relate that he was likewise a cobbler, whose son having made a considerable fortune by agencies and dealings in confiscated property, begot, by a common strumpet, daughter of one Antiochus, a baker, a child who afterwards became a Roman knight. This dissonance of opinions I submit to my readers, who may believe what they will.

Certain it is, that Publius Vitellius, of Nuceria, whether of an ancient family or of mean parentage, was a Roman knight and a procurator to Augustus. He left behind him four sons, all men of very high quality, who had the same cognomen but the different praenomina of Aulus, Quintus, Publius, and Lucius. Aulus died during his consulship, which dignity he bore jointly with Domitius, the father of Nero Caesar. He was a man of very luxurious tastes and much spoken of for his magnificent banquets. Quintus was displaced from his senator's estate, when, upon a motion made by Tiberius, a decree was passed that all such senators as were thought incompetent should be culled out and removed. Publius, an intimate friend and companion of Germanicus, prosecuted his enemy and murderer, Cnaeus Piso, and procured sentence against him. After he had been made praetor, being arrested among the accomplices of Sejanus and delivered into the hands of his brother to be confined in his house, he opened a vein with a penknife, intending to bleed himself to death; but afterwards, not so much from repenting the resolution he had made as to comply with the entreaties of his friends, he suffered his wound to be bound up and cured. He died a natural death, however, during his imprisonment.

Lucius, after his consulship, was made governor of Syria and by his politic management not only brought Artabanus, king of the Parthians, to give him an interview but to worship the standards of the Roman legions. He afterwards filled two ordinary consulships and also the censorship jointly with the emperor Claudius. While that prince was absent upon his expedition into Britain, he also had the charge of the whole Empire. He was a harmless person, honest and industrious, howbeit blemished with a very bad name because of the love he bore an abandoned freedwoman, whose spittle, mixed with honey, he used as a remedy, anointing his throat and jaws with it, and that not privately nor seldom but daily and in public. He was besides much given to flattery and it was he who, by his example, gave rise to the worship of Caius Caesar as a god; for, upon his return from Syria, he would not presume to come into his presence otherwise than with his head covered, turning himself about and then falling prostrate before his feet. And because he would omit no artificial means to curry favour with Claudius, a prince entirely in the thrall of his wife and freedmen, he begged of Messalina, as if it were the greatest gift she could bestow upon him, that she would have the grace to permit him to remove her shoes; and the right shoe, which he had drawn off, he carried about him constantly betwixt his toga and his tunic and from time to time would take it out and kiss it vehemently. He likewise worshipped golden images of Narcissus and Pallas among his household gods. It was he who, when Claudius exhibited the secular games, mingled with his congratulations this expression, 'May you often do the same.'

## 3

He died of palsy the next day after he was taken down with it: leaving behind him two sons, whom he had by his wife, Sextilia, a woman highly esteemed for her virtue, and of noble descent. He lived to see them both consuls the same year and during the whole year also; the younger succeeding the elder for the last six months. The senate honoured him after his decease with a funeral at the public expense and with a statue in the rostra, which had this inscription upon the base: 'One who was steadfast in his loyalty to the prince.' The emperor Aulus Vitellius, son of this Lucius, was born upon the eighth of the kalends of October or, as some say, upon the seventh of the ides of September, in the consulship of Drusus Caesar and Norbanus Flaccus. His nativity, as foretold by the astrologers, inspired his parents with such horror, that his father endeavoured in every way possible to prevent his being sent governor into any of the provinces, while he was alive: and his mother, when he was sent to the legions in Germany by Galba, and also when he became emperor, at once lamented him as ruined forever. His childhood and youth he spent at Capri, among the strumpets and catamites that Tiberius kept there; and he was himself constantly hailed by the name of Spintria (those devisers of unnatural lewdnesses), and it was thought that by suffering the abuse of his own body by the emperor he had secured his father's advancement.

## 4

In the subsequent years of his life, stained as he was with all manner of shameful villainies, he waxed very powerful at court, having grown into familiar acquaintance with Caius Caligula because of his love of chariot-running and with Claudius for his affection toward dice play. But he was in even greater favour with Nero, not only for these same things, but because of a special service which he had performed for him. For, when Nero presided in the games instituted by himself, though he was extremely desirous to perform among the harpers, yet his modesty would not permit him, notwithstanding the people entreated much for it; and upon his leaving the theatre, Vitellius pretended to be an ambassador sent at the earnest wish of the people and so brought him in the end to yield to their entreaties.

## 5

By the favour of these three princes he was not only advanced to the highest offices of state, but to the greatest dignities of the sacred order; after which he held the proconsulship of Africa and had the superintendence of the public works, in which appointment his conduct, and hence his reputation, were very different. For he governed the province during two years with singular integrity; and in the latter year he acted as deputy to his brother, who succeeded him. But in his office in the city, he was said to have secretly stolen the gifts and ornaments of the temples and to have exchanged brass and tin for gold and silver.

## 6

He took to wife Petronia, the daughter of a man of consular rank, by whom he had a son, blind in one eye, who was called Petronianus. The mother being willing to appoint this youth her heir upon condition that he should be released from his father's authority, he discharged him accordingly; but shortly after, as was believed, murdered him, charging him with a design upon his life and pretending that he had, from consciousness of his guilt, drank the poison he had prepared for his father. Soon afterwards, he married Galeria Fundana, the daughter of a man of praetorian rank, by whom he had both sons and daughters; but one of the male children had such an impediment in his speech and stammered so excessively that he was little better than if he had been dumb.

## 7                                            A.U.C. 821

He was sent by Galba into Lower Germany, contrary to his expectation. It is supposed that he was furthered in this appointment by the interest of Titus Junius, a man very mighty in those days: whose friendship he had long before gained by favouring the same set of charioteers with him in the Circensian games. But Galba openly declared that none were less to be feared than those who thought of nothing but their victuals and that even his hungry belly and greedy appetite must be satisfied with the plenty of that province; so that it was evident he was chosen more out of contempt than because of any especial grace. Certain it is, that when he was to set out he had no money for the expense of his journey; he being at that time so much straitened in his circumstance that he was obliged to put his wife and children, whom he left at Rome, into a poor lodging which he hired for them, in order that he might let his own house for the remainder of the year; and he took from his mother's ear a pearl, which he pawned to defray his expenses on the road. A crowd of creditors who were waiting to stop him, and among them the people of Sineussa and Formia whose taxes he had converted to his own use, he got rid of by terrifying them with the apprehension of false charges: suing one of them, a certain freedman, who was very noisy in demanding a debt of him, under pretence that he had kicked him; which action he would not withdraw, until he had wrung from the freedman fifty thousand sesterces.

Upon his arrival in the province, the army, which was disaffected to Galba and eager to revolt, received him with open arms as a gift of the gods; for he was the son of a man who had been thrice consul, he was in the prime and flower of life, and of an easy, prodigal disposition. This opinion, which had been long entertained of him, Vitellius confirmed by some late proofs; kissing all the common soldiers whom he met with all along the road and showing himself courteous and affable in the inns and stables, even to the muleteers and travellers, asking them in a morning if they had got their breakfasts and letting them see, by belching, that he had got his.

Now when he came into the camp he denied no man's suit; nay, he pardoned all who stood under sentence, or were in disgrace of any kind. Whereupon, before one month had passed, without respect to the day or season, he was called by the soldiers out of his bedchamber, although it was evening, and he in undress, and unanimously saluted by the name of Emperor. He was then carried round the most considerable towns in the neighbourhood, with the sword of the Divine Julius in his hand, which had been taken by some person out of the temple of Mars and presented to him when he was first saluted. Nor did he return to the praetorium until his dining room was in flames from the chimney's taking fire. Upon this accident, all being in consternation at this adverse and ominous occurrence: 'Be of good cheer!' he cried, 'it shines brightly upon us.' And this was all he said to the soldiers. The army of the Upper Province likewise, which had before declared against Galba for the senate, joining in the proceedings, he very eagerly accepted the cognomen of Germanicus, offered him by the unanimous consent of both armies; but deferred assuming that of Augustus and refused forever that of Caesar.

9

When news came to him that Galba was slain, having settled his affairs in Germany he divided his troops into two bodies, intending to send one of them before him against Otho and to follow with the other himself. The army he sent forward had a lucky omen: for suddenly an eagle came flying up to them on the right, and having hovered round the standards, flew gently before them on their road. But, on the other hand, when he began his own march, all the equestrian statues, which were erected for him in several places, fell suddenly down with their legs broken; and the laurel crown which he had put on as emblematical of auspicious fortune, fell off his head into a river. Soon afterwards, at Vienne, as he was upon the tribunal administering justice, a cock perched upon his shoulder and afterwards upon his head. These prodigious sights prefigured an event correspondent thereto: for the empire which had been secured for him by his lieutenants he himself was not able to hold.

## 10

Of the victory at Bedriacum and the death of Otho, he heard while he was yet in Gaul: and without the least delay, by a single proclamation, he disbanded all the praetorian cohorts, as having, by their repeated treasons, set a dangerous example to the rest of the army; their arms he commanded them to deliver to his tribunes. A hundred and twenty of them, under whose hands he had found petitions presented to Otho, for rewards of their service in the murder of Galba, he ordered to be sought out and executed. This was indeed a worthy and magnificent beginning of his reign and such as gave good hope of his proving an excellent prince, had he not managed his other affairs more in accordance with his own natural disposition and the course of his former life than with his majesty as an emperor. For, having begun his march, he rode through every city on his route in a triumphal fashion: and sailed down the great rivers in ships fitted most luxuriously and adorned with crowns of various kinds. He fared most sumptuously at table, being served with all manner of dainty foods: observing no discipline either of household servants or of soldiers, but turning all their outrages to mere jests; and they, not content with the provision everywhere made for them at the public expense, committed every kind of robbery and insult upon the inhabitants, setting slaves at liberty as they pleased, and if any dared to make resistance, dealing blows and abuse, frequently wounds, and sometimes outright slaughter among them.

When he reached the fields on which the battles were fought, some of those around him being horrified at the corrupt bodies of the dead, he had the audacity to encourage them with this accursed speech: 'That an enemy slain had a very good smell, especially if he were a fellow citizen.' Howbeit, to qualify the offensiveness of the stench, he quaffed in public a goblet of wine and with equal vanity and insolence distributed a large quantity of it among his troops. On beholding a stone with an inscription upon it to the memory of Otho, he said, 'it was a mausoleum good enough for such a prince.' He also sent the poniard, with which Otho killed himself, to the colony of Agrippina, to be dedicated to Mars. Upon the Appennine hills he celebrated a Bacchanalian feast.

## II

At last he entered the city with trumpets blaring, in his general's cloak, and girded with his sword, amid a display of standards and banners; his attendants being all in the military habit, and the arms of the soldiers unsheathed. Acting more and more in flagrant disrespect of all laws, both divine and human, he assumed the office of Pontifex Maximus, upon the day of the defeat at the Allia; ordered the magistrates to be elected for ten years of office; and made himself consul for life. And that no man might doubt what pattern he chose to follow in his government of the empire, he made his offerings to the shade of Nero in the midst of the Campus Martius, and with a full assembly of the public priests attending him. At a solemn entertainment he desired a harper who pleased the company much, to sing something in praise of Domitius; and upon his beginning some songs of Nero's, he started up in presence of the whole assembly and could not refrain from leaping for joy and clapping his hands.

## 12

Having in this manner begun his rule, he administered his affairs during the greater part of the time entirely according to the pleasure and advice of the vilest among the players and charioteers, and especially of his freedman Asiaticus. This man had, when young, abused his own body with him in mutual filthiness; but afterwards, in loathing of that abominable vice, had run away. His master, some time after, finding him at Puteoli selling a sour liquor called posca, made of water and vinegar, seized him and put him in chains, but soon released him, and kept him in his former relation. After which, being a second time offended with his contumacy and sullen behaviour, he sold him to a strolling fencing master; and then, when the fellow was to have been brought up to play his part at the conclusion of an entertainment of gladiators, he suddenly carried him off and at length, upon his being advanced to the government of a province, gave him his freedom. The first day of his reign as he sat at supper, he dubbed him knight of Rome and gave him the gold ring: notwithstanding that, on the morning of the same day, when all about him entreated for that favour in his behalf, he professed the utmost abhorrence of casting so foul a blot on the equestrian order.

## 13

He was given most of all to excessive feeding and to cruelty. He always ate three meals a day, sometimes four: breakfast, dinner, supper, and a drunken revel after all, which he was able to bear very well, by reason of regular vomiting. His manner was to send word that he would breakfast with one friend, dine with another, etc., and all in one day. None ever entertained him at a cost of less than four hundred thousand sesterces. The most notorious one of all was a set banquet given him by his brother at which, it is said, there were served up no less than two thousand choice fishes and seven thousand birds. Yet even this feast, sumptuous as it was, he himself surpassed at one he gave upon the first use of a dish which had been made for him and which, for its extraordinary size, he called 'The Shield of Minerva'. In this dish there were tossed up together the livers of charfish, the brains of pheasants and peacocks, with the tongues of flamingos, and the entrails of lampreys, all of which had been brought in ships of war as far as from the Carpathian Sea and the Spanish Straits. He was not only a man of prodigious appetite, but he would gratify it likewise at unseasonable times, and with any gross stuff that came in his way; so that, at a sacrifice, he would snatch from the fire flesh and cakes and devour them on the spot. When he travelled, he would stop at every inn along the road and fall to viands piping hot, or cold and left over from the day before, sometimes half eaten, just as fortune served him.

## 14

He delighted to put to death or otherwise punish anyone at all, without distinction of persons or occasions: and he treated in this manner several noblemen, his schoolfellows and companions, whom he had by flattery enticed into his society, as if he were on the point of inviting them to share the empire with him. To one he gave poison with his own hand, in a cup of cold water which he called for in a fever. Of the usurers, notaries, and publicans, who had ever at any time demanded a debt of him at Rome, or any toll or custom upon the road, he hardly spared one. One of these, while in the very act of saluting him, he ordered for execution, but immediately sent for him back; and when all about him commended his clemency, he commanded the man to be slain before his face, saying, 'I would feed my eyes.' Two sons who interceded for their father, he ordered to be executed with him. A Roman knight, upon being dragged away for execution, cried out, 'Sir, I have made you my heir!' Whereupon he desired that the will be produced; and finding that a freedman had been made joint heir with him, he commanded that both he and the freedman should have their throats cut. He put to death some of the common people only for railing aloud at the blue party in the Circensian games; supposing it to be done in contempt of himself and the hope of a revolution in the government. There were no persons with whom he dealt more harshly than with jugglers and astrologers; and as soon as anyone of them was informed against, he put him to death without the formality of a trial. He was exasperated with them because, after his proclamation by which he commanded all astrologers to quit Rome and Italy also, before the kalends of October, a bill was immediately posted about the city, with the following words: 'Take Notice' (in imitation of the form of the public edicts, which began with the words Bonum Factum), 'The Chaldaeans also decree that Vitellius Germanicus shall be no more, by the day of the said kalends.' He was even suspected of being accessory to his mother's death, by forbidding sustenance to be given her when she was unwell; a German witch, whom he held to be oracular, having told him, 'that he would long reign in security if he survived his mother'. But others say, that being quite weary of the state of affairs and apprehensive of the future, she obtained without difficulty a dose of poison from her son.

## 15

In the eighth month of his reign, the troops both in Moesia and Pannonia revolted from him; as did likewise, of the armies beyond sea, those in Judaea and Syria, some of which swore allegiance to Vespasian as emperor in his own presence, and others in his absence. In order, therefore, to retain the favour and affection of the people, Vitellius lavished on all around whatever he had it in his power to bestow, both publicly and privately, in the most extravagant manner. He also levied soldiers in the city, and promised all who enlisted as volunteers, not only their discharge after the victory was gained, but all the rewards due to veterans who had served their full time in wars. The enemy now pressing hotly forward both by sea and land, on one hand he opposed against them his brother with a fleet, the new levies, and a body of gladiators, and in another quarter the troops and generals who were engaged at Bedriacum. But being discomfited in open field or secretly betrayed at every turn, he agreed with Flavius Sabinus, Vespasian's brother, to abdicate, on condition of having his life spared and a hundred millions of sesterces granted him; and he immediately, upon the palace steps, publicly declared to a large body of soldiers there assembled, 'that he resigned the government, which he had accepted against his will'; but they all remonstrating against it, he put off the conclusion of the treaty. Next day, early in the morning, he came down to the Forum in a very mean habit, and with many tears repeated the speech, from a writing which he held in his hand; but the soldiers and people both, interrupting him a second time and exhorting him not to be cast down, but to rely on their zealous assistance, he took courage again, and forced Sabinus, with the rest of the Flavian party, who now thought themselves secure, to retreat into the Capitol where he destroyed them all by setting fire to the temple of Jupiter, while he beheld the contest and the fire from Tiberius' house where he was feasting. Not long after, repenting of what he had done, and laying all the fault upon others, he called a public assembly: where he swore, and compelled all the rest to take the same oath, 'that he and they would hold nothing more sacred than the public peace'. Then, drawing a dagger from his side, he presented it first to the consul and, upon his refusing it, to the magistrates, and then to every one of the senators; but none of them being willing to accept it, he went away, as if he meant to lay it up in the temple of Concord. But some crying out to him, 'You are Concord', he came back again, and said that he would not only keep his weapon, but for the future use the surname of Concord.

## 16

He advised the senate to send ambassadors, accompanied by the Vestal Virgins, to crave peace, or at least, some longer time to consult upon the point. The next day, while he was waiting for an answer, word was brought to him by a spy that the enemy was advancing. Immediately, therefore, throwing himself into a small litter, borne by hand, with only two attendants, a baker and a cook, he privately withdrew to his father's house, on the Aventine hill, intending to escape thence into Campania. Soon after, upon a groundless report flying around that the enemy was willing to come to terms, he suffered himself to be brought back to the palace; where, finding nobody, and those who were with him slinking away, he girded round his waist a belt full of gold pieces, and then ran into the porter's lodge, tying the dog before the door, and piling up against it the bed and bedding.

## 17

By this time the forerunners of the enemy's army had broken into the palace, and meeting with nobody, searched, as was natural, every corner. Being dragged by them out of his cell, and asked 'who he was?' (for they did not recognise him), 'and if he knew where Vitellius was?' he deceived them by a lie. But at last being recognised, he begged hard to be detained in custody, even were it in a prison; pretending to have something to say which concerned Vespasian's security. Nevertheless he was dragged half naked into the Forum, with his hands tied behind him, a rope about his neck, and his clothes torn, amid the most scornful abuse, both by word and deed, and then along the Via Sacra; his head being held back by the hair, in the manner of condemned criminals, and the point of a sword put under his chin, that he might hold up his face to public view; some of the mob, meanwhile, pelting him with dung and mud, while others called him 'an incendiary and glutton'. They also upbraided him with the defects of his person, for he was monstrously tall, and had a face usually very red with hard drinking, a large belly, and one thigh weak, by reason of a chariot having run against him, during his attendance upon Caius Caligula at a race. At length, upon the Gemonian Steps, he was tortured and mangled by slow degrees, and then dragged by a hook into the Tiber.

## 18

Thus he perished, with his brother and son, in the fifty-seventh year of his age, and so verified the prediction of those who had foretold him that by the sign which had been seen at Vienne, as before related, he would fall into the hands of a Gaul. For he was seized by Antoninus Primus, a general of the adverse party, who was born at Toulouse, and, when a boy, had the surname of Becco, which signifies a cock's beak.

# T. Flavius Vespasianus Augustus

## I

The empire, which had wavered so long in a doubtful and unsettled state, induced by the rebellion and violent death of its last three princes, was at length re-established in peace and security by the Flavian family. This house was, I must needs say, of obscure descent, and could boast of no ancestral honours; howbeit the commonwealth had no cause to regret its ascendancy, though it is acknowledged that Domitian met with the just reward of his avarice and cruelty. Titus Flavius Petro, a townsman of Reate, the original seat of the Flavian family, and a centurion, siding in the civil war with Pompey, (but whether he served voluntarily or was called forth, it is not known), fled out of the battle of Pharsalia and went home; where, having at last obtained his pardon and discharge, he became a collector of the money raised by public sales in the way of auction. His son, surnamed Sabinus, was never engaged in the military service, though some say he was a centurion of the first order, and others, that while he held that rank, he was discharged on account of his ill health. This Sabinus was a publican, and received the tax of the fortieth penny in Asia. And there were remaining, at the time of the advancement of the family, several statues, which had been erected to him by the cities of that province, with this inscription: 'To the honest Tax-farmer'. He afterwards turned usurer among the Helvetii, and there died, leaving behind him his wife, Vespasia Polla, and two sons which he had by her; the elder of whom, Sabinus, came to be prefect of the city, and the younger, Vespasian, to be emperor. Polla, descended of a good family at Nursia, was the daughter of Vespasius Pollio, who was thrice appointed military tribune, and at last prefect of the camp; and her brother was a senator of praetorian dignity. There is to this day, about six miles from Nursia, on the road to Spoletum, a place on the summit of a hill, called Vespasiae, where are several monuments of the Vespasii, a sufficient proof of the nobility and antiquity of the race. I cannot deny that some have alleged that Petro's father was a native of Gallia Transpadana, whose employment was to hire labouring people who used to emigrate every year from the country of the Umbria into that of the Sabines, to assist them in their husbandry, but who settled at last in the town of Reate, and there married. But I could never find (make what search I would) the least evidence to persuade me of the truth of this report.

2

Vespasian, the emperor, was born in the country of the Sabines beyond Reate, in a little country seat called Phalacrine, upon the fifth of the kalends of December, in the evening, in the consulship of Quintus Sulpicius Camerinus and Caius Poppaeus Sabinus, five years before the death of Augustus. He was brought up under the care of Tertulla, his grandmother by the father's side, upon an estate belonging to the family at Cosa in the Volscian territory. When he became emperor, he used frequently to visit the place where he had spent his infancy, the house being kept just as it had been in former times, that his eyes might miss nothing of what they were wont to see there. And he so loved the memory of his grandmother that on all solemn occasions and festival days, he constantly drank out of a silver cup which she had been accustomed to use. After assuming the virile gown, in the seventeenth year of his age, he refused for a long time the senator's toga, though his brother had obtained it; nor could he be persuaded to sue for it by anyone but his mother. She at length forced him to it, more by taunts and reproaches, than by her entreaties and authority; calling him now and then, in taunting fashion, his brother's footman. He served as military tribune in Thrace. When made quaestor, the province of Crete and Cyrene fell to him by lot. He was candidate for the aedileship and soon after for the praetorship, but met with a repulse in the former case; though at last, with much difficulty, he came in sixth on the poll-books. Howbeit, the office of praetor he carried upon his first canvas, standing among the highest at the poll. Being highly displeased with the senate and desirous to gain, by all possible means, the favour of Caius Caligula, he earnestly demanded and obtained leave to exhibit extraordinary games in honour of the emperor's victory in Germany;

and urged the senate to augment the punishment of the conspirators against his life by exposing their dead bodies unburied. He likewise gave him thanks in that august assembly for the honour of being admitted to his table.

## 3

Amid these events he married Flavia Domitilla, a freedwoman of Statilius Capella, a Roman knight of Sabrata in Africa, who had been committed to his care and given the Latin rights; and who was soon afterwards declared fully and freely a citizen of Rome, on a trial before the Court of Recovery, brought by her father Flavius Liberalis, a native of Ferentium, but no more than secretary to a quaestor. By her he had three children, Titus, Domitianus, and Domitilla. He outlived his wife and daughter whom he buried while he was yet a private citizen. After his wife's death, he recalled his former concubine Caenis, the freedwoman of Antonia, together with her amanuensis; and her he kept, after he was emperor, almost as if she had been his lawful wife.

## 4                                          A.U.C. 804

Under the emperor Claudius, by the interest of Narcissus, he was sent to Germany in command of a legion; whence being removed into Britain, he engaged the enemy in thirty battles. He reduced under subjection to the Romans two very powerful tribes and above twenty great towns, with the Isle of Wight, which lies close to the coast of Britain; partly under the command of Aulus Plautius, the consular lieutenant, and partly under Claudius himself. For this achievement he received the triumphal ornaments, and in a short time after two priesthoods, besides the consulship, which he held during the two last months of the year. The interval between that and his proconsulship, he lived a quiet life in a retired place, for fear of Agrippina, who still had great power over her son (Nero), and hated all the friends of Narcissus, who was then dead. Afterwards he got by lot the province of Africa, which he governed with much honour and reputation, notwithstanding that once, in an insurrection at Adrumetum, he was pelted with turnips. It is certain that he returned thence nothing richer; for his credit was so low that he was obliged to mortgage his whole property to his brother; and of necessity, for the maintenance of his estate and dignity, he went so low as to trade in mules; for which reason, he was commonly called 'the Muleteer'. He is said likewise to have been convicted of extorting from a young man of fashion two hundred thousand sesterces for procuring him the broad stripe, contrary to the wishes of his father, and was sharply rebuked for it. While in attendance upon Nero in Achaia, he frequently withdrew from the theatre while Nero was singing; or, if he remained, fell asleep; which gave so much offence, that he was not only excluded from his society, but forbidden to salute him in public. Upon this, he withdrew to a small, remote town, where he lay skulking, in constant fear of his life, until a province, with an army, was offered to him.

There had been spread throughout the East, and for long believed among men, a saying that there should come forth from Judaea one whom destiny decreed should be lord of the whole world: which prophecy (as events showed), referred to a Roman emperor; but the Jews, taking it to themselves, rebelled, and having slain their governor, Gessius Florus, put to flight also the lieutenant of Syria, Cestius Gallus, a man of consular rank, who was advancing to his assistance, and took from him an eagle, the standard of one of his legions. To suppress this revolt, because there was need of a stronger army and a valiant general, who might be safely trusted in an affair of so great consequence, Vespasian was chosen in preference to all others as a man of approved valour and activity and one who, because of the obscurity of his origin and name, was not to be feared in high places. Two legions, therefore, eight squadrons of horse, and ten cohorts, being added to the former troops in Judaea, he, taking with him his eldest son as lieutenant, as soon as he arrived in his province, turned the eyes of the neighbouring provinces upon him by immediately reforming the discipline of the camp and engaging the enemy once or twice with such resolution, that, in the attack of a castle, he had his knee hurt by the stroke of a stone and received several arrows in his shield.

5

After the deaths of Nero and Galba, while Otho and Vitellius strove for the sovereignty, he had good hope of the empire, conceived long before, from the following tokens: upon an estate belonging to the Flavian family, in the neighbourhood of Rome, there was an old oak, sacred to Mars, which, at the three childbirths of Vespasia, put out each time a new branch, foreshadowing the future fortune of each child. The first was small and slender, and quickly withered away; and therefore the girl born at that time did not live the year to an end. The second became vigorous, which portended great felicity; but the third reached the proportions of a tree. Whereupon his father Sabinus, encouraged by these omens, which were confirmed by the augurs, told his mother, 'that her grandson would be emperor of Rome'; at which she laughed heartily, marvelling, she said, 'that her son should be in his dotage while she continued still in full possession of her powers'.

Afterwards in his aedileship, when Caius Caesar, being angry with him for not taking care to have the streets kept clean, ordered the soldiers to fill the bosom of his gown with mud, some persons at that time interpreted it as a sign that the government, being trampled under foot and deserted in some civil commotion, would fall under his protection, and as it were into his bosom. Once as he sat at dinner, a strange dog brought in a man's right hand, and laid it under the table: this being as everyone knows, the sign of sovereign power. Another time, while he was at supper, a plough ox, having shaken the yoke off his neck, broke into the room; and after he had driven away all the attendants, on a sudden, as if he was weary, lay down at Vespasian's feet as he reclined upon his couch and gently put his neck under him. A cypress tree, in a field belonging to the family, was plucked up by the roots, without any force of tempest, and laid flat upon the ground; but on the following day it rose again, greener and stronger than before.

He dreamt in Achaia that he and his should begin to prosper when Nero had a tooth drawn; and it happened that the day after, a surgeon coming into the hall showed him a tooth which he had just extracted from Nero. In Judaea, upon his consulting the oracle of the divinity at Carmel, the answer was so encouraging as to assure him of success in anything he undertook, however great or important it might be. And when Josephus, the historian, one of the noble prisoners, was put in chains, he confidently affirmed that he should be released in a very short time by the same Vespasian, who would first become emperor. Some omens, no less significant, were likewise mentioned in the news from Rome and among others, that Nero, towards the close of his days, was commanded in a dream to carry Jupiter's sacred chariot out of the sanctuary where it stood, to Vespasian's house, and conduct it thence into the circus. Also, not long afterwards, as Galba was going to the election in which he was created consul for the second time, a statue of the Divine Julius turned towards the east. And in the field of Bedriacum, before the battle began, two eagles engaged in the sight of the army; and one of them being overcome, a third came at the very instant from the east and drove the victor away.

6

Yet for all this he attempted no enterprise, though friends and soldiers were very ready to aid him and even press him to action, until he was drawn to it by the unexpected favours of some persons, who, as it fell out, were both unknown to him and at a distance. Two thousand men, drawn out of the legions in the Moesian army, had been sent to the assistance of Otho. While they were upon their march, news came that he had been vanquished and had laid violent hands upon himself, notwithstanding which, they continued their march as far as Aquileia, pretending that they gave no credit to the report, where, after they had, by vantage of opportunities offered and uncontrolled liberty, committed all manner of robberies and outrageous acts, fearing to be called to an account on their return and punished therefore, resolved upon choosing and creating an emperor. For they counted themselves in no way inferior to the army which made Galba emperor, nor to the praetorian troops which had set up Otho, nor the army in Germany to whom Vitellius owed his advancement. Having proposed, therefore, all the consular lieutenants, and some taking exception to one for this cause and another for that at last some of the third legion, which a little before Nero's death had been removed out of Syria into Moesia, highly extolled Vespasian, and all the rest assenting thereto, his name was immediately inscribed on their standards. But for a time the project was suspended, the troops being brought to submit to Vitellius a little longer.

But when the fact was once divulged, Tiberius Alexander, governor of Egypt, first compelled the legions under his command to swear obedience to Vespasian as their emperor, on the kalends of July, which was observed ever after as the day of his accession to the empire; and upon the fifth of the ides of the same month, the army in Judaea, where he then was, swore allegiance to him. The enterprise was very much advanced by a copy of a letter, (whether true or false, I know not), that was circulated, and said to have been written by Otho, before his decease, to Vespasian, recommending to him in the most urgent terms to avenge his death and entreating him to come to the aid of the commonwealth: and also by a rumour that Vitellius, after his success against Otho, proposed to change the winter quarters of the legions and remove those in Germany to a less hazardous station and a warmer climate. Moreover, among the governors of provinces, Licinius Mucianus dropping the grudge arising from a jealousy of which he had hitherto made no secret, promised to join him with the Syrian army; and, among the allied kings, Vologaesus, king of the Parthians, offered him a reinforcement of forty thousand archers.

# 7

Vespasian, therefore, having undertaken a civil war and sent forward his generals and forces into Italy, passed over to Alexandria to obtain possession of the key of Egypt. Here having entered alone, without attendants, the temple of Serapis, to take the auspices respecting the establishment of his power, and having done his utmost to propitiate the deity, upon turning round, he thought he saw Basilides, his freedman, who offered him the sacred leaves, chaplets, and cakes, according to the usage of the place; although no one had admitted him, and he had long laboured under a muscular infirmity, which scarcely enabled him to set one foot before another, and he was known, withal, to be a long way off. And immediately letters arrived with intelligence that Vitellius' troops had been defeated at Cremona and he himself slain at Rome. The only thing that he now wanted (being, as one would say, a prince unlooked-for, and new to the empire), was something to impart to him countenance, authority, and a kind of royal majesty. But even that came on apace, by this occurrence: a poor commoner who was blind, and another who was lame, came both together before him when he was seated on the tribunal, imploring him to heal them, and saying that they had been admonished in a dream by the god Serapis to crave his help, in this manner, that he would restore to the one his sight, if he did but anoint his eyes with his spittle, and strengthen the leg of the other, if he vouchsafed only to touch it with his heel. At first, hardly believing that the thing would find success, he dared not put it to the venture; at length, through the persuasion of his friends, openly before the whole assembly, he essayed both means, and neither missed of its effect. About the same time, at Tegea in Arcadia, by the direction of some soothsayers, several vessels of ancient workmanship were dug out of a consecrated place; and among them was an effigy resembling, for all the world, Vespasian.

## 8                                                    A.U.C. 823

Thus qualified as he was, and graced with so great fame, he returned to Rome; and after his triumph over the Jews, he added eight consulships to his former one. He took upon himself likewise the censorship, and all during his reign he held nothing closer to his heart than first to restore order in the state, which had been brought almost to utter decay, and then to adorn and improve it. The soldiers, some presuming boldly on their victory, and others disheartened by the disgrace of their overthrow, had fallen into every species of audacity and licentiousness. Nay, the provinces, too, and free cities, and some kingdoms in alliance with Rome, were all in a discordant state. He, therefore, disbanded many of Vitellius' soldiers, and punished others; and so far was he from granting any extraordinary favours to the sharers of his success, that it was late before he paid the gratuities due to them by law. That he might let slip no opportunity of reforming the discipline of the army, upon a young man's coming to him smelling of sweet perfumes to give him thanks for having appointed him to command a squadron of horse, he turned away his head in disgust, and, giving him this sharp reprimand, 'I had rather you had smelt of garlic,' revoked his commission. When the men belonging to the fleet, who travelled by turns from Ostia and Puteoli to Rome, petitioned for an addition to their pay, under the name of shoe money, thinking that it would answer little purpose to send them away without a reply, he ordered them for the future to run barefoot; and so they have done ever since. He deprived of their liberties Achaia, Lycia, Rhodes, Byzantium, and Samos, and reduced them to the form of provinces; Thrace, also, and Cilicia, as well as Comagene, which until that time had been under the government of kings. He stationed some legions in Cappadocia on account of the frequent inroads of the barbarians, and, instead of a Roman knight, appointed as governor there a man of consular rank. The city of Rome being much blemished by the ruins of houses which had been burnt down long before, he gave leave to any one who would to take possession of the void ground and build upon it, if the proprietors should hesitate to perform the work themselves. He took upon himself the re-edifying of the Capitol, and was the foremost to put his hand to clearing the ground of the rubbish, yea, and carried some of it away upon his own shoulder. And he undertook likewise to restore the three thousand tables of brass which had been destroyed in the fire which consumed the Capitol; searching in all quarters for copies of those curious and ancient records, in which were contained the decrees of the senate, almost from the building of the city, as well as the acts of the people, relative to alliances, treaties, and privileges granted to any person.

## 9

He built also new works: namely, the temple of peace near the Forum, that of Claudius on the Caelian mount, which had been begun by Agrippina but almost entirely demolished by Nero; and an amphitheatre in the centre of the city, which he understood that Augustus had projected. He purified the senatorian and equestrian orders, which had been much reduced by the havoc made among them at several times and was fallen into disrepute by neglect. Having removed the most unworthy persons, he chose in their room the most honourable persons in Italy and the provinces. And to let it be known that those two orders differed not so much in privileges as in dignity, he declared publicly, when some dispute arose between a senator and a Roman knight, 'that senators ought not to be provoked with foul language, unless they were the aggressors, and then it was fair and lawful to return it'.

## 10

The business of the courts had greatly accumulated, partly from old lawsuits which, on account of the interruption that had been given to the course of justice, still remained undecided, and partly from the accession of new suits arising out of the disorder of the times. He, therefore, chose commissioners by lot to provide for the restitution of what had been seized by violence during the war, and others with extraordinary jurisdiction to decide causes belonging to the centumviri and reduce them to as small a number as possible, for the dispatch of which, otherwise, the lives of the litigants could scarcely allow sufficient time.

## 11

Lust and prodigality, from the lack of restraint which had long prevailed, had taken a mighty hold upon the city. He, therefore, obtained a decree of the senate, that a woman who formed a union with the slave of another person, should be accounted a bondwoman herself; and that usurers should not be allowed to take proceedings at law for the recovery of money lent to young men while they lived in their father's family, not even after their fathers were dead. In all other affairs, from the beginning of his empire to the very end, he ruled with great moderation and clemency.

## 12

His former low estate he dissimulated not at any time; nay, he would often make mention of it himself. When some affected to trace his pedigree to the founders of Reate and a companion of Hercules, whose monument is still to be seen on the Salarian road, he mocked and laughed them to scorn. And so indifferent was he to external and adventitious ornaments that, on the day of his triumph (which his son Titus shared with him), being quite tired of the lengthy and tedious march, he could not forbear saying, 'he was rightly served, for having in his old age been so silly as to desire a triumph; as if it was either due to his ancestors, or had ever been expected by himself.' Nor would he for a long time accept the tribunician authority or the title of

Father of his Country. And the custom of searching those who came to salute him he dropped even in the time of the civil war.

## 13

The frank speech of his friends, the figurative allusions of advocates pleading at the bar, and the unmannerly rudeness of philosophers, he bore with great mildness. Licinius Mucianus, a man notorious for his wantonness, but presuming confidently on his great services, treated him very disrespectfully, yet he reproved him only privately; and when complaining of his conduct to a common friend of theirs, he concluded with these words, 'However, I am a man.' When Salvius Liberalis, in pleading the cause of a rich man under prosecution, was so bold as to say, 'What is it to Caesar, if Hipparchus possesses a hundred millions of sesterces?' he commended him for it. Demetrius, the Cynic philosopher, who had been sentenced to banishment, meeting him on the road, and not deigning to rise or salute him, but rather barking at him, I know not in what words, he only called a cur.

## 14

Wrongs and affronts offered to him, he never bore in mind nor avenged. He arranged a marriage for the daughter of Vitellius into a very noble house and gave her, beside, a rich dowry and equipage. Being in great fear and dismay after he was forbidden the court in the time of Nero, and asking those about him what he should do or whither he should go, one of those whose office it was to introduce people to the emperor, thrusting him out, bade him go to Morbonia which (there being no such place), was a courtly way of wishing him ill. But when this same person came afterwards to ask his forgiveness, he gave no further vent to his anger than to give him the same message in almost the very words. So far was he from contriving the overthrow or death of any person through fear or suspicion that, when his friends counselled him to beware of Mettius Pompusianus, because it was commonly believed, on his nativity being cast, that he was destined by fate to the empire, he made him consul, promising for him that he would not forget the benefit conferred.

## 15

There is scarcely to be found an innocent person who is known to have been punished in his reign, unless in his absence and without his knowledge, or at least against his will. Although Helvidius Priscus, the philosopher, was the only man who presumed to salute him on his return from Syria by his private name of Vespasian and, when he came to be praetor, omitted any mark of honour to him or even any mention of him in his edicts, yet he was not angry until Helvidius proceeded to inveigh against him in the most insolent terms. Then indeed he banished him, and afterwards ordered him to be executed; yet he would gladly have saved him notwithstanding and accordingly sped messengers on the way to fetch back the executioners; and he would have saved his life had he not been deceived by a false report that he was already dispatched. He never rejoiced at the death of any man; nay, he would even weep and sigh at the just punishment of malefactors.

## 16

The only thing for which he might deservedly be blamed was covetousness. For, not content with reviving the imposts which had been repealed in the time of Galba, he imposed new and onerous taxes, augmented the tribute of the provinces and doubled that of some of them. He likewise openly engaged in a traffic, which is discreditable even to a private individual, namely that of buying great quantities of goods for the purpose of retailing them again to advantage. Nay, he made no scruple of selling the great offices of the state to suitors for them, and also pardons to persons under prosecution, whether they were innocent or guilty. It is believed that if any of his procurators were more greedy or unscrupulous than the others, he promoted them to higher offices with the view of squeezing them after they had become rich. It was a common saying, that he used them as sponges, because it was his practice, as we may say, to wet them when dry and squeeze them when wet. Some write that he was by nature most covetous and was upbraided with it by an old herdsman of his who, upon the emperor's refusing to enfranchise him gratis, (which he humbly craved of him on his advancement to the empire), cried out, 'that the fox changed his hair, but not his nature'. Some, on the contrary, are of opinion that he was driven to his rapacious proceedings by necessity and the extreme poverty of the treasury and exchequer, of which he took public notice in the beginning of his reign; declaring that 'no less than four hundred thousand millions of sesterces were wanting to carry on the government.' This is the more likely to be true, because he used to the best purposes what he procured by bad means.

## 17

To all ranks of men he was most liberal. He made up to several senators the estate required by law to qualify them for that dignity. He relieved likewise such men of consular rank as were poor, with a yearly allowance of five hundred thousand sesterces; and rebuilt, in a better manner than before, several cities in different parts of the empire which had been damaged by earthquakes or fires.

## 18

He set great store by scholars and artists and encouraged them above all others. He was the first who, out of his own coffers, granted to the Latin and Greek professors of rhetoric the yearly stipend of a hundred thousand sesterces each. He also bought the freedom of fine poets and artists, and gave a noble gratuity to the restorer of the Venus of Cos and to another artist who repaired the Colossus. Some person offering to convey some immense columns into the Capitol at a small expense by a mechanical contrivance, he rewarded him very handsomely for his invention, but would not accept his service, saying, 'Suffer me to find maintenance for the poor people.'

## 19

In the games during which the stage scenery of the theatre of Marcellus was dedicated he revived the old musical entertainments. He gave Apollinaris, the tragedian, four hundred thousand sesterces, and to Terpinus and Diodorus, the harpers, two hundred thousand; to some a hundred thousand; and the least he gave to any of the performers was forty thousand, besides many gold crowns. He entertained company constantly at his table and often in great state and very sumptuously, in order to help the butchers and all those who sold victuals. As in the Saturnalia he made presents to the men which they were to carry away with them, so did he to the women upon the kalends of March. Yet for all this he could not wholly avoid the infamous note of his former avarice. The Alexandrians called him constantly Cybiosactes; a name which had been given to one of their kings who was sordidly avaricious. Nay, at his funeral Favo, the principal mimic, personating him and imitating, as actors do, both his manner of speaking and his gestures, asked aloud of the procurators how much his funeral and the procession would cost. And being answered, 'ten millions of sesterces,' he cried out, 'give him but a hundred thousand sesterces, and they might throw his body into the Tiber!'

## 20

He was of middle stature, well set, and with limbs compact and strongly made. His countenance was like that of a man in the act of straining himself. Whereupon, one of those witty fellows, upon the emperor's request that he make a jest respecting himself, retorted, 'That I will – when you have finished your business at the stool.' His health was excellent, though he did nothing more to preserve it than vigorously rub his neck and other parts of his body at regular times, in the tennis court attached to the baths, besides fasting one day in every month.

## 21

This order of life he maintained for the most part. After he became emperor, he used to wake very early, often before daybreak. Having read over his letters, and the briefs of all the departments of the government offices, he admitted his friends; and while they were paying him their salutations, he would put on his shoes and dress himself without aid. Then, when he had dispatched such business as was brought before him, he rode out, and afterwards retired to rest, lying on his couch with one of his concubines, of whom he kept several after the death of Caenis. Coming out of his private apartments, he passed to the bath and then entered the supper room.

They say that he was never more pleasant and indulgent than at that time: and such opportunities as these, his attendants always waited for when they had any favour to ask.

## 22

At supper, and indeed at all times he was very free and merry with his friends; being much given to humour, but of a low order, and not forbearing at times to use very ribald language. Yet there are many ingenious conceits of his extant, among which are these. Being once reminded by Mestrius Florus, that *plaustra* was a more proper pronunciation than *plostra*, he saluted him the next day by the name of Flaurus; which name, being derived from a Greek word meaning 'worthless', gave a happy point to the retort. Having yielded at length to a certain woman who was enamoured of him and ready, as it were, to die for pure love, he admitted her to his bed; and when she had given him four hundred thousand sesterces for lying with her, and his steward desired to know how he would have the sum entered in his accounts, he said: 'For Vespasian's being seduced.'

## 23

He quoted Greek verses very aptly; as, in referring to a tall man, who had enormous parts:

> Still shaking, as he strode, his vast long spear.

And of Cerylus, a freedman, who being very rich, had begun to pass himself off as freeborn, to elude the exchequer at his decease, and assumed the name of Laches, he said:

> Ah, Laches, Laches! when thou art no more,
> Thou'lt Cerylus be called, just as before.

Most of all he affected a kind of humour upon his own unseemly means of raising money, perhaps in order to wipe off the odium by light words and turn it all to jest. One of his ministers, whom he loved dearly, made suit in behalf of some person as his brother, for a stewardship. And when he had put off granting him his petition, he sent for the candidate, and having exacted from him as much money as he had agreed to give his friend at court, he appointed him without further delay, to the office. The minister interposing himself again, 'You must,' said he, 'find another brother; for the one you adopted is in truth mine.'

Suspecting once, during a journey, that his mule driver had alighted to shoe his mules only in order to have an opportunity for allowing a person they met, who was engaged in a lawsuit, to speak to him, he asked him how much he got for shoeing his mules, and insisted on having a share of the profit. When his son Titus blamed him for laying a tax even upon the sanitary arrangements, he applied to his son's nose a piece of the money he received in the first instalment and asked him if he was offended with the smell. When he answered no, 'And yet,' said he, 'it is derived from urine.'

Some ambassadors brought him word that there was decreed for him, at the common expense, a statue of giant-like proportions, that would cost no small sum of money. He commanded them to pay it down immediately, holding out the hollow of his hand, and saying, 'there was a base ready for the statue'. Not even when he was in fear and peril of death could he forbear jesting. For when, among other prodigies, the mausoleum of the Caesars suddenly flew open and a blazing star appeared in the heavens: one of the prodigies, he said, concerned Julia Calvina, who was of the family of Augustus; and the other, the king of the Parthians, who wore his hair long. And in the very first access of his disease, 'Methinks,' said he, 'I am deifying,' in allusion to the apotheosis of the emperors.

## 24

In his ninth consulship, being assailed in Campania with some light symptoms of his sickness, and immediately returning to the city, he soon afterwards went thence to Cutiliae, and his estates in the country about Reate, where he used constantly to spend the summer. Here, though his malady was much aggravated, and he also injured his bowels by too free use of cold waters, he nevertheless executed the functions of emperor and even gave audience to ambassadors in bed. At last, being taken ill of a diarrhoea, to such a degree that he was ready to swoon, he cried out, 'An emperor ought to die standing.' As he was endeavouring to rise, he died in the hands of those who were helping him up, upon the eighth of the kalends of July, being sixty-nine years, one month, and seven days old.

## 25

All writers agree in this, that so confident was he of his own horoscope and that of his children that, after several conspiracies against him, he told the senate that either his sons would succeed him, or nobody. It is said, moreover, that he dreamed once that he saw a balance standing in the middle of the porch of the Palatine house, exactly poised; in one scale of which stood Claudius and Nero, in the other, himself and his sons. And it fell out so indeed; for the reigns of the two parties were precisely of the same duration.

# *Titus Flavius Vespasianus Augustus*

I

Titus, surnamed as his father was, Vespasianus, was the darling and delight of mankind, so richly endowed was he with natural grace, genius, and good fortune. To win, as he did, the favour of all, after he became emperor, was no easy accomplishment, considering that before that time, and even during his father's reign, he could not avoid the hatred and ill will of the world. This Titus, I say, was born upon the third of the kalends of January in the year remarkable for the death of Caius Caligula, near the Septizonium, in a poor ill-favoured house, and a very small and dark room, which still remains to be seen.

2

He received his education in the palace with Britannicus (son of Claudius and Messalina), and was instructed in the same arts under the same masters. It was at this time, men say, that a physiognomist being introduced by Narcissus, the freedman of Claudius, to examine the features of Britannicus positively affirmed that he would never become emperor, but that Titus, who stood by, would. Now these two were so familiar, that Titus being next him at table, is thought to have tasted of the same cup of poison whereof Britannicus drank and died; whereupon he fell into a grievous disease that troubled him long and occasioned him great suffering. In remembrance of all these things, he afterwards erected a golden statue of Britannicus in the Palatium, and dedicated to him an equestrian statue of ivory; attending it in the Circensian procession, in which it is still carried to this day.

## 3

From his very childhood, there shone forth in him the noblest gifts both of body and mind, and these grew in strength as he advanced in years. He had a fine countenance and physique, which combined a certain majesty with grace and beauty: and was very strong, though not tall, and inclined somewhat to stoutness. He was gifted with an excellent memory and a capacity for all the arts of peace and war; he was a perfect master of the use of arms and a good horseman; very ready in the Latin and Greek tongues, both in verse and prose, and such was the facility he possessed in both, that he would harangue and versify extempore. Nor was he unskilled in music, for he could both sing and play upon the harp sweetly and proficiently. I have also heard men say that he could write shorthand very swiftly, striving in sport and merriment with his own secretaries in the imitation of any handwriting he saw; and would often say that he would have made a notable forger.

## 4

In the rank of military tribune, he served both in Germany and Britain, receiving great commendation for his industry, and no less for his modesty and reputation; as appears from the great number of statues, with honourable inscriptions, erected to him in various parts of these provinces. After serving in the wars, he pleaded causes in court, but with less assiduity than applause. About the same time, he married Arrecina, the daughter of Tertullus, who was only a knight, but had formerly been prefect of the praetorian guards. After her death, he married Marcia Furnilla, but afterwards divorced her, taking from her their daughter. Upon the expiration of his quaestorship, he was raised to the rank of commander of a legion, and took the two strong cities of Tarichaea and Gamala in Judaea; and having his horse killed under him in a battle, he mounted another, whose rider he had met and slain.

# 5

Soon afterwards, when Galba came to be emperor, being sent to congratulate him upon his advancement, he drew all men's eyes upon him, wherever he came; it being the common opinion that the emperor had sent for him with a design to adopt him for his son. But finding all things again in confusion, he turned back upon the road; and going to consult the oracle of Venus at Paphos about his voyage, he received assurances of obtaining the empire for himself. These hopes were speedily strengthened, and being left to finish the reduction of Judaea, in the final assault of Jerusalem, he slew seven of the enemy, with a like number of arrows, and won the city upon the birthday of his daughter. So great was the joy and love of the soldiers that, in their congratulations, they saluted him with one voice by the title of Emperor; and upon his quitting the province soon afterwards, would needs have detained him earnestly begging him, and that not without threats, 'either to stay, or take them all with him'. Upon this rose the suspicion of his being engaged in a project to revolt against his father and claim for himself the government of the East; and the suspicion was augmented when, on his way to Alexandria, he wore a diadem at the consecration of the ox Apis at Memphis: which he did only in accordance with the ancient religious usage of the country, yet there were those who construed it otherwise. Making, therefore, what haste he could into Italy, he arrived first at Rhegium, and sailing thence in a merchant ship to Puteoli, went to Rome with all possible speed and lightly equipped. Presenting himself unexpectedly to his father, he said, by way of checking the false rumours concerning him, 'I am come, father; I am come.'

# 6

From that time forward he constantly carried himself as his father's colleague, and, indeed, as regent of the empire. He triumphed with his father, bore jointly with him the office of censor, and was, besides, his colleague not only in the tribunician authority, but in seven consulships. Taking upon himself the care and inspection of all offices, he dictated letters, wrote proclamations in his father's name, and pronounced his speeches in the senate in place of the quaestor.

He likewise assumed the command of the praetorian guards, although no one but a Roman knight had ever before been their prefect. In this office he conducted himself with much violence, taking off without scruple or delay all those he had most reason to suspect, after he had secretly sent his emissaries into the theatres and camp, to demand, as if by general consent, that the suspected persons should be delivered up to punishment. Among these, he invited to supper Aulus Caecina, a man of consular rank, whom he commanded to be stabbed, immediately he had gone out of the room. I must needs say that he was driven to this proceeding by an imminent danger; for he had discovered a writing under the hand of Caecina, containing an account of a plot hatched among the soldiers. By these acts, though he provided for his future security, yet for the present he so much inflamed the hatred of the people, that scarcely anyone ever came to the empire with a more unpopular character or more generally disliked.

## 7

Besides his cruelty, he was suspected also of riotous living, as he often continued feasting until midnight with the most spendthrift of his companions; and of wanton lust, likewise, on account of the number of catamites and eunuchs that he kept about him, and the love that he was noted to bear to Queen Berenice, to whom it was said that he promised marriage. There was, moreover, suspicion of plunder and avarice; for it is certain that, in causes which came before his father, he used to offer his interest for sale, and take bribes. In short, men both believed and reported him to be another Nero. But this bad name turned out in the end to his profit, and enhanced his praises to the highest pitch when he was found to possess no vicious propensities but, on the contrary, the noblest virtues. The banquets that he gave were pleasant merriments, rather than sumptuous orgies; and he surrounded himself with such fine friends that the succeeding princes adopted them as most serviceable to themselves and the state. He immediately sent away Berenice from the city, much against both their wills. Some of his old eunuchs, though such skilful dancers that they bore an uncontrollable sway upon the stage, he was so far from treating with any extraordinary favour that he would not so much as witness their performances in the crowded theatre. He violated no citizen's rights; and if ever man refrained from injustice, he did; nay, he would not accept the allowable and customary offerings. Yet in munificence he was inferior to none of the princes before him. Having dedicated his amphitheatre, the Colosseum, and built some warm baths close by it with great expedition, he entertained the people with splendid spectacles. He likewise exhibited a naval fight in the old Naumachia, besides a combat of gladiators; and in one day brought into the theatre five thousand wild beasts of all kinds.

# 8

He was by nature most kind and gracious; for whereas all the emperors after Tiberius, according to the example he had set them, would not admit the grants made by former princes to be valid unless they received their own sanction, he confirmed them all by one general edict, without waiting for any applications to be made. Of all who sued for any favour he sent none away without hope. And when his ministers remonstrated with him that he promised more than he was able to perform: 'What!' said he, 'there ought no man to depart from the speech of a prince sad and disconsolate.' Calling to mind one time as he sat at supper that he had done nothing for any man that day, he uttered this memorable and praiseworthy saying, 'My friends, I have lost a day.'

He treated the people on all occasions with so much courtesy that, on his presenting them with a show of gladiators, he declared that he would set it forth, not to please himself, but to delight the beholders; and accordingly he did so. He denied them nothing and very frankly encouraged them to ask what they pleased. Espousing the cause of the Thracian party among the gladiators, he frequently joined in the popular demonstrations in their favour, but without compromising his dignity or doing injustice. And to omit no occasion of gaining in popular favour, he sometimes made use himself of the baths he had erected and admitted the common people with him.

There fell in his reign some dreadful accidents: an eruption of Mount Vesuvius, in Campania, and a fire in Rome, which raged for three days and three nights; besides a plague, such as was scarcely ever known before. Amid these many great calamities he showed not only princely concern, but even a fatherly affection, for his people; one while comforting them by his proclamations, and another while relieving them to the utmost of his power. For repairing the losses in Campania, he chose commissioners by lot, from among the men of consular rank. The estates of those who had perished by the eruption of Vesuvius and who had left no heirs, he applied to the repair of the ruined cities. As to the public buildings destroyed by fire in the City, he openly proclaimed that nobody should be a loser but himself. Accordingly, he applied all the ornaments of his palaces to the decoration of the temples and purposes of public utility, and appointed several men of the equestrian order to superintend the work. For the relief and cure of the people during the plague, he employed, in the way of sacrifice and medicine, all means both human and divine. Among the adversities of those times may be reckoned the informers and their agents, a tribe of miscreants who had grown up under the licence of former reigns. These he commanded to be scourged or beaten with sticks in the Forum and then, after he had compelled them to pass through the amphitheatre as a public spectacle, ordered them to be sold for slaves, or else banished to some barren islands. And to restrain such as might, at any time, follow their practices, he made a law, among others, prohibiting actions to be successively brought under different statutes for the same cause, or the state of affairs of deceased persons to be inquired into after a certain term of years.

## 9

Having proclaimed that he accepted the office of Pontifex Maximus for the purpose of keeping his hands undefiled, he made good his word. For after that time, he was never the author of any man's death, nor accessory thereto (albeit he lacked not sometimes just cause of revenge), but swore devoutly that he would rather die himself than do others to death. Two men of patrician rank being convicted of aspiring to the empire, he only advised them to desist, saying that the sovereign power was disposed of by fate, and promised them that if there was anything else they desired of him he would grant it. He also dispatched messengers to the mother of one of them, who was at a great distance and in deep distress over her son, to assure her of his safety. The men themselves he not only invited to sup with him, but next day, at a show of gladiators, purposely placed them close by him; and handed to them the arms of the combatants which had been presented to him for his inspection. It is said, moreover, that having had their nativities cast, he assured them, 'that a great calamity was impending on both of them, but from another hand, and not from his'; and so it fell out indeed. Though his own brother was continually plotting against him, almost openly stirring up the armies to rebellion and contriving to get away, yet he could not endure to execute him, or to banish him from his presence; nor did he treat him with less honour than before; but, as he had always done from the first day of his imperial dignity, he constantly declared him to be his partner in government, and his successor; at other times, begging him privately, with tears and prayers, 'that he would return the affection he had for him'.

## 10

Amid this blessed course of life he was cut short by an untimely death, to the greater loss of mankind than of himself. At the close of the public spectacles, he shed abundant tears, and then retired into the Sabine country, more sad than he usually was, because, when he was sacrificing, the victim had broken loose and escaped; and also because in fair and clear weather it had thundered. At the first resting place on the road, being seized with a fever and carried forward in a litter, they say that he drew back the curtains and looked up to heaven, complaining very piteously that his life should be taken from him who had not deserved to die; for there was no action of his that he could repent of, save one. What that one was, he neither uttered himself, nor is it easy for any man to guess. Some think that he alluded to an intimate association which he had formerly with his brother's wife. But Domitia devoutly swore that he had never had such dealings with her: which she would never have done, had there been any truth in the report; nay, she would rather have boasted of it, as she was ready enough to glory in all her shameful intrigues.

## 11

He departed this world in the same villa where his father had died before him, upon the ides of September, two years, two months, and twenty days after he had succeeded his father; and in the one-and-fortieth year of his age. When his death became known to the people, they mourned for him as for a private and domestic sorrow. The senate assembled in haste, before they could be summoned by proclamation, and locking the doors of their house at first, but afterwards opening them, gave him such thanks and heaped upon him such praises, now he was dead, as they never had done while he was alive and present among them.

# Titus Flavius Domitianus

Domitian was born upon the ninth of the kalends of November, when his father was consul-elect and was to enter upon his office the month following. His birth took place in the sixth region of the city at the Pomegranate, in the house which he afterwards converted into a temple of the Flavian family. His childhood and youth, so the report goes, were spent in so much poverty and infamy, that he owned not so much as one piece of plate; and it is well known that Clodius Pollio, a man of praetorian rank, against whom there is a poem of Nero's extant entitled Luscio, kept a note in his handwriting which he sometimes produced, in which Domitian promised him the use of his body for one night. Some likewise have said that he had similar relations with Nerva, who succeeded him. In the war with Vitellius he fled into the Capitol with his uncle Sabinus and a part of the troops they had in the city. But the enemy breaking in and the temple being set on fire, he hid himself all night with the sacristan; and early the next morning, disguised as a priest of Isis, and mixing with the worshippers belonging to that vain superstition, he passed over the Tiber, with only one attendant, to the house of a woman who was the mother of one of his schoolfellows, and lurked there so close that, though the enemy, who were at his heels, searched very strictly after him, they could not discover him. At last, after the victory of his party, he showed himself, and being generally saluted by the name of Caesar, he assumed the office of praetor of the City, with consular authority, but in fact had nothing but the name; for the jurisdiction he transferred to his next colleague. But he used his absolute power so licentiously that even then he showed what kind of prince he was likely to prove. And not to recite every particular, after he had brought dishonour to the wives of many men of distinction, he took Domitia Longina from her husband, Aelias

Lamia, and married her; and in one day disposed of above twenty offices in the city and the provinces; upon which Vespasian said several times, that 'he marvelled that he did not send him a successor too'.

2

He likewise designed an expedition into Gaul and Germany, notwithstanding that none was necessary, and his father's friends advised him against it; and this he did only because he yearned to equal his brother in achievements and reputation. But for this he was sharply rebuked, and that he might the more effectually be reminded of his age and position, was made to live with his father, and his litter had to follow his father's and brother's carriage, as often as they went abroad; but he attended them in their triumph for the conquest of Judaea, mounted on a white horse. Of the six consulships which he held, only one was ordinary; and that he obtained by the cession and interest of his brother. He greatly affected a modest behaviour and, above all, a taste for poetry; insomuch, that he rehearsed his performances in public, though it was an art he had formerly little cultivated, and which he afterwards despised and abandoned. Yet, devoted as he was at this time to poetical pursuits, when Vologaesus, king of the Parthians, desired succours against the Alani, with one of Vespasian's sons to command them, he laboured with might and main to procure for himself that appointment. But the scheme proving abortive, he endeavoured by presents and promises to engage other kings of the East to make a similar request. After his father's death, he was for some time in doubt whether he should not offer the soldiers a donative double to that of his brother, and made no scruple of saying frequently, 'that he had been left his partner in the empire, but that his father's will had been treacherously laid aside'. From that time forward, he was constantly engaged in plots against his brother, both publicly and privately; until, his brother falling dangerously ill, he ordered all his attendants to leave him, under pretence of his being dead, before the breath had really left his body; and, at his decease, paid him no other honour than that of enrolling him among the gods; and he often carped at his memory, in sneering fashion, both in speeches and in edicts.

## 3

In the beginning of his reign, he used to retire into a secret place for one hour every day, and there do nothing else but catch flies, and stick them through the body with a sharp pin. When someone, therefore, inquired whether anybody was with Caesar, Vibius Crispus made answer, not impertinently, 'No, not so much as a fly.' Soon after his advancement, his wife Domitia, by whom he had a son in his second consulship, and whom the year following he complimented with the title of Augusta, falling madly in love with Paris, the actor, he put her away; but within a short time afterwards, being unable to bear the separation he took her home again, pretending that the people had called upon him to do so. In the administration of the empire, he conducted himself for a good while in a variable manner, as one composed of an equal mixture of vices and virtues, until at length he turned his virtues also into vices: being (so far as we may conjecture), over and above his natural inclination, made covetous by want, and cruel by fear.

## 4

He exhibited, at frequent intervals, magnificent and costly shows, not only in the amphitheatre, but also in the circus; in which, beside the usual races with chariots drawn by two or four horses abreast, he represented a battle between both horse and foot, and a sea fight in the amphitheatre. The people were also entertained with the chase of wild beasts and the combat of gladiators, even in the night time, by torchlight; nor did men only take part in these spectacles, but women also. He regularly attended the games given by the quaestors, which had been disused for some time, but were revived by him; and upon those occasions, always gave the people the liberty of demanding two pairs of gladiators out of his own school, who appeared last in court uniforms. At all the shows of gladiators, there always stood at his feet a little boy dressed in scarlet, with a prodigiously small head, with whom he used to confer often, and sometimes on serious matters. Certain it is, he was overheard asking him 'what he thought of the last appointment in the provinces, namely that of making Mettius Rufus governor of Egypt'.

He exhibited naval fights, performed by fleets almost as numerous as those usually employed in real engagements; making a vast lake near the Tiber and building seats around it; and these he would witness himself during the greatest storms and showers that might rage. He set forth also the Secular games, computing not from the year in which they had been exhibited by Claudius, but from the time of Augustus' celebration of them. In these, upon the day of the Circensian sports, in order to have a hundred races performed, he reduced each course from seven rounds to five. He likewise instituted, in honour of Jupiter Capitolinus, a solemn contest in music to be performed every five years; besides horse racing and gymnastic exercises, with more prizes than are at present allowed. Herein the concurrents strove also for the prize in elocution, both Greek and Latin; and besides single harpers, there were others who played concerted pieces or solos, without vocal accompaniment. Young girls also ran races in the stadium, at which he presided in his sandals, dressed in a purple robe, made after the Grecian fashion, and wearing upon his head a golden crown bearing the images of Jupiter, Juno, and Minerva; with the flamen of Jupiter, and the college of priests sitting by his side in the same dress, excepting only that their crowns had also his own image on them.

He likewise celebrated every year upon the Alban mount the festival of Minerva, for whom he had appointed a college of priests, out of which were chosen by lot persons to preside as governors over the college; these were obliged to entertain the people with extraordinary chases of wild beasts, and stage-plays, beside contests for prizes in oratory and poetry. At the festival of the Seven Hills, he distributed large hampers of provisions to the senatorian and equestrian orders, and small baskets to the common people, encouraging them to eat by falling to himself. The day after, he scattered among the people a variety of cakes and other delicacies to be scrambled for; and upon the greater part of them falling amidst the seats of the crowd, he ordered five hundred tickets to be thrown into each range of benches belonging to the senatorian and equestrian orders.

## 5

Many noble and stately buildings which had been consumed by fire, he rebuilt; and among them the Capitol, which had been burnt down a second time; but all the inscriptions were in his own name, without any credit being given to the original founders. He likewise erected a new temple in the Capitol to Jupiter Custos, and a Forum, which is now called Nerva's, as also the temple of the Flavian family, a stadium, for races both of men and horses, an odeum, for musical performances, and a naumachia, for naval battles; out of the stone dug from which, the sides of the Circus Maximus, which had been burnt down, were rebuilt.

## 6

He undertook several expeditions, some voluntarily, and some from necessity. That against the Catti was unprovoked, but that against the Carmatians was necessary; an entire legion, with its commander, having been cut off by them. He sent two expeditions against the Dacians; the first upon the defeat of Oppius Sabinus, a man of consular rank; and the other, upon that of Cornelius Fuscus, prefect of the praetorian cohorts, to whom he had entrusted the conduct of the war. After several battles with the Catti and Dacians, he celebrated a double triumph. But for his victories over the Sarmatians, he only bore in procession the laurel crown to Jupiter Capitolinus. The civil war stirred up by Lucius Antonius, governor of Upper Germany, he dispatched, without being personally present at it, with wonderful good fortune; for, at the very moment of joining battle, the Rhine suddenly thawing, the troops of the barbarians which were ready to join L. Antonius, were prevented from crossing the river. Of this victory he had intelligence by presages, before the messengers arrived with the news. For upon the very day the battle was fought, a splendid eagle spread its wings round his statue at Rome, and made a great flapping noise in token of much joy. And shortly after a rumour became common that Antonius was slain; nay, many avouched confidently that they saw his head brought to the city.

## 7

He introduced many innovations in matters of common practice. The dole of viands distributed in little baskets in lieu of a public supper, he abolished, and revived the old custom of regular and complete suppers. To the four former parties in the Circensian games, he added two new ones who wore gold and scarlet. He prohibited the players from acting in the theatre, but permitted them the free and lawful exercise of their art in private houses. He gave order that no males should be gelded; and reduced the price of the eunuchs who were still left in the hands of the dealers in slaves. On the occasion of a great plenitude of wine, and as much scarcity of corn, supposing that the tillage of the ground was neglected for the sake of attending too much to the cultivation of vineyards, he published a proclamation forbidding the planting of any new vines in Italy, and ordering the vines in the provinces to be cut down, nowhere permitting more than one half of them to remain. However, he did not persist in the full execution of this act. Some of the greatest offices he conferred upon his freedmen and soldiers. He forbad two legions to be quartered in the same camp, and more than a thousand sesterces to be deposited by any soldier with the standards; because it was thought that Lucius Antonius had been stimulated in his late project by the large sum deposited in the military chest by the two legions which he had in the same winter quarters. He made an addition to the soldiers' stipend, of three gold pieces a year.

## 8

In the administration of justice he was precise and energetic. Many a time, sitting out of course in the Forum, he reversed the definitive sentences of the One Hundred, given through favour or selfish interest. He occasionally cautioned the judges of the Court of Recovery to beware of being too ready to admit claims for freedom brought before them. He set a mark of infamy upon judges who were convicted of taking bribes, as well as upon their assessors. He likewise persuaded the tribunes of the people to prosecute a corrupt aedile for extortion, and to desire the senate to appoint judges for his trial. He likewise took such effectual care in punishing magistrates of the city and governors of provinces, guilty of malversation, that they never were at any time more moderate or more just. Most of these, since his reign, we have seen prosecuted for crimes of various kinds. Having taken upon himself the reformation of the public manners, he restrained the licence of the populace in sitting promiscuously with the knights in the theatre. Defamatory libels, published to injure persons of rank, of either sex, he suppressed, and not without visiting shame and ignominy upon the authors. He expelled a man of quaestorian rank from the senate for practising mimicry and dancing. From women of dishonest life, he took away the privilege and use of their litters; as also the right of receiving legacies or inheriting estates. He struck out of the list of judges a Roman knight for taking back his wife whom he had divorced and prosecuted for adultery. He condemned several men of the senatorian and equestrian orders, upon the ancient Scantinian law against pederasty or sodomy. The loose crimes of the Vestal Virgins, which had been overlooked by his father and brother, he punished severely, but in different ways: namely, offences committed before his reign, with death, and those since its commencement, according to the ancient custom, that is, to be let down into some underground place, and there starved to death; for, having given liberty to the two sisters called Ocellatae, to choose the mode of death which they preferred, and banished those who had deflowered them, he afterwards commanded that Cornelia Maximilla, the president of the vestals, who had formerly been acquitted upon a charge of incontinence, and a long time after was again prosecuted and condemned, should be buried alive; and those who had been guilty with her, beaten to death with rods in the Comitium; excepting only a man of praetorian rank, to whom, because he confessed the fact while the case was dubious, and it was not established against him, though the witnesses had been put to the torture, he granted the favour of exile. And to preserve pure and undefiled the reverence due to the gods, he ordered the soldiers to demolish a tomb which one of his freedmen had erected for his son out of the stones designed for the temple of Jupiter Capitolinus, and to sink in the sea the bones and relics buried there.

# 9

At first he abhorred bloodshed and slaughter so much that, before his father's arrival in Rome, calling to mind the verse of Virgil,

*Impia quam caesis gens est epulata juvencis,*

> Ere impious man, restrained from blood in vain,
> Began to feast on flesh of bullocks slain,

he designed to have published a proclamation, 'to forbid the sacrifice of oxen'. Before his accession to the imperial authority, and during some time afterwards, he scarcely ever gave the least grounds for being suspected of covetousness or avarice; but, on the contrary, he often afforded proofs, not only of his justice, but his liberality. To all about him he was generous even to profusion, and recommended nothing more earnestly to them than to avoid doing anything base or beggarly. He would not accept the property left him by those who had children. He also set aside a legacy bequeathed by the will of Ruscus Caepio, who had ordered his heir 'to make a present yearly to each of the senators upon their first assembling'. He exonerated all those who had been under prosecution from the treasury for above five years before; and would not suffer suit to be renewed, unless it was done within a year, and on condition that the prosecutor should be banished if he could not make good his cause. The secretaries of the quaestors having engaged in trade, according to custom, but contrary to the Clodian law, he pardoned them for what was past. Such portions of land as had been left when it was divided among the veteran soldiers, he granted to the ancient possessors, as belonging to them by prescription. He put a stop to false prosecutions in the exchequer, by severely punishing the prosecutors and this saying of his was much quoted: 'A prince who does not punish informers, encourages them.'

# 10

But he did not long continue in this course of clemency and justice, although he sooner fell into cruelty than into avarice. He put to death a scholar of Paris, the pantomimic, though but a child and ill at the time, only because, both in person and the practice of his art, he resembled his master; and he did likewise Hermogenes of Tarsus for some oblique reflections in his History; besides crucifying the scribes who had copied the work. One who was master of a band of gladiators happening to say, 'that a Thrax was a match for a Murmillo, but not so for the exhibitor of the games', he ordered him be dragged from the benches into the arena, and exposed to the dogs, with this label upon him, 'a Parmularian (one who favoured the Thrax party) guilty of talking impiously'. He put to death many senators, and among them several men of consular rank. In this number were Civica Cerealis, when he was proconsul in Africa, Salvidienus Orfitus, and Acilius Glabrio in exile, under the pretence of their planning to revolt again him. The rest he punished upon very trivial occasions; Aelius Lamia for some jocular expressions, which were of old date and perfectly innocent; because, upon Domitian's commending his voice, after he had taken his wife from him, he replied, 'Alas! I hold my tongue.' And when Titus advised him to take another wife, he answered him thus: 'What! have you a mind to marry again?'

Salvius Cocceianus was condemned to death for keeping the birthday of his uncle Otho, the emperor; Mettius Pompusianus, because he was commonly reported to have an imperial nativity, and to carry about with him a map of the world upon vellum, with the speeches of kings and generals extracted out of Titus Livius, and for giving his slaves the names of Mago and Hannibal; Sallustius Lucullus, lieutenant in Britain, for suffering some lances of a new invention to be called 'Lucullean'; and Junius Rusticus, for publishing a treatise in praise of Paetus Thrasea and Helvidius Priscus, and calling them both 'most upright men'. Upon this occasion, he likewise banished all the philosophers from the city and Italy. He put to death the younger Helvidius for writing a farce, in which, under the character of Paris and Oenone, he reflected upon his having divorced his wife; and also Flavius Sabinus, one of his cousins, because, upon his being chosen at the consular election to that office, the public crier had, by a blunder, proclaimed him to the people not consul, but emperor.

Becoming still more cruel after his victory in the civil war, he employed the utmost industry to discover those of the adverse party who absconded: many of them he racked with a newly devised torture, inserting fire through their private parts; and some he dismembered by cutting off their hands. Certain it is, that only two of any note were pardoned, namely a tribune who wore the narrow stripe, and a centurion; who, to clear themselves from the charge of being concerned in any rebellious project, proved themselves to have been guilty of prostitution, and consequently incapable of exercising any influence either over the general or the soldiers.

## II

Now in his cruelties he was not only excessive, but also subtle and crafty, pouncing upon his victims when they least expected it. He sent for a certain collector of his rents the very day before he crucified him, and invited him to come into his own bedchamber, where he made him sit down upon the bed beside him; and dismissed him in a very merry, light-hearted manner, deigning him also the favour of a plate of meat from his own table. When he was on the point of condemning to death Aretinus Clemens, a man of consular rank, and one of his friends and emissaries, he retained him about his person the same or greater favour than ever; until at last, as they were riding together in the same litter, upon seeing the man who had informed against him, he said, 'What sayest thou, Clemens, shall we hear tomorrow what this base slave shall have to say?' Treating with disdain and contempt the patience of men, he never pronounced a heavy sentence without some preface that promised clemency; so that there was not a surer sign of some horrible end than a mild and gentle beginning. Some person who stood accused of treason, he brought into the senate, and when he had declared that 'he should prove that day how dear he was to the senate', he so influenced them, that they condemned the accused to be punished according to the ancient custom; that is, to have their necks locked in pillory, and so be beaten to death with rods. Then, as if horrified by the cruelty of the punishment, he would intercede in these words (for is not impertinent to give them just as he delivered them), 'Permit me, Conscript Fathers, so far to prevail upon your affection for me, however extraordinary the request may seem, as to grant the condemned criminals the favour of dying in the manner they choose; for by this you shall spare your own eyes, and all the world shall know that I was present in the senate.'

## 12

Having emptied his coffers by the expense of his buildings and public spectacles, and the increased stipend granted to the soldiers, he made an attempt at the reduction of the army, in order to lessen the military charges. But perceiving that he would thereby expose himself to the insults of the barbarians and still be unrelieved of his burdens, he plunged into every manner of robbery and extortion to raise money. The estates of the living and the dead were sequestered upon any charge, by whomsoever preferred. It was sufficient, if any word or deed whatsoever were charged against a man, to make it high treason against the prince. Inheritances, were they never so far off, and no matter to whom they belonged, were confiscated, in case but one person should come forth and say, 'that he had made the emperor his heir'. Besides these exactions, the poll tax on the Jews was levied with extreme rigour, both on those who lived after the manner of Jews in the city, without publicly professing themselves to be such, and on those who, concealing their origin, avoided paying the tribute imposed upon that people. I remember, when I was a youth, to have been present when an old man, ninety years of age, was stripped naked by the procurator, in a very crowded court, that it might be determined whether he was circumcised or not.

From his very youth Domitian was neither civil nor kind, but of a forward, audacious bent, and excessive both in word and deed. When Caenis, his father's concubine, upon her return from Istria, offered him her lips to kiss, as she had been used to do, he presented his hand. Being indignant that his brother's son-in-law should be attended by servants clad in white, he cried out, as if they aped the imperial livery:

> Too many princes are not good.

## 13

But once he mounted the imperial seat, he had the impudence to boast in the senate, 'that it was he who had given the empire to his father and brother both, and they had but delivered it back to him'. And upon taking his wife again, after divorcing her, he gave out by proclamation, 'that he had recalled her to his couch', as if his bed were consecrated, like that on which the images of the gods reposed. He was not a little pleased, too, at hearing the acclamations of the people in the amphitheatre on a day of festival, 'All happiness to our lord and lady.' But when, during the celebration of the Capitoline trial of skill, the whole concourse of people entreated him with one voice to restore Palfurius Sura to his place in the senate from which he had been long before expelled (he having then carried away the prize of eloquence from all the orators who had contended for it), he did not vouchsafe to give them an answer, but only commanded silence, by the voice of the crier. With equal arrogance, when he dictated the form of a letter to be used by his procurators, he began it thus: 'Our lord and god commands so and so'; when it became a rule that no one should style him otherwise either in writing or speaking. He suffered no statues to be erected for him in the Capitol, unless they were of gold and silver, and of a stated weight. He built so many fine gates and arches, surmounted by representations of chariots drawn by four horses and other triumphal ornaments, in different quarters of the city, that a wit inscribed on one of the arches the Greek word meaning 'it is enough', thus making a play on its similar sound to the word for 'an arch'.

He filled the office of consul seventeen times, more than any man had ever assumed before him, and for the seven middle occasions in successive years; but in scarcely any of them had he more than the title; for he never continued in office beyond the kalends of May, and for the most part only till the ides of January. After his two triumphs, when he assumed the cognomen of Germanicus, he called the months of September and October, Germanicus and Domitian, after his own names, because he commenced his reign in the one and was born in the other.

# 14

By this course of life, becoming both hated and feared by all men, he was surprised in the end, and murdered by his friend and favourite freedmen who, together with his wife, conspired his death. He had long before suspected the very year and day, as well as the manner, of his death; for when he was but a youth the Chaldaean astrologers had told him all. His father once laughed at him, sitting at supper, for refusing to eat some mushrooms, saying that if he knew his fate, he would be afraid of the sword instead. Being, therefore, always stricken with fear and lowness of spirits at the least suspicion of danger, he was moved, it is credibly reported, to withdraw the edict ordering the destruction of the vines, chiefly because the copies of it which were dispersed had the following lines written upon them:

> Gnaw thou my root, yet shall my juice suffice
> To pour on Caesar's head in sacrifice.

It was from the same apprehension and fear, that he refused a new honour, one that had never been devised before, offered to him by the senate, though he was ordinarily greedy of all such compliments. What they decreed was this: that as often as he held the consulship, Roman knights, chosen by lot, should walk before him, clad in the Trabea, with lances in their hands, among his lictors and apparitors. As the time of the danger which he dreaded drew near, he became daily more and more perplexed; insomuch that he lined the walls of the porticos in which he used to walk with the stone called Phengites, brought from Cappadocia, which was as hard as marble, white and translucent; by the reflection of which he could see every object behind him. He seldom gave an audience to persons in custody, unless in private, being alone, and he himself holding their chains in his hand. He condemned to death Epaphroditus, his secretary, because it was believed that he had assisted Nero, when utterly forsaken, to kill himself; and by this means he hoped to persuade his servants that the life of a master was not to be attempted, in any emergency.

## 15

To conclude, his last victim was Flavius Clemens, his cousin-german, who is thought by some to have been a convert to the Christian religion, a man most contemptible for his slothfulness and negligence, whose sons, then of very tender age, he had openly avowed would be his successors; and, discarding their former names, had ordered one to be called Vespasian, and the other Domitian. Nevertheless, he suddenly killed him, upon a very slender suspicion (of Jewish manners), when he was scarcely out of his consulship. By this deed, more than anything else, he hastened his own destruction. For the space of eight months, there was so much lightning at Rome, seen and reported to him, that at last he cried out, 'Let him now strike whom he will,' meaning God or Jupiter. The Capitol was struck, as were also the temple of the Flavian family, with the Palatine house, and his own bedchamber. The tablet also, inscribed upon the base of his triumphal statue was carried away by the fury of the tempest, and fell upon a neighbouring monument. The tree which just before the advancement of Vespasian had been prostrated and rose again, suddenly fell a second time. The goddess Fortune of Praeneste, to whom it was his custom on New Year's Day to commend the empire for the ensuing year, and who had always given him a favourable reply, now in this last year delivered a most woeful one, and not without mention of blood. He dreamt that Minerva, whom he worshipped even to a superstitious excess, was withdrawing from her sanctuary, saying that she could not protect him any longer, because she was disarmed by Jupiter.

But nothing so much disquieted him as an answer given by Ascletario, the astrologer, and the accident that happened to him. This Ascletario had been informed against, and did not deny his having predicted that which by his art and learning he foresaw. Domitian asked him what end he thought he should come to himself. And when he made answer, that his destiny was to be torn to pieces by dogs, he ordered him immediately to be slain, and in order to prove the rashness and uncertainty of his art, caused him to be very carefully buried. But in the execution of this order, it chanced that the funeral pile was blown down by a sudden tempest, and the body, half burnt, was rent piecemeal by dogs; which, being observed by Latinus, the comic actor, as he chanced to pass that way, he told it, among the other news of the day, to the emperor at supper.

## 16

The day before his death, he ordered some dates, served up at table, to be kept till the next day, adding, 'if I have the luck to use them'. And turning to those who were nearest him, he said, 'Tomorrow the moon in Aquarius will be bloody instead of watery, and an event will happen which will be much talked of all the world over.' About midnight, he was so terrified that he leaped out of bed. That morning he tried and passed sentence on a soothsayer sent from Germany, who being consulted about the lightning, foretold from it a change in the government. And as he scratched an ulcerous tumour on his forehead, seeing the blood run down his face, he said, 'Would this were all that is to befall me!' Then, upon his asking the time of the day, instead of telling him the fifth hour, which was the one he feared, false word was brought to him that it was the sixth. Overjoyed at this information, as if all danger were now passed, and hastening to cherish his body and make much of himself, he was stopped by Parthenius, his chamberlain, who told him that a person was come to wait upon him about a matter of great consequence, which would admit of no delay. Ordering all persons to leave him, therefore, he retired into his chamber, and was there murdered.

## 17

Touching the manner and means of his death, this much is of common report: the conspirators being in some doubt when and where they should attack him, whether while he was in the bath, or at supper, Stephanus, a steward of Domitilla's, then under prosecution for defrauding his mistress, offered them his counsel and help; and wrapping up his left arm, as if it was hurt, in wool and bandages for some days, to prevent suspicion, at the hour appointed he secreted a dagger in them. Pretending then to make a discovery of a conspiracy, and being for that reason admitted, he presented to the emperor a memorial, and while he was reading it in great astonishment, stabbed him in the groin. But Domitian, though wounded, making resistance, Clodianus, one of his guards, Maximus, a freedman of Parthenius', Saturius, his principal chamberlain, with some gladiators, fell upon him, and stabbed him in seven places. A boy who had the charge of the lares in his bedchamber, and was then in attendance as usual, gave these further particulars: that he was ordered by Domitian, upon receiving his first wound, to reach him a dagger which lay under his pillow, and call in his domestics; but that he found nothing at the head of the bed, excepting the hilt of a poniard, and that all the doors were fastened: that the emperor in the meantime got hold of Stephanus, and throwing him upon the ground, struggled a long time with him; one while endeavouring to wrench the dagger from him, another while, though his fingers were hurt and mangled, to pluck out his eyes.

He was killed upon the fourteenth of the kalends of October, in the forty-fifth year of his age, and the fifteenth of his reign. His corpse was carried out upon a common bier by the public bearers, and buried by his nurse Phyllis, at his suburban villa on the Latin Way. But she afterwards privately conveyed his remains to the temple of the Flavian family and mingled them with the ashes of Julia, the daughter of Titus, whom she had also nursed.

## 18

He was tall in stature, his countenance modest, and inclined to ruddiness, with large eyes, though his sight was dim. His presence was graceful and comely, especially in his youth, excepting only that his toes were bent somewhat inward. In course of time, he became disfigured by baldness, corpulence, and the slenderness of his legs, which were reduced by a long illness. He was so sensible of how much the modesty of his countenance recommended him, that he once made boast to the senate, 'Thus far you have approved both of my disposition and my countenance.' His baldness irked him so much, that he considered it an affront to himself if any other person was twitted with it, either in jest or in earnest; though in a small tract he published, addressed to a friend, 'concerning the preservation of the hair', he uses for their mutual consolation the words following:

'Seest thou my graceful mien, my stately form?

and yet the fate of my hair awaits me; yet with a stout heart I endure that the bush of my head disappears in my fresh youth. And this would I have you know, that nothing is more pleasing, and nothing more fleeting, than beauty.'

## 19

He so disliked exertion and fatigue, that he scarcely ever walked through the city on foot. In his expeditions and on a march, he seldom rode on horseback, but was generally carried in a litter. He had no disposition toward the exercise of arms, but delighted in the use of the bow and arrow. Many persons have seen him often kill a hundred wild animals, of various kinds, at his Alban retreat, and fix his arrows in their heads with such dexterity, that he could, in two shots, plant them, like a pair of horns, in front. He would sometimes direct his arrows against the hand of a boy standing at a distance, with his fingers apart; and such was his precision that they all passed through the void spaces between the fingers, doing the boy no harm at all.

## 20

In the beginning of his empire, he neglected the study of all liberal sciences, though he took care to restore, at a huge expense, the libraries which had been burnt down; collecting manuscripts from all parts, and sending scribes to Alexandria, either to copy or correct them. Yet he never gave himself the trouble of reading history or poetry, or of employing his pen even for private purposes. Except for the commentaries and acts of Tiberius Caesar, he never read anything. His letters, speeches, and edicts, were all drawn up for him by others; though he could converse with elegance, and sometimes voiced memorable original sentiments. As for example: 'Would that I were as fair and well favoured as Maecius fancies himself to be.' And of the head of someone whose hair was reddish and sprinkled with grey, he said, 'that it was snow mixed with mead'. It was his saying that the lot of princes was very miserable, for they were never credited with the discovery of a conspiracy, unless they were slain first.

## 21

When he had leisure, he amused himself with dice, even on days that were not festivals, and in the morning. He went to the bath early, and made a plentiful dinner, insomuch that he seldom ate more at supper than a Matian apple, to which he added a draught of wine, out of a small flask. He gave frequent and sumptuous banquets, but they were short, for he never prolonged them after sunset, and held no revel afterwards. For, till bed time, he did nothing else but walk by himself in his own chamber.

## 22

In fleshly lust he was excessive; and the ordinary use of Venus, as if it was a kind of exercise, he called Clinopale, or bed-wrestling. It was commonly reported that he himself used, with pincers, to depilate his concubines, and to swim about in company with the lowest prostitutes. His brother's daughter, Julia, was offered him in marriage when she was a virgin; but being at that time enamoured of Domitia, he resolutely refused her. Yet not long afterwards, when she was given to another, he was ready enough to solicit her favours, and that even while Titus was living. But after she was bereft of father and husband both, he loved her with most ardent affection, and that openly; insomuch that he was the occasion of her death, by forcing her to miscarry when she was with child by him.

## 23

The people took his death very indifferently, but the soldiers felt it to the very heart; and immediately endeavoured to have him ranked among the gods. They were also ready to revenge his loss, if there had been any to take the lead. However, they soon after effected it, by resolutely demanding the punishment of all those who had been concerned in his assassination. On the contrary, the senate was so overjoyed, that they met in all haste, and in a full assembly reviled his memory in the most bitter terms; ordering ladders to be brought in, and his shields and images to be pulled down before their eyes and dashed in pieces upon the floor of the senate house; passing at the same time a decree to obliterate his titles everywhere, and abolish all memory of him. A few months before his death, a raven on the Capitol uttered these words: 'All will be well.' Some person gave this interpretation of the prodigy:

> *Nuper Tarpeio quae sedit culmine cornix,*
> *'Est bene,' non potuit dicere; dixit, 'Erit.'*

> Late croaked a raven from Tarpeia's height,
> 'All is not yet, but shortly will be, right.'

It is reported likewise that Domitian dreamed that a golden excrescence grew out of the back of his neck, which he considered as a certain sign of happy days for the empire after him. And so it fell out shortly after: such was the just and moderate conduct of the emperors succeeding him.